WESTERN EUROPE:
ECONOMIC AND SOCIAL CHANGE SINCE 1945

WESTERN EUROPE:

ECONOMIC AND SOCIAL CHANGE SINCE 1945

Edited by

Max-Stephan Schulze

LONGMAN
London and New York

Addison Wesley Longman Limited
Edinburgh Gate,
Harlow, Essex CM20 2JE, United Kingdom
and Associated Companies throughout the world

Published in the United States of America
by Addison Wesley Longman, New York

First published 1999

ISBN 0-582-29199-2 PPR

British Library Cataloguing in Publication Data

A catalogue entry for this title is
available from the British Library

Library of Congress Cataloging-in-Publication Data

Western Europe : economic and social change since 1945 / edited by Max-
    Stephan Schulze.
        p.   cm.
        Includes bibliographical references and index.
        ISBN 0-582-29199-2 (pbk.)
        1. Europe, Western—Economic conditions—1945–   2. Europe,
    Western—Social conditions—1945–   I. Schulze, Max-Stephan.
    HC240.W433   1998
    330.94′055—dc21   98–26233
                                                                CIP

Set by 35 in 10.5/12.5pt Baskerville
Produced by Addison Wesley Longman Singapore (Pte) Ltd.,
Printed in Singapore

Contents

List of Plates

List of Figures

List of Tables

Acknowledgements

The publishers would like to thank the following for their permission to reproduce illustrative material: Archive für Kunst und Geschichte for plates 2.1, 2.2 and 9.1; Associated Press for plates 6.2, 12.1 and 12.2; BAA Heathrow for plate 13.2; BFI Stills, Posters and Designs for plate 4.1; Chorley & Hanford Limited for plates 14.1 and 14.2; *The Economist* for plates 7.1 and 8.1; Nick Garland, the Telegraph Group and the Centre for the Study of Cartoons and Caricatures, University of Kent for plate 9.2. © Telegraph Group Limited, London, 1992; Horst Haitzinger for plate 18.2; Heathrow press office for plate 13.1; Hulton Getty Picture Collection for plates 6.1, 11.1, 17.2, 19.1 and 19.2; Museum of London for plate 5.1; National Archives and Records Administration for plates 3.1, 16.1 and 17.1; 'PA' News for plate 8.1; *Pravda* for plate 3.2; Tony Stone Images for plates 6.3, 15.1, 15.2 and 20.1.

The publishers would also like to thank the copyright holders of the following tables and figures for permission to reproduce their material: Academic Press for figure 10.2 (M.S. Teitelbaum and J.M. Winter, *The Fear of Population Decline*, Orlando, 1985); Arnold for table 14.3 (A.G. Champion, *Counterurbanization: The Changing Pace and Nature of Population Deconcentration*, London, 1989); Blackwell Publishers for table 5.3 (N.F.R. Crafts, 'Productivity growth reconsidered', *Economic Policy* 13 (1992)) and table 8.2 (G. Peters, *The Politics of Taxation*, Oxford, 1991); Edward Elgar Publishing Limited and David Coates for table 6.2 (D. Coates (ed.), *Economic and Industrial Performance in Europe: A Report Prepared for the Centre for Industrial Policy and Performance, University of Leeds*, Cheltenham, 1995); Her Majesty's Stationary Office for table 3.2 (*Western Cooperation: A Reference Handbook*, London, 1956). Crown copyright is reproduced with the permission of the Controller of Her Majesty's Stationery Office; Routledge for tables 6.1 and 6.3 (I. Laveson and J.W. Wheeler, *Western Europe in Transition: Structural Change and Adjustment Policies in Industrial Countries*, Croom Helm, London, 1980) Gianni Toniolo for figure 19.1 (N. Rossi, A. Sorgato, G. Toniolo, 'I conto economici italiani: una ricastruzione statistica, 1890–1990', *Rivista di Storia Economiche* 10 (1993)); Yale University Press for table 16.4 (K. Burk and A. Cairncross, *Goodbye Great Britain: The 1976 IMF Crisis*, London, 1992).

Whilst every effort has been made to trace the owners of copyright material, in a few cases this has proved problematic, and so we take this opportunity to offer our apologies to any copyright holders whose rights we may have unwittingly infringed.

1 Introduction

Max-Stephan Schulze

Since the end of the Second World War, western Europe's total output rose fivefold and per capita output increased more than three times. In 1946, European Gross Domestic Product per head was less than half that of the United States. By the mid-1970s, incomes in western Europe had reached about three-quarters the US levels and the gap continued to narrow thereafter, albeit at a slower rate. The growth of GDP per head may be a crude proxy for the rise in the 'standard of living', but there is no doubt that the increase in material prosperity was probably *the* major characteristic of economic and social development in western Europe since 1945.

This impression is confirmed, for instance, when we look at measures such as life expectancy and infant mortality. In 1950, the average male in western Europe had a life expectancy at birth of about 64 years; half a century later this had risen to 74 years. Similarly, females' life expectancy at birth rose from 68 years in 1950 to 80 years by the mid-1990s. An even more dramatic change can be observed in infant mortality which fell by nearly 85 per cent between 1950 and 1994.

In contrast to the years before the war, increasing prosperity was, broadly speaking, common across western Europe – with important political implications. This book is concerned with the causes and consequences of the common European experience and is written primarily for the non-specialist reader. Each chapter provides an outline of historical development, some specific examples or case studies, and a summary of historical debate. A brief annotated bibliography at the end of each chapter offers a guide to further reading.

The structure of the book is designed to encourage readers to approach the main problems in post-war European economic development from both a thematic and a chronological perspective. There are three broad sections.

Part One traces the course of the European economy since 1945 and starts with an account of the impact of war on human and physical resources. This is followed by a discussion of post-war reconstruction and the beginnings of European economic integration. Of the next two chapters, the first explores the pattern and origins of rapid economic expansion during the Great Boom that stretched from the early 1950s to the early 1970s. The second examines the slow-down in economic growth, the problem of inflation and the rise in unemployment that occurred in the 20 years since. The extent, the causes and the economic consequences of structural change since 1945, including the issue of 'deindustrialization', are discussed in Chapter 6. This is followed by the analysis of the development of western Europe's foreign trade and payments from the 1950s. The rise of the welfare state in post-war Europe and the debates about its long-term viability are examined in Chapter 8. Chapter 9 deals with the 'institutionalization' of economic integration in the European Community since 1958.

Part Two explores long-term forces of economic and social change. Chapter 10 analyses the causes and consequences of demographic change since 1945 and asks whether demographic behaviour in different countries converged over time to a European 'norm'. The next chapter looks at the extent and changing nature of European immigration and examines its causes and economic consequences. Emphasizing the importance of distinct national traditions, Chapter 12 reflects on post-war educational reform in Europe as a response to perceived labour market requirements and increasing social aspirations. The next chapter offers an assessment of the social and economic consequences of technological and demand changes in transport and communications. Chapter 14, on the process of urbanization, analyses the relationship between structural change in the European economy and changes in the spatial distribution of production and consumption.

Adopting a country by country approach, Part Three considers the aims, priorities, conditions and outcomes of national economic policies in the Benelux countries, Britain, France, Germany, Italy, Scandinavia and Spain respectively.

Finally, the conclusion of this book seeks to place post-war economic change and integration in western Europe into a long-term historical perspective that takes account of development in the late nineteenth century and the inter-war period.

PART ONE: THE EUROPEAN ECONOMY SINCE 1945

2 The Legacy of the Second World War

Peter Howlett

Economic Growth during the War

Wartime disruption both to geographical boundaries and to the price mechanism makes it difficult to give a precise account of the growth of the national economies during the Second World War, particularly in 1944 and 1945 when a lot of economic activity in continental Europe probably moved into the unrecorded informal sector. However, Angus Maddison has estimated a consistent set of real data covering our economies for this period and these are shown in Table 2.1.[1] Not surprisingly, those economies which experienced land fighting ended the war with levels of real GDP below their pre-war level, whereas the war enhanced the levels of real GDP of those economies that avoided land fighting (the UK and the neutral economies).

Apart from the neutrals, the only economies which appear to have received overall sustained stimulation from the war were the UK and Germany. At their respective peaks they had a level of real GDP 27 per cent (in 1943) and 24 per cent (in 1944) higher than it had been in 1938. The decline in UK real GDP after 1943, reflecting the fact that munitions production had reached the level necessary to launch the liberation of Europe, was fairly steady, but in Germany the devastation that came with the land war which culminated in defeat brought a dramatic decline in real GDP of almost a third in 1945. By contrast the performance of the other major combatant, Italy, was consistently poor: real GDP peaked as early as 1940 (and even then it was only 8 per cent higher than in 1938) and it declined rapidly after the Allied invasion in 1943.

The occupied countries, France, Belgium, Denmark, the Netherlands and Norway, all experienced a similar pattern of invasion and occupation leading to a decline in real GDP in 1940. Of these economies Denmark was the quickest to recover and indeed in 1944 its level of real GDP exceeded its 1938 level (although it subsequently fell back in 1945). Following its liberation in the summer of 1944 Belgium also started to revive but there was no recovery in the other occupied economies until the last year of the war. Occupation was most severe for France and the Netherlands: by 1944 both had seen real GDP reduced to about half its pre-war level and the gains made in 1945 were modest.

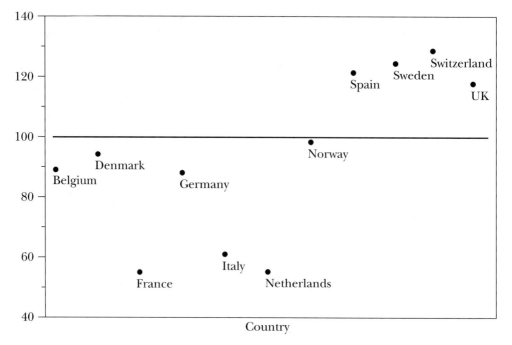

Figure 2.1. Real GDP in 1945 (1938 = 100). *Source:* calculated from A. Maddison, *Monitoring the World Economy 1820–1992* (Paris, 1995).

Table 2.1. Real Gross Domestic Product, 1939–45 (1938 = 100)

	1939	**1940**	**1941**	**1942**	**1943**	**1944**	**1945**
Germany	109	110	117	119	121	124	88
Italy	107	108	107	105	95	77	61
UK	101	111	121	124	127	122	117
France	107	88	70	63	60	50	55
Belgium	107	94	89	81	80	84	89
Denmark	105	90	81	83	92	102	94
Netherlands	107	94	89	81	79	53	55
Norway	105	95	98	94	92	87	98
Spain	106	115	115	122	125	130	121
Sweden	107	104	105	112	117	121	124
Switzerland	100	101	100	98	97	99	128

Source: calculated from Maddison, *Monitoring the World Economy*, pp. 162–3, 181, 183–4; Maddison derived his real GDP figures using a purchasing power parity method based on 1990 prices.

Furthermore, Table 2.1 overstates the actual living standards enjoyed by those in the occupied economies because it does not take into account their exploitation by Germany. The occupied economies were subject to occupation levies by Germany. France, in particular, suffered, transferring about a third of its output to Germany during the period of occupation and supplying more than 40 per cent of the total foreign occupation income received by Germany.

For Germany the foreign contribution amounted to about one-seventh of GDP and it helped to ensure that the reduction in German living standards was small.[2] Germany also used its position to impose highly favourable exchange rates on other continental economies and to boost its imports of industrial and agricultural goods from the western occupied countries (for example, it has been estimated that during the occupation Belgium supplied between two-thirds and three-quarters of its manufacturing output directly to Germany); and as a last resort it could simply seize what it needed from them (indeed, many of the goods and services provided to Germany by the occupied countries were never paid for).

Of the neutral countries, the war proved beneficial for Spain and Sweden which were both important suppliers to the German economy; in particular, Swedish iron ore was a key strategic input for the German war economy. By 1945 Swedish real GDP was 24 per cent higher than it had been in 1938 and at its peak in 1944 Spain had seen a gain of 30 per cent. The geographical position of Switzerland made it more dependent on German goodwill and the curtailment of Swiss imports partly explains its sluggish wartime performance. However, 1945 brought a marked upturn in Swiss fortunes and real GDP increased sharply.

The Impact of the War on the Structure of GDP

Most of the economies involved in the war underwent a marked shift in the composition of their GDP as government expenditure expanded at the expense of consumption, investment and net exports. In the UK and Germany the expansion of the state sector mainly reflected the need to finance their massive war effort. In both countries the state came to dominate the economy, although in Germany the trend had begun before the war and its extent went much further: in 1939 about a third of German national income was already devoted to the war effort, with the UK devoting less than half that amount; by 1943 the German figure had risen to about 70 per cent (and it was probably even higher in 1944) and the UK had peaked at 55 per cent. In contrast, the weaker commitment of Mussolini to the war was reflected by the fact that at its peak, in 1941, the Italian economy devoted less than a quarter of GDP to the war effort.

In the occupied economies the expansion of the state sector reflected the enlarged bureaucracy needed to administer them and the high level of the occupation levies. Although during the war state expenditure also grew in the neutral economies, it did not come to dominate economic activity to the same extent; for example, in the case of Sweden government expenditure as a percentage of GDP increased from 9 per cent in 1938 to 14 per cent between 1941 and 1943.

In a peacetime economy consumption typically dominates GDP but the massive expansion of the government sector and the changes in output this entailed inevitably meant that consumption contracted severely, for example in the UK the share of consumption in GDP fell from 79 per cent in 1938 to 52 per cent in 1943. Germany had already experienced a marked decline in private consumption in the 1930s, from 71 per cent of national income in 1928 to 59 per cent in 1938, but this did not prevent real per capita consumption falling a further 30 per cent between 1938 and 1944 (compared to a 14.5 per cent decline in Britain between 1938 and 1943). However, until 1943 most of the increase in German government expenditure came not from squeezing domestic consumers but from squeezing the consumers in the occupied economies. This in turn added to the burden on the occupied economies: in France, for example, consumption was less than half of its pre-war level (Belgium and the Netherlands suffered similar, if slightly less severe, fates whilst Denmark was the least affected of the occupied economies).

Investment often contracts in wartime because the danger of damage by enemy action makes any new investment extremely risky, and war also acts to discourage and curtail trade (shipping blockades and the bombing or sabotage of key transportation links being an important form of economic warfare). Furthermore, both investment and trade came to be dominated by the war needs of the state. In both Germany and the UK civilian house building was squeezed in order to increase the allocation of investment resources to war production. The UK lost its continental markets during the war whilst British naval superiority cut Germany off from its non-continental markets. Furthermore, the loss of shipping due to warfare meant that shipping capacity was a key constraint and it had to be carefully controlled by the state. Finally, it has already been pointed out that Germany drew on external resources to boost its ability to wage war and the UK was no different: it ran down its own considerable foreign assets and it also received substantial wartime aid from Canada and, particularly, the USA.

The Pattern and Volume of Trade

The war had a dramatic impact on trading patterns; for example, the pre-war trend of German policy, which had been to increase its trade with central and south-east Europe, was reversed and trade was reorientated to the western economies which produced the range and quality of goods needed in a modern war economy. The wartime domination of western continental European trade by Germany is shown in Table 2.2: in terms of imports, the importance of German supplies increased dramatically for all the economies shown whilst in terms of exports the orientation to Germany of the occupied economies in particular was even more marked. The rise in the importance of Germany to wartime Swedish trade largely reflected the mining of the Skagerrak by the Germans in April 1940; this effectively cut Sweden off from the west, which it had previously relied on for 70 per cent of its trade. The general experience of a massive expansion in the importance of trade with Germany did, however, mask another important

Table 2.2. Trade of western European economies with Germany, 1938 and 1943

	1938		1943	
	I	**E**	**I**	**E**
Italy	27	21	60	48
Belgium	11	12	45	77
Denmark	25	20	71	74
France	7	6	60	82
Netherlands	21	15	68	84
Norway	18	16	68	72
Sweden	24	18	51	47
Switzerland	23	16	31	37

Note: I = imports from Germany as a percentage of total imports; E = exports to Germany as a percentage of total exports.

Source: calculated from B.R. Mitchell, *International Historical Statistics: Europe 1750–1988* (Houndmills, 3rd edition, 1992), pp. 558–62, 574, 582, 591, 607, 611, 615, 638, 641; based on nominal value in local currency.

wartime development: trade between other western European economies (with the exception of some Scandinavian trade) collapsed.

For many economies this collapse either compounded the problems caused by the inter-war depression or wiped out the hard-won gains of the late 1930s, as Figure 2.2 illustrates. By 1938 only the three Scandinavian economies had restored their export volumes to their 1929 level and of these Denmark and Norway would both suffer serious setbacks in the war; Belgium had almost restored its export volume to the 1929 level prior to the war, but by 1946 its export level had been reduced by more than 60 per cent compared to 1938. Figure 2.2 clearly demonstrates the devastating impact the war had on the defeated powers and the occupied economies. Germany fared worst, with an export volume in 1946 that was only 7 per cent of its 1938 level, whilst several of the former occupied economies were exporting less than half their 1938 volume.

Only the UK, Sweden and Switzerland had restored or exceeded their 1938 volume of exports by 1946 (although Switzerland would take another two years to again achieve the 1929 level of exports and the UK would take another three years). The other western European economies had to wait until 1949–50 to achieve this goal (by which time most had also matched their 1929 export volume level), with the exception of (West) Germany which needed an extra year (and it would not reach its 1929 export volume level until the mid-1950s).

One problem facing Germany was the demands of its ally Italy. By 1938 Germany was the main trading partner of Italy, but the relationship was not to the benefit of Germany since Italy wanted scarce raw materials from Germany but in

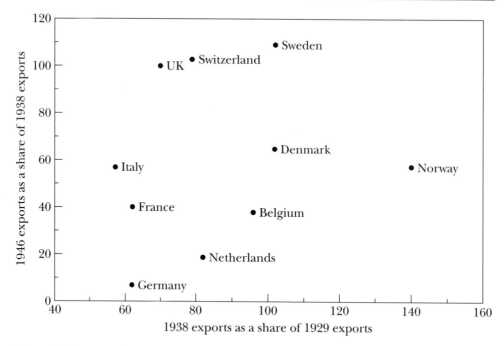

Figure 2.2. Impact of the 1930s depression and the Second World War on export volumes. *Source:* A. Maddison, *Dynamic Forces in Capitalist Development* (Oxford, 1991), pp. 316–19 (export volume in 1913 = 100).

return supplied non-strategic goods. Table 2.2 shows that in 1943 Italian dependence on Germany for imports was on a par with that of the occupied economies but Italy exported a much smaller share of its total exports to Germany. Thus, the Italian economy was a potential drag on the German wartime effort, although the latter effectively resisted most of the important demands of the former.

The wartime loss of non-European supplies increased the strain on several economies. The main UK exports to Norway, for example, had been textiles and coal; whilst the loss of the former was not serious, the loss of the latter (which was not replaced by Germany) did adversely affect the performance of the Norwegian economy. Indeed, the loss of raw material imports and the enforced increase of their own raw material exports to Germany was one of the chief factors behind the wartime decline in the GDP of the occupied economies. On the other hand, the increase of raw material exports to Germany partially explains the rather better wartime performance of both Spain and Sweden.

The loss of European supplies adversely affected the UK: Europe had accounted for a fifth of all pre-war British imports but by 1941 it accounted for a mere 0.2 per cent. One consequence was that the UK became more reliant on North America for its imports: imports from North America increased from just over a fifth of total imports in 1938 to almost half in 1945. Britain was also adversely affected by the wartime inflation which saw export prices increase by 85 per cent and import prices double. Thus, although the volume of British imports fell by almost a third during the war, the import bill rose by almost a fifth.

The Distribution of Labour

Details about wartime changes in the distribution of the workforce are sketchy for most of these economies. The German and British labour markets were dominated by the massive expansion of the wartime armed forces. In Germany the size of the armed forces increased from 1.4 million personnel in 1939 to 13 million by the end of the war; in the UK it increased from just under half a million in 1939 to just over 5 million in 1945. In both economies this in turn led to a mobilization of civilian labour, particularly female labour, to replace men taken into the armed forces.

In focus: The Wartime Mobilization of Women

The war brought about an expansion of the armed forces in all the combatant nations and a direct consequence of this was that men were removed from the civilian labour force in very large numbers. This loss, particularly the loss of industrial labour, had to be replaced and an obvious source of replacement labour was women. In both Germany and Britain the war saw the expansion of female employment in traditionally male preserves such as engineering, chemicals, and iron and steel.

Traditionally historians have contrasted the successful British effort to mobilize women for the war effort with the German failure to utilize properly its female labour reserves.[1] Table 2.3 shows that the number of women in the

Table 2.3. Female civilian labour force: Germany and the UK, 1939–45 (excluding armed forces and foreign workers)

	Number (in 000s)		Percentage of total	
	Germany	**UK**	**Germany**	**UK**
1939	14,626	5,094	37.4	26.4
1940	14,386	5,517	41.3	30.0
1941	14,167	6,005	42.7	33.5
1942	14,437	6,608	46.1	36.8
1943	14,806	6,792	48.9	38.8
1944	14,808	6,640	51.1	39.0
1945		6,331		38.2

Sources: German figures from L.J. Rupp, *Mobilizing Women for War* (Princeton, 1978), pp. 185, 187; UK figures calculated from Central Statistical Office with P. Howlett, *Fighting with Figures* (London, 1995), p. 38.

1. This case study is based on: L.J. Rupp, *Mobilizing Women for War* (Princeton, 1978), pp. 74–114, 167–81; A.S. Milward, *War, Economy and Society 1939–1945* (London, 1977), pp. 219–21; R.J. Overy, *War and Economy in the Third Reich* (Oxford, 1994), especially pp. 303–11.

The Wartime Mobilization of Women (continued)

civilian labour force in Britain increased by a third between 1939 and 1943 whereas in Germany numbers were relatively static. These numbers also support the view that whereas Nazi ideology dissuaded German women from the workforce in order to protect the sanctity and stability of the family, the British fully embraced compulsion by passing laws to allow them to conscript and direct female workers (although in practice these were used mainly to direct young unmarried women to the war industries). Thus, we have the apparent irony that the less democratic society adopted the more liberal approach to the labour market.

The traditional view of the mobilization of female workers in Germany has, though, been criticized. First, consider the actual number of women mobilized in each economy: the minimum number of women in the German civilian labour force was 14.2 million in 1941 but the maximum in the UK was only 6.8 million in 1943 (Table 2.3), a discrepancy that is not fully explicable by the larger German population. In Germany, unlike Britain and despite Nazi ideology, the number of women in the labour force had increased by more than 3 million between 1933 and 1939. Amongst the industrialized countries of the 1930s Germany had the highest proportion of women in the labour force (the higher pre-war female participation rate of Germany compared to Britain is not a surprise in the context of the national labour markets – Germany had reached conditions of full employment in 1938 whereas in Britain unemployment was still above one million in mid-1940). The right-hand half of Table 2.3 shows that in 1939 women made up 37 per cent of the civilian labour force in Germany, had exceeded 40 per cent in 1940, and by 1944 more than half of all workers in the indigenous German civilian labour force was female; in Britain, at their peak women accounted for only 39 per cent of the civilian labour force.

Although this suggests that Germany was far better than Britain in utilizing female labour to replace its lost civilian male labour (which is the reverse of the story told by the absolute numbers), it is misleading as it ignores the 3 million foreign workers drafted into the German economy during the war. If these are taken into account then the share of German female labour increased from 37.1 per cent in 1939 to 40.6 per cent at its peak in 1942. Thus, it seems that in terms of the overall civilian economy both countries mobilized female workers to roughly the same degree (that is, female workers came to account for approximately four out of every ten workers in both economies).

Within the civilian labour force there was a redistribution of labour to the munitions and related industries. In Britain the share of workers in such industries increased from 17 per cent of civilian employment in 1939 to 30 per cent in 1943; whilst in Germany their share of industrial employment increased from 34 per cent in 1939 to 45 per cent in 1943. In both economies this

expansion was matched by a contraction of employment in the consumer industries. In Germany the pressure on the civilian labour market was greatly eased by
the use of foreign labour which at its peak numbered more than seven million
workers.

Within the occupied economies the initial impact of German invasion was
to greatly increase unemployment. This was because of the disruption of both
raw material supplies and transportation and distribution systems, compounded
by the loss of workers fleeing the oncoming armies. However, despite production remaining at low levels in most of the occupied economies, unemployment
levels gradually recovered – although this often reflected the introduction of
compulsory short-time working which effectively replaced unemployment with
overemployment. Increasingly many of these workers came to work, either directly
or indirectly, on orders for the German economy (it has been estimated that in
France approximately 3 million workers were so employed).[3] Many workers in
Sweden and Switzerland were likewise employed.

In focus: Foreign Labour in the German Economy

Foreign labour played an important part in the German war economy and its
growth is shown in Figure 2.3. Civilian foreign labour had played a small but

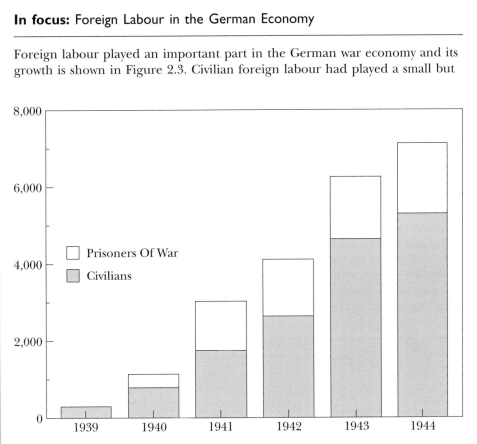

Figure 2.3. Foreign workers in Germany on 31 May annually, 1939–44 (000s).
Source: A.S. Milward, *War, Economy and Society 1939–45*, p. 223.

Foreign Labour in the German Economy (continued)

Plate 2.1. 'Youth of France . . . make the right choice!' A German propaganda poster aimed at recruiting workers in occupied France (about 1940). Young people were offered the 'choice' between prospering in German factories and allying themselves with an England that was heading for defeat.

significant role in the pre-war period but during the war this expanded: between 1940 and 1941 it increased by almost 1 million, and between 1941 and 1943 it increased by a further 2.9 million. These workers were initially attracted to Germany by carrots (offers of higher wages) and sticks (for example, withholding unemployment benefit from workers who refused to go to Germany). As the pressure on the German economy intensified in 1942 the German authorities started to close down factories in the occupied economies that were not directly contributing to the war effort. This was followed by the introduction of direct compulsion (which had previously been used in eastern Europe) to deport workers from France, Belgium and the Netherlands to Germany. The civilian workers were supplemented by prisoners of war (of whom 1.8 million were working in Germany by 1944) and by foreigners in concentration camps so that at the peak the total number of foreign workers in Germany exceeded 7 million, accounting for approximately a fifth of the total German labour force.

Foreign Labour in the German Economy (continued)

Plate 2.2. A young Ukrainian forced worker in a Siemens plant (1943). There were more than 7 million foreign workers in Germany in 1944, and most were drafted in by direct compulsion in the occupied countries.

Foreign Labour in the German Economy (continued)

There was also a shift in the distribution of foreigners employed in the German economy: before 1942 the bulk of foreigners were employed in agriculture (approximately 60 per cent in 1940, mainly Polish workers, and just under half in 1941) but that year witnessed a sharp rise in the number employed in industry and by 1943 these constituted the largest group (45 per cent). The importance of this can be seen from the fact that in 1940 foreign workers accounted for under 3 per cent of the German industrial labour force but by 1944 they accounted for almost 30 per cent.

The bulk of these foreign workers came from central and eastern Europe (Poland in particular being a key source) and, with the exception of the Italians, all came from economies that had been conquered by Germany or, like Slovakia, were effectively German satellites. Until the beginning of 1943 Italian workers were the largest group of western European workers in Germany (their numbers peaking at over 200,000 in mid-1942) but as the need in the Italian economy for skilled workers grew, coupled with the relatively poor treatment of their workers in Germany and rising wage levels in Italy (particularly in agriculture), their numbers diminished and by late 1943 there were barely 100,000 Italian workers left in Germany. The Netherlands was another important source of foreign labour in the early years of the war but from 1942 onwards Belgium and particularly France became more important: compulsory drafting was introduced in Belgium in October 1942 and over the next six months 215,000 workers were transferred to Germany; by April 1944 there were more than 630,000 civilian male French workers in Germany (which represented more than 10 per cent of all Frenchmen aged between 18 and 50). Norway, on the other hand, proved to be a net importer of labour during the war.

Trends in Industry and Agriculture

Trends in industrial production during the war were similar to those in real GDP per capita: in the UK, Germany (at least until 1944) and the neutral economies industrial production rose whereas in the occupied economies and Italy it fell. In the occupied economies (where the decline in industrial production was between one-third and two-thirds) a key problem was the disruption of energy supplies, particularly of coal and oil. For example, despite the fact that Belgian coal was important to the economies of Germany, France and Italy, its output declined during the occupation (from 30 million tonnes in 1941 to 25 million tonnes in 1943) and coal exports fell by almost half (from 4 million tonnes to 2.2 million tonnes). Furthermore, France, Norway and Denmark had previously relied on Britain for a significant proportion of their coal fuel supplies and this loss was not made good by Germany (which lacked the capacity to replace the

British supplies). One long-term consequence of this situation is that the loss of British coal supplies made French industry more dependent on the Ruhr and this would eventually help to underpin the creation of the European Coal and Steel Community in 1951, which was itself an important step towards creating the new post-war Europe.

The pattern of industrial production changed during the war in all economies, including the neutrals, to reflect the vastly increased demand for munitions. The general trend was for engineering, iron and steel, metallurgical and non-metallurgical industries to expand their production along with the more obvious war industries such as aircraft, shipbuilding, armaments and chemicals. The neutral economies became an important source of supply for Germany as they were safe from the threat of disruption by allied air attacks. Of particular importance was the Swedish provision of iron ore, ball-bearings, paper-pulp, paper and wood products and the Swiss provision of engineering goods and armaments. The UK supply of munitions (particularly of aircraft, tanks, small arms and landing craft and ships) and machine tools was greatly boosted by American goods supplied under Lend–Lease aid provided by the USA.

A corollary of the expansion of the munitions and related industries was the contraction of the consumer goods industries. This contraction was often part of a deliberate state policy to release more resources for the war industries. In contrast, many German consumer industries initially increased their output (although this situation was reversed in the latter stages of the war) and the consumption of consumer goods by the German population was further boosted by supplies from the occupied economies. However, the orientation of the German economy towards war production had proceeded further than in any other economy prior to the outbreak of war. Thus, between 1936 and 1939 the war-related industries accounted for two-thirds of all industrial investment and by 1939 a quarter of the German labour force was working on military orders.

The agricultural sector usually plays a key role in wartime because of the need to ensure an adequate food supply: in the Second World War an estimated one million Europeans, mainly in central and eastern Europe, died of starvation. The food supply came under pressure because trade disruption reduced the flow of imported foodstuffs. These supply problems were exacerbated by rising demand which was fuelled by increasing employment and real incomes in Germany, the UK and the neutral economies and by the increased burden placed on the occupied countries by Germany. Originally, Germany had hoped that eastern Europe would become its food basket, but between 1940 and 1943 France, Denmark and even Italy supplied more food to Germany than Russia; France in particular became a key source of food for the wartime German economy.

Agricultural production in wartime western Europe witnessed a general trend away from livestock farming to arable farming as the latter produced a higher calorific output per hectare. In Britain, for example, net domestic output by calories increased by over 90 per cent which enabled it to cut its calorific dependence on imports by three-quarters. The war also witnessed increased mechanization in agriculture in the non-occupied economies.

The pressures on food supply, and concerns about inflation, led to the state taking control of food supply and distribution, even in the neutral economies, and food rationing became the norm. Such policies were probably most successful in Switzerland and the UK, where popular support for such policies was also probably strongest and policing the easiest. Even in the occupied economies, however, where farmers were often reluctant to follow policies imposed by Germany, state policy was relatively successful in at least maintaining a minimum food supply to the population (although only in Denmark and the Netherlands did the food supply increase during the war). The operation of a black market was also a useful valve in the occupied economies, especially Belgium, for releasing some of the inherent economic, political and social pressures.

The Economic Legacy of the War

Figure 2.1 emphasizes that one wartime legacy for the western European economies, other than the UK and the neutral countries, was the need to restore real GDP to its pre-war levels. The drive for restoration could be seen as a potential source of stimulation to post-war Europe. Given that the Second World War was more destructive in economic terms than the First World War, it was likely that the post-war recovery would be more rapid (simply because it was starting from a relatively lower base) and so it proved. The speed at which an economy achieved restoration was, in general, correlated with the shock the war had induced. Thus, the restoration of pre-war levels of real GDP was achieved in 1946 by Denmark and Norway, in 1947 by Belgium and the Netherlands, and in 1949 by France and Italy.

The most notable exception was Germany, which did not restore pre-war levels until 1951, and this was because, unlike these other economies, German real GDP decreased significantly in 1946 (at which time it was only 52 per cent of its 1938 level – some estimates even suggest a much lower figure). The only other economy to suffer a decline after the war was the UK whose real GDP fell continuously from 1943 to 1947 (although even in the latter year it was still 10 per cent higher than it had been in 1938). Spain is also a special case, because although it had been neutral during the war it had previously suffered its own bloody Civil War (1936–39), and despite the stimulation it received from the Second World War it did not exceed its 1935 level of real GDP until 1951 (see Chapter 21).

The loss of life attributable to the Second World War and the Holocaust amounted to at least 40 million people. This was more than three times the loss incurred in the First World War. Most of the war-induced deaths occurred in central and eastern Europe, and the western economies (with the exception of Germany and Austria) suffered relatively small losses: Denmark and Norway suffered minimal casualties; Belgium witnessed just over 100,000 war-related deaths (equal to about 1.3 per cent of its pre-war population), Italy approximately a quarter of a million (0.6 per cent), the UK 362,000 (0.8 per cent), France approximately half a million (1.4 per cent); of these economies, the more than 200,000 casualties suffered by the Netherlands was the highest in proportional terms (2.4 per cent). German losses were on a much larger scale: over 6 million Germans (9 per cent) died as a direct result of the war.

In demographic terms another important legacy of the war was the mass movement of people: the defeat of Germany brought in its wake the migration of 25 million people, probably the greatest such migration in European history. Migration in the west was dominated by the influx of refugees to Germany: by 1950 Germany had absorbed 10 million refugees (mainly ethnic Germans), three-quarters of them going to West Germany. Given that one of the aims of Nazi ideology and expansionism was to increase the 'living space' of Germans, it is ironic that this post-war 'resettlement' of German populations in Germany increased the 'living space' of non-German populations and condensed that of Germans.

The war also adversely affected the quality of human capital: in the immediate post-war years the UN thought that the most serious problem facing Europe was the shortage of managers, technicians and skilled workers. This problem was particularly acute in the former occupied economies because during the war there had been de-skilling of experienced workers (due to mobilization and by their being forced to work in occupations unrelated to their training) and young workers had not been trained. In Germany the problem was exacerbated by the self-inflicted wounds of the Holocaust by which the state systematically killed a large number of its own able-bodied and skilled citizens. Given that modern economic growth theory emphasizes the role of human capital in achieving long-term growth, it is likely that efforts to make good this particular weakness were an important source of post-war growth. In this regard West Germany benefitted from the post-war migration which provided the economy with a cheap, flexible and relatively skilled pool of labour.

In terms of physical capital the Second World War caused more damage to Europe than the First World War: extensive bombing – particularly of the two main European combatants, i.e. Germany and the UK – destroyed factories, housing and transportation systems; merchant shipping was lost to submarine warfare (the German and Italian merchant fleets were virtually destroyed and the UK lost its position as the largest fleet to the USA); and livestock was also destroyed on a large scale. The damage to the housing stock was most severe in Germany (where about a fifth of the pre-war stock was destroyed) but it was also significant (5–9 per cent of the pre-war stock) in Italy, Belgium, France, the Netherlands and the UK. The situation was compounded by the virtual cessation of non-war-related building during the hostilities. However, after the war the general desire to make good the wartime damage led to increased investment in house building, except in France and Italy, and this was an important component of the post-war investment boom that underpinned recovery and growth. Furthermore, some economies, most notably Germany, ended the war with a larger industrial capital stock due to wartime investment in the munitions and related industries and this too aided post-war recovery.

Many economies also saw their net foreign assets decline: the UK saw a pre-war positive balance of $21 billion turn into a debt of $2 billion in 1947, the pre-war French assets of $3.9 billion were wiped out, whilst Dutch assets of $4.8 billion were cut in half. Germany, on the other hand, did relatively well: a net debtor of $2 billion in 1938, it made no service payments on that debt until 1953 and even then the pre-war debts were scaled down.[4] The war also left Europe facing a balance of payments crisis in general and a severe dollar shortage in particular. The need to solve this problem came to dominate economic policy in the immediate post-war years.

Historiographical Interpretations

The Second World War ended with Germany defeated and the UK victorious, but in the post-war period West Germany would be near the top of the growth league of the major industrial powers (just behind Japan, another defeated power) while the UK would languish near the bottom of the league (along with the USA). This has led some historians to conclude that defeat in war was actually beneficial to long-term growth. In this section we shall consider two variations of this argument: one focusing on capital (the capital legacy debate) and one focusing on institutional change (the Olson debate).

It has been argued that the wartime destruction of the capital stock of the defeated powers, and to a lesser extent the occupied economies, meant that in the post-war period these economies invested in new plant and machinery which embodied the latest technology. This gave them a competitive edge over economies such as the UK which did not engage in such investment and thus explained their better post-war growth record. Although this argument has some superficial appeal, it does not stand up to close historical scrutiny; for example, economic studies show that the utilization of machinery rather than its age is a more important factor in explaining differences in economic productivity across economies.

More importantly most economic historians, following the lead of a 1953 UN report, have argued that despite wartime destruction, increases in industrial capacity during the war meant that the capital stock of Europe was greater after the war than it had been before the war. Furthermore, much of the wartime investment was geared towards industries which were to prove important in the post-war period, such as the car and aircraft industries, engineering, chemicals, metal manufacturing and, crucially, machine tools. Finally, the war had also acted as a catalyst for technical innovation in the aircraft industry, in chemicals, in medicine, in synthetic materials, in metallurgy and in atomic energy. Thus, at the end of the war there was a backlog of technical innovations that could be applied to the peacetime economies and whose potential remained to be exploited.

Olson's theory of institutional sclerosis starts by proposing that vested interest groups (such as trade unions and employer cartels) come to dominate the economy.[5] Over time their actions have a detrimental impact on the economy: first, through the rent they extract from the economy for their members (for example, higher wages for trade union members or higher prices for the goods of the cartel members); and secondly, in the obstacles they put in the way of economic progress in an effort to protect the vested interest of their own group. They thus exert a sclerotic influence on the economy resulting in decelerating rates of growth. War can be good if it helps to sweep away the existing vested interests and thus remove the obstacles to new ideas, people and organizational forms which can allow the economy to fulfil its potential more easily. For Olson, the defeat of Germany in the Second World War did just that and thus helps to explain its impressive post-war record, whereas in victorious Britain there was no such institutional new broom and thus the sclerotic tendencies of the British economy continued.

The Olson argument is controversial and indeed there is evidence that the war reinforced or created certain tendencies that Olson would identify as sclerotic: it is argued that it encouraged the growth of cartels and trade associations in Europe and that it intensified existing state–business relations; it is also clear that it led to the increased protection of agriculture in post-war Europe (the Common Agricultural Policy of the European Economic Community can be traced back to state intervention in the management of wartime agriculture and food supply). However, the war also opened the way for new ideas and modes of production; for example, it led to a more widespread European embrace of American methods of standardized mass production, and in particular the demonstration of the failure and danger of autarky in the inter-war and war years did pave the way for greater willingness to create more openness in international trade and for nations to cooperate with one another.

The post-war world also saw a proliferation of international institutions, such as the International Monetary Fund, the World Bank, the General Agreement on Tariffs and Trade, and the Bretton Woods system, whose aim was to create a more stable and freer international economy. Within western Europe the most important institutional legacy of the war would be the European Economic Community and its attendant bodies at whose core lay a Franco-German alliance. This alliance was important because the economic conflict between France and Germany had been a significant contributory factor to the two World Wars of the first half of the twentieth century; its creation would usher in an unprecedented economic golden age for western Europe.

Bibliographical Note

The economic history literature on western Europe in the Second World War is dominated by Alan Milward: his *War, Economy and Society 1939–1945* (London, 1977) is the outstanding comparative wartime study; it is ably supported by his books on *The German Economy at War* (London, 1965), *The New Order and the French Economy* (London, 1970) and *The Fascist Economy in Norway* (Oxford, 1972). Other useful comparative wartime studies include G. Ránki, *The Economics of the Second World War* (Vienna, 1993), M. Harrison (ed.), *Economic Mobilisation for World War II* (forthcoming) and Jun Sakudo and Takao Shiba (eds), *World War II and the Transformation of Business Systems* (Tokyo, 1994). A concise introduction to the wartime economies of Europe is provided by the chapter in Derek H. Aldcroft, *The European Economy 1914–1990* (3rd edn, London, 1993).

With the exception of Germany the literature on individual economies is surprisingly thin. Probably the most useful of the books on the German economy are B.A. Carroll, *Design for Total War: Arms and Economics in the Third Reich* (The Hague, 1968) and R.J. Overy, *War and Economy in the Third Reich* (Oxford, 1994), the latter being a series of collected papers by the historian who has most successfully challenged Milward's view of the German war economy. Useful sources for other economies are: W.K. Hancock and M.M. Gowing, *The British War Economy* (London, 1949), and P. Howlett, 'The wartime economy, 1939–1945', pp. 1–31 in Roderick Floud and Donald McCloskey (eds), *The Economic History of Britain since 1700* (2nd edn), *Volume 3: 1939–1992* (Cambridge, 1994); Angela Raspin, *The Italian War Economy, 1940–1943* (New York and London, 1986); see also the relevant chapters in Vera Zamagni, *The Economic History of Italy, 1860–1990* (Oxford, 1993); John Gillingham, *Belgian Business in the Nazi New Order* (Ghent, 1977); and M. Fritz, I. Nygren, S. Olsson and U. Olsson, *The Adaptable Nation* (Stockholm, 1982).

Notes

1. A. Maddison, *Monitoring the World Economy 1820–1992* (Paris, 1995). The data were calculated on the basis of the post-war territory of each economy. The only serious problem this poses is that Germany refers to West Germany, although the relative shifts shown are not out of line with other independent estimates for wartime Germany.

2. A.S. Milward, *War, Economy and Society 1939–1945* (London, 1977), pp. 135–49.

3. A.S. Milward, *The New Order and the French Economy* (London, 1970), pp. 291–3.

4. Maddison, *Monitoring the World Economy*, p. 71.

5. M. Olson, *The Rise and Decline of Nations* (New Haven, 1982).

3 Reconstruction and the Beginnings of European Integration

Till Geiger

After a decade of economic crisis and war, most western European politicians rejected previous policy regimes of limited state intervention and/or autarkic trade policy. Despite significant differences, governments across western Europe adopted expansionary domestic reconstruction programmes and ambitious welfare reforms. Given this broad consensus, this chapter emphasizes the shared problems of post-war reconstruction rather than the different national experiences.

Reconstruction, Emergency Relief and the Collapse of Intra-European Trade

At the end of the Second World War, the nation states of western Europe faced similar domestic challenges of accomplishing the transition from war to peace and of reconstructing the domestic economy. To assist the process of domestic reconstruction, the American and British governments took the lead in organizing emergency relief to the war-torn regions of Europe and in re-establishing international trade relations. Confronted with these problems, policy-makers in war-torn Europe faced crucial decisions which would determine the pace of economic recovery. With hindsight, the prospects for a speedy recovery of western Europe were excellent given the considerable potential for catch-up growth (compare Chapters 2 and 4). At the time, however, many Europeans felt rather pessimistic about the continent's economic prospects.

Liberation (or defeat) did not end economic hardship for most Europeans. Among the demographic and economic consequences of the Second World War outlined in Chapter 2, the shortage of food and the large number of displaced persons presented the most immediate problem for Allied military authorities and new-formed governments. Civilian food rations declined in some areas to less than 1000 calories per day. As a consequence of wartime policy, domestic

Plate 3.1. Photograph by David Seymour of a hungry child, orphaned by the war, waiting to receive her milk ration. The acute shortage of food left millions of urban people living at subsistence level. The food crisis became worse in 1947 following an extremely harsh winter.

agriculture could not manage to supply sufficient food for the starving consumers. Moreover, the extensive damage to the transport system severely disrupted not only food distribution, but also industrial production. Many firms found their efforts to convert to peacetime production frustrated by the shortage of raw materials and coal. Faced with these problems, many Europeans relied on the black market to supplement their meagre rations or obtain fuel. Moreover, wartime inflation had undermined the value of the national currency.

As a consequence of general economic disruption, most European economies disintegrated into localized economies based on barter exchange. To some extent, the widespread experience of deprivation undermined people's trust in government economic policy and capitalism. Distrusting the market, citizens increasingly defied economic controls and government rationing.[1]

Therefore, a primary objective of most governments became the restoration of national integration of economic activity.[2] To increase domestic food production, governments introduced agricultural support payments to farmers to discourage them from selling food on the black market. In an attempt to contain the high inflation, some governments decided to eradicate the monetary overhang by a currency reform (for example, Belgium in 1946; West Germany in 1948) or a strict monetary policy (for example, Italy after 1948). To tackle the housing crisis, most governments supported the construction of new apartment blocks and houses on the outskirts of bomb-damaged cities. Moreover, many countries set about reforming social security arrangements for their population. Through these policy measures, governments attempted to restore the functioning of the market economy at home.

The international community assisted these efforts to overcome the immediate economic crisis by providing roughly $2.6 billion of short-term emergency relief, mainly to eastern European countries. Most of this assistance was distributed through the United Nations Relief and Rehabilitation Administration (UNRRA) and financed imports of food supplies, raw materials and coal from the United States or other European countries. At the same time, UNRRA assisted in the resettlement of the thousands of displaced persons at the end of the war. While making an important contribution, the national governments anxiously guarded against any attempts by UNRRA officials to interfere in domestic affairs (such as treatment of displaced persons) or economic policy (such as in the distribution of economic aid).

During the war, American and British experts attempted to address the thorny issue of re-establishing international payments, finance and trade. After the experience of the international financial crisis and the destructive trade wars of the inter-war period, the consensus favoured the creation of new international institutions to oversee a new international economic order. As Chapter 2 showed, the Second World War further disrupted the established pattern of intra-European trade and left most European countries with considerable debts. These negotiations culminated in the Bretton Woods agreement creating the International Monetary Fund and the International Bank for Reconstruction and Development (better known as the World Bank). Throughout the negotiations, the American government was primarily interested in re-establishing an international payments system based on fixed exchange rates and currency convertibility. Therefore, American negotiators insisted that all signatories make their currency convertible after a period of five years. However, most European countries supported the Bretton Woods agreement in the expectation of generous reconstruction loans from the American government. When these loans failed to materialize after 1945, most European governments continued to maintain the existing over-valued

Table 3.1. Level of industrial production in selected European countries (1938 = 100)

	1946				1947		
	Q1	**Q2**	**Q3**	**Q4**	**Q1**	**Q2**	**Q3**
Belgium	77	85	93	99	99	106	102
Denmark	93	86	97	100	99	100	108
France	75	88	82	94	95	104	96
West Germany	22	26	31	31	24	33	37
Italy	34	55	65	61	49	65	76
Netherlands	62	68	76	83	81	88	91
United Kingdom	101	102	100	115	103	110	109
Total incl. Germany	68	74	76	83	78	85	86
Total excl. Germany	80	87	88	98	93	100	99

Note: Q1 = first quarter, Q2 = second quarter, etc.

Source: United Nations Economic Commission for Europe, Research and Planning Division, *A Survey of the Economic Situation and Prospects of Europe* (Geneva, 1948), Table 1, p. 3.

exchange rates, thereby reducing the price of dollar imports. As a consequence, the new international financial order remained irrelevant to resolving the problems of transition from war to peace and economic reconstruction. Moreover, governments failed in their attempts to create an International Trade Organization due mainly to the opposition of the American Congress and important interest groups in the United States. (For a more detailed discussion of the post-war payments systems, see Chapter 7.)

In most European countries, industrial output recovered to its pre-war level by the spring of 1947 – except in Italy, the Netherlands and western Germany. Despite this promising start, European recovery appeared to stagnate in the spring and summer of 1947 (see Table 3.1).[3] Given the disappointing rate of progress, it became obvious that domestic resources would not suffice to complete the ambitious reconstruction programmes of most countries. Despite recognizing the need for European economic integration, European governments resisted moves to coordinate their reconstruction efforts, because such steps might undermine domestic plans. Inter-governmental cooperation through the United Nations Economic Commission for Europe (UNECE) remained limited to the allocation of coal, timber and steel to ease the immediate post-war shortages. At the same time, European governments curtailed their imports from neighbouring countries in order to preserve their foreign currency reserves. As a consequence, trade between European countries remained significantly below pre-war levels (see Chapter 2). Instead, European economies looked to the United States for much-needed machine tools and raw materials. Given dwindling dollar reserves, economic recovery in most European countries depended on the ability to finance these vital imports. This phenomenon became known as the 'dollar gap'.

In focus: The Dollar Gap

Among economists, the dollar shortage was a controversial concept referring to what might have been more aptly termed a 'persistent disequilibrium in the balances of payments' of the western European economies.[1] While the balance of payments of most western European countries remained in constant deficit, the United States' balance of payments displayed a persistent surplus. The controversy centred on the nature of the disequilibrium and policy solution.

Due to the upheaval of the Second World War, most western European countries suffered from internal inflationary pressure. Put simply, total demand for goods (i.e. consumption, investment, government expenditure and exports) exceeded the available domestic supply of goods. Domestic production of goods could not be expanded quickly in the short term for a variety of reasons (for example, shortage of raw materials, lack of vital spare parts, retraining of the workers). Therefore, to correct this internal imbalance between demand (Y^D) and supply (Y^S), governments had two options: either to reduce any component of demand through austerity measures or to allow prices to rise. Austerity measures might include restrictive monetary policy, controls on investment and exports, and rationing of consumer goods. Allowing prices to rise might redistribute income and wealth from those on fixed incomes or relying on state benefits (such as pensioners, the unemployed, savers) to industrialists and owners of fixed assets. However, austerity measures as well as inflation might create disincentives for producers to increase production and invest in new factories and therefore run counter to the reconstruction objectives. Moreover, either economic policy might prove unpopular with large sections of the population. At the same time, the popular demands for social welfare reform constrained the ability of governments to significantly reduce government expenditures in the immediate post-war future.

An alternative course of action would be to purchase additional products abroad. Through imports (I), countries increase the domestic supply (Y^S). In the immediate post-war period, the United States became the only possible source for additional goods. The Belgian government, for example, sought to satisfy the inflated domestic demand through increased imports. Once internal balance had been restored ($Y^D = Y^S + I$), the government imposed a restrictive policy regime to stabilize the economy. Kindleberger described this deflationary approach as 'killing the cat [i.e. inflation] by stuffing it with cream [i.e. imports]'.[2] To pursue such economic policy, countries needed a

1. Charles Poor Kindleberger, 'The European Recovery Program', in *Marshall Plan Days* (Boston: Allen & Unwin, 1987), p. 65. The following case study draws heavily on this chapter which was originally published in the 1953 edition of Kindleberger's *International Economics*.
2. Kindleberger, 'Belgium after World War II: an experiment in supply-side economics', in *Marshall Plan Days*, p. 230.

The Dollar Gap (continued)

large dollar currency reserve (R) or needed to earn sufficient dollars through exporting goods (X). Many western European governments argued that the deterioration in their terms of trade (the ratio of import prices to export prices) had significantly reduced their export earnings. This adverse change in the terms of trade resulted from prices of raw materials increasing far more rapidly than the price of manufactured goods during the Second World War and post-war restocking boom. As exports reduced the goods available for domestic consumption, government measures to increase exports would prove unpopular with domestic consumers. In most European countries, export earnings proved insufficient to finance the level of desired imports, resulting in major external deficits. To correct an external imbalance, governments had two further options: either to increase overseas borrowing or to devalue the exchange rate. Given their economic state, western European countries lacked the ability to borrow from foreign financial institutions unless they could convince the American government to offer financial support. Under normal economic conditions, devaluation would resolve an external imbalance by increasing the price of imports and thereby reducing the demand for foreign goods. At the same time, domestic goods would be cheaper for foreign consumers and would lead to increased exports. To some extent, the controversy over the dollar gap centres on whether a massive devaluation in conjunction with domestic deflation would have been sufficient to cure the external and internal disequilibrium. Figure 3.1 illustrates the economic problem.

In the immediate post-war period, widespread shortages fuelled the demand for dollar imports (line i). As a consequence, the price of imports mattered less than obtaining additional goods. In Figure 3.1, the reduced influence of the import price is captured in the steep incline of line i. However, a country might not be able to afford to purchase all the imports it wants to buy, because it lacks the foreign currency reserves. As a consequence, the country's effective demand for imports (line d_1) would fall short of its propensity to import (line i) regardless of the exchange rate. At the prevailing exchange rate (r_1), the country in Figure 3.1 could afford a smaller quantity of imports (I) than the actual demand for imports $(I + I^d)$.[3] If a country decided to finance its imports out of reserves, additional overseas borrowing and financial aid, its government would have an interest in keeping the price of dollar imports down as much as possible. Therefore, it overvalues its own currency by setting the lowest possible exchange rate in terms of dollars (line r_1). At this exchange rate, Figure 3.1 assumes the country would not export at all.

---

3. Indeed, the dollar gap corresponds to the shaded rectangle assuming that the equilibrium exchange rate (r_e) would yield the required dollar earnings for the necessary dollar imports.

The Dollar Gap (continued)

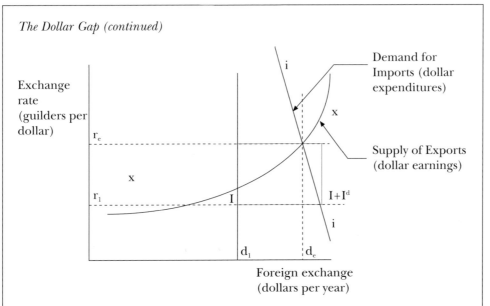

Figure 3.1. The dollar gap.

The question is whether a country could increase its export earnings sufficiently to finance its desired imports by raising the price of dollar imports (or devaluing its currency) rather than relying on financial aid. In Figure 3.1, this is represented by the line r_e. At this equilibrium exchange rate, import plans equal export earnings. Therefore, the country would have regained external balance and there would be no 'dollar gap'.

A number of influential economists have argued that western European countries should follow this policy description. To achieve external balance, governments should devalue their currencies, while balancing their budgets in order to remedy the internal disequilibrium. However, such a policy would adversely affect living standards in the short term and, therefore, would prove unpopular with electorates who had rejected such austerity measures in recent elections.

Crucially, the success of a devaluation would depend on the elasticity of export demand. Given the shortages of consumer goods in the domestic economy, producers lacked the incentive to export while local consumers screamed for more goods. Unless other countries liberalized imports, a country might be unable to increase exports sufficiently to finance necessary imports at the increased prices after devaluation. If one western European country devalued, others would follow suit and thereby limit the positive impact on ability to export of the first country to devalue. When the British government devalued sterling in September 1949, most western European governments followed suit, hoping to increase their dollar exports. In this

The Dollar Gap (continued)

context, many western European critics pointed to the inconsistencies of American foreign economic policy. Despite the prowess of the American economy, American tariffs and non-tariff barriers remained fairly high, leading to a persistent surplus in the American balance of payments. This protectionist stance presented a major barrier for western European producers trying to increase exports to the United States. Therefore, some critics demanded that the United States should reduce its trade barriers and revalue the dollar, thus reducing the price of imports from Europe. However, American governments encountered fierce political opposition to any attempt to reduce trade restrictions.

Given domestic opposition to trade liberalization, governments failed to overcome this disequilibrium in world trade by a general realignment of currencies (devaluation of western European currencies and revaluation of the dollar). As a consequence, the dollar shortage remained a serious problem for western European governments. For the Truman Administration, the ERP offered a creative solution to the economic problem of western European reconstruction and the recovery of the world economy. First, the ERP closed the dollar gap, sustaining the economic recovery boom and political stability in western Europe. Second, American aid smoothed the road to the liberalization of trade and international finance on a regional and eventually on a world basis.

The Marshall Plan

For American observers, the process of western European reconstruction seemed to be balanced on a knife edge. Unless European nations decided to cooperate, their reconstruction efforts might stall, leaving Europe economically dependent on American aid. To break this potential deadlock, the American Secretary of State, George C. Marshall, announced the new aid programme in July 1947. After drawing a dramatic picture of the economic situation in Europe, Marshall offered that the Truman Administration would assist a joint European recovery programme if European governments requested such financial assistance.

Following Marshall's announcement, the British Foreign Secretary, Ernest Bevin, and his French counterpart, Georges Bidault, seized the initiative, inviting all European governments (except Spain) to discuss the American offer at a hastily convened conference in Paris. When the Conference on European Economic Co-operation (CEEC) convened for its opening sessions on 16 July 1947, 16 western European and Scandinavian governments sent delegates indicating their willingness to work together in drawing up a joint recovery programme.[4] However, significant differences soon emerged between the positions of most European governments and the Truman Administration. Believing in the advantages

Plate 3.2. 'Before and after the Paris Conference.' 'They assembled – they rejoiced – they pressed forward – they lamented.' This *Pravda* cartoon of the 1947 Conference on European Economic Co-operation offers a Soviet view of the realities of the European Recovery Programme.

of a large single market, American officials encouraged the formation of a European customs union. Despite massive American pressure behind the scenes, a number of western European countries indicated their opposition to any such plan. For the British government, the creation of a customs union would undermine its traditional trading links with the Commonwealth. The Irish and several Scandinavian countries saw a customs union as a threat to national sovereignty.

In the end, the CEEC decided to set up a working party to study the feasibility of a customs union. From the perspective of the Truman Administration, the CEEC failed to agree a recovery programme which amounted to little more than a collection of national aid requests. Far from coordinating their domestic reconstruction projects, most western European governments planned the expansion of the national economy without consideration of the economic impact on neighbouring countries. For example, taken together the planned expansion of the domestic steel industries threatened to lead to an over-expansion of steel-making capacity in western Europe. Moreover, to close the dollar gap by the end of Marshall aid in 1952, the CEEC's final report estimated that European economies would require about $22 billion. Based on this estimated dollar gap, the report asked the American government to contribute about $19 billion towards financing the continued import of goods from the dollar area. From the start, this figure seemed unrealistically high to American officials.

Based on the CEEC's report, the Truman Administration drew up the European Recovery Program (ERP) for congressional approval. To ensure passage through Congress, the American government scaled down the original aid requests considerably. While approving the ERP in the spring of 1948, Congress further reduced the amount of aid available and insisted on the creation of a new separate government department, the European Co-Operation Administration (ECA). To assist the ECA in administering the available monies, the CEEC set up a permanent Organisation for European Economic Co-Operation (OEEC). In light of the congressional cuts to the ERP, the OEEC Council appointed a committee to review the national aid requests. Based on their careful examination of each country's aid request, the committee adjusted national aid requests taking into account the impact of reconstruction plans on neighbouring economies. Despite the involvement of the OEEC member states, the ECA retained control over the final allocation and the ultimate use of ERP funds in the recipient country.

ERP funds allowed western Europe to continue importing American foodstuffs, raw materials and machinery. Before the Marshall Plan, the continuation of European reconstruction had been to some extent doubtful given the dependence on American imports and the limited currency reserves. However, it would be wrong to suggest that continued western European recovery depended on ERP funds. By the summer of 1947, industrial production in many western European countries had reached pre-war levels (see Table 3.1). In all likelihood, Europe's recovery would have continued even without Marshall aid – albeit at a slower rate. For the most part, ERP freed western European governments from the immediate worry of financing American imports to sustain rapid economic recovery.

At home, the recipient government would sell the imported goods on to firms and consumers. Under the provisions of the ERP, the receipts from these sales accrued to the recipient government as counterpart funds. With the permission of the local ECA mission, recipient governments could use the counterpart funds to finance essential investments to improve, for example, domestic infrastructure.

Table 3.2. Allotment summary of European Recovery Program aid, 3 April 1948 to 30 June 1951 ($ million)

Country	Total
Austria	560.8
Belgium and Luxembourg	546.6
Denmark	256.9
France	2,401.0
Germany (Federal Republic)	1,297.3
Greece	515.1
Iceland	23.7
Irish Republic	146.2
Italy	1,297.3
Netherlands	977.7
Norway	231.7
Portugal	50.5
Sweden	118.5
Trieste	33.4
Turkey	144.7
United Kingdom	2,713.6
European Payments Union: Capital Fund	350.0
Total	11,664.7

Note: Total does not include freight charges and administrative expenditures as well as Interim Aid which provided emergency relief to some European countries before the ERP started. Therefore, the total funds allocated to European countries are less than the overall ERP expenditure total of $13.7 million mentioned in the text.

Source: Central Office of Information, *Western Co-operation: A Reference Handbook* (London, 1956), Table 3, p. 3.

In some countries (such as France, West Germany and the Netherlands), counterpart funds made a significant contribution to long-term economic development. For example, counterpart funds financed a large proportion of new electricity generation capacity in West Germany. However, a number of countries resented having to obtain ECA permission to use counterpart funds. Instead, the British government preferred repaying the national debt.

Between 1947 and 1952, the United States spent $13.7 billion under the ERP. For four and a half years, the American people decided to allocate on an annual basis up to 2.3 per cent of GNP towards assisting European recovery and economic development. In this respect, the ERP far exceeded the proportion of national income spent as aid to the Third World by any industrialized country today. At a national level, the contribution of ERP grants varied considerably. In a number of countries (such as Austria and the Netherlands), Marshall aid made a crucial difference to economic recovery and long-term economic development. To some extent, the economic policy choices of the recipient government influenced the effectiveness of the American economic aid.

The European Payments Union and Recovery of Intra-European trade

However, the real importance of the ERP lay in revitalizing intra-European trade. During the first two years of the ERP, the distinct lack of progress towards European economic integration concerned ECA officials. Rather than importing goods from neighbouring economies, most governments remained primarily interested in obtaining dollars to finance the import of American goods. To jump-start intra-European trade, the OEEC devised an intra-European payments scheme supported by ERP funds in October 1948. Under its terms, the countries planning a trade surplus with other OEEC countries had to provide their trading partners with a line of credit (or drawing rights) in the amount of the trade surplus. Through exercising these drawing rights, the country with the trade deficit could import goods without paying for them. Surplus countries had to finance the drawing rights from the national ERP grant. Effectively, the deficit country could increase its own share of ERP funding by importing from other OEEC member states. Given these favourable terms, deficit countries increased their imports from other OEEC countries utilizing the additional credit. Surplus countries disliked the scheme, because their eventual ERP grant available for domestic reconstruction depended on the extent to which deficit countries exercised their drawing rights. Given these shortcomings, the payments agreement was only renewed with some modifications after massive pressure from the ECA in September 1949. However, this second intra-European payments agreement also failed to encourage the resumption of intra-European trade on a significant scale, and discussions almost immediately began on replacing the existing scheme with a regional multilateral payments system.

The proposed regional payments system allowed for the limited convertibility of currencies among the signatories. At the outset, Britain opposed the proposals, because its membership would permit the other members of the Sterling Area to trade with OEEC countries through the British account. Under the proposed arrangements, Britain might have to advance other member states the funds to import raw materials from the Sterling Area. To overcome its opposition, the Truman Administration promised additional financial support to the British government. With the last hurdle out of the way, the European Payments Union (EPU) started operations in July/August 1950. In contrast to the previous payments agreements, each member state received a quota based on the volume of its intra-European trade in 1949. Under the agreement, the balances resulting from a member state's commercial trade were totalled up on a monthly basis. Provided it stayed within its quota, a member state with an overall deficit would be obliged to pay a rising proportion of its deficit with the EPU. In reverse, members with a surplus balance received a proportion of balance in gold or dollars. This arrangement created an incentive for deficit countries to remain within their quota. If a country experienced temporary or persistent payments problems, the Management Board of the EPU advised the member government on economic policy and could recommend the temporary suspension of trade liberalization. Except for the start-up capital, the EPU operated independently of the ERP and did not affect the distribution of ERP grants to OEEC member states. The EPU facilitated intra-European trade by restoring limited convertibility between European countries, while allowing member states to maintain their import controls from the dollar area. (On the importance of the EPU, see also Chapter 7.[5])

In the absence of a regional payments system, the foreign exchange controls meant that most OEEC member states continued to restrict the inflow of foreign manufactured goods through import quotas. Through imposing import quotas, government departments prioritized the importation of essential items for domestic reconstruction. During the first two years of the ERP, most OEEC member states remained reluctant to liberalize trade while other states continued to maintain their import quotas. At first, governments tried to reduce quotas on a product-by-product basis. When this procedure proved ineffectual, the OEEC Council agreed to set overall percentage targets for the liberalization of foreign trade. This alternative approach allowed governments to determine which products would no longer be subject to import quotas. At the same time as setting up the EPU (July 1950), the OEEC member states agreed to abandon quotas for 50 per cent of their foreign trade, leading to an instantaneous expansion of intra-European trade. Within the first year, intra-European trade grew by 41 per cent. By 1956, intra-European imports had increased to more than twice their pre-liberalization level. Over the next few years, existing quotas were reduced further by similar across-the-board cuts.

The progressive liberalization of intra-European trade established and sustained a virtuous cycle of economic growth through the expansion of trade. Through increased trade, the western European economies became progressively more integrated. At the centre of the emerging western European economy, the West German economy provided a growing market for the neighbouring economies. In turn, growing export earnings enabled European countries to increase their imports of German machine tools. Rapid expansion of production encouraged firms to invest in larger factories to supply the emerging European market. Increased confidence convinced many western European politicians of the potential benefits of further economic integration.

American financial support proved crucial in the setting-up of the EPU which enabled the step-by-step liberalization of intra-European trade. By tolerating the continued discrimination against dollar goods, successive American governments laid the foundations for the phenomenal growth of western European economies in the 1950s. The success of the incremental liberalization of intra-European trade made further economic integration desirable, paving the way for the creation of the European Economic Community in 1958. (See also Chapter 9.)

First Steps towards European Integration

The progress towards European economic integration occurred incrementally in the immediate post-war period. Indeed, the process seemed painstakingly slow to the considerable number of enthusiasts for the idea of a united Europe. Having considerable support among post-war leaders, the idea of European unity reflected the rejection of the immediate past by European elites. Many politicians attributed the outbreak of the Second World War to an aggressive political and economic nationalism of the inter-war period. Following this logic, the creation of a united Europe would eradicate the root cause of international antagonism by replacing the existing nation states. However, after the end of the war, the pressing problems of reconstruction forced governments to concentrate on domestic issues and pushed these grand ideas off the political agenda.

While most governments acknowledged the advantages of political and economic cooperation, western European politicians resisted surrendering any sovereignty. For example, the difficulties in liberalizing intra-European trade reflected this reluctance to diminish national control over economic policy.[6] Given the economic upheavals of the immediate post-war years, rescinding control over foreign trade carried considerable political risks as long as neighbouring countries continued to pursue extremely protectionist policies. In this context, the unilateral abolition of exchange controls would have led to an unstoppable outflow of hard currency reserves, undermining domestic reconstruction. As a consequence, most cooperation between European states occurred within the framework of intergovernmental institutions like the UNECE or the OEEC which permitted governments to reserve their right to reject the advice or decisions of these bodies.

An illustration of this development is the fate of the post-war movement to create a united Europe. This move originated from the Congress of Europe held in The Hague in 1948 which called on western European governments to embark on setting up an economic and political union. However, the political activists behind The Hague Congress immediately lost the initiative to the national governments which established the Council of Europe in 1949. Eager to preserve their prerogative, governments ensured that the real power within the new institution rested with the Council of Ministers rather than the Consultative Assembly. As a consequence, the Council of Europe failed to develop into a federal European state as many in the European Movement had hoped. In contrast to the 'federalist' aspirations, a number of countries sought to restrict the powers of European institutions to narrowly defined functions on an inter-governmental basis. Given the need for consensus among the signatories, this 'functionalist' position determined the pace of integration.

The 'functionalist' approach presumed governments would continue to co-operate at the European level. However, this limited integration offered little guarantee that governments would not terminate European cooperation at a future date. This possibility called into question the reconstruction plans of some European governments which assumed unhindered access to the European market. For example, the Monnet Plan envisaged the expansion of the French steel industry, but relied on the unrestricted ability to import Ruhr coal. After unsuccessful attempts to internationalize control of the Ruhr, the French foreign minister, Robert Schuman, suggested the creation of a common market for coal and steel supervised by a supra-national authority on 9 May 1950. In contrast to the previous proposals to impose outside control over Ruhr coal, the Schuman Plan envisaged the partial surrender of national control over domestic coal and steel industries. For France, these proposals would secure access to Ruhr coal on equal terms to West German consumers. From the West German perspective, the Schuman Plan was attractive for two reasons. First, such an agreement would end Allied restrictions on West German steel production. Moreover, the proposals represented a recognition of the newly created Federal Republic of Germany. After a short period of intense discussion, the British government rejected the Schuman Plan because ministers found it impossible to accept the proposed supra-national authority. In the end, five nations – Belgium, West Germany, Italy, Luxembourg and the Netherlands – accepted the French invitation and started negotiating the Treaty of Paris, creating the European Coal and Steel Community (ECSC) on 18 April 1951.

In the first years of its operation, the High Authority of the ECSC achieved the creation of a common market for coal and steel by removing tariffs, quotas, and other restrictions. Under the umbrella of the ECSC, member states cooperated successfully, confirming that a supra-national institution need not work against the national interest. To some extent, the rapid growth of the west European economy smoothed the integration of national steel industries. Due to this favourable economic development, the ECSC did not have to oversee the contraction of the European steel industries as many had feared at the outset. Nevertheless, member states extended the original mandate of the ECSC to include social questions and rehabilitation of coal-mining areas. Despite this deepening of cooperation, the limited scope for trade-offs between member states offered few possibilities to advance further the process of European economic integration. On balance, the successful cooperation made member states more inclined to take economic integration further by creating the Common Market in 1958 (see Chapter 9).

Conclusion

In the immediate post-war period, western European governments found themselves caught in a Catch-22 situation. Domestic reconstruction necessitated the import of food, raw materials and machinery from the United States. Therefore, most governments protected their hard currency reserves through a wide array of exchange controls and import quotas. While most countries would have benefited from trading with neighbouring economies, the need for preserving dollar reserves weighed against such intra-European trade. Eventually, western European governments overcame this vicious circle with the assistance of the American Marshall Plan initiative. ERP aid facilitated the gradual liberalization of intra-

European trade, sparking the sustained economic boom in western Europe in the 1950s. Based on the experience of economic cooperation (OEEC, EPU, ECSC), a number of governments became convinced that their political and economic interests would be best served by creating a Common Market.

Historiography

For most of the early post-war period, historical accounts portrayed the Marshall Plan as the crucial impetus for western European recovery and as saving western Europe from the clutches of Soviet imperialism. Since the late 1950s, historians have challenged these early histories, highlighting the American security interests behind the decision to assist western Europe. As archival records became accessible, European historians also challenged American accounts of this period, emphasing the importance of domestic reconstruction programmes.

Debates among historians have focused on five questions. Was there an economic crisis in 1947? Did Europe 'need' the ERP? Did American dollars 'rescue' Europe? Did the Marshall Plan resolve the disintegration of the western European economy? Was there an American 'empire'?

As shown above, western European recovery started to falter after a promising start in the winter of 1947. Due to an exceptionally severe winter, industrial production stagnated in the first two quarters of 1947 (see Table 3.1). Against the background of a general coal shortage throughout Europe, ice and snow led to the closure of factories and electrical power stoppages. Given their limited currency reserves, western European countries could not afford to import large quantities of American coal and demanded increased exports from the limited coal production of the Ruhr. However, an expansion of Ruhr coal production depended on the improved availability of food and consumer goods in West Germany. Overcoming these impediments to European recovery required a radical new approach which would restore normal trading relationships between European economies. Recent American studies have documented that the Secretary of State, George Marshall, perceived these economic problems as an impending crisis and dramatized their severity to ensure the passage of the ERP.

Alan Milward and other European historians have challenged this view by drawing attention to the way in which national reconstruction programmes triggered the impending economic crisis. Milward's analysis showed that European governments continued purchasing American products for domestic reconstruction, deliberately running down their dollar reserves. To some extent, they gambled that the American government would eventually finance European payment deficits with the United States. By cutting imports from the dollar area, western European countries could have continued to reconstruct their economies, albeit at a slower pace. Therefore, the sense of impending economic crisis resulted from the considerable drain on the dollar reserves by the expansionary domestic reconstruction programmes. For reasons of domestic politics, European governments shied away from adopting an alternative economic strategy of austerity, devaluation and deflation which would have led to unemployment and slower economic growth. In a sense, this position argues that the ERP was not strictly necessary for western European reconstruction.

Through the ERP, the Truman Administration provided western Europe with the dollars to finance its imports of American goods. In the 1980s, some observers have suggested that European governments could have borrowed the needed dollars from American private banks or issued bonds on Wall Street. Such suggestions ignore the economic circumstances after 1945. After the First World War, European countries had financed their reconstruction mainly through borrowing from American banks and Wall Street. This heavy borrowing directly contributed to the world economic crisis following the Great Crash of 1929. Given the experience of the inter-war period, most American banks remained reluctant to lend any money to European countries or firms until the mid-1950s. In the absence of private finance, the ERP sustained the recovery process of the western European economy.

The contribution of ERP grants and loans varied significantly from country to country. On balance, the macro-economic contribution to many economies seems to have been small. In the last decade, arguments among historians have focused on whether ERP funds provided the crucial margin for economic recovery. This debate is far from resolved. Some historians have tried to demonstrate the importance of ERP grants for a particular industry or investment project. Given their restricted scope, such micro-economic studies are unable to resolve this dispute. While the contribution to national economies is in some doubt, few historians and observers would dispute the instrumental role of the Marshall Plan in kick-starting intra-European trade.

American sponsorship of European reconstruction was motivated by more than sheer generosity as early accounts suggested. To some extent, considerations of national security influenced the decision to help Europe to help itself. Concerned about growing Soviet control of eastern Europe, American policymakers suggested that a strategy of economic containment would prevent any further Soviet expansionism. The rationale of the containment strategy was that economic assistance would raise living standards and thereby reduce the popularity of national Communist parties in western Europe. By defeating the Communist challenge, American foreign economic policy would check the expansion of the Soviet empire. Against the background of the American involvement in the Vietnam War, American revisionist historians challenged this interpretation, highlighting the extent of American interventionism in this period. In response to the inadequacy of the Bretton Woods system, the ERP should be seen as an expansionary programme to prevent the collapse of the capitalist world economy. Implicitly, the revisionist position assumes that the American economy would have slumped without the western European export demand. Through the ERP, the Truman Administration ensured American economic domination of western Europe.

More recent studies by European historians provide yet another perspective on the ERP. Their analyses show that national governments pursued primarily national objectives and seemed apt at using American aid to their own advantage. All these interpretations are not necessarily incompatible. A consensus interpretation might suggest that the ERP provided a 'creative solution' to the failure of the Bretton Woods institutions to overcome the transitional problems of reconstruction. Given domestic resistance to reducing American tariffs or to revaluing the dollar, the ERP provided a gradualist approach to establishing a new multilateral world economic order. In this sense, the ERP might be interpreted as a gift in exchange for which the western European governments accepted American economic leadership.

Bibliographical Note

A good starting point for further reading are the following textbooks: David Ellwood, *Rebuilding Europe: Western Europe, America and Postwar Reconstruction* (London, 1992) and John Killick, *The United States and European Reconstruction, 1945–1960* (Edinburgh, 1997). At a more advanced level, the seminal studies of Alan Milward are essential reading for an understanding of the recent debates about western European reconstruction and integration: Alan S. Milward, *The Reconstruction of Western Europe, 1945–51* (London, 1984); and Alan S. Milward, *The European Rescue of the Nation-State* (London, 1992).

The economic surveys of UNECE provide a contemporary account of western Europe's economic problems which is still useful to historians. Of particular interest is the 1953 report which provides a comprehensive analysis of economic developments since 1945: United Nations Economic Commission for Europe, Research and Planning Division, *Economic Survey of Europe since the War: A Reappraisal of Problems and Prospects* (Geneva, 1953).

There are a growing number of accounts on particular aspects of this period. On the European Recovery Program, the most comprehensive economic assessment is Imanuel Wexler, *The Marshall Plan Revisited: The European Recovery Program in Economic Perspective* (Westport, 1983). For a detailed analysis of the political and diplomatic background of the European Recovery Program consult Michael J. Hogan, *The Marshall Plan: America, Britain, and the Reconstruction of Western Europe* (Cambridge, 1987). The most detailed account of the operations of the EPU is Jacob Kaplan and Günther Schleiminger, *The European Payments Union: Financial Diplomacy in the 1950s* (Oxford, 1989). On the origins of the ECSC, a perceptive study is John Gillingham, *Coal, Steel, and the Rebirth of Europe, 1945–1955: The Germans and French from Ruhr Conflict to Economic Community* (Cambridge, 1991).

Notes

1. See Rainer Gries, *Die Rationen-Gesellschaft: Versorgungskampf und Vergleichsmentalität: Leipzig, München und Köln nach dem Kriege* (Münster: Westfälisches Dampfboot, 1991), pp. 323–35. As E.P. Thompson observed: 'People starve: their survivors think differently about the market'; see Edward P. Thompson, *On the Poverty of Theory* (London, 1978), p. 11.

2. On the concept of national integration, see Gunnar Myrdal, *An International Economy: Problems and Prospects* (London, 1955), pp. 16–31.

3. United Nations Economic Commission for Europe, Research and Planning Division, *A Survey of the Economic Situation and Prospects of Europe* (Geneva, 1948), pp. 3–10. This perception of crisis is discussed in more detail in the review of the historiography at the end of this chapter.

4. The Soviet Union and its eastern European allies declined the invitation because their governments found the American conditions for Marshall aid unacceptable.

5. Arguably, regional monetary cooperation eventually led to the concerted approach to restore full convertibility between the dollar and the European currencies in 1958; see Chapter 7 and Jacob Kaplan and Günther Schleiminger, *The European Payments Union: Financial Diplomacy in the 1950s* (Oxford, 1989).

6. If a country signs an agreement on trade liberalization, the government negotiates away its freedom to impose trade restrictions or to raise tariffs. Free trade amounts to the abrogation of national sovereignty in foreign economic policy.

4 The Great Boom: 1950–73

N.F.R. Crafts

Introduction

The years from the early 1950s to the early 1970s were a period of outstanding economic success for western Europe. This was an era of rapid economic growth, low unemployment and modest inflation which has, not surprisingly, often been called a Golden Age. Workers, both skilled and unskilled, and the owners of firms all shared in the benefits. This experience was way beyond the wildest dreams of even the most optimistic pundit or policymaker in the late 1940s. For a while the escape from the nightmare of the 1930s seemed to be complete, and only towards the end of the period did doubts about the continued vitality of the European economies start to resurface.

Although all western European economies enjoyed faster growth and much lower unemployment than in the 1930s or in the past 20 years, success was not uniform. Thus while West Germany marvelled at the *Wirtschaftswunder*, by the early 1960s the British 'chattering classes' had discovered the 'British Disease'. Two obvious – but as yet unsettled – questions arise which will be examined in the later parts of the chapter.

(1) Why was growth during the Golden Age so much faster than either before or since?

(2) What explains the relative success and failure in economic growth among European countries at this time?

A moment's thought suggests that answers to these questions can be facilitated by considering a further controversial issue, namely, why did the Golden Age come to an end during the 1970s?

Accounting for trends in unemployment and inflation is rather less difficult than explaining trends in growth. Both the low unemployment of the 1950s and 1960s and the rise in unemployment after the Golden Age can be understood quite readily within the framework of standard economic models of the labour market. Similarly, recourse to fairly standard ideas in macroeconomics can illuminate the onset of rapid inflation at the end of the boom years. By contrast, theorizing about growth is less fully developed and the unusual historical situation of the early post-war period makes the use of standard ideas a little too facile.

The Economic Environment during the Golden Age

In retrospect, several key features of the economic environment during the 1950s and 1960s appear to have been particularly conducive to the outstanding economic performance of the time. Later on, these favourable attributes either faded or, in some cases, disappeared altogether. Four points are particularly worth noting.

(1) Since 1913 the European economies had experienced two world wars and the economic dislocation of the depression and trade wars of the 1930s. This meant that growth had been below trend and that an opportunity existed for rapid growth through correcting policy errors and repairing damaged economies.

(2) Moreover, the United States had built up a large productivity lead based on the use of more advanced technology and generally larger-scale production than prevailed in Europe. By 1950, this stood at an all-time high and output per person employed in American manufacturing was 2.5 times the British level, 2.75 times the West German level and 3.1 times the French level.[1] In an era when technology transfer was to become easier this offered the possibility of a period of rapid 'catch-up' growth.

(3) The years from the early 1950s through to the early 1970s were a period when energy and other raw materials seemed to be in elastic supply and their prices remained low. The traumatic OPEC oil price shocks of 1973/74 and 1979/80, which altogether raised the nominal price of oil from $2.1 to $35.5 per barrel, symbolize the 1970s as a decade when commodity prices soared and macroeconomic management suddenly became a great deal more difficult (see Chapter 5).

(4) Pressures arising from competition with rapidly growing Asian economies were completely absent in the 1950s. As late as 1965, the developed countries still accounted for 93 per cent of all manufactured exports and the de-industrialization of European economies was yet to begin.

Although the post-war environment presented European economies with substantial opportunities once the immediate difficulties of post-war reconstruction had been overcome, nevertheless to exploit this potential it was necessary to establish an appropriate policy framework. Here, clearly, there were important differences between countries to which we shall return later, but there were also a number of general tendencies which should be recognized.

(1) The Golden Age was accompanied by multilateral trade liberalization and economic integration through the establishment of the EEC and EFTA. This increased competition facilitated the transfer of technology, improved the allocation of resources and encouraged larger-scale production (see Chapters 7 and 9).

(2) The early post-war period was notable for widespread attempts at rapprochement between labour and capital which might serve to encourage wage moderation on the one hand in return for high investment on the other hand. These attempts generally took the form of moves towards 'corporatism' and were buttressed by expansion of the Welfare State (see Chapter 8).

(3) Macroeconomic policy was based on a return to fixed exchange rates under the auspices of the Bretton Woods system. This was constructed with a view to obviating the adverse demand and price shocks of the inter-war period and thus to be conducive to investment while providing a framework which would offer counter-inflationary discipline.

(4) Although throughout western Europe there had been a move further away from *laissez faire* towards a mixed economy with a greater role for the state, nevertheless on balance governments worked with the market economy rather than against it. The distortions created by policy intervention were much less severe than in other parts of the world where long-term outcomes were very disappointing, such as in Latin America or, even more obviously, eastern Europe.

The Golden Age in Comparative Perspective

This section contains a basic statistical outline of economic performance during the great boom. The exceptional nature of this phase is highlighted by presenting comparative data for earlier and later years. The periodization adopted is quite conventional for a general overview but it should be remembered that countries do differ and, in a more detailed study, would deserve to be given individual treatment. For example, in France, 1954–76 has been singled out as the '*vingt glorieuses*'.[2]

Table 4.1 concentrates on economic growth measured in terms of real gross domestic product per person. Information on levels of real GDP/person is also

Plate 4.1. By the late 1950s growing prosperity in western Europe was sufficiently widespread for audiences to enjoy a heady, if largely vicarious, taste of hedonism in films such as Federico Fellini's *La Dolce Vita* (1959). Its barbed but affectionate portrait of decadent cafe society, though specifically about the Roman film world, proved to have a more general resonance: it was one of the first foreign-language films to break out of the art-house circuit in the USA and the English-speaking world, and find a wider public, and helped promote a sense of the social and cultural renaissance of western Europe after the era of postwar austerity.

Table 4.1. Levels and rates of growth of real GDP per person ($1990 international; per cent per year)

(a) 1913–50	GDP/person		Growth rate
	1913	1950	
1. Australia	5,505	7,218	0.7
2. USA	5,307	9,573	1.6
3. New Zealand	5,115	8,495	1.4
4. UK	5,032	6,847	0.8
5. Canada	4,213	7,047	1.4
6. Switzerland	4,207	8,939	2.1
7. Belgium	4,130	5,346	0.7
8. Netherlands	3,950	5,850	1.1
9. Germany	3,833	4,281	0.3
10. Denmark	3,764	6,683	1.6
11. Austria	3,488	3,731	0.2
12. France	3,452	5,221	1.1
13. Sweden	3,096	6,738	2.1
14. Ireland	2,733	3,518	0.7
15. Italy	2,507	3,425	0.8
16. Norway	2,275	4,969	2.1
17. Spain	2,255	2,397	0.2
18. Finland	2,050	4,131	1.9
19. Greece	1,621	1,951	0.5
20. Portugal	1,354	2,132	1.2
21. Japan	1,334	1,873	0.9
22. South Korea	948	876	−0.2
23. Taiwan	794	922	0.4

(b) 1950–73	GDP/person		Growth rate
	1950	1973	
1. USA	9,573	16,607	2.4
2. Switzerland	8,939	17,953	3.1
3. New Zealand	8,495	12,575	1.7
4. Australia	7,218	12,485	2.4
5. Canada	7,047	13,644	2.9
6. UK	6,847	11,992	2.5
7. Sweden	6,738	13,494	3.1
8. Denmark	6,683	13,416	3.1
9. Netherlands	5,850	12,763	3.4
10. Belgium	5,346	11,905	3.5
11. France	5,221	12,940	4.0
12. Norway	4,969	10,229	3.2
13. Germany	4,281	13,152	5.0
14. Finland	4,131	10,768	4.3

Table 4.1 (cont'd)

(b) 1950–73	GDP/person		Growth rate
	1950	1973	
15. Austria	3,731	11,308	4.9
16. Ireland	3,518	7,023	3.1
17. Italy	3,425	10,409	5.0
18. Spain	2,397	8,739	5.8
19. Portugal	2,132	7,568	5.7
20. Singapore	2,038	5,412	4.3
21. Hong Kong	1,962	6,768	5.5
22. Greece	1,951	7,779	6.2
23. Japan	1,873	11,017	8.0
24. Taiwan	922	3,669	6.2
25. South Korea	876	2,840	5.2

(c) 1973–94	GDP/person		Growth rate
	1973	1994	
1. Switzerland	17,953	20,830	0.7
2. USA	16,607	22,569	1.5
3. Canada	13,644	18,350	1.4
4. Sweden	13,494	16,710	1.0
5. Denmark	13,416	19,305	1.8
6. Germany	13,152	19,097	1.8
7. France	12,940	17,968	1.6
8. Netherlands	12,763	17,152	1.4
9. New Zealand	12,575	15,085	0.9
10. Australia	12,485	17,107	1.5
11. UK	11,992	16,371	1.5
12. Belgium	11,905	17,225	1.8
13. Austria	11,308	17,285	2.0
14. Japan	11,017	19,505	2.8
15. Finland	10,768	14,779	1.5
16. Italy	10,409	16,404	2.2
17. Norway	10,229	18,372	2.8
18. Spain	8,739	12,544	1.7
19. Greece	7,779	10,165	1.3
20. Portugal	7,568	11,083	1.8
21. Ireland	7,023	12,624	2.8
22. Hong Kong	6,768	19,592	5.2
23. Singapore	5,412	18,797	6.1
24. Taiwan	3,669	12,985	6.2
25. South Korea	2,840	11,235	6.8

Sources: A. Maddison, *Monitoring the World Economy, 1820–1992* (Paris, 1995) and Asian Development Bank, *Asian Development Outlook* (Oxford, 1995).

presented. These are measured in 'international dollars' using exchange rates adjusted for differences in price levels or, as the jargon goes, at 'purchasing power parity'. Measurement of both levels and rates of growth of real GDP is quite difficult and, while the broad outline of the estimates in Table 4.1 is probably reliable enough for our purposes, the precise detail should be regarded as open to some question.

The most obvious feature of Table 4.1 is the very strong growth performance of western Europe during the 1950–73 period. Even countries, like the UK, in which growth was relatively slow recorded growth rates which were higher than ever before. Equally clear is the marked slow-down in growth subsequently. A growth rate of 2 per cent per year is well above average for European countries in the recent past but would have been at the bottom of the league during the Golden Age. By contrast, fast growth in Hong Kong and Singapore has been sustained, with the result that in terms of levels of GDP per person they have now overtaken most of Europe.

During the boom years there is a strong inverse correlation between a country's initial level of productivity and subsequent growth performance. This is highlighted in Table 4.1 by listing countries in rank order of real GDP per person in 1950. It is clear that countries at the bottom of the table on average grow faster than countries at the top. The rationale for this might be that those at the bottom had greater scope for catch-up growth, being initially more backward. At the same time, the correlation is by no means perfect and some countries do rather better or worse than their rank order position might predict; for example, on this basis, France and West Germany seem to be winners while the UK and Ireland appear to be losers. It is also noticeable that this inverse correlation is absent prior to 1950 and, among European countries, rather weak after 1973.

Table 4.2 reviews indicators of short-term macroeconomic performance. Here the main statistical difficulty lies in the unemployment figures. Both over time and across countries there are major differences in the way that unemployment is counted. For recent years the OECD provides standardized estimates which try to correct for discrepancies but even here experts typically argue for further fine-tuning. For the inter-war years we are on much less secure ground and the comparability of the estimates in Table 4.2 either between countries or with the post-war data must be regarded as very problematic. Despite these problems, there is no doubt that Europe in the Golden Age was blessed with much lower unemployment than either in the troubled 1930s or during the difficult adjustments of recent years. The explanation for this is considered in detail below.

On inflation, the outcome is a little less impressive. Both to nineteenth century and to 1990s eyes inflation appears somewhat high. Actually, here it is necessary to distinguish between the 1950s and early 1960s when, following the inflation of the Korean War, prices rose only very slowly, and the later 1960s when a number of inflationary pressures built up prior to the notorious OPEC oil price shock. At that time membership of the Bretton Woods fixed exchange rate system led to Europe importing inflation from monetary expansion by the United States, while

Table 4.2. Standardized unemployment rates and inflation rates (per cent)

	1929–38	1955–73	1980–95
(a) Unemployment			
Australia	12.9	2.8	8.2
Austria	12.0	1.7	4.4
Belgium	8.0	3.5	9.8
Canada	12.3	5.5	9.6
Denmark	10.6	3.2	9.7
Finland	3.9	2.5	7.8
France	na	2.5	9.6
Germany	8.5	1.8	6.1
Italy	na	4.7	7.5
Japan	na	1.7	2.5
Netherlands	8.0	2.4	8.6
Norway	7.8	2.0	3.8
Sweden	5.3	1.6	4.1
Switzerland	2.8	0.5	2.1
UK	11.1	3.3	9.7
USA	16.7	5.3	6.9
(b) Inflation			
Australia	−1.4	5.9	6.0
Austria	−0.7	4.6	3.8
Belgium	−0.7	4.5	4.0
Canada	−1.7	4.6	4.2
Denmark	0.6	6.9	4.7
Finland	−1.3	7.8	5.7
France	1.4	6.7	5.4
Germany	−1.9	4.0	3.2
Italy	−0.2	7.5	9.4
Japan	1.2	6.0	1.8
Netherlands	−1.8	5.8	2.3
Norway	0.4	5.5	5.3
Sweden	−0.2	6.0	6.8
Switzerland	−1.6	4.2	3.6
UK	−0.7	7.5	6.3
USA	−1.8	4.3	4.3

Sources: inter-war estimates from A. Maddison, *Dynamic Forces in Capitalist Development* (Oxford, 1991), post-war estimates from R. Layard, S. Nickell and R. Jackman, *The Unemployment Crisis* (Oxford, 1994) updated using OECD, *Economic Outlook.*

domestic wage pressures were increasing with growing militancy on the part of workers. The inflation of the 1970s is both a symptom and a cause of the strains and, in some cases, the breakdown of the post-war 'social contract' between capital and labour.

In focus: The Low Unemployment Interlude

From the vantage point of the 1990s the low unemployment that Europe experienced in the 1950s and 1960s appears both highly enviable and no longer attainable. How could things have been so different during the Golden Age? Explanations in the textbooks of the time, written from a Keynesian standpoint, stressed the role of demand conditions and contrasted the strong growth in investment and exports of the early post-war years with the depressed situation in the 1930s. This analysis is now generally agreed to be simplistic although adequate demand is, of course, necessary to sustain low levels of unemployment.

In explaining medium-term trends in unemployment, the key is to examine influences on equilibrium in the labour market. Unemployment operates to reduce wage aspirations and can be seen as responding to pressures on the labour market to create a balance between workers' wage demands and employers' ability to pay. Wage demands will also depend on factors such as the system of wage bargaining and the generosity of unemployment benefits which both influence bargaining power and also tend to set a floor level for market wages.

A good deal of research effort has been devoted to estimating equilibrium levels of unemployment for different post-war periods in European countries. This literature is unanimous that these levels were low everywhere in the 1960s but had risen substantially in much of Europe by the 1980s, such that most of the rise in unemployment and the variations in unemployment outcomes across countries can be accounted for in this way. One widely cited set of estimates puts equilibrium unemployment in France, West Germany and the UK at 1.8, 0.5 and 2.6 per cent respectively in the 1960s compared with 7.8, 4.0 and 7.9 per cent respectively in the 1980s. By contrast, over the same interval, equilibrium unemployment in Norway and Sweden was estimated to have risen only from 2.1 to 2.5 per cent and from 1.6 to 2.4 per cent respectively.[1]

In this framework, the low unemployment of the early post-war period would be attributed to effective 'social contracts' between capital and labour, to relatively low levels of tax and benefits, all of which limited wage pressures, and to low prices for imported commodities and rapid productivity growth which sustained employers' profitability. By the 1970s, all these factors changed in a direction which tended to push up the level of unemployment which would balance target and feasible real wages. The required change in unemployment tended to be lower in countries like Sweden where employers' and workers' bargaining was highly coordinated and real wage pressures were better contained.

To this basic story, two more points can be added. First, there is a strong element of persistence in unemployment. Good times tend to improve the

1. R. Layard, S. Nickell and R. Jackman, *Unemployment* (Oxford, 1991), p. 436.

The Low Unemployment Interlude (continued)

work experience and employability of the workforce and vice versa. In times of low unemployment such as the 1950s relatively small increases in unemployment are needed to restrain wages because the unemployed are on average potentially highly employable. After a series of adverse shocks this will tend to be much less true; thus the after-effect of the 1970s was a permanent increase in equilibrium unemployment even when the pressures of the period subsided, just as the high employment of wartime left a favourable legacy to the 1950s.

Second, the problem of the unskilled needs to be highlighted. In the early post-war period demand for these workers remained buoyant but, since the mid 1970s, technological changes and de-industrialization have undermined their position, pushing down equilibrium wages for the unskilled. How serious this has been for unemployment in different countries has varied, depending on their benefit systems and the skills base of their workforce. Countries with strong training systems and limited duration of benefits such as Sweden have been better placed to cope than, say, the UK with open-ended benefits and many workers with little human capital.

Table 4.3 confirms that the boom years were characterized by very rapid growth of exports and by high investment rates. These features can certainly be seen as contributing to the strong demand of the post-war years and contrast strongly with the difficult 1930s. Both investment and export demand are clearly less strong in the years since the Golden Age. At the same time, Table 4.3 also has important implications for the supply side of the European economies.

Exports grew much faster than did output, reflecting an increasing openness to international trade during the Golden Age. The protectionism of the inter-war years was being reversed and real transport costs were falling. Trade growth had a number of positive effects on the growth potential of European economies and tended to promote catch-up. The stimulus came from greater exposure to international competition, faster diffusion of new types of capital goods, and the favourable impact of wider markets on incentives to innovate and to adopt large-scale methods of production. In turn, successful product innovation was a key to rapid export growth.

Investment is also important for growth as it represents the way in which the capital stock is increased and it is a vital part of exploiting the opportunities which technological change offers. The high rate of investment in the Golden Age was sustained by continued profitability, but it was threatened in the 1970s when profits were squeezed by the adverse shocks of the period and as diminishing returns became more apparent while opportunities for catch-up growth were gradually exhausted. Nevertheless, although investment rates have fallen since the 1960s and are now well below those of the fast-growing East Asian economies, the investment rates of recent years generally remain quite high by pre-war standards.

Table 4.3. Growth of exports and rate of investment

	1930–38	1960–73	1980–93
(a) Growth of export volume (% per year)			
Australia	4.1	6.7	5.7
Austria	−2.4	9.3	4.5
Belgium	−0.5	10.8	4.0
Canada	−0.1	9.4	5.4
Denmark	0.2	6.8	4.4
Finland	2.5	6.5	3.5
France	−4.0	9.1	3.7
Germany	−3.6	9.6	4.3
Italy	−4.1	11.9	3.6
Japan	9.6	14.9	6.0
Netherlands	−1.9	10.6	3.9
Sweden	0.3	7.9	3.4
UK	−2.9	5.5	2.9
USA	−2.1	6.8	5.6
(b) Non-residential investment/GDP (%)			
Australia	10.8	20.2	18.2
Austria		21.1	18.8
Belgium		16.5	14.2
Canada	10.4	16.9	14.8
Denmark		16.5	13.4
Finland		20.0	17.4
France	12.1	16.3	14.8
Germany	9.8	19.6	16.2
Italy		16.6	14.8
Japan	13.6	26.5	24.0
Netherlands	14.0	19.8	14.8
Sweden		16.8	14.0
UK	6.0	14.6	13.7
USA	9.8	13.5	13.9

Sources: exports growth from Maddison, *Dynamic Forces in Capitalist Development* and OECD, *Economic Outlook*; investment estimates from T. van de Klundert and A. van Schaik, 'On the historical continuity of the process of economic growth', in B. van Ark and N.F.R. Crafts (eds), *Quantitative Aspects of Postwar European Economic Growth* (Cambridge, 1996) and OECD, *Historical Statistics, 1960–1993*.

Attempts have been made to quantify the contribution of different changes on the supply side to economic growth. In Table 4.4 the sources of growth are divided into two: growth of 'Total Factor Input' (TFI) and growth of 'Total Factor Productivity' (TFP). For example, growth of real GDP of 5.99 per cent per year in West Germany in 1950–73 is broken down into a TFI component of 2.71 per cent per year (of which capital stock growth contributed 2.20 percentage

Table 4.4. The supply-side sources of growth (per cent per annum)

	France	Germany	UK
(a) 1913–50			
GDP	1.15	1.28	1.29
Total factor input	0.48	1.00	0.94
Non-residential capital	0.63	0.59	0.72
Total factor productivity	0.67	0.28	0.35
Catch-up effect	0.00	0.00	0.00
Foreign trade effect	0.03	−0.13	0.01
Structural effect	0.04	0.20	−0.04
Scale effect	0.03	0.04	0.04
(b) 1950–73			
GDP	5.02	5.99	2.96
Total factor input	1.96	2.71	1.71
Non-residential capital	1.59	2.20	1.64
Total factor productivity	3.06	3.28	1.25
Catch-up effect	0.46	0.62	0.08
Foreign trade effect	0.37	0.48	0.32
Structural effect	0.36	0.36	0.10
Scale effect	0.15	0.18	0.09
(c) 1973–92			
GDP	2.26	2.30	1.59
Total factor input	1.61	0.77	0.96
Non-residential capital	1.26	0.93	0.93
Total factor productivity	0.65	1.53	0.63
Catch-up effect	0.31	0.31	0.20
Foreign trade effect	0.12	0.15	0.15
Structural effect	0.15	0.20	−0.09
Scale effect	0.07	0.07	0.05

Sources: derived from Maddison, *Dynamic Forces in Capitalist Development* and A. Maddison, 'Macroeconomic accounts for European countries', in van Ark and Crafts (eds), *Quantitative Aspects of Postwar European Economic Growth.*

points) and a TFP component of 3.28 percentage points. The former measures the contribution of increases in the stock of capital and in the amount of labour, which in some cases is negative, reflecting declines in hours worked per person per year. The latter measures increases in output over and above those attributable to growth of factors of production resulting from greater efficiency in the utilization of resources and better technological knowledge.

Angus Maddison, whose estimates form the basis of Table 4.4, identifies four specific components of TFP growth – growth from technological catching-up of the United States, from better utilization of resources due to trade liberalization, from structural shifts away from low productivity sectors like traditional agriculture, and from cost reductions associated with increases in the scale of production. In West Germany in 1950–73 these sum to 1.64 of the 3.28 percentage points TFP growth per year. The remainder of TFP growth comes from unspecified sources including innovations and improvements in knowledge.

Detailed estimates are available for only a few countries and they are based on quite strong assumptions. Nevertheless, the message that comes from the results reported in Table 4.4 is well worth considering. Three points in particular should be noted.

(1) The acceleration of growth in the Golden Age and the subsequent slow-down owed a great deal to changes in TFP growth but changes in the rate of growth of the capital stock also play an important part.

(2) The rapid TFP growth of the Golden Age was based to a substantial extent on factors which were essentially transitory (catch-up, foreign trade and structural effects) in the sense that their impact was bound to weaken as their scope was exhausted.

(3) Relatively slow British growth in the Golden Age is partly explained by lower possibilities for catch-up and structural change in an economy which already had few agricultural workers in 1950 and which had a relatively high initial income level. At the same time, slow TFP growth in Britain is by no means fully explained by these factors and also seems to have resulted from a failure in the effective development and application of new products and processes.

In focus: Technology Transfer

In recent decades, reductions in the technology gap between the leader and follower countries have come to be a key feature of catch-up growth. It is important to recognize that this was much less the case prior to World War II; improvements in the international diffusion and application of technological knowledge were an important part of the acceleration of European growth during the Golden Age. In particular, European countries were able to assimilate American technology much more effectively than in the early twentieth century.

America's rise to technological leadership was based on a number of unique advantages which were consolidated and further developed by the investment strategies to which they gave rise. American technological progress was strongly conditioned by abundant natural resources, reflected for example in the low price and rapid spread of electrification of production processes, and by a large, relatively homogeneous domestic market conducive to the development of mass production methods, epitomized by the success

Technology Transfer (continued)

of Henry Ford. A crucial element in technological advance came from experience-based learning which spread via networks of personal contacts.

A shift away from European style craft-based methods of production was expedited by the development of large corporations and managerially intensive production methods pioneered by companies like Dupont. The large market, which offered the prospect of big sales volumes over which to spread fixed costs, encouraged firms to develop in-house research and development in sectors like chemicals and electricals where science paid off. College education became much more common than in Europe and new disciplines such as chemical engineering and management science were established.

Initially, American methods were frequently inappropriate – and not cost-effective – in the different circumstances prevailing in Europe. Moreover, transfer of technology was hampered by the importance of 'tacit' (as opposed to explicitly documented) knowledge in the practical application of new ideas and by the relative weakness of tertiary education in Europe. After mid-century, these various obstacles to technology transfer were reduced.

Trade liberalization and moves towards economic integration in Europe created a wider market. Linked to this, American direct investment in Europe blossomed and multinational companies proved to be a powerful and relatively low cost mode of diffusing technology; 310 American manufacturing subsidiaries were set up in Britain between 1950 and 1962 compared with 233 in the whole inter-war period.[1] Improvements in communications and in European education, together with a trend towards greater codification of scientific knowledge, started to transform national networks for the spread of information into international ones. Natural resource endowments diminished in importance as technological progress became less dependent on them and more dependent on investments in human capital and scientific research.

To take full advantage of these increased opportunities for technological catch-up, countries needed an appropriate policy framework and adequate 'social capability'; catch-up was not automatic. Development of an infrastructure to support rapid diffusion of technology was more important than pursuit of grandiose projects, and the spur of competition among firms seems generally to have been more powerful than interventionism as an effective stimulus to rapid adoption of new methods from abroad, as Japanese experience also confirms.[2]

1. G. Jones and F. Bostock, 'US multinationals in Britain before 1962', University of Reading Discussion Paper in International Investment and Business Studies No. 214 (1996), p. 9.
2. A. Goto, 'Technology importation: Japan's postwar experience', in Y. Kosai (ed.), *The Japanese Experience of Economic Reforms* (London, 1993), pp. 277–304.

Compared probably with any previous era, a hallmark of the Golden Age was the much reduced economic insecurity felt by the average European citizen (*cf.* Chapter 8). Obviously, this came in large part from the rapid economic growth and the low unemployment of the period. For many workers, however, these features were accentuated by trends in both the pre-tax and post-tax and benefit income distribution towards reduced inequality. In part, this reflected the technological and trade environments but in addition government now played a larger role than hitherto. An increased size of government reduced exposure to business cycle downturns but also provided expanded welfare state provision. Table 4.5 shows that the overall size of the government budget (outlays) was typically over 30 per cent of GDP by the 1960s, funded by taxation (receipts) rather than borrowing, a proportion that would have been quite unthinkable a century earlier. A larger state budget and a better safety net were key ingredients of European post-war settlements and, despite right-wing fears to the contrary, the tax implications do not seem to have created severe disincentives to investment and growth.

The end of the Golden Age heralded a further rapid rise in government spending such that, in the recent past, outlays of around 60 per cent of GDP have been seen in several countries while 45 per cent or more has become quite usual in Europe. Rising outlays reflected both greater purchases of goods and services but also, and generally to a greater extent, increased transfer payments to compensate for unemployment, old age, and so on. After the 1960s, fiscal arithmetic seems to have become a good deal less favourable and the assumptions on which the post-war welfare states had been established were undermined by demographic and labour market changes (see Chapter 10), by the slow-down in economic growth and by policy responses to the shocks of the 1970s. By the 1980s, it seemed that the welfare state structures might ultimately be unsustainable. At the same time, there was quite general concern that Europe had become locked into high levels of government spending which might be a serious impediment to growth through some combination of budget deficits that pushed up interest rates and higher taxation that discouraged investment.

Here then is a final illustration of what has been an underlying theme in this account of the Golden Age, namely, that the early post-war years saw the coming together of a number of mutually reinforcing elements promoting favourable economic performance in all dimensions but that from the late 1960s this unravelled. The post-war settlement was conducive to rapid growth, low unemployment and economic security but was also underpinned by these outcomes. The very success of the reconstruction of post-war Europe carried with it the seeds of the eventual destruction of some of the pillars on which it rested as catch-up and cheap energy were used up, diminishing returns to investment became apparent, the initial balance between capital and labour was disturbed and the realignment of exchange rates became a more pressing problem. Undoubtedly, serious policy errors were made in the 1970s but in the nature of things the Great Boom could not have continued indefinitely.

Table 4.5. Government consumption, social security transfers, government outlays and tax receipts (per cent of GDP)

	Consumption	Transfers	Outlays	Receipts
(a) 1960–73				
Australia	13.0	5.6	24.4	25.3
Austria	14.0	14.9	38.7	38.7
Belgium	13.2	13.5	36.0	25.3
Canada	16.1	7.3	31.6	30.1
Denmark	17.6	9.5	33.8	35.4
Finland	14.0	6.6	30.3	32.6
France	14.6	15.5	38.0	37.7
Germany	17.1	12.8	37.5	37.6
Italy	13.5	11.9	33.7	30.2
Japan	7.9	4.5	19.5	20.0
Netherlands	14.3	na	40.8	39.5
Norway	15.7	10.3	36.7	40.2
Sweden	19.5	10.0	38.9	41.7
Switzerland	10.4	7.3	20.3	24.9
UK	17.5	7.8	36.7	34.8
USA	17.8	6.3	29.4	27.5
(b) 1980–93				
Australia	18.0	9.5	34.5	33.5
Austria	18.5	20.2	51.0	47.3
Belgium	16.4	24.6	59.8	51.1
Canada	20.3	12.5	46.6	40.1
Denmark	26.1	17.8	59.5	56.0
Finland	20.6	16.0	47.2	47.4
France	18.8	21.5	50.7	46.5
Germany	21.4	16.1	47.8	44.9
Italy	16.6	17.3	50.6	39.6
Japan	9.5	11.1	32.9	31.6
Netherlands	15.7	26.4	59.8	54.1
Norway	20.2	na	na	na
Sweden	27.9	19.4	64.0	59.7
Switzerland	13.4	14.0	31.3	34.2
UK	21.4	12.9	44.6	40.4
USA	17.9	11.4	36.3	31.4

Source: OECD, *Historical Statistics, 1960–93.*

Debates and Interpretations

It was once debated whether the growth of the Golden Age was really special. An influential contribution by Janossy argued that the Great Boom was simply a recovery to a pre-existing trend growth path from which Europe had been diverted by war and depression.[3] Although reconstruction did play an important part in the first phase of the boom, it is now accepted both that this view is rejected by standard econometric tests and that we can identify aspects of post-war growth which were unprecedented – for example, the extent of technology transfer and the rate of investment in R & D. The current controversy is rather about why growth was so fast. The debate centres not on the proximate sources of growth such as TFP growth which are the concern of growth accounting as in Table 4.4, but on the underlying determinants of growth performance.

There are three main reasons why this is difficult to resolve. First, a monocausal explanation for fast growth is unlikely; this was a multi-faceted process and assessing the relative contributions of different factors is contentious, particularly given that theoretical ideas in this area continue to evolve. Second, there are considerable problems of measurement which stand in the way of quantitative analysis; for example, measurement of the disincentive effects of taxation on growth is still in its infancy. Third, there can easily be disputes over directions of causality which may indeed often be two-way; for example, more investment may be good for growth, but equally, better growth prospects stimulate investment.

One hotly debated point has been the relative importance of 'demand' and 'supply' factors in promoting rapid growth. Writers in the Keynesian tradition such as Boltho continue to stress that macroeconomic policy in the Golden Age was much more conducive to strong investment than it had been during the inter-war period and that the period was relatively free of adverse demand shocks, unlike the 1970s.[4] This school of thought tends to put greater emphasis on the existence of a suitable policy framework and its role in establishing favourable expectations rather than on the attempts made by some governments (including that of the UK) to smooth out fluctuations in demand by active fiscal policy. There is some evidence to suggest that in the post-war period unpredictable monetary policy has had an adverse effect on growth, but there has not yet been a satisfactory test of the joint hypotheses that monetary policy was more predictable than in the inter-war period and that this had a substantial impact on investment and growth.

Even if it is argued that 'demand' conditions were important, it should be remembered that they worked through inducing changes on the supply side of the economy – more rapid growth in the quantity and perhaps quality of the capital stock – to produce faster growth. Alternative 'supply' interpretations stress different reasons for strong productivity growth.

A very influential, yet highly controversial, hypothesis is that of Olson and the Eurosclerosis school.[5] They argue that in mature democracies growth tends to be held back by interest groups which try to prevent reallocations of resources towards dynamic sectors and away from declining industries and which pursue sectional interests at the expense of jeopardizing incentives to invest and innovate. Such interest groups are difficult to organize effectively but tend slowly to proliferate as stable political conditions are maintained. War, foreign invasion and episodes of totalitarian government tend to purge society of these sclerotic tendencies and to create a period where the political economy of growth is more favourable. Similarly, widening of markets – such as through European economic integration – tends to change the locus of lobbying activities and to give a breathing space until reorganization has been achieved.

In this view, the 1940s and 1950s generally reduced Eurosclerosis, especially in some fast-growing countries, but by the 1970s and 1980s the problem had returned and was reflected in a resurgence of protectionism, pressures to expand the public sector and a diversion of talent from entrepreneurship to rent-seeking. Olson's hypotheses have, however, been strongly criticized by those who argue that the weakening of interest groups prior to the Golden Age was much less general than suggested. Econometric tests of the hypothesis have also produced negative results; across countries there is no robust relationship between the date of the last shock to stable democracy and post-war growth performance. The real, unresolved problem with both criticisms, as well as Olson's original hypothesis, is one of measurement – how to quantify the strength of the sclerotic tendencies.

An alternative perspective, which overlaps that of Olson in some respects, has recently been proposed by Eichengreen.[6] This stresses that the post-war period saw a general shift in Europe towards institutional arrangements which reassured firms that the profitability of investment and innovation would not be threatened by workers' attempts to hijack the returns, and which promised employees that wage moderation would be rewarded by growth in productivity and long-run living standards. This required appropriate commitment and monitoring mechanisms, coordination across sectors and a clear realization that bad behaviour would be costly. Eichengreen sees centralization of wage bargaining, trade liberalization and the realization that rapid catch-up growth could be achieved as key underpinnings of successful 'social contracts'. A common theme in both Eichengreen and Olson's lines of argument is that where organizations are 'encompassing', that is, represent broad groups, it is much better for growth than where they are 'sectional', because they have to be concerned about the general effects of their actions and cannot afford to act as free-riders. Both Eichengreen and Olson also tend to see such arrangements as prone to degenerate over time.

It is certainly the case that post-war Europe saw changes in wage bargaining arrangements and moves towards 'social contracts', as Eichengreen says, and the logic of the models that say this might be good for growth (and low unemployment) is appealing. Table 4.6 is derived from a book whose central themes echo these arguments and bears out the story, at least if taken at face value. It is much harder to quantify the effects on investment and growth and significant effects have not yet been shown. It should be added that summary classification of wage bargaining systems is itself a controversial area. The problems here are once again of measurement and also in this case of the direction of causation – was fast productivity growth good for social contracts or the other way around?

In Table 4.6, the terms 'corporatist' and 'neo-corporatist' describe varieties of wage-setting systems characterized by a relatively high degree of national coordination in bargaining and by a mutual sharing of responsibility between the state and high-level worker and employer organizations which are likely to be encompassing, whereas decentralized collective bargaining will be sectional.

Table 4.6. A classification of industrial relations systems

	1925	1938	1950
Corporatism	A, D, E	CH, DK, N, S	A, B, DK, N, NL, S
Collective bargaining			
Neo-corporatist	CH	B, NL	CH, D
Decentralized	B, DK, N, NL, S, UK	IRL, UK	IRL, UK
Contestation	F, FIN, IRL	FIN, F	FIN, F, IT
Authoritarian	IT, P	A, D, E, IT, P	E, P

	1963	1975	1990
Corporatism	A, B, DK, N, NL, S	A, B, CH, D, DK, N, NL, S	A, CH, D, FIN, N, S
Collective bargaining			
Neo-corporatist	CH, D	FIN	B, DK, NL
Decentralized	IRL, UK	IRL, IT, UK	IRL, F, IT
Contestation	FIN, F, IT	E, F, P	E, P, UK
Authoritarian	E, P		

Note: the abbreviations are as follows: A = Austria, B = Belgium, CH = Switzerland, D = Germany, DK = Denmark, E = Spain, FIN = Finland, F = France, IRL = Ireland, IT = Italy, N = Norway, NL = Netherlands, P = Portugal, S = Sweden.

Source: derived from C. Crouch, *Industrial Relations and European State Traditions* (Oxford, 1993).

'Contestation' reflects a situation where collective bargaining arrangements are relatively unstructured or institutionalized, while in 'authoritarian' cases unions are generally repressed.

Table 4.6 is suggestive of Eichengreen's main theme. In 1950, it is noticeable that, relative to 1925, there were more countries classified as 'corporatist' or 'neo-corporatist' and fewer with decentralized collective bargaining. It is also striking that Ireland and the UK, which Table 4.2 suggested were countries whose growth was disappointing during the Golden Age, are the two cases that fall into this latter category. This is an example of variations in institutions across European countries which may have affected growth and which reflect differences both of historical legacy and of policy towards reform. It is perhaps an important aspect of what Abramovitz famously termed 'social capability' for growth and catching-up.[7]

While there is widespread agreement among economic historians that 'social capability' is central to explaining why growth rates differed in the Golden Age, there is no consensus on what exactly were its major components. The ability to modernize and to assimilate ideas from abroad is influenced by vested interests, by education systems, by incentive structures and thus by institutions and policy. Although, obviously, 'social capability' was high throughout western Europe relative to many other parts of the world, it is important to recognize that there was considerable heterogeneity within Europe. Finding out how much this mattered and why it persisted are central tasks for further research.

To get a flavour of what might be involved, compare the UK and West Germany, relatively a 'loser' and a 'winner' respectively in Golden Age growth.

Apart from having different industrial relations systems, the literature has also highlighted several other important differences including:

- *corporate governance* where the relative unimportance of outside shareholders in West Germany may have allowed a less short-termist attitude to investment;
- *industrial policy* where the British badly mishandled control of nationalized industries and went further down the unsuccessful route of fostering 'national champions';
- *taxation* where the British system was characterized by much higher marginal direct tax rates which may have discouraged investment;
- *vocational training* where West German 'corporatist' institutions delivered more skills by solving problems of market failure linked to employers' fears that the workers they trained would be poached and workers' fears that their investment in acquiring skills would go unrewarded.

To account for the existence of these contrasts one might partly appeal to history, partly to the implications of war and its aftermath and partly to political constraints which circumscribed policy reform.

Explaining the growth experience of the Golden Age looks set to become one of the staple controversies of quantitative economic history on a par with 'Did Victorian Britain fail?' and 'Why and how was Prometheus Unbound?'. This should not be taken to indicate that progress in the debates is not possible but rather that this is a fascinating and complex set of issues.

Bibliographical Note

The best introductory book on the Great Boom is H. van der Wee, *Prosperity and Upheaval: the World Economy 1945–1980* (London, 1987). N.F.R. Crafts and G. Toniolo (eds), *Economic Growth in Europe since 1945* (Cambridge, 1996) is more sophisticated and contains restatements of the Eichengreen and Olson theories on post-war growth, while A. Maddison, *Dynamic Forces in Capitalist Development* (Oxford, 1991) gives an overview of phases in economic growth together with a fairly accessible discussion of growth accounting.

Key ideas on unemployment are simply explained in R. Floud and D. McCloskey (eds), *The Economic History of Britain since 1700*, vol. 3 (Cambridge, 1994), Chapter 7, while R. Nelson and G. Wright, 'The rise and fall of American technological leadership', *Journal of Economic Literature* (1992) is an excellent survey of issues relating to technological transfer. Finally, the classic reference on catch-up growth is M. Abramovitz, 'Catching up, forging ahead, and falling behind', *Journal of Economic History*, 46 (1986).

Notes

1. S. Broadberry, 'Convergence: what the historical record shows', in B. van Ark and N.F.R. Crafts (eds), *Quantitative Aspects of Postwar European Economic Growth* (Cambridge, 1996).

2. P. Sicsic and C. Wyplosz, 'France', in N.F.R. Crafts and G. Toniolo (eds), *Economic Growth in Europe since 1945* (Cambridge, 1996), p. 219.

3. F. Janossy, *The End of the Economic Miracle* (White Plains, NY, 1969).

4. A. Boltho, 'Economic growth', in A. Boltho (ed.), *The European Economy: Growth and Crisis* (Oxford, 1982).

5. M. Olson, *The Rise and Decline of Nations* (New Haven, CT, 1982).

6. B. Eichengreen, 'Institutions and economic growth: Europe after World War II', in Crafts and Toniolo (eds), *Economic Growth in Europe since 1945*.

7. M. Abramovitz, 'Catching up, forging ahead, and falling behind', *Journal of Economic History*, 46 (1986).

5 The Search for Economic Stability: Western Europe since 1973

Nicholas Woodward

Before the Oil Crisis

With the first oil crisis, 1973 has often been presented as the great turning point in post-war European economic history. According to conventional histories, the two previous decades had been a period of outstanding economic success; long-run economic growth had been at an all-time high, while unemployment and inflation had been low. Following the oil crisis, however, the economic environment became less favourable and the European economy proved unable to adjust readily to the changed conditions. Faced with these problems, governments responded by introducing new economic policies, but these came too slowly and were often misdirected. The result was a deterioration in economic performance.

Although this account has much to recommend it, the tendency to identify 1973 as the turning point is probably misplaced, because in the years immediately preceding the oil crisis there were already signs that the economic environment was deteriorating. One of the first indications of this came in the late 1960s when European inflation began to rise. The main reason for this was that the Vietnam war had generated a demand inflation in the United States which was then transmitted to the other industrialized countries. The result was that an inflationary momentum was allowed to build up that eventually European governments would feel obliged to choke off.

One of the casualties of the higher inflation was the adjustable peg of the Bretton Woods system. This was finally abandoned in March 1973 in favour of floating exchange rates. Although many of the worst fears about floating did not materialize, it was to have some important consequences over the next decade and

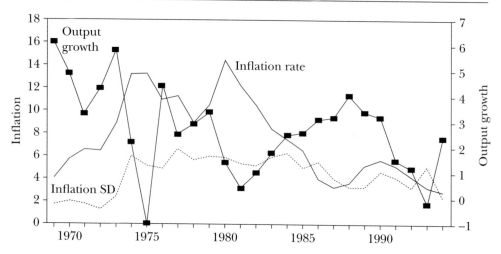

Note: The SD (standard deviation) measures the dispersion of inflation within Europe. The interpretation is that roughly two-thirds of the countries will lie within one standard deviation either side of the average.

Figure 5.1. European inflation and output growth (per cent change per annum). *Source:* OECD, *Economic Outlook,* various issues.

beyond. First, it removed a financial discipline on governments. Some countries adopted over-expansionary financial policies so that during the 1970s large inflation differences emerged within Europe (Figure 5.1). Another consequence was that it led to a much greater degree of exchange rate volatility, particularly between the European currencies and the dollar. As the exchange rate movements were not always linked to relative price changes, large swings in price competitiveness occured in both the 1970s and 1980s. This posed a major problem for policy-makers, especially those in West Germany and Switzerland.

Apart from Vietnam, another reason for the higher inflation in the early 1970s was that western Europe experienced a series of wage explosions. These started in France in 1968 and then spread to a number of other countries, an important development because it seemed to signal a shift away from wage moderation. This had been a key feature of the 1950s and 1960s, since it had enabled governments to maintain low levels of unemployment without the fear that inflationary problems would emerge. At the same time, it led to high levels of profitability that, in turn, underpinned the investment boom which had been one of the causes of the high rate of economic growth and low unemployment.

Faced with higher inflation and rising wage costs, a number of countries adopted deflationary policies in 1970/71. However, it soon became clear in some countries that wage settlements were less responsive to demand pressures than hitherto, as a result of which the attempt to reduce inflation was partially (and temporarily) abandoned. The decline in wage responsiveness was to pose problems over the next decade because it implied that the restoration of low inflation would bring fairly high costs in terms of unemployment and lost output. Consequently,

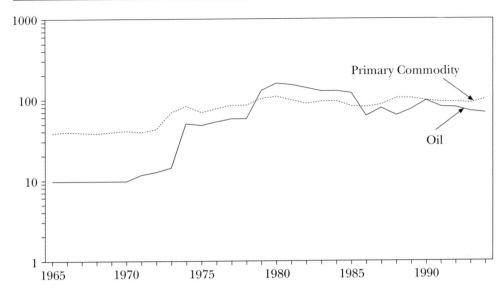

Figure 5.2. Average oil and non-fuel primary commodity prices (1990 = 100). *Source:* IMF, *Financial Statistics,* Annual Supplements.

governments were to be faced with painful choices between inflation and unemployment control.

Thus by the early 1970s the European economies were in a less healthy position than they had been a decade before. Nevertheless, there was no great sense of despondency at the time. By later standards, the problems were still relatively modest, but, in any case, in 1971 the world economy entered a synchronized, if short-lived, boom, that brought down unemployment and accelerated short-run growth.

In the event, the boom proved unsustainable as further inflationary problems reappeared. In part, this was due to overheating domestic conditions, so that in early 1973 a number of European countries began to apply restrictive measures. At the same time, the boom helped to drive up the price of imported raw materials and foodstuffs which rose at an unprecedented rate (Figure 5.2).[1] Thus, already by mid-1973, before the oil crisis, the European economy was heading for a period of stagflation: high inflation coupled with higher unemployment and lower growth.

From OPEC I to OPEC 2: 1973–79

These stagflationary problems, however, were aggravated in the second half of 1973 by the first oil crisis. This was an immediate consequence of the policies of the Organization of Petroleum Exporting Countries (OPEC). In retaliation for the pro-Israeli stance of the industrialized countries during the Yom Kippur war in the autumn of 1973, OPEC first introduced an oil embargo, although, with the exception of the Netherlands,[2] this was soon lifted. This was followed by a series of oil price increases (OPEC 1). The result was that between the autumn of 1973

Table 5.1. Oil dependency, 1971 (oil requirements as a percentage of primary energy requirements)

Country	Oil requirements	Country	Oil requirements
Belgium	63.7	UK	45.6
France	66.4	OECD Europe	61.5
West Germany	54.9	Canada	53.4
Italy	79.7	Japan	75.2
Netherlands	60.4	USA	45.4

Source: OECD, *Economic Outlook*, December 1973.

and the spring of 1974, the nominal price of crude oil rose by over 400 per cent (Figure 5.2).

Although requirements differed (Table 5.1), Europe was relatively dependent on imported oil. This, coupled with the size of the price increase, created some major difficulties for the European economies. Indeed in 1974 Europe faced its most serious crisis since 1950. Three specific problems emerged. For some countries, the first and most immediate problem was a large balance of trade deficit. In the long run, of course, this would have to be eliminated by reducing consumption in favour of higher exports. But in the interim the deficit would have to be financed by borrowing from countries with surpluses. In the event, this financing problem proved less difficult than was feared, as surplus countries lent to deficit ones through the usual international capital flows.

The second difficulty was that OPEC 1 threatened to raise inflation that was already considered to be too high. In principle, of course, there was no reason why OPEC 1 should have had a permanent impact on inflation. The increase in oil prices was a once-and-for-all event. Inflation, therefore, should have risen in the short term, only to fall back again. The danger was, however, that the increase in oil prices would have a more sustained impact by either raising inflationary expectations or encouraging labour to push for higher wages in order to resist the inevitable decline in living standards.

Finally, higher oil prices threatened to raise unemployment by redistributing world income towards the OPEC countries which in the short term had a low propensity to spend. Linked with this, the higher energy prices would encourage producers to discontinue certain lines of production and to scrap part of their capital which, in turn, would reduce the demand for labour. There was also the danger that the overall reaction of the industrialized countries to OPEC 1 would be highly deflationary, as individual countries tried to correct their balance of payments and inflationary difficulties.

Obviously, therefore, the capacity of Europe to deal with the crisis would depend crucially upon the degree of economic flexibility. If a major contraction was to be avoided, firms would have to invest heavily and restructure their production rapidly towards areas where demand was buoyant. At the same time labour would have to be occupationally and geographically mobile, and would have to be prepared to accept reductions in living standards, otherwise profits and investment

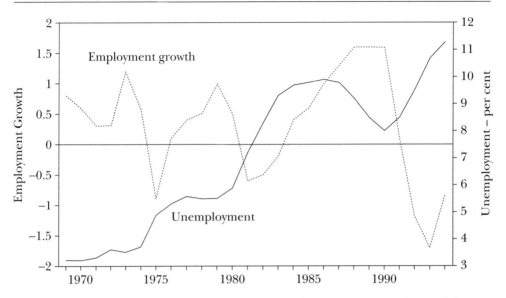

Figure 5.3. European employment growth and unemployment. *Source:* as Figure 5.1.

would fall and governments would be obliged to choke off inflationary problems by adopting contractionary policies.

The oil crisis also posed a major policy dilemma for governments – whether to adopt *accommodating* demand policies to contain unemployment or *extinguishing* measures to reduce inflation and improve the balance of payments. There was no clear-cut prescription. It all depended on the weight individual countries attached to their short-run unemployment and inflation goals, and on the circumstances in which they found themselves in the mid-1970s. In the event, the policy reaction varied from country to country. Switzerland and West Germany, for example, attached a high priority to controlling inflation and maintained tight monetary policies. Sweden, by contrast, gave a higher priority to unemployment and introduced accommodating policies and special employment measures, confident that with its flexible wage-bargaining system the inflationary consequences would not be too severe. As a result Sweden was one of the few countries which had lower open unemployment at the end of the 1970s than at the beginning. France, Italy and the UK also tried to follow a relatively expansionary line in the mid-1970s. They, however, were much less successful and were later forced to adopt extinguishing policies, whether because of debt, inflationary or currency problems.

Overall, there was a marked deterioration in the performance of the European economy in the mid-1970s. Inflation, which had averaged just under 7 per cent in the early 1970s, rose to over 13 per cent in 1974/75. After this it declined, although in 1979 it was still 10 per cent. Output also fell after 1973 and Europe entered its most severe downturn since the 1930s (Figure 5.1). Nevertheless, the slump was fairly short-lived, the recovery starting in 1975. However, with the exception of 1976, this proved to be disappointing and European unemployment, which rose to over 5 per cent in 1977, remained persistently high throughout the decade (Figure 5.3). To some extent, this was due to low investment

Plate 5.1. A used car lot in 1974. This picture was taken in Britain, but across the whole of western Europe consumers, and producers alike, felt the impact of soaring petrol prices and often actual shortages. One response was to downgrade to smaller cars.

and low profitability. However, governments were also unable to adopt highly expansionary policies because of a persistent fear of either reigniting inflation or aggravating government debt problems, which had emerged with the boom and slump years earlier in the decade.

To counter these problems, of course, new policies were introduced. On the financial front, much has been made of the rise of monetarism in the mid/late 1970s and the associated demise of demand management. In reality, however, things were not so simple. It is true that a number of European countries introduced money supply targets in the mid/late 1970s in the hope that this would influence inflationary expectations. But the targets were not always ambitious and sometimes were ignored.[3] Fiscal policy, the manipulation of taxation and government expenditure, also continued to be used selectively, as and when conditions allowed.

On the supply side, the primary emphasis was in containing unemployment. Consequently, in an attempt to moderate wage pressures, a number of governments introduced formal or informal incomes policies which were viewed as an alternative to deflation. At the same time there was a marked expansion of industrial subsidies. Special labour market measures, such as employment subsidies and government employment and early retirement schemes, were also introduced, along with employment protection policies, the aim of which was to reduce lay-offs. It was assumed at the time that such policies were bound to be effective in containing unemployment. Recently, however, economists have be-

Table 5.2. Misery index (sum of consumer price inflation rate and unemployment rate)

	1973	1979	1990	1995	Change 1973–79	Change 1979–90	Change 1990–95
Austria	8.5	5.4	6.5	8.1	−3.1	1.1	1.6
Belgium	9.3	11.8	12.1	14.5	2.5	0.3	2.4
Denmark	10.3	15.8	12.2	12.1	5.5	−3.6	−0.1
Finland	12.3	13.5	9.6	18.2	1.2	−3.9	8.6
France	10.0	16.8	12.3	13.3	6.8	−4.5	1.0
Germany	7.9	7.4	8.9	11.2	−0.5	1.5	2.3
Greece	17.5	14.0	27.4	19.3	−3.5	13.4	−8.1
Ireland	17.1	20.4	16.5	15.4	3.3	−3.9	−1.1
Italy	17.2	22.6	17.6	17.4	5.4	−5.0	−0.2
Netherlands	11.1	9.8	9.4	9.0	−1.3	−0.4	−0.4
Norway	9.0	6.7	9.3	7.4	−2.3	2.6	−1.9
Portugal	13.7	32.1	28.1	11.3	18.4	−4.0	−16.8
Spain	13.3	24.2	23.0	27.6	10.9	−1.2	4.6
Sweden	8.7	8.9	12.2	10.4	0.2	3.3	−1.8
Switzerland	8.7	3.9	5.9	6.0	−4.8	2.0	0.1
UK	11.3	17.9	15.4	11.6	6.6	−2.5	−3.8

Source: As for Figure 5.1.

come sceptical about their long-term consequences. Such policies, it is argued, do little, if anything, to improve economic flexibility which was essential if the European economies were to adapt to the more difficult circumstances. Industrial and employment subsidies, for example, were often targeted at declining industries with few growth prospects, and, by reducing the risks of bankruptcy, may have encouraged higher wage settlements. Similarly, employment protection policies, although leading to fewer lay-offs in the short run, increase the costs of employment and may, therefore, discourage firms from creating jobs.

Perhaps it is not surprising, therefore, that at the end of the decade European economic performance was worse than before the oil crisis. Nevertheless, performance varied quite considerably within Europe. Table 5.2, for example, shows the 'misery index' – the sum of the inflation and unemployment rates. On this measure, the best performers were Austria, West Germany, the Netherlands, Sweden and Switzerland, while Ireland, Italy, Portugal, Spain and the UK were the worst.

Why did some countries perform better than others? Probably, the most important factor was the flexibility of wage bargaining arrangements.[4] It is no coincidence, for example, that Austria, West Germany (see box), Norway, Sweden and Switzerland were countries with a relatively high degree of social cohesion in which wages responsed readily to deteriorating economic conditions. In such countries, therefore, both profits and investment held up fairly well, and the authorities were able either to adopt extinguishing policies without the danger that unemployment would rise rapidly, or to adopt accommodating policies without the fear of explosive inflation.

In focus: West Germany and the First Oil Crisis

As the main text shows, West Germany was able to adapt better than the other large western European economies. The important question is: why?

Part of the answer is that Germany acted promptly. In the wake of the oil crisis, the Bundesbank, despite opposition from the trade unions, adopted a fairly tight monetary policy. One consequence was that the Deutschmark appreciated. This partially offset the increase in dollar-denominated oil prices. At the same time, however, the appreciation forced German manufacturers to cut their costs and to bargain more intensively over wages. The consequence was that German inflation rose only marginally in 1974, after which it declined steadily and by 1978 was lower than it had been at the beginning of the decade. Inevitably, however, the appreciation aggravated the decline in export demand, already under way because of the world slump. Unemployment, therefore, rose sharply in the mid-1970s, although the Federal government partially offset this by adopting expansionary fiscal policies.

Nevertheless, the German economy turned up in 1975 and, with inflation under control, the authorities had some flexibility in stimulating the economy. Thus both expansionary fiscal and monetary policies were adopted at various times in the recovery years. The result was that by 1979 unemployment was back down to 3.3 per cent, high by earlier post-war German standards, but below the level of the other large countries.

The moral of the story would seem to be that governments should act decisively when confronted with OPEC-type disturbances to eliminate inflation. However, that interpretation needs to be qualified, because Germany in part owed its relative success to other factors. First, it benefited from the tight policies that were adopted *before* the oil crisis. In 1972/73, when the world boom was at its peak, the German authorities made deliberate attempts to reduce the growth of demand which was regarded as dangerously inflationary. The result was that Germany went into the oil crisis with a large balance of trade surplus and relatively low inflation, both of which eased subsequent adjustment problems.

Institutional and historical factors also help explain Germany's relative success. For example, one consequence of the experience in the 1920s and 1940s was that the electorate was sensitive to the prospect of high inflation. This helped to win support for counter-inflation policies and allowed the Federal Government to adopt a long-term strategy. Germany also benefited from the independence of the Bundesbank and from its cautious monetary policies in the 1960s. This lent credibility to the deflationary policies and helped to bring inflation down quickly. Finally, Germany was assisted by a consensual wage bargaining system and cooperative labour movement. Consequently during the mid-1970s, when orders were declining and profitability low, there was less resistance to lower wage increases.

Fighting Stagflation: 1979–90

In the early 1980s, European governments were again asked to make painful choices. The immediate cause of this was the second oil crisis – OPEC 2. This was a direct consequence of the Iranian Revolution at the beginning of 1979, which reduced the supply of oil at a time when demand was increasing. The result was that oil prices rose by 130 per cent between the end of 1978 and May 1980. This was less than in 1973/74, although the real income transfer to the OPEC countries, expressed as a percentage of national income, was about the same.

The second oil crisis posed the same problems as OPEC 1. In some respects the European countries were better placed to deal with it: unlike 1973, it had not been preceded by an unsustainable boom, wages had been increasing at a relatively moderate rate and the company sector was in a more healthy financial situation.[5] Nevertheless, the European economy was starting from a higher inflation and unemployment base. The projections for world oil reserves were also more pessimistic.

It was partly because of this that the immediate response of the European countries to OPEC 2 was the introduction of extinguishing monetary policies (Figure 5.4). Thus by 1979 Europe was heading for another period of stagflation that was aggravated by the introduction of tight monetary policies by the US Federal Reserve in June 1979. This pushed the US into a severe downturn in 1981–82 which, in view of its prominence in the world economy, was bound to have knock-on effects for Europe.

Nevertheless, on balance, Europe dealt quite successfully with OPEC 2. On this occasion the distribution of trade imbalances was less marked, and wages

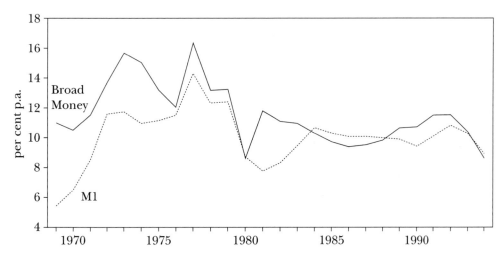

Note: M1 – narrow money – includes assets which can be used to make payments, such as current account bank deposits and notes. Broad money includes M1 plus assets which can be converted quickly into money such as deposit accounts.

Figure 5.4. European monetary growth: three-year moving average. *Source:* as Figure 5.1.

rose less rapidly in response to higher prices, so that profits held up fairly well. This did not prevent inflation, which peaked at over 12 per cent, from rising. But it came down quickly and remained at a fairly low level for the rest of the 1980s (Figure 5.1). Furthermore, although Europe experienced a serious downturn in the early 1980s, this was less marked than in the mid-1970s. The most disappointing aspect of performance, therefore, was unemployment which increased quite rapidly in the early 1980s, a rise that continued into the middle of the decade.

Whether governments could have done much to contain the rise in unemployment through more expansionary policies is an open question. It was increasingly argued in the early 1980s that the underlying level of unemployment had risen over the previous decade because of structural changes within the economy, and this limited the ability to introduce expansionary measures without an early acceleration of inflation. Whether or not this was true, it is evident that by the early 1980s the approach to financial policy had shifted in a more conservative direction, as demand management was downgraded in favour of reducing budget deficits and maintaining price stability.

Indicative of the New Conservative Macroeconomics, as it was known, was the Organisation for Economic Co-operation and Development (OECD) meeting of Economics and Finance Ministers in May 1983 when it was agreed that financial policy should henceforth be set in a medium-term framework, rather than responding to short-run goals such as unemployment. Nevertheless, a change in attitude had been evident at least four years earlier. At this time the argument was frequently voiced that sustained expansion would not be possible again until debt and inflationary difficulties were eliminated. There was also a feeling that those countries that had adopted extinguishing policies in the mid-1970s had performed better subsequently.

Symptomatic of the change in attitude had been the formation of the Exchange Rate Mechanism (ERM) within the European Monetary System (EMS) in March 1979, which aimed to stabilize exchange rates between Community members (see Chapter 9). The formation of EMS was prompted by a number of motives: that it would aid the cause of monetary unification and, particularly attractive from the West German point of view, that it would reduce exchange rate volatility. But another important consideration was that it would provide an anchor for financial policy and impose a discipline on wage bargainers and governments alike. This was an important consideration for the French authorities, which, along with West Germany, co-sponsored the scheme.

Nevertheless, in 1979 it was probably the United Kingdom, which did not join the ERM until 1990, that adopted the new conservative approach most enthusiastically. Following the election of the Thatcher government in May 1979, the central policy priority became the reduction of inflation coupled with a shift away from demand management towards a system of planned monetary growth. Consequently, both monetary and fiscal policy were planned over the medium term through an extension of targeting. In fact, the government missed its targets and the targeting policy soon became quite flexible. Nevertheless, both monetary and fiscal policy became extremely restrictive during the slump, indicative of the change in stance.[6]

West Germany also moved increasingly in a conservative direction in 1982, although this was motivated primarily by a desire to reduce the size of the budget deficit. The latter had risen because at the 1978 Bonn Group 7 summit the German authorities had been persuaded, against their better judgement, to adopt an expansionary fiscal stance. By the early 1980s, however, German economic performance had deteriorated, and it was felt that this was at least partly due to the public deficit which had reduced the incentive to invest.

Restrictive financial policies, however, were not confined to the UK and West Germany. To a greater or lesser extent, most European governments moved in a conservative direction in the early 1980s. For example, both Ireland and Italy, both of which had experienced high inflation in the 1970s, adopted more restrictive policies. In 1979 they both joined the ERM which imposed a monetary discipline on their governments. Ireland also carried out a fiscal consolidation between 1981 and 1983.

Only France seriously questioned the drift towards conservative financial policies at this time. Following the election of President Mitterrand in 1981, the decision was made to adopt relatively expansionary policies. This was supplemented with a range of supply-side measures, including an incomes policy, an increase in the minimum wage, shorter working hours and improvements in the statutory position of trade unions. Although the policy was not a complete failure, the programme was abandoned in 1983 as inflationary problems re-emerged and France was faced with a foreign exchange crisis. To a large extent, this was a predictable outcome because the labour market measures had, if anything, reduced the growth of productive capacity at a time when demand was expanding. After 1983, therefore, French financial policy shifted in a conservative direction. Fiscal policy became tight and France adopted a non-accommodating stance within the ERM. Eventually, from 1988 this gave way to an ultra-hard currency policy – the *franc fort* – the aim of which was to improve French competitiveness by securing lower rates of inflation than West Germany.[7]

Nevertheless, it would be wrong to make too much of the severity of the new conservative policies, because, following the slump of 1980/81, the European economy expanded continuously until the end of the decade, an unusually long period of recovery. In part, this was due to the conservative financial policies in the early 1980s that had paved the way for a sustained expansion. Thereafter, economic expansion was kept more or less in line with the growth of productive capacity. The result was that European inflation remained low for the rest of the decade (Figure 5.1).

The world economy was also free of further oil price shocks, although at the time of the Gulf war in 1990 there was some apprehension about a possible OPEC 3 – an event which fortunately did not materialize. In fact, oil prices declined from 1981, experiencing a sharp fall in 1986. Thereafter, prices recovered but were still lower in 1990 than they had been a decade earlier (Figure 5.2).

Table 5.3. Total factor productivity growth (per cent per annum)

	1960–73	1973–79	1979–88
Austria	3.4	1.4	0.7
Belgium	3.7	1.5	1.1
Denmark	2.8	1.2	0.8
Finland	3.4	1.7	2.3
France	3.9	1.7	1.5
West Germany	2.7	2.0	0.7
Greece	5.8	1.5	−0.7
Italy	4.6	2.2	1.0
Netherlands	3.1	2.0	0.6
Norway	3.6	−0.4	1.4
Spain	4.2	1.7	2.1
Sweden	2.5	0.3	0.9
Switzerland	1.6	−0.9	0.2
UK	2.2	0.5	1.9

Source: N.F.R. Crafts, 'Productivity growth reconsidered', *Economic Policy*, no. 15 (Oct. 1992).

Linked with this there was a sustained growth of trade, at a lower rate than in the early 1970s but sustained nonetheless.

Even so, it should not be assumed that Europe was free of problems after 1981. Exchange rates, especially against the dollar, remained volatile and became a source of uncertainty. Similarly, large budget deficits in the USA drove up European real (i.e. adjusted for inflation) interest rates, which, in turn, discouraged investment. Another shock emanating from the USA was the October 1987 stock market crash, which threatened to push the world economy into another downturn. The 1980s was also a decade in which structural and technological change was quite rapid, as activity shifted increasingly towards the service sector, the information revolution progressed and competition from low wage Less Developed Countries, especially those of east Asia, intensified. Such change obliged European producers to adapt their production patterns.

Despite the long boom and low inflation, however, economic performance in the 1980s is usually considered to have been disappointing. In part, this is because unemployment was persistently high, an issue to which we shall return. The long-run growth of productivity, and hence living standards, was also quite low. Thus many countries experienced lower growth in the 1980s than in the 1970s, while no countries could match the growth record of the 1960s (Table 5.3).

Why growth should have been relatively low in the 1980s has been a source of dispute. One view, which has attracted a good deal of support, has been that the slow-down was inevitable, the result of fewer opportunities to grow through catch-up (see Chapter 4). Thus, according to this view, growth in the 1950s and 1960s had been rapid because it had been possible to imitate technologies and organizational methods already pioneered in the US, the economic leader. By the 1970s and 1980s, however, as a result of rapid growth in previous decades, catch-up opportunities had declined. An alternative argument was that the problem reflected 'Eurosclerosis'. According to this view, European institutions were not sufficiently flexible to deal with the greater economic turbulence of the 1970s and 1980s. In part this lack of flexibility was due to the policy stance of the 1950s and 1960s – industrial subsidies, permissive competition policies, generous welfare provision, for example – that had left Europe with sluggish product and labour markets.

Whatever its merit, the Eurosclerosis argument was widely accepted by international bodies, such as the OECD, and more importantly by European governments. In the second half of the 1980s, therefore, policy switched towards the introduction of liberal supply-side measures, the aim of which was to improve the flexibility of the European economies. Undoubtedly, the main Community initiative was the single market agreement of 1987, which was designed to eliminate all non-tariff barriers and border technicalities in the EC by 1992. Although the main aim of this was to further economic integration, it was anticipated that the single market would have a significant impact on intra-community competition and trade. Lower costs and prices would follow, which, in turn, would give a boost to growth and employment. Indeed, the Cecchini Report of 1988 estimated that consumer prices might fall by as much as 6 per cent, and somewhere between 1.8 and 5 million new jobs would be generated.[8]

Country-specific policies were even more important. Such policies were pursued most enthusiastically in the UK, although, as the 1990 OECD Report *Progress in Structural Change* shows, all European countries were active. In view of the numerous measures, it is only possible to give a flavour of those that were introduced. They included the following.

(1) *Financial deregulation*: This embraced the abolition of exchange and credit controls, the deregulation of banking and measures to stimulate the growth of equity markets. The aim of these was to inject competiton into the financial system and to reduce the privileged access to finance which some companies enjoyed.

(2) *Tax reform*: This incorporated reductions in the rate of personal and corporate taxation, a switch from direct to indirect taxation and a reduction of tax distortions. The aim of these measures was to increase saving and to improve employment and production incentives.

(3) *Competition policies*: These included more active monopolies and mergers policies and the deregulation of certain markets to improve opportunities for entry. Such policies were based on the belief that strong competitive pressures act as a stimulus to change in both product and labour markets.

(4) *Industrial policies*: The main emphasis here was the reduction of industrial subsidies, combined with a switch away from industrial support for declining industries in favour of sunrise industries, small firms and research and development.

(5) *Privatization measures*:   The aim of these was to expose public sector enterprises to greater financial and competitive pressures. Measures have included denationalization schemes and contracting-out of public sector services.

(6) *Labour market reforms*:   The aim of these was to encourage greater mobility, enhance wage flexibility and encourage job creation. The measures included the reform of unemployment benefit schemes, an extension of retraining programmes, modification of minimum wage and employment protection laws, and trade union reforms.

Stagnation: the 1990s

Despite the policy reforms of the 1980s, however, performance in the first half of the 1990s has been mixed. On the plus side, it has continued to be a period of low inflation. Indeed, by the middle of the decade inflation was lower than it had been in the late 1960s (Figure 5.1). In part, this was a consequence of a continued determination on the part of governments to keep inflation firmly under control through fairly tight monetary policies (Figure 5.4). For most countries, the main discipline has been the ERM, although a number of countries – Finland, Spain, Sweden and the UK – have also moved towards explicit policies of inflation targeting, and most European countries have increased the autonomy of their central banks in anticipation of the European Monetary Union. Such autonomy, it is argued, has tended to lower inflationary expectations with favourable consequences for both inflation and interest rates.

Primary commodity and oil prices (Figure 5.2) continued to have a benign impact on inflation in the 1990s. Nevertheless, at the time of writing (spring 1997) the markets remain nervous about the prospects for oil prices. In recent years the size of the oil glut, which has kept prices relatively low over the past decade, has declined. Furthermore, the risks of instability in Saudi Arabia, which has played an important position in maintaining world oil supplies, have increased.

Yet another reason for the low inflation has been that the period since 1990 has been one of low growth. Following the respectable rates of expansion in the late 1980s, there was a slow-down between 1990 and 1992 (Figure 5.1). This was a consequence of uncertainty associated with the Gulf war coupled with recessions in the US and the UK, both of which had experienced inflationary difficulties in the late 1980s and were obliged to introduce tight financial policies. The UK experienced a particularly prolonged downturn, in part because of the emergence of debt problems, themselves a consequence of the financial deregulation in the 1980s.

In 1992 there was a further decline, as Europe entered another severe slump. To some extent, this was a consequence of German reunification in 1990 which threatened to create new inflationary problems. As a result the Bundesbank was forced to introduce tight monetary policies, which had knock-on effects for the rest of Europe. A recovery then emerged in 1994. But it was uneven: strong in

Table 5.4. Unemployment rates (per cent) besed on commonly used definitions of unemployment

	1973	1979	1990	1994	Change 1973–90
Austria	0.9	1.7	3.2	4.4	2.3
Belgium	2.3	7.3	8.7	12.9	6.4
Denmark	1.0	6.2	9.6	12.1	8.6
Finland	1.6	6.0	3.5	18.4	1.9
France	2.7	6.0	8.9	12.2	6.2
Germany	1.0	3.3	6.2	9.6	5.2
Greece	2.0	1.9	7.0	9.6	5.0
Ireland	5.7	7.1	13.2	14.2	7.5
Italy	6.4	7.8	11.5	11.3	5.1
Netherlands	3.1	5.6	6.9	7.6	3.8
Norway	1.5	1.9	5.2	5.4	3.7
Portugal	2.2	8.2	14.7	6.9	12.5
Spain	1.9	8.6	16.3	24.2	14.4
Sweden	2.0	1.7	1.7	8.0	−0.3
Switzerland	0.0	0.3	0.5	4.7	0.5
UK	2.1	4.5	5.9	9.2	3.8

Source: As for Figure 5.1.

1994, only to weaken in 1995 and 1996. This weak recovery was due partly to the Japanese economy, which had been uncharacteristically flat since 1992, and to another short recession in the US. Recovery was also slowed down by the need for the European countries to adopt fairly tight fiscal policies in order to reduce their budget deficits to 3 per cent of national income, which was a condition for joining the European Monetary Union, due to be established in 1999.

Inevitably, the slow growth has resulted in another rise in unemployment (Figure 5.3). In 1973 average unemployment had been 3 per cent, in 1979 5.5 per cent, and by 1990, despite eight years of recovery, it was 8 per cent. However, by 1995, following the slump, it had risen to over 11 per cent. This was associated with a high incidence of long-term unemployment, and exceptionally high unemployment rates for the unskilled and younger workers.

Of course, unemployment has varied considerably within Europe (Table 5.4). In 1994, for example, the worst-placed countries were Spain (24 per cent), Finland (18 per cent) and Ireland (14 per cent). But even the best-placed countries – Austria (4 per cent), Netherlands (8 per cent), Norway (5 per cent) and Switzerland (5 per cent) – had higher unemployment rates than in 1973. The record has also been inferior to those of Japan and North America. In the US, for example, unemployment rose from 4.9 per cent in 1973 to 6.1 per cent in 1994. For Japan the figures were 1.3 per cent and 2.9 per cent. It is clear, moreover, that European unemployment was a consequence of a poor job creation record.

For example, in the second half of the 1970s US employment grew at 1.7 per cent per annum, Japan's employment grew at 0.9 per cent while Europe experienced zero growth. In the 1980s the US grew at 2.7 per cent, Japan at 1.0 per cent and Europe at 0.9 per cent.

The Unemployment Problem

Not surprisingly, reducing unemployment has become the main policy priority of the 1990s. Why has it risen over the past 20 years? Although economists differ about the specific details, there is widespread agreement that it has been a multi-causal problem. In part the unemployment has been a consequence of the three economic slumps which have taken place since 1973 and which, by post-war standards, have been particularly severe. These slumps, moreover, have been accompanied by an increase in the number of long-term unemployed, who tend to have low re-employment probabilities. At the same time, in the face of overseas competition and structural and technological change, there has been a decline in the demand for unskilled labour, pointing to an increase in mismatch unemployment.[9]

Thus since the mid-1970s the employment environment has become more difficult. This, however, does not inevitably imply that unemployment had to increase. As we have seen, North America and Japan, which have also been subject to the disturbances, have experienced very little increase in unemployment. The reason is that they have had flexible labour markets. Thus in the face of economic disturbances, it is essential that wages – nominal, real and relative – are flexible to provide employers with the incentive to create jobs, governments the incentive to adopt expansionary policies and labour the incentives to move to high-growth areas. Linked with this, labour needs to be occupationally and geographically mobile. Ultimately, of course, the degree of flexibility will depend upon institutions and government policies – the design of wage bargaining systems, the strength of trade unions, the coverage and effectiveness of manpower policies, for example.

However, in view of the persistence of unemployment since the mid-1970s, the European labour market has not been sufficiently flexible. This much has been widely recognized in Europe. For example, in its submission to the G7 jobs conference at Lille in 1996, the European Commission argued that a small part of the unemployment problem might be due to inadequate aggregate demand, but the main source of the problem was an inability to create jobs in the new high-tech sectors and inadequate labour (occupational and geographic) mobility, in the face of rapid organizational and technological change and intensive competition from abroad.

There has, moreover, been some agreement about the necessary direction of future reform. There has been fairly wide agreement that in Europe there is only limited room for reflationary measures, and that debt problems need to be eliminated in order to stimulate investment. The main emphasis of reform, however, needs to be on the supply side, to improve international competitiveness and the adaptability of the labour force. The latter policies, it is now conceded, were not given a sufficiently high profile in the 1980s. For example, the 1993 European Commission white paper on *Employment Growth and Competitiveness* argued that a broad-based approach to unemployment policy was now necessary, which should include a large number of labour market measures, such as the introduction of advanced vocational training throughout people's working lives, revival of the rented housing market to stimulate geographic mobility, less generous unemployment benefits to improve the incentives to move and retrain, and increased spending on active manpower measures to improve the employability of the long-term unemployed and unskilled workers.

Nevertheless, there has been a difference of opinion within Europe about the need to deregulate the labour market. One option is to adopt the 'Anglo-Saxon' model, where the emphasis has been on an unregulated labour market, relatively free of rigidities. This was the route taken by the United Kingdom in the 1980s when there was a shift away from consensual labour market policies. Incomes policies were abandoned in favour of trade union reform, reforms of the unemployment benefit system, interviews for long-term unemployed (Restart), abolition of minimum wages (Wage Councils) and a weakening of unfair dismissal protection. The policy, moreover, seems to have been a qualified success. Doubts, it is true, have been expressed about the growth of part-time employment and the continued problems of the long-term unemployed and unskilled workers, sometimes attributed to education and training weaknesses. Nevertheless, since the early 1980s Britain has experienced greater wage flexibility with a relative improvement in its position in the European job creation and unemployment leagues.

However, the other European countries have been reluctant to embrace these reforms. The issue first surfaced at the Maastricht negotiations in 1991 when Britain opted out of the social charter, arguing that excessive rigidity had been the cause of the poor European job creation record. The continental countries, however, doubt whether the Anglo-Saxon approach is the answer. It may create numerous jobs, they argue, but these have often been of low quality, offering limited job security and with low skill requirements. They also claim that job creation has been achieved through low real-wage growth and unacceptable levels of inequality that have often forced reluctant secondary workers into the labour market to make up family earnings.

They have preferred, therefore, to persevere with what is sometimes called the European approach, where the main emphasis has been consensual wage bargaining: strong trade unions, welfare support and extensive dialogue between labour, employers and government. This approach, it is argued, is a more humane, less extreme alternative to securing wage moderation and a flexible labour market. Consequently, for the foreseeable future unemployment policy in Europe is likely to remain broadly based and to eschew drastic reform of the institutional structure. It will be interesting to see whether it will be able to check and reverse the rise in unemployment over the next few years.

Bibliographical Note

Not surprisingly, the period since 1973 lacks a definitive economic history. Nevertheless, there is no shortage of information about the European economies. The Organisation for Economic Co-operation and Development publishes a biannual *Economic Outlook*, which gives an overall picture for the industrialized world as well as comments and forecasts for the individual countries. The OECD also publishes occasional *Economic Surveys* on individual countries. The *Financial Times* and *The Economist*, both of which are now available on CD-Rom, also include occasional country surveys and day-to-day reports. Slightly more difficult, but still accessible, is the journal *Economic Policy: A European Forum*, which includes articles on specific topics and countries. Useful readings on European issues will also be found in A. Boltho (ed.), *The European Economy* (Oxford, 1981), N.F.R. Crafts and G. Toniolo (eds), *Economic Growth in Europe since 1945* (Cambridge, 1996) and the two volumes edited by David Dyker, *The European Economy* and *The National Economies of Europe* (London, 1992).

Notes

1. To some extent the European Community countries were isolated from the impact of the import inflation by the Common Agricultural Policy. On the determinants of primary commodity prices, see C.L. Gilbert, 'Primary commodity prices and inflation', *Oxford Review of Economic Policy*, Vol. 16 (1990), no. 4, pp. 77–99.

2. This lasted until March 1974.

3. N. Thygesen, 'Monetary policy', in A. Botho (ed.), *The European Economy* (Oxford, 1981).

4. S.W. Black, 'Learning from adversity: policy responses to two oil shocks', *Princeton Essays in International Finance*, no. 160 (Dec. 1985).

5. J. Llewellyn, 'Resource prices and macroeconomic policies: lessons from the two oil shocks', *OECD Economic Studies*, no. 1 (Autumn 1983).

6. On the new conservative macroeconomics, see the symposium in *Economic Policy*, no. 5 (Oct. 1987).

7. On French macroeconomic policy, see J. Sachs and C. Wyplosz, 'The economic consequences of President Mitterrand', *Economic Policy*, no. 2 (April 1986), pp. 262–322; and O.J. Blanchard and P.A. Muet, 'Competitiveness through disinflation', *Economic Policy*, no. 16 (April 1993), pp. 11–56.

8. P. Cecchini, *The European Challenge, 1992* (Aldershot, 1988).

9. See, for example, R. Layard, S. Nickell and R. Jackman, *Unemployment* (Oxford, 1991).

6 Industrial and Structural Change

Maurice Kirby

It is conventional for economists and economic historians to define the process of structural adaptation in national economies in terms of the changing distribution of resources between the primary, secondary and tertiary sectors. Whilst the primary sector embraces all activities relating to the exploitation of raw materials in agriculture and mining, the secondary, or industrial sector, includes both the processing of materials and the production of goods. The tertiary sector refers to services of all kinds whether they are delivered under public or private auspices. Their range is therefore considerable, incorporating transport and distribution networks, the delivery of professional services, such as insurance and banking, and central and local government bureaucracies. In relation to the process of long-run economic growth, there is an accepted historical generalization that rising per capita incomes in western capitalist economies have been dependent largely upon resource transfers from agriculture to industry, the latter being consistent mainly with the manufacturing sector. The broad interpretation of the rise of the secondary sector is that it has reflected the changing distribution of final demand in response to increases in income and changes in consumer tastes. Thus in terms of elementary economic theory, the agricultural sector has declined relatively as per capita incomes have risen because the income elasticity of demand for food is typically less than one, while manufacturing expands because the elasticity of demand for its products is usually greater than one. Rising incomes have also been viewed as a critical factor in determining the rate of expansion of the tertiary sector. As consumers become wealthier their pattern of demand is likely to diversify from a preponderance of expenditures on food and goods to encompass rising purchases of services, both personal and collective. Again, this reflects an income elasticity of demand which is greater for services than for goods, so that as national income rises a greater proportion of national resources will be devoted to the tertiary sector. Rising expenditures on transport and distribution networks, financial services, and health and education provision, are also indicative of the growing complexity and sophistication of economies and societies over time (see Chapters 13 and 14).

The factors which have served to propel structural change have been many and varied. In addition to rising real incomes and changing tastes, the development of national and international trade has been a decisive influence, fully reflecting the evolution of comparative trading advantage and shifting national industry competitiveness in relation to productivity trends and costs of production. Political and social developments have also played a significant role, not least in precipitating and sustaining the rise of that part of the tertiary sector dominated by central and local government services. In these respects, it is only necessary to refer to the decline of *laissez-faire* social and economic policies during the course of the twentieth century in response to the rise of left-of-centre political parties, these trends culminating after 1945 in the creation of welfare states and mixed private and public sector economies. All of these influences may be viewed as operating over an extended period. However, structural change can also be a short-term phenomenon in response to macroeconomic shocks, sudden discontinuities in economic policy, rapid technological change and dramatic shifts in international competitive advantage. The 1970s and 1980s provide excellent examples in each category, as evidenced by the oil crises of 1973–74 and 1979, the rapid development of North Sea oil and gas, the election of governments committed to deregulation and market forces, and the ease of international technology transfer in favour of the rapidly developing industrial economies of the Pacific rim. Indeed, in the western European context after 1945 structural change has been more rapid than at any time in the modern industrial era, so much so that it became fashionable after 1970 to refer to the rise of the 'service economy' as a result of the income elasticities referred to above. Accelerating developments after that date gave added credence to the concept of a 'post-industrial society', insofar as the 1970s and 1980s witnessed the onset of 'deindustrialization' in western economies. A notable phenomenon in relation to British experience, deindustrialization (whether defined in terms of the declining proportion of industrial employment in total employment, or the proportionate reduction in the contribution of industrial output to gross domestic product) was experienced to a greater or lesser extent by all of the economies of western Europe. Viewed by some as a cause for concern, given the alleged primacy of manufacturing industry in sustaining economic growth and real living standards, to others deindustrialization was inevitable if not desirable, fully reflecting shifting patterns of competitive advantage and consistent also with the ongoing expansion of the tertiary sector, both public and private.

In order to elucidate the process of structural change in western Europe, the first substantive section of the chapter provides a historical outline of the principal sectoral developments. It begins with a description of the main trends before ranging in detail across agriculture, industry and services. The second section assesses the key interpretations of structural change with a particular focus on the causes and consequences of deindustrialization. The final section offers some concluding remarks, setting the western European experience after 1945 in historical context.

Table 6.1. Structure of employment in western Europe, 1950–70 (percentage share: I = Agriculture, II = Industry, III = Services)

	1950			1960			1970		
	I	**II**	**III**	**I**	**II**	**III**	**I**	**II**	**III**
Austria	34.0	35.4	30.6	24.2	39.7	36.1	18.8	40.3	40.9
Belgium	10.1	46.8	43.1	8.4	45.3	46.3	4.6	42.1	53.3
Denmark	25.1	33.3	41.6	17.8	36.1	46.1	11.3	37.1	51.7
France	28.3	34.9	36.8	21.4	36.2	42.4	13.9	38.5	47.6
West Germany	22.2	43.0	34.8	13.8	48.2	38.0	8.5	48.4	43.1
Italy	45.4	28.6	26.0	32.2	36.3	31.5	19.1	43.0	37.9
Netherlands	13.9	40.2	45.9	11.1	39.1	49.8	7.0	37.7	55.3
Norway	29.8	33.2	37.0	20.9	34.5	44.7	13.5	36.1	50.4
UK	5.1	46.5	48.4	4.1	47.8	48.1	3.2	44.1	52.7

Source: I. Lateson and J.W. Wheeler (eds), *Western Economies in Transition: Structural Change and Adjustment Policies in Industrial Countries* (London, 1980), Table 3.2, p. 47.

The Direction of Structural Change: An Overview

Tables 6.1–6.6 are illustrative of the direction of structural change in western Europe in the decades after 1950. The focus is on changes in the structure of employment and the distribution of Gross Domestic Product (total output) between the primary, secondary and tertiary sectors. In order to highlight the onset of deindustrialization and the expansion of the service sector, both public and private, Tables 6.1–6.4 are divided chronologically in the mid-1970s. In these respects, the distinctive experience of the UK is set out in Table 6.5, whilst Table 6.6 identifies trends in government expenditure as a percentage of GDP after 1974.

Table 6.1, covering the period from 1950 to 1970, confirms the general pattern of structural change in western Europe in the so-called 'golden age' of economic growth (see Chapter 4). All of the named countries experienced consistent reductions in the share of agriculture in the total labour force. The opposite trend is observable in the case of services, and whilst there are three cases of marginal decline in industrial employment (Belgium, the Netherlands and the UK), the general pattern is consistent with an overall increase in the percentage of industrial employment. Table 6.2 provides a detailed picture of sectoral changes in employment for the period 1974–91. Again, there are consistent patterns, notably the continuing fall in the proportion of agricultural employment, complemented in these years by proportionate reductions in manufacturing employment. Coincidentally, all countries experienced significant increases in the proportion of the labour force engaged in the service sector, broadly defined.

Tables 6.3 and 6.4 provide a mirror image of the trends in employment structure, insofar as they highlight the changing distribution of GDP from 1950 through to 1991. Whilst the general diminution in the relative status of agriculture

Table 6.2. Employment by major industrial sectors in western Europe, 1974–91 (percentage shares; list of sectors: 1 Agriculture, hunting, forestry and fishing; 2 Mining and quarrying; 3 Manufacturing; 4 Electricity, gas and water; 5 Construction; 6 Wholesale and retail trade, restaurants and hotels; 7 Transport, storage and communications; 8 Financing, insurance, real estate and business services; 9 Community, social and personal services. Figures in parentheses have been calculated as residuals)

Sector	Austria			Belgium			Denmark		
	1974	1981	1991	1974	1981	1991	1974	1981	1991
1	13.01	10.27	7.39	3.91	3.19	2.66	9.70	7.40	5.76
2	1.13	0.49	0.35	1.04	0.79	0.19	0.13	0.09	0.08
3	30.35	29.73	27.00	31.68	24.70	20.92	23.75	21.49	20.69
4	1.07	1.13	1.16	0.90	0.93	0.81	0.60	0.68	0.77
5	8.67	8.68	8.58	7.98	7.32	6.59	8.03	7.32	6.46
6	16.11	17.58	19.09	16.10	16.36	17.28	14.69	14.34	14.73
7	6.70	6.41	6.47	7.22	7.77	7.03	7.13	6.94	7.04
8	4.54	5.15	6.70	5.49	6.39	9.12	6.15	6.68	9.24
9	18.41	20.56	23.27	25.67	32.55	35.40	29.82	35.06	35.23

Sector	France			Germany			Italy		
	1974	1981	1991	1974	1981	1991	1974	1981	1991
1	10.66	8.45	5.77	7.01	5.16	3.35	17.54	13.42	8.51
2	0.87	0.63	0.37	–	0.94	0.64	–	1.09	1.06
3	28.31	25.10	20.92	46.66	33.33	31.18	39.26	26.19	22.10
4	0.80	0.91	0.93	–	0.82	0.90	–	–	–
5	9.35	8.54	7.26	46.32	7.87	6.49	43.20	10.28	9.14
6	15.60	16.20	17.35	–	15.56	16.65	–	19.23	21.77
7	6.01	6.22	6.45	–	5.94	5.91	–	5.65	5.37
8	6.19	7.64	10.22	–	6.08	8.50	–	2.75	4.68
9	22.20	26.32	30.73	–	24.31	26.38	–	(21.39)	(27.37)

Sector	Netherlands			Norway			United Kingdom		
	1974	1981	1991	1974	1981	1991	1974	1981	1991
1	5.67	4.87	4.58	10.61	8.36	5.90	2.82	2.66	2.27
2	0.17	0.16	0.22	0.61	0.68	1.07	1.44	1.46	0.72
3	25.00	20.94	18.27	23.76	19.83	14.95	32.38	26.51	20.13
4	0.93	0.89	0.69	1.09	1.10	1.07	1.40	1.46	1.09
5	8.79	7.93	6.53	8.91	7.68	6.61	6.82	6.36	6.72
6	17.22	17.53	17.79	16.67	17.36	18.00	18.04	19.60	20.09
7	6.12	6.33	6.30	9.88	9.15	8.24	6.33	6.36	5.97
8	7.50	9.23	10.66	4.36	5.21	7.78	6.52	7.92	12.34
9	(28.61)	(32.12)	(34.96)	(24.11)	(30.63)	(36.38)	24.24	27.68	30.67

Source: D. Coates (ed.), *Economic and Industrial Performance in Europe* (Aldershot, 1995), Table 3.1, pp. 108–9, Tables 4.1–4.3, pp. 141–43.

Table 6.3. Percentage distribution of Gross Domestic Product at current prices (percentage shares: I = Agriculture, II = Industry, III = Services)

	1950			1976		
	I	II	III	I	II	III
Austria	17.8	49.6	32.6	5.1	44.1	50.8
Denmark	21.0	36.0	43.0	7.2	37.7	55.1
France	14.7	47.3	38.0	5.2	41.7	53.1
Germany	10.4	49.8	39.8	2.9	49.4	47.7
Italy	25.3	33.3	41.4	8.2	44.6	47.2
Netherlands	14.2	39.8	46.0	4.7[a]	41.2[a]	54.1[a]
Norway	15.1	31.7	53.2	6.5	38.1	55.4
UK	5.8	45.5	48.7	2.9	41.2	55.9

Note: [a]1974 figure.

Source: Lateson and Wheeler (eds), *Western Economies in Transition*, Table 3.4, p. 51.

Table 6.4. Output shares in GDP by sector, 1974–91 (percentage output shares; sectors as in Table 6.2)

Sector	Austria			Belgium			Denmark			France		
	1974	1981	1991	1974	1981	1991	1974	1981	1991	1974	1981	1991
1	4.3	4.1	3.5	2.9	2.6	2.2	7.5	7.8	8.1	7.7	5.3	5.2
2	0.8	0.7	0.4	0.6	0.4	0.1	0.1	0.4	4.9	1.0	1.0	0.7
3	34.4	33.1	33.0	27.5	27.1	28.9	24.7	25.4	22.1	38.7	30.1	26.1
4	3.4	3.7	3.5	2.1	3.3	3.1	1.3	1.7	1.8	4.7	2.5	3.1
5	11.8	9.6	8.1	9.5	7.9	7.1	11.8	8.2	5.9	11.4	8.6	7.7
6	20.0	19.8	20.6	23.5	21.3	17.7	18.0	18.0	18.1	26.0	17.9	17.6
7	6.1	6.8	7.7	10.5	9.4	10.0	10.2	10.7	12.0	13.8	7.5	9.3
8	15.1	17.9	18.7	5.1	6.9	7.8	20.0	21.1	21.7	34.0	21.6	23.0
9	4.2	4.3	4.7	18.2	21.1	23.2	6.4	6.6	5.4	10.8	5.5	7.3

Sector	Germany			Italy			Norway		
	1974	1981	1991	1974	1981	1991	1974	1981	1991
1	2.4	2.1	2.1	5.7	5.7	4.6	5.2	4.4	3.5
2	1.8	1.2	0.7	0.0	0.0	0.0	2.9	19.2	36.5
3	41.7	38.8	35.4	28.2	28.0	28.2	31.2	19.3	13.4
4	3.0	3.3	3.2	6.0	6.2	5.2	4.9	4.7	3.9
5	8.1	7.1	5.7	10.1	8.3	6.9	7.7	7.3	4.9
6	12.5	12.2	11.8	21.7	22.2	21.8	15.1	14.4	10.3
7	5.9	6.7	7.3	5.5	6.0	6.8	11.4	40.5	10.9
8	12.6	14.6	15.6	22.8	23.9	26.5	15.2	14.4	11.9
9	11.9	14.0	18.2	–	–	–	6.5	5.8	4.7

Sources: Coates (ed.), *Economic and Industrial Performance in Europe*, Table 3.3, pp. 112–13; OECD, *National Accounts*, various issues.

Table 6.5. Percentage shares of Gross Domestic Product in the UK at current prices, 1973–91

	1973	1979	1986	1988	1990	1991
Primary	4.2	6.7	5.3	3.8	3.3	3.7
Agriculture, forestry and fishing	2.9	2.2	1.7	1.3	1.4	1.7
Coal and coke	1.1	1.3	1.0	0.7	0.5	0.6
Extraction of mineral oil and natural gas	–	3.2	2.6	1.8	1.4	1.4
Secondary	40.9	36.7	32.2	31.3	31.3	29.8
Mineral oil processing	0.4	0.6	0.7	0.3	0.4	0.4
Manufacturing	30.0	27.3	23.0	22.4	21.2	19.9
Construction	7.3	0.6	5.8	6.2	7.2	6.4
Other energy and water supply	2.8	2.6	2.7	2.4	2.5	3.1
Tertiary	54.9	56.5	62.3	64.8	65.4	66.4
Distribution, hotels, catering, repairs	13.1	12.7	13.3	13.2	13.9	13.9
Transport	4.7	4.8	4.3	} 6.9	} 6.7	} 6.6
Communication	2.3	2.5	2.6			
Banking, finance, insurance, business services and leasing	10.7	11.0	15.0	18.4	17.3	16.8
Ownership of dwellings	5.1	5.8	5.5	5.1	6.1	6.6
Public administration, national defence and compulsory social security	6.1	6.1	6.9	6.5	6.3	6.6
Education and health services	7.7	8.1	8.6	8.5	9.0	9.5
Other services	5.1	5.7	6.1	6.2	6.1	6.4

Sources: Central Statistical Office, *National Income and Expenditure* 'Blue Book', various editions, 1983, 1985, 1987, 1989, 1992, CSO, London.

is again observable, at least until the mid-1970s, the share of industry in total output was variable. On the other hand, the expansion of the service sector was a feature common to all countries. For the period from the mid-1970s to 1991, inter-country experience was less consistent, especially in relation to manufacturing. Whilst there was general continuity in trends in agriculture and services in all countries, there was a twofold division in relation to the share of manufacturing in total output. In Austria, Belgium, Denmark and Italy there was broad stability in the share of manufacturing, whereas there were significant reductions in France and West Germany, with Norway experiencing a major fall.

Table 6.5 sets out in greater detail the UK experience from the 1970s to 1991. Two trends are outstanding: first, the substantial reduction in the percentage share of manufacturing in GDP from a figure in 1973 which was already considerably below that in the two most comparable European economies – France and West Germany – and second, the surge forward of the tertiary sector. By the early 1990s the latter was the predominant element in Britain's economic structure, accounting for virtually two-thirds of total output. It is significant that the prime source of expansion up to the late 1980s was private sector financial services, with

Table 6.6. Total outlays of government as a percentage of GDP, 1974–90

	1974	**1980**	**1981**	**1982**	**1983**	**1984**
Austria	41.9	48.9	50.3	50.9	51.2	50.8
Belgium	39.4	59.0	64.2	64.2	64.1	62.8
Denmark	45.9	56.2	59.8	61.2	61.6	60.3
France	39.3	46.1	48.7	50.4	51.4	52.0
West Germany	44.6	48.5	49.4	49.6	48.5	48.1
Italy	37.9	41.7	45.8	47.4	48.6	49.4
Netherlands	47.9	57.5	59.7	61.6	62.2	61.0
Norway	44.6	48.3	47.9	48.3	48.4	46.3
United Kingdom	44.8	44.8	47.5	47.0	46.7	47.3
	1985	**1986**	**1987**	**1988**	**1989**	**1990**
Austria	51.7	52.4	52.7	51.1	50.0	49.6
Belgium	62.5	61.8	60.1	57.7	55.7	55.2
Denmark	59.3	55.7	57.3	59.4	59.4	58.4
France	52.2	51.4	50.9	50.2	49.4	49.9
West Germany	47.6	47.0	47.3	46.9	45.5	46.0
Italy	50.9	50.7	50.2	50.4	51.5	53.0
Netherlands	59.7	59.6	60.8	58.3	55.9	55.6
Norway	45.6	49.9	51.1	53.7	54.6	na
United Kingdom	46.2	45.2	43.1	41.3	41.2	42.1

Source: OECD, *Economic Outlook, Historical Statistics 1960–1990,* Table 6.5, p. 68.

only marginal increases in other tertiary services. In overall terms, these trends manifest in the British economy have been viewed as the most extreme example of 'deindustrialization' in modern capitalist economies, giving rise to a vigorous and ongoing public debate as to its ultimate consequences for national economic well-being.

Table 6.6 sheds further light on the evolution of the tertiary economy. Covering the period from 1974 to 1990, it underscores the growth of government activity in relation to GDP. In view of the substantial controversy in Britain on the merits and demerits of the expanded state, especially in the context of deindustrialization and the rise of 'Thatcherism' after 1980, it is instructive to note that throughout the period British governmental outlays never exceeded 48 per cent of GDP, whilst in three cases (Belgium, Denmark and the Netherlands) the total exceeded 60 per cent.

Agriculture in Western Europe

Although total output in agriculture grew more slowly than in industry after 1945, the post-war decades marked a significant discontinuity in relation to the inter-war period. In the first instance, investment was well above the pre-war

Plate 6.1. Agriculture in 1947. This photograph is from Germany (it was taken in Hanover on 7 August), but it could just as well have been taken in many other countries across continental Europe. Note the use of oxen instead of the more expensive horses, and, by present standards, the large number of farmhands involved. Most here are women, because of the absence of their menfolk in the aftermath of the war.

Plate 6.2. Agriculture in 1997. Structural change in the European economy meant that, by the end of the twentieth century, only a small percentage of the total labour force in Europe was employed in the production of foodstuffs.

average. Notable increases occurred in the UK, West Germany, France, the Netherlands, the Scandinavian countries, and Italy. In some cases – the UK, France and Italy – this was partly a response to government incentives, augmented by rising real incomes of agriculture producers. As for the visible fruits of higher investment, this was well reflected in the onward march of mechanization complemented by the increased use of fertilizers, pesticides and insecticides. In the former case the most spectacular manifestation of the heightened efficiency of farming operations was the rise in the number of tractors. The UK had led the way in their use before 1939 so that the post-war expansion in numbers was relatively small – from 325,000 in 1950 to 443,000 in 1962 – but elsewhere, as in France and West Germany, huge increases were registered, in the former case from 142,000 to 900,000 and in the latter from 139,463 to 960,000 over the same period.

Other technological advances after 1945 embraced improvements in seed selection and animal breeding. From the early 1960s, moreover, the capital intensity of farming accelerated further in response to 'industrialized' feeding methods for livestock. The result of all of these developments was to boost the level of agricultural productivity, so much so that by the early 1960s the marginal productivity of labour in Belgium and Danish agriculture was approaching the levels in manufacturing industry. By that time, there was every reason to believe that agricultural labour productivity in western Europe as a whole exceeded that in industry by a margin of up to 15 per cent.[1] It is important to note, however, that these increases in productivity were not matched by equivalent increases in output. The key explanation for this is to be found in the elasticities of demand referred to above. If there had been a greater equivalence in demand elasticities for agricultural and industrial produce then it is possible that agriculture could have played a significant role in European economic growth. In the post-war years, however, the prospects for greater sales, other than to provide for additional population, were bleak. High nutritional and production standards provide one explanation as do the limited opportunities for overseas sales in view of the outstanding comparative advantage enjoyed by staple food exporters in North and South America and Australasia. The net effect, therefore, was that although western European agricultural output was expanding this failed to match the growth in productivity. The inevitable result was the declining share of agriculture in total output, as indicated in the statistical tables.

These circumstances also explain the sustained outflow of labour from the agricultural sector in favour of industry and services. Although this was not a new phenomenon after 1945, the rate of transfer accelerated markedly in the post-war decades up to 1970. In France, for example, departures from agriculture for urban employment averaged 90,000 per annum in the 1950s and 1960s, resulting in a fall in the share of agriculture in total employment from 28.3 per cent in 1950 to only 13.9 per cent in 1970. By 1991 the equivalent figure was less than 6 per cent. Equally spectacular falls were recorded in West Germany and Italy. The one exception to the general trend was the UK, but only on account of the

In focus: The Survival of Family Farms

On the eve of the Second World War, small-scale peasant farms dependent upon family labour and with a limited commitment to production for the market, remained the most representative form of agricultural enterprise in continental Europe. After 1945, however, subsistence agriculture was subject to a combination of economic, social and political influences which were to render its future problematical. First and foremost was the fact of non-viability in commercial terms. According to an OECD survey carried out in 1960, more than 50 per cent of farms were economically non-viable in France, West Germany, Italy, the Netherlands and Norway on account of their failure to provide their owners with an adequate standard of living.[1] Although the succeeding decades witnessed a general European-wide reduction in fragmentation, as late as the early 1980s more than 40 per cent of all farms in Belgium, West Germany, Italy and the Netherlands were smaller than 10 hectares. Small-scale farming is not always inconsistent with efficiency, as in the case of Belgium and the Netherlands where the average size of farms is heavily influenced by intensive market gardening. But in general terms, fragmentation of holdings represented a substantial institutional barrier to the achievement of scale economies and higher incomes for farmers.

In the light of these factors all western European governments embarked on interventionist policies with respect to their agricultural sectors. By the 1960s two trends were in evidence.[2] In the first instance there was the desire to shield peasant farmers from the most extreme elements of international competition in order to prevent the return of rural distress on the scale of the 1930s. It is salutary to remember that in most European countries agricultural interests enjoyed substantial political influence, independent of any governmental preferences for protectionism on strategic or balance of payments grounds. Thus, in France and West Germany, for example, 'pro-peasant' policies were the order of the day in the 1950s and 1960s, with both countries committed to the establishment of economic and social parity between agriculture and other sectors. Similar considerations were at work in Denmark and the Netherlands. Even in the UK, where commercial farming had penetrated furthest, governments felt obliged to protect and sustain small-scale farmers, not least in the Celtic uplands where elements of subsistence farming continued to exist after 1950.

The principal measures of support for agricultural incomes took the form of price controls and direct payments. The former were exemplified in the Common Agricultural Policy of the European Union which, from its inception, has guaranteed prices sufficiently above world market levels to

1. OECD, *Agriculture and Economic Growth* (Paris, 1960).
2. A.M. Williams, *The Western European Economy: A Geography of Post-War Development* (London, 1987), pp. 112–44.

The Survival of Family Farms (continued)

sustain the interests of small-scale producers. There can be no doubt that the policy has been successful both in stabilizing prices and in providing adequate living standards for farmers in general. In these respects, agricultural support has played a critical role in retarding structural change in European agriculture to the benefit of small-scale family farms. In the absence of price support the flight from rural to urban areas would have been even more rapid in response to declining real living standards and foreclosure. The costs to the wider community have, however, been considerable in terms of the encouragement to excess production (leading to the infamous food mountains and wine lakes of the European Union), retarded productivity growth and higher prices to consumers. But this is to ignore the central fact that agricultural policies have been framed on political and social, as well as economic grounds.

relatively early reduction in agricultural employment observable before 1914. Even here, however, the 5.1 per cent recorded in 1950 had fallen to a minuscule 2 per cent by the early 1990s.

Industry in Western Europe

In a magisterial survey of European economic growth in the later nineteenth and twentieth centuries, the Swedish economist, Ingvar Svennilson, concluded that on the eve of the First World War the European economies were confronted by an emergent problem of structural transformation *vis-à-vis* the most dynamic economy of the time – the United States.[2] According to Svennilson the latter possessed the greatest potential for economic growth and rising living standards by virtue of the development of dynamic manufacturing sectors in the provision of capital equipment and consumer durable goods. Enjoying access to a rapidly expanding domestic market of continental proportions, American industrialists had already begun to make the transition to high-throughput mass production technology at the behest of corporate forms of business organization. In this light the survival and prosperity of European industry was dependent upon its ability to withstand the American competitive challenge in respect of both product and process innovations. Although the inter-war years witnessed the beginnings of structural diversification in Europe away from the old staple industries (coalmining, cotton and wool textiles, heavy engineering and shipbuilding) in favour of high value chemicals, artificial fibres, motor vehicles, light machine tools and electrical products, the really decisive structural shifts in favour of the growth industries of the twentieth century had to await the period after 1945. The supply-side innovations conducive to structural transformation may have been *in situ* by that date, but it was only in the post-war decades that they could come to fruition in a general context of expanding markets at home and abroad, trade liberalization and rising real incomes. Indeed, the period from 1950 to 1970 has been designated as the 'golden age' of western economic growth, characterized by extraordinarily rapid growth in world trade, institutional stability and full employment.[3] The key explanations for this phenomenon are highlighted in Chapters 4 and 7. All that needs to be said in the present context is that in terms of Svennilson's analysis, this period was consistent with a process of structural convergence as the economies of western Europe evolved to match the high growth potential of the US economy already observable before 1939.

In this respect there were continuities with experience before 1939, but the three post-war decades witnessed substantial acceleration in the rate of structural change in Europe. In the manufacturing sector there were two main developments, first the expansion of consumer durable industries and secondly the upsurge in output of 'producers' or investment goods. In the former case a combination of full employment, rising real incomes and the availability of hire purchase interacted with supply-side innovations to underwrite expanding production and sales. In relative terms, however, the main growth thrust was in favour of capital goods, notably in West Germany, Belgium, Italy, France and the UK. In West Germany, for example, the index of production for consumption goods rose from 100 to 178 in the period 1950–63/64, whilst that for investment goods rose from 100 to 249. For Italy the equivalent figures were 209 and 243 and for Belgium 152 and 177 – less spectacular than in West Germany but still denoting the overall trend.[4] At the forefront of expansion was a range of technologically advanced industries which were able to take advantage of a cluster of innovations from the 1930s. Petrochemicals, chemical engineering, synthetic materials, heavy electricals and electronics were the principal beneficiaries. All of them grew rapidly in response to expanding domestic markets, but extra impetus was provided by buoyant overseas sales in view of the high international demand for capital goods after 1950.

If the upsurge in growth of these modern sectors represented a discontinuity in Europe's industrial structure, over the divide of the Second World War, one notable pre-war trend which continued was the growth of concentration and increasing scale of enterprise in a spectrum of industries. Growth was especially marked in the chemical, petroleum and petrochemical industries. An excellent example is ICI, founded in 1926 as a result of the merger of the three largest firms in the British chemical industry. This was the greatest merger in British industry between the wars, but ICI's growth was most spectacular after 1945 in terms of assets and turnover, with the firm enjoying three-fold increases in the period to 1965. In Germany, ICI's inter-war rival, I.G. Farben, was broken up after the war, but by the mid-1960s the succeeding firms – Farbenfabriken Bayer, Farbwerke Hoechst, and Badische Anilin- und Soda Fabrik – had each attained a size almost as large as I.G. Farben itself in 1938. Similar developments, albeit on a lesser scale, were observable in the French and Italian chemical industries. Large-scale firms were also characteristic of the petroleum and artificial fibres industries. In the former case, Shell and BP in Britain, the French Compagnie Française des Pétroles, and the Italian ENI had total domestic sales of petrol in

1963 in excess of total national sales in 1938, whilst in artificial fibres sustained expansion in the scale of operations occurred in the British Courtaulds company, the Dutch Algemene Kurstzijde Urie, the German Vereinigte Glanzstoff and the Italian firm, Snia Viscosa.

In analysing these trends, business historians have concentrated attention on a variety of causal factors ranging from access to technical and managerial economies of scale to a conscious European desire to emulate corporate managerial structures in the USA. Whilst such influences were operative before 1939, the constellation of factors in their favour in the post-war decades were more urgent and compelling in view of the rapidity of market expansion and accelerating research and development costs in science-based industries. The role of government was a further precipitating factor. In the UK, for example, the formation of the Industrial Reorganisation Corporation as a 'merger broker' in 1966 by the then Labour Government was tantamount to official recognition that British manufacturing industry in general was vulnerable to the loss of competitive advantage as a result of relative fragmentation of ownership. Public ownership of industry and the economics of military defence procurement – both of them exemplified in British and French experience after 1945 – also provided a powerful impetus to both concentration of ownership and an increased scale of operations. In the British case, governmental underwriting of oligopolies in manufacturing industry and of natural monopoly in nationalized utilities sat uneasily with a commitment to pro-competition policies in the name of economic efficiency and consumer welfare. Yet as long as governments were concerned to sustain a viable industrial base in the face of the international competitive power of American corporate enterprise, the encouragement to big businesses in the form of 'national champions' was understandable.

It is a point well taken, however, that despite the emergence of dominant corporations, most manufacturing firms in western Europe remained small. In West Germany the number of firms in industry and commerce employing less than five persons was 81 per cent of the total in 1950 and as high as 76 per cent in 1961. In the British case, in the 1950s there may have been a decline in the number of firms employing fewer than 25 persons, but the reduction was concentrated in the 5–10 employee range with possible increases in the numbers employing 11–24 persons. In effect, therefore, countries such as Britain, France, West Germany and Italy possessed dualistic industrial structures with innumerable minnows swimming in the company of whales. Indeed, in some cases the opposite ends of the size spectrum could enjoy a complementary relationship, as in the case of large engineering firms subcontracting component orders to adjacent small-scale workshops in extensive urban conurbations such as the West Midlands in England and the Ruhr in West Germany.

In the light of the general governmental approbation of large-scale firms in the period to 1970, it is instructive to note that in the two succeeding decades a diametrically opposed view came to prominence whereby official encouragement was given to the foundation and nurturing of small businesses. It is by no means coincidental that the early 1970s witnessed the end of the 'golden age' of western economic growth, as evidenced by the onset of stagflation and macroeconomic instability. In these circumstances the commercial performance of large-scale corporate firms in a variety of industrial sectors began to falter, resulting in widespread redundancies and foreclosures. Encouragement to small-firm formation by means of tax incentives and subsidies was looked upon with favour as a means to employment creation and also as a seedbed for innovation. Small-scale firms were also viewed as a route to reinvigorated entrepreneurism, thereby providing an offset to the risk aversion of large-scale firms.[5] Whilst European experience provides some excellent examples of the resilience and dynamism of small-scale family-owned enterprises after 1970, most notably in the textile districts of northern Italy, the expansion of employment in small manufacturing firms could not offset the loss of jobs in larger firms subject to an increasingly exacting business environment.

The growth slow-down in western economies is conventionally dated from the onset of the first oil crisis in 1973–74 in which the international price of oil, denoted in dollars, rose by 400 per cent (see Chapter 5). The two succeeding decades witnessed profound structural changes in the economies of western Europe. As Tables 6.2, 6.4 and 6.5 indicate, the most visible of these changes was the relative decline of the manufacturing sector in its share of GDP and total employment. A range of sectors was affected, from old-established industries such as coalmining and iron and steel, to the growth sectors of the post-1945 period, notably motor vehicles, petrochemicals and parts of the electronics industry. In aggregate terms, the relevant trends were not uniform across countries. This is exemplified in the case of the share of manufacturing in GDP. Of the seven countries identified in Table 6.4, Austria and Denmark experienced marginal declines, whilst there was virtual stability in Belgium and Italy. The largest reductions were experienced in France, West Germany and Norway, although in the Norwegian case it should be noted that the substantial reduction in the share of manufacturing in total output was complemented by an exponential rise in the share of extractive industries, from 2.9 per cent in 1974 to 36.5 per cent in 1990. This was a direct consequence of the impact of natural resource exploitation on a relatively small economy following the discovery of oil in the North Sea in the later 1960s.

By the early 1980s the trend towards manufacturing contraction in western Europe was sufficiently established to give rise to the doom-laden concept of deindustrialization, denoting the onset of severe structural imbalance in the light of the widely held assumption that manufacturing industry fulfilled a pivotal role in underpinning economic growth and rising living standards. Concerns over deindustrialization were registered most explicitly within the UK. This is hardly surprising, given the distinctive trends identified in Table 6.5. As the statistics indicate, manufacturing output and employment fell more rapidly in the UK than in any other European economy, with notable falls in the period 1979–81. In these years alone manufacturing output fell by 17 per cent at the same time as there were commensurate falls in employment. A further serious consequence of deindustrialization was that from the early 1980s onwards the UK balance of trade in manufacturing exhibited a mounting deficit large enough by the end of the decade to dominate the current account balance of payments as a whole. If there was a positive side to these developments, it was reflected in the so-called UK 'productivity miracle' of the 1980s whereby the drastic shedding of labour in manufacturing and the closure of marginal productive units facilitated a sustained movement towards western European productivity norms in general and those of West Germany in particular.[6]

Before proceeding to analyse the development of the tertiary sector in western Europe it is appropriate to comment on the range of governmental responses to the overall trend towards deindustrialization after 1970, bearing in mind that the latter provoked social and economic strains to which governments were bound to respond. Whilst the scope of intervention and the deployment of policy instruments varied from country to country, the period to the mid-1980s was characterized by mounting state intervention in industrial structures.[7] At one level governments responded to the problem of industrial recession via macroeconomic policies designed to promote employment. However, it is more pertinent in the present context to focus on industrial policy *per se*, i.e. instruments of microeconomic intervention, designed to retard or accelerate the process of structural adjustment. In the former case tax reliefs and subsidies were on a rising trajectory after 1973 with the lion's share of aid being directed towards ailing sectors, such as iron and steel and shipbuilding. Coincidentally, many European governments sought to diversify industrial structures via direct subsidies to R&D in high growth sectors. In this respect the general area of microelectronics loomed large, especially in Denmark, Belgium, the Netherlands, Sweden and the UK. A further area in which government intervention played a defensive role was foreign trade. Whilst the 1970s and 1980s experienced tariff reductions in OECD countries in general, the whole of the period was overlain by the rise of non-tariff barriers to trade. As in the case of financial aid, the major recipients of this form of assistance were traditional industrial sectors such as steel, textiles and clothing, although the motor vehicle industry was also singled out for special treatment. Indeed, in this latter case, approximately 50 per cent of its trade in western Europe was subject to non-tariff barriers by 1983, compared with only 1 per cent a decade earlier. Quantitative non-tariff barriers were also complemented by product-specific price and technical regulations as well as explicit preferences for domestic producers in public procurement. At the same time, trade distortions were enhanced by sector-specific export subsidies.

By the mid-1990s a substantial degree of consensus had emerged amongst economists and policy advisors as to the results of interventionist industrial policies. In the light of Svennilson's conception of desirable structure change, it has been argued that subsidies and other protective measures 'distorted competition and blurred market signals', and in so doing locked economic resources into sub-optimal uses.[8] Insofar as industrial policies buttressed the position of low growth sectors in the name of short-term social and political objectives, economic welfare was reduced at the same time as the management of public finances was rendered more difficult. In relation to the safeguarding of jobs, moreover, the empirical record demonstrates clearly that employment trends in protected sectors did not differ significantly between western European countries irrespective of the policy mix. To the extent that governmental aid facilitated excessively high wage levels in strongly unionized industries such as motor vehicles and steel, the resulting distortion of relative factor prices may have encouraged the substitution of capital for labour at the expense of employment. If there were no clear benefits arising from protectionism, a similar judgement has been applied to the promotion of new industrial sectors. In the case of France and the UK, for example, an authoritative OECD-sponsored survey concluded that the strategy of 'picking winners' in presumed growth sectors – writ large in both countries in the later 1970s – failed to produce demonstrable international competitive advantage, and even when successful, the relevant firms had been heavily dependent upon government procurement.[9]

For all of the above reasons, the development of European industrial policies during the course of the 1980s marked a reversal of previous trends. Far from governments seeking to bolster declining sectors and to subsidize growth points for the future, the accent was on deregulation to permit the operation of market forces, a consideration which, in the guise of privatization, also applied to public utilities and 'lame-duck' nationalized firms in the manufacturing sector. In these respects substantial programmes were implemented in the UK and France in the 1980s, with Italy and West Germany following suit towards the end of the decade. At the same time, direct subsidies to declining industrial sectors were run down. This was especially the case in the UK and the Netherlands. In the former, it is conventional to refer to the election of a Conservative government in 1979 committed to the reinvigoration of a free-market economy with a drastically reduced scale of strategic intervention in the belief that the pre-existing trend of state intervention had introduced rigidities within the economic system at the expense of efficiency and welfare criteria. In the Netherlands, however, the reversal in policy was equally abrupt: from 1982 until the end of the decade 'defensive' intervention in favour of declining sectors was halved at the same time as investment subsidies were progressively eliminated.

In focus: The Iron and Steel Industry

In the post-1945 period the iron and steel industry maintained its position as one of the most important industries in western Europe. It participated fully in the demand-led expansion of the 'golden age' and availed itself of a sequence of supply-side innovations conducive to greater efficiency. In the two decades after 1950 output increased in all European countries, although differential growth rates were observable at an early stage. In the British case production increased by 50 per cent compared with two-fold increases in France and West Germany. More impressive, at least in terms of growth rates, was the development of steel making capacity in southern Europe, notably in Italy and Spain. At the same time, the scale of output increased dramatically. In the inter-war period iron and steel plants with productive capacity of less than one million tonnes per annum were the norm, whereas by the early

The Iron and Steel Industry (continued)

1980s the minimum efficient scale of production in response to optimal blast furnace and rolling mill techniques was in the range 3–10 million tonnes.

But if the iron and steel industry was a beneficiary of the 'golden age' in terms of market expansion, the period after 1973 was afflicted by fluctuations in demand in response to profound market uncertainty. In the years from 1974 to 1984 European output fell by 30 per cent in the face of a constellation of demand and supply-side factors. In this respect, the effects of global recession were exacerbated by longer-term influences. These included the declining use of steel on the part of established manufacturing sectors such as motor vehicles, and the fact that expanding sectors, primarily electronics and computers, made limited use of the material. The post-1970 decades also witnessed the onset of intense competition both at home and abroad from eastern European producers and developing economies such as Mexico, Brazil and South Korea, enjoying access to lower wages and up-to-date plant. To compound the situation, the onset of falling demand after 1974 coincided with the coming to fruition of long-term investment plans in the western European industry so that the remainder of the decade was marked by sub-optimal working as surplus capacity increased.

Given the high level of state ownership in the industry, governmental responses to falling prices and profits were characterized by a combination of protectionism and subsidization as well as restructuring and diversification. In the former category, most governments subsidized their national industries by writing off or carrying large debts, or by offering low interest loans. By 1977 the industry's crisis was severe enough to provoke action by the European Community in the form of the Davignon Plan which provided for the run-down of capacity and coordinated price increases. As the recession deepened in 1980 the Community took the power to set mandatory quotas and production targets, as well as agreeing to the gradual elimination of subsidies. As a result, capacity within the Community as a whole fell from 169 million tonnes in 1980 to 142 million tonnes in 1985. Particularly severe falls were registered in the UK and France as a result of enforced restructuring. In both countries the relevant industries were assisted by governmental curbs on trade union power, thus paving the way for extensive redundancies after major strike action. In the British case, the reduction in capacity was reflected in a dramatic fall in the labour force, from 220,000 in 1974 to only 54,000 in 1986, by which time UK productivity levels approximated to the best in Europe. Whilst diversification strategies in favour of high-quality special steels aided the West German and French industries, this was in marked contrast to experience in the UK where the British Steel Company remained historically committed to basic steel production. The experience of the iron and steel industry is thus illustrative of several of the trends noted in this section – sustained market expansion in the 'golden age', followed by recession, the latter consistent with deindustrialization, and provoking a variety of governmental responses.

The Tertiary Sector

The tertiary, or service sector can be classified in a number of ways. One simple division is between the private and public sectors, the former producing output with a marketable value (and therefore contributing directly to GDP) and the latter reflecting the non-market orientation of public bureaucracies, broadly defined. A more helpful subdivision for the purposes of exposition is to follow the approach adopted by Gershuny and Miles whereby the service sector is divided into four categories: distribution (transport, wholesale and retail trades), producer (financial, research and marketing services), social (health, education, etc.) and personal (domestic services, boundaries, entertainment, etc.).[10] Across western Europe as a whole the service sector as a proportion of total employment and GDP has been growing at the expense of the primary and secondary sectors since at least the end of the nineteenth century. In these respects there was an element of continuity across the divide of the Second World War. Tables 6.1 and 6.3 confirm the overall trends in favour of the service sector during the 'golden age', whilst Tables 6.2, 6.4 and 6.6 provide a disaggregated view of sectoral trends in services from the mid-1970s onwards. In general terms the accelerated decline in manufacturing in this period was complemented by service sector expansion. By the early 1980s, services accounted for 50 per cent or more of employment in all of the major economies of western Europe. Equally significant was the expanding percentage of services in GDP, accounting for more than 60 per cent in the UK, Sweden, Belgium, the Netherlands and France. In Denmark the figure was as high as 72 per cent. The major exceptions were Norway (55 per cent), West Germany (52 per cent) and Italy (54 per cent). In the Norwegian case the relatively low percentage was fully reflective of the impact of natural resource exploitation in a small economy, whilst in West Germany and Italy it was an indication of the success of these countries in resisting the trend towards deindustrialization observable elsewhere.

Reference has already been made to the income elasticities of demand which point towards the secular expansion of the service sector. In relation to financial and business services, as consumers become wealthier they are likely to seek more financial advice and the services forthcoming may be viewed as an alternative to consumption and as a means of bringing expenditure forward. Moreover, the increasing globalization of business after 1970 has given rise to new demands for services in the form of international advertising and marketing. Indeed, there is evidence to suggest that in an increasingly complex world economy both government and industry subcontracted out for specific business services which were formerly performed in-house. This trend in itself encouraged the formation of new firms in the service sector within western Europe. The dominant share of this new business was captured by London, reflecting the capital's long-standing comparative advantage in international finance, but substantial growth was also registered in Amsterdam, Paris, Zürich and Frankfurt.[11]

As for the expanded role of the state, Table 6.6, depicting government outlays as a percentage of GDP after 1974, points to the fact that the upsurge in govern-

Plate 6.3. The Lloyds building in London. Over the last half century, a rising proportion of national income has been generated in services and, especially, financial services. London's 'City' continued to be Europe's main centre of service-sector activities such as international finance, banking and insurance.

ment expenditure was very much a phenomenon of the 1970s and early 1980s. In this period, acceleration in the rate of public expenditure in relation to GDP was predicated on the assumption that it was essential in sustaining economic growth and stability, especially in view of the need to correct pervasive market failure

manifesting itself in a rising trend in unemployment. From the early 1980s onwards, however, the expansion of the public sector began to slow down as governments and their electorates adopted a more sceptical view of the merits of the
expanded state. One critical factor was the ongoing international recession which
ultimately served to reduce governmental revenues at the same time as public
sector deficits mounted. As stagflation persisted, moreover, the relative growth of
a sector insulated from market forces came to be seen as harmful to economic
efficiency and growth. As early as 1980 an OECD-sponsored conference referred
to 'the welfare state in crisis' in view of mounting concerns about the relative
over-provision of public goods at the expense of real wealth producers in the
private sector.[12] In policy terms, the earliest and most extreme reaction to these
developments occurred in the UK following the election of Margaret Thatcher's
Conservative government in 1979, committed to 'rolling back the frontiers of
the state' via budgetary reductions in order to release resources to a newly
invigorated private sector. This was the essence of 'Thatcherism'. The statistics in
Table 6.6 bear testimony to the government's resolve, but it is instructive to note
that the reining back of government outlays as a proportion of GDP was a general
phenomenon, with the exceptions of Italy and Norway.

Interpretations of Structural Change

The preceding sections have pointed to the substantial structural changes which
have taken place in the western European economies since 1945. Whilst there
were obvious continuities with the pre-war period, in the decline of agriculture
and the growth of services, for example, the characteristic feature of the post-war
years was the rapid pace of structural change. 'Deruralization' with respect to
agriculture had been occurring in western Europe since the later nineteenth
century, but it is the magnitude of the decline after 1950 which is striking – in
employment terms (taking the index of farm employment in 1950 as 100), in the
period to 1962, 35 per cent in Belgium, 33 per cent in West Germany, 31 per
cent in France, and 28 per cent in Italy. Transfers from agriculture on this
scale were in principle dependent upon the availability of non-farm employment
in order to overcome the resistance of the agricultural population to movement
from the land, and also to avoid subsidizing low-income farmers to the extent
that their incentive to move was impaired. The provision of non-agricultural employment was clearly dependent upon adequate demand for non-farm products
and services and either the provision of extra non-farm capital or more labour-
intensive use of capital. As indicated already, these conditions were amply fulfilled
in the 'golden age' of western economic growth due to a complex of factors –
political, economic and institutional – which were conducive to the maintenance
of high levels of aggregate demand and capital investment.

Whilst the explanation for the diminution of the agricultural sector is relatively straightforward, this cannot be said of the phenomenon of deindustrialization
and the accelerated growth of the service sector. The profound structural changes

of the 1970s and 1980s were the product of many and complex factors. At the most elementary level, changing income elasticities of demand in a situation of rising real incomes for consumers clearly had a role to play. The approaching end of the life cycle of numerous traditional manufactures in advanced industrial economies meant that certain types of production – often assisted by rapid international technology transfers – moved to lower-wage countries, with less unionized or non-unionized labour, many of them on the Pacific rim. As for the expansion of market services, one possible explanation arises from the distinction between services directly linked to the production of goods and 'free-standing' services. Whilst the share of market services in households' final consumption rose strongly between 1975 and 1982, a European Community survey of 1983 showed that bought-in services by the manufacturing sector clearly exceeded that of manufacturing value added.[13] This was a direct reflection of the withdrawal of firms from service activities formerly performed in-house, and to that extent it could have been a key factor in explaining the expansion of market services. Further contributions to the decline of manufacturing were the oil shocks of 1973–74 and 1979–80. The resulting increases in world oil prices raised the cost of energy inputs but in a situation where real wages in western Europe were relatively inflexible. This meant that industrial enterprises bore the brunt of higher oil bills, especially after the first oil shock. The evidence suggests that manufacturing industry could pass on higher production costs only at the expense of the price competitiveness of its products in relation to those economies relatively unaffected by the oil shock.

There remains to be considered the case of the UK which, as noted already, was most severely affected by the trend towards deindustrialization after the early 1970s. In this respect a considerable public debate arose as to the reasons for the unusually severe contraction of British manufacturing industry.[14] One early and controversial explanation focused on the notion of 'crowding out', insofar as a rapidly rising trend of government expenditure after the 1960s in order to facilitate the expansion of public sector services, deprived the industrial base of capital and labour. The resulting competition for resources between the private and public sectors set in train a wage/price spiral which adversely affected price competitiveness. The mounting costs of the expanded state were also reflected in rising levels of personal and corporate taxation. These developments eroded further the competitiveness of manufacturing industry, in the former case via compensatory (and inflationary) wage and salary demands and in the latter via reduced corporate profits with knock-on effects on the level of investment.

Whilst it is true that this interpretation of the structural problems of the British economy helped to validate the Conservative government's attempts to rein back public expenditure after 1979, its empirical foundations have proved to be weak. Quite apart from the fact that other European countries experienced an acceleration in public sector growth over the same period, there is little evidence to suggest that British industry was starved of either capital or labour. Specific skill shortages have existed from time to time, but the great majority of new recruits to the public sector were females, whilst a majority of the unemployed in manufacturing industry were males. Similarly, with regard to capital funding, the effective company taxation rate was falling throughout the relevant period and this, together with the report of the Wilson Committee on financial institutions, underlined the fact that there was little, if any, evidence of capital starvation on the part of manufacturing industry.[15]

If the 'crowding out' hypothesis with respect to structural change in the British economy has given rise to substantial criticisms, it might be thought that an explanation of deindustrialization founded on the growing contribution to the economy of North Sea oil after 1975 – a short-term factor *par excellence* – would be far less contentious. This is not, however, the case. The build-up of oil production in the later 1970s led to an appreciation in the value of the pound in its new (and temporary) guise as a petro-currency. It is plausible to argue, therefore, that the sudden acceleration in the loss of manufacturing capacity (17 per cent in the period 1979–81) was the direct result of declining price competitiveness. The problem with this explanation, however, is that the manufacturing sector had already experienced substantial contraction before 1979, and the election of the Conservative government in that year was a contributory factor in its own right to manufacturing decline. In this latter context the new government's commitment to the restraint of inflation by restrictive monetary and fiscal policies renders it doubly difficult to unravel the North Sea oil effect.[16]

The fact that deindustrialization was well under way in the UK before North Sea oil began to exert a significant impact on the economy, together with the inadequacies of the 'crowding out' hypothesis, inevitably focuses attention on the longer-term causes of the contraction in manufacturing industry. Constraints of space preclude extensive commentary on this theme. It is sufficient to say that the literature concerning Britain's relative decline as a manufacturing nation is vast. Explanatory factors have embraced long-standing institutional and cultural antipathies to industrial modernization, deficiencies in educational and entrepreneurial standards, misallocation of investment and research and development resources, and an economic policy environment in which the needs of the industrial base have been subordinated consistently to overriding macroeconomic concerns.[17] At a more prosaic level it is legitimate to argue that all of these factors have impacted adversely on the price and non-price competitiveness of British manufactures. In relation to the latter, there is a broad consensus among economists that the ability of the continental European economies to resist the trend towards deindustrialization after 1970 was dependent upon superior non-price competitiveness in the areas of product design, reliability in performance, delivery dates and after-sales service.

Conclusion

This chapter has reviewed the main structural changes that have taken place in the economies of western Europe since 1945, whilst noting the sheer rapidity of the adjustment process and commenting on the main causal factors. It should be clear that structural change can have positive and negative effects at the level of national economies. In the former context, economic growth and rising living standards have clearly been dependent upon resource transfers from agriculture to the manufacturing sector where the scope for productivity gains is relatively high. So too, in relation to the rise of the service sector, this can be viewed as a consequence of the process of economic development in which the secondary sector becomes more and more reliant for its efficient functioning on a range of sophisticated market services. It is also possible that deindustrialization can have positive aspects. Even if there is a relative decline in the importance of the manufacturing sector, the resulting structural changes need not be a source of concern as long as it continues to grow in absolute terms, thereby helping to sustain full employment and a sufficient volume of exports to balance a country's desire for imports. Moreover, if labour displaced from manufacturing as a result of productivity growth is being absorbed in the service sector, this may be consistent with increased leisure time and a higher quality of life. On the negative side, however, deindustrialization may be on such a scale that it prevents the attainment of national economic policy goals. In contrast to the continental European economies, British experience was outstanding in this respect. In the 1970s the loss of jobs in UK manufacturing had been largely offset by the creation of extra employment, principally in the public services. During the 1980s, however, there was an overall increase in unemployment, with particular concentrations in the industrial districts of northern England, Wales and Scotland. Whereas in the 1970s the growth of service sector employment was equally distributed between regions, this was not the case in the 1980s. In that decade the growth in the tertiary sector was propelled mainly by the expansion of financial services where the relevant firms generated roughly double the number of jobs in the south of England compared with those regions most severely affected by structural unemployment in the manufacturing sector. These facts serve to underline the uniqueness of Britain's experience as an advanced capitalist economy in the later twentieth century.

Bibliographical Note

The Organisation for Economic Cooperation and Development (OECD) has published a sequence of commentaries on structural change in the western capitalist economies. These are as follows: *Structural Reform Measures in Agriculture* (Paris, 1972); *Structural Adjustment and Economic Performance* (Paris, 1987); and *Economies in Transition: Structural Adjustment in OECD Countries* (Paris, 1989). The most up-to-date commentary on European industry is provided by Peter Johnson (ed.), *European Industries: Structure, Context and Performance* (Cheltenham, 1993), whilst the seminal analysis of the shedding of labour from agriculture is set out in Edward F. Denison, *Why Growth Rates Differ* (Washington DC, 1967). An excellent account of the expansion of the tertiary sector is contained in J.I. Gershuny and I.D. Miles, *The New Service Economy: The Transformation of Employment in Industrial Society* (London, 1983). On the issue of deindustrialization with specific reference to British experience see N.F.R. Crafts, *Can Deindustrialisation Seriously Damage Your Wealth?* (London, 1993) and Mark Cook and Nigel M. Healey, *Growth and Structural Change*

(London, 1995). Finally, M.M. Postan, *An Economic History of Western Europe, 1945–1964* (London, 1967) is still a valuable source on the shape and form of structural change in the two post-war dacades.

Notes

1. M.M. Postan, *An Economic History of Western Europe, 1945–1964* (London, 1967), p. 177.

2. Ingvar Svennilson, *Growth and Stagnation in the European Economy* (Geneva, 1954).

3. N.F.R. Crafts, 'The golden years of economic growth in Western Europe, 1950–1973', *Economic History Review*, vol. XLVIII (1995), pp. 429–47.

4. M.M. Postan, *An Economic History of Western Europe, 1945–1964* (London, 1967), p. 188.

5. D.J. Storey, *Entrepreneurship and the New Firm* (London, 1982).

6. N.F.R. Crafts, *Can Deindustrialisation Seriously Damage Your Wealth?*, (London, 1993).

7. OECD, *Economies in Transition: Structural Adjustment in OECD Countries* (Paris, 1989), pp. 137–47.

8. *Ibid.*, p. 141.

9. OECD, *Structural Adjustment and Economic Performance* (Paris, 1987).

10. J.I. Gershuny and I.D. Miles, *The New Service Economy: the transformation of Employment in Industrial Societies* (London, 1983).

11. Commission of the European Community, *European Economy* (Brussels, September, 1985).

12. OECD, *The Welfare State in Crisis* (Paris, 1981).

13. Commission of the European Community, *European Economy*, no. 18, (Brussels, 1983).

14. M.W. Kirby, 'The economic record', in Terry Gourvish and Alan O'Day (eds), *Britain since 1945* (London, 1991), pp. 11–37.

15. H.M. Treasury, *Evidence on the Financing of Trade and Industry to the [Wilson] Committee to Review the Functioning of Financial Institutions*, vol. 1 (1977).

16. C. Bean, 'The impact of North Sea oil', in R. Dornbusch and R. Layard (eds), *The Performance of the UK Economy* (London, 1987), pp. 64–96.

17. The following provide useful surveys: B.W.E. Alford, *British Economic Performance, 1945–1975* (London, 1988); Michael Dintenfass, *The Decline of Industrial Britain, 1870–1980* (London, 1992).

7 Foreign Trade and Payments in Western Europe

Catherine R. Schenk

The two decades after 1950 witnessed a global increase in the volume of international trade which far outstripped the increase in world output.[1] This phenomenal expansion was facilitated by relaxations in controls both on trade itself and on international payments. Western European countries were major participants in this economic expansion, registering unprecedented rates of growth in trade and output. This 'golden age' came to a sharp end in the early 1970s, when the post-war payments system disintegrated and protectionism returned as a tool of trade policy. Although avoiding a return to controls on trade among themselves, the economic performance of western Europe in the two decades since 1970 has been much more uneven.

Trade within Europe

Trade among western European countries grew very quickly through the recovery from the Second World War and continued until the 1980s. From 1950 to 1958, as the Organisation for European Economic Co-operation (OEEC) liberalized its trade, intra-European imports grew from US$845 million to US$1943 million.[2] Much of this increase was the result of expanded trade with West Germany, driven by that country's dramatic post-war recovery. Exports from all European countries to West Germany grew much faster than their exports to the rest of Europe or to the rest of the world,[3] and by 1955 Germany was absorbing at least 10 per cent of the exports of every west European nation except for Portugal and the UK. As well as providing an attractive market for European manufactures, West Germany was also able to run persistent trade surpluses from exports of engineering goods which helped to re-equip European industry.

After the beginning of the European customs union in 1958 (European Economic Community), trade within Europe continued to expand, due both to the

Table 7.1. Intra-EEC(12) trade (average annual percentage change)

	Total	Bel/L	Dk	Ger	Fr	Italy	Neth	UK	Ire	Port	Spain
(a) Imports											
1960–70	10.3	11.1	9.3	11.4	11.7	12.2	11.4	5.5	9.9	11.2	20.6
1970–80	16.2	16.3	12.4	16.3	17.8	17.0	15.2	14.7	17.3	15.8	17.8
1980–90	7.3	6.7	6.1	7.2	7.0	7.1	6.8	7.5	7.4	11.1	10.5
(b) Exports											
1960–70	10.4	11.9	8.4	11.6	10.0	13.7	11.3	6.4	10.1	11.3	12.6
1970–80	15.6	14.9	14.0	15.0	16.3	15.6	16.3	15.6	18.5	13.4	20.1
1980–90	8.1	7.2	8.6	8.6	8.1	9.1	7.3	5.8	11.8	14.5	11.9

Note: The EEC(12) are the countries listed plus Greece.

Source: EEC, *External Trade Statistical Yearbook 1991.*

Table 7.2. Members' share of intra-EEC(12) trade (per cent)

	Total	Bel/L	Dk	Ger	Fr	Italy	Neth	UK	Ire	Port	Spain
(a) Imports											
1960	100	8.5	3.9	21.6	13.4	10.1	9.7	27.2	1.4	1.2	1.5
1970	100	9.1	3.5	24.0	15.2	12.0	10.8	17.4	1.3	1.3	3.8
1980	100	9.3	2.5	24.2	17.4	12.9	9.9	15.4	1.4	1.2	4.4
1990	100	8.7	2.3	23.9	17.0	12.7	9.5	15.6	1.4	1.7	5.9
(b) Exports											
1960	100	8.7	3.4	26.4	15.9	8.4	9.3	23.9	1.0	0.8	1.7
1970	100	10.0	2.8	29.4	15.3	11.4	10.1	16.6	1.0	0.8	2.1
1980	100	9.3	2.5	27.9	16.1	11.3	10.7	16.5	1.2	0.7	3.0
1990	100	8.6	2.6	29.3	16.1	12.4	9.9	13.3	1.7	1.2	4.3

Source: As for Table 7.1.

rapid growth of European economies and the reduction in trade barriers. As a result, trade within Europe grew faster than trade of European countries with the outside world, although this was less true of the 1970s when oil imports made up a larger proportion of European imports.

Table 7.1 shows the growth of the value of trade among 12 EEC countries from 1960 to 1990 and Table 7.2 shows the relative importance of each country in that trade. Trade within Europe expanded by over 10 per cent per annum in the 1960s compared with a growth rate of less than 8 per cent in trade between Europe and the rest of the world in this decade. This pattern was repeated in the 1980s when intra-European trade grew about a third faster than trade with the rest of the world. During the inflation and recession of the 1970s, the value of trade within and outside Europe grew at about the same rate, around 16 per cent

Table 7.3. Intra-European trade as a percentage of total trade

	Total	Bel/L	Dk	Ger	Fr	Italy	Neth	UK	Ire	Port	Spain
(a) Imports											
1960	37.9	56.6	54.5	39.7	35.0	36.8	54.1	22.3	64.0	51.6	35.5
1970	50.3	66.3	48.7	51.7	56.0	47.5	63.4	29.4	70.1	52.6	40.9
1980	49.2	61.6	50.3	49.4	52.0	46.2	54.7	40.9	75.3	54.3	31.3
1990	58.8	70.7	53.7	54.1	64.8	57.4	59.9	51.0	70.8	69.1	59.1
(b) Exports											
1960	40.8	60.7	57.1	40.3	38.5	40.1	61.2	22.9	80.8	38.5	58.4
1970	53.4	75.2	44.2	49.8	58.1	51.7	72.6	32.7	74.3	43.8	49.6
1980	55.7	73.2	51.6	51.1	55.4	51.6	73.5	45.0	76.0	58.6	52.2
1990	60.7	75.1	52.1	53.6	62.7	58.2	76.5	52.6	74.8	73.5	64.9

Source: As for Table 7.1.

per annum. Also apparent in Table 7.1 is the relatively slow growth in intra-European trade during the 1960s in Denmark, the UK and Ireland which were not part of the EEC during this decade. The impact of membership of the EEC is also suggested by the relatively rapid increase in Spain's and Portugal's trade with the rest of Europe in the 1980s.

In Table 7.2 West Germany stands out as the most important market for both imports and exports. The prominence of Italy and France in European trade increased over the first three decades of the EEC's existence while that of the UK declined. Table 7.3 shows that European trade has been particularly important for the smaller European nations such as Ireland, Portugal, and the Benelux countries. The most dramatic change is evident in the increasing importance of the European market for the UK between 1960 and 1990, largely as a result of the reduction in trade with the Commonwealth and joining the EEC in 1973.

Interestingly, the creation of a customs union in western Europe appears to have encouraged trade in similar goods between members rather than specialization in production. It has been estimated that 71 per cent of the increase in trade within the EEC in 1959–67 was intra-industry trade, especially within the machinery and transport equipment sectors and later in chemicals and consumer durables.[4]

Trade of Europe with the Rest of the World

The importance of markets outside Europe varied widely for OEEC countries after the Second World War. The UK had substantial trade with the Commonwealth and the USA during the 1950s due in part to Britain's historical ties with these countries and also to preferential tariff and quota arrangements. Over the course of the decade, however, as trade barriers were relaxed, Britain's trade

Table 7.4. Trade of EEC(12) with other countries (percentage share)

	USA		Japan		L. America		EFTA		OPEC	
	Imp.	Exp.	Imp.	Exp.	Imp.	Exp.	Imp.	Exp.	Imp.	Exp.
1960	20.4	13.6	1.4	1.2	9.6	8.3	15.0	21.5	14.4	11.1
1970	21.7	18.0	3.4	2.6	7.9	6.7	17.4	25.1	16.3	7.5
1980	16.9	12.8	4.9	2.2	5.8	6.1	17.0	25.5	27.2	18.1
1990	18.4	18.2	10.0	5.4	5.5	3.6	23.5	26.5	9.7	8.4

Source: As for Table 7.1.

began to realign itself to the faster growing European market. Nevertheless, by 1960 the UK was still conducting about 75 per cent of its trade outside Europe.

As noted above, trade outside Europe grew more slowly than intra-European trade and only the larger European states were heavily involved. The UK accounted for over one-third of European trade with the outside world in 1960, but by 1990 the UK had given way to West Germany which then accounted for 35 per cent of this trade. This reflected the shift in relative competitiveness of German and British exports. Table 7.4 shows that, as might be expected, the European Free Trade Association (EFTA) countries were the major target for EEC exports and they eventually came to supplant the USA as the major source of imports. This was due in part to the bilateral trade agreements negotiated between the EEC and EFTA members in 1973 which reduced tariff barriers on industrial trade. In the last decade, Japan has become an increasingly important source of imports, which reflects that country's growing importance in world production. The OPEC countries (such as Saudi Arabia) also occupied a large proportion of European trade, especially through the oil price inflation of the 1970s and early 1980s.

Trade Liberalization and Economic Growth

The liberalization of trade barriers among European countries in the post-war period was driven by recognition of the political and economic crises caused by the protectionism of the inter-war period. Trade policy was thus directly linked to the European post-war goals of growth, prosperity and political stability.

In theory, trade is linked to growth through specialization and comparative advantage. With free trade, countries and regions are able to specialize in making goods of which they are the most efficient producers and to import the goods of which they are relatively high-cost producers. This allows the most efficient allocation of resources and so the best prospects for growth overall. The ability to export also increases the size of the market for a country's products which, in turn, allows the exploitation of economies of scale, since producing for a large market generally allows a reduction in unit costs. Again, trade generates more efficient production and offers the greatest potential for economic growth, while trade barriers tend to distort the use of scarce resources, raise the cost of production and so hinder growth. A third and more intangible link is that a highly competitive environment may provide an impetus for firms to pursue technological and other innovations which accelerate growth. Conversely, firms operating behind protective trade barriers may be lulled into complacent inefficiency.

There is no doubt that the trade liberalization of the 1950s accelerated the recovery of western Europe. As noted above, the rapid expansion of West German production created demand for other European manufactures as well as providing the engineering goods to re-equip European industry. Through trade, individual states reinforced each other's growth. In the first seven years of the EEC, the average annual growth rate of members' nominal GNP was 9.8 per cent; this rose to 13.4 per cent in the following eight years to 1972. The UK, which tended to align its trade to the slower-growing Commonwealth and American markets, did not take full advantage of this reinforcing effect and the UK growth performance was weaker through this period partly as a result.

Europe's trade and growth was also influenced by the boom which all industrialized countries experienced in the 1950s and 1960s. This so-called 'Long Boom' was in part created by the liberalization of trade barriers under the auspices of the General Agreement on Tariffs and Trade (GATT). The Kennedy Round of the GATT, which lasted from 1964 to 1967, achieved a reduction in tariff barriers of over one-third on products which accounted for close to 75 per cent of world trade. This was followed by more modest reductions agreed during the Tokyo Round from 1973 to 1979 which brought the EEC's average tariff level down to 4.7 per cent compared to 4.3 per cent for the USA and 2.9 per cent for Japan. The net result was a freeing-up of trade on industrial products which has benefited developed countries such as those in western Europe by increasing the potential market for their products and reducing the costs of imports for consumers. Tariff barriers on agricultural products were not similarly reduced because of the protectionist stance of American and European governments with respect to their domestic farming. It is only very recently under the Uruguay Round of the GATT that agricultural trade has become more central to the negotiations.

While the European states were recovering and growing quickly it was relatively easy for governments to commit themselves to opening their markets to the rigours of international competition. When growth slowed and unemployment increased in the 1970s, competition from producers in other countries was often seen as a threat to the continued prosperity of voters, and calls for trade protection increased. The result has been an increase in non-tariff barriers to trade by European states, especially against products from low-cost Asian producers. Western Europe has been the target of such controls (for example, in 1982 the USA restricted imports of European steel) as well as using them against their trading partners (for example, since 1980 the EEC has limited imports of cars from Japan). The direction of causation between trade and growth, therefore, is not always easy to determine. While the rise of this 'New Protectionism' has accompanied slower growth in Europe, in some senses it has been a result of the international recession as well as a cause.

In focus: The Effect of Integration on Industry – The European
Automobile Industry

With the integration of European markets and the global spread of
multinational enterprises, the pattern of international trade in Europe has
become increasingly complex. An example of the rise of 'Europeanized'
production is the automobile industry since 1958.

Soon after the end of the Second World War there were large protected
motor industries in the UK, Germany, France and Italy. Before 1958 the
tariffs on imported cars ranged from 17 per cent in West Germany to 33.3
per cent in the UK and 45 per cent in Italy. By 1968 there were no tariffs on
intra-EEC trade in cars, but imports from outside the customs union were set
a tariff of 17.6 per cent. These changes in tariffs naturally had an impact on
the geographical distribution of the industry. In 1950, half of the motor
vehicles produced in the four major producing countries were made in the
UK but by 1960 West Germany was the major manufacturer in Europe,
accounting for 37 per cent of production. By 1970, after the removal of trade
barriers within the EEC, the UK share of European production had fallen to
17.5 per cent, giving way to France which increased its share to 26 per cent.
Certainly, the loss of Britain's market share cannot be attributed solely to its
initial exclusion from the Common Market, but it should be noted that in
a very short space of time the continental motor vehicle industry had
flourished under the supportive conditions of rising incomes and tariff
protection.

The fast-growing European market also attracted foreign investment, from
the USA in particular. In 1967 'Ford of Europe' was created to produce cars
specifically for the burgeoning European market. The following year Ford
began production of the Escort simultaneously in the UK and West Germany,
and in 1969 production of the first specifically 'European' model, the Capri,
was begun. In the 1970s Ford moved most of its design and development
activity from Britain to West Germany to take advantage of faster-growing
productivity on the continent.

Britain was not the only non-EEC country to be affected by trade
patterns within Europe. In the 1970s, Spain was a rapidly growing market
for automobiles but was tightly protected under the Franco regime which
imposed a 30 per cent tariff on imported parts, limited foreign ownership to
50 per cent, and insisted on local content of production to at least 95 per
cent of a car's value. Eventually a compromise was reached which allowed
Ford to have 100 per cent ownership of its Spanish subsidiary and reduced
import tariffs to 5 per cent. In return, Ford ensured 66 per cent local content
of production and agreed to export at least 67 per cent of output to protect
domestic producers such as Seat. In 1974, Ford began producing the Fiesta
there and Spain became a rapidly growing car producer.

The Swedish firm Volvo also took advantage of the growing European
market. In 1960 65 per cent of its cars were sold in Scandinavia and 20 per

The Effect of Integration on Industry – The European Automobile Industry (continued)

cent in North America. By 1970, however, 30 per cent were sold in Europe, at the expense of the Scandinavian share. In order to penetrate the EEC market Volvo opened an assembly plant in Belgium where labour costs were low and there were significant government incentives for inward investment.

The identification of a European-wide market for cars also led to attempts at cooperation among European firms. In 1968 Citroën and Fiat agreed to coordinate their planning, investment, research, purchasing and sales in Europe. Citroën was a weak partner, however, and Fiat withdrew from the alliance in 1973, giving way to the Peugeot take-over of Citroën the following year. Such concentration of ownership through acquisition has been characteristic of the post-war motor industry as European producers were forced to respond to the slump in demand after the 1973 oil price rises and increasing competition from the USA and Japan. Amalgamation promised greater economies of scale and the benefits of rationalizing production. The concentration of ownership is still not reflected in the names of cars, however. For example, BMW continued to use the Rover marque after buying the British company in 1994.

Increasingly from the 1970s, international trade facilitated specialization of production, and companies maintained production and sales sites throughout the region. This had the advantage of spreading risk (for example of labour unrest or currency fluctuations) while reaching a broader base of customers through reduced transport costs. Specialization at plant level also allowed economies of scale and exploitation of labour cost differentials. In the 1970s the Ford Fiesta, for example, contained engines from Valencia and transmissions from Bordeaux. Fiestas were made simultaneously in Saarland (West Germany) and some were assembled in Dagenham for the British market. In the 1980s, the updated Fiesta was planned by an Anglo-German team of designers, assembled in Germany and Spain using engine blocks from Dagenham and carburettors from Northern Ireland. Belgium became a major assembly location for Ford, General Motors, Volkswagen, British Leyland, Volvo and the major French firms, which took advantage of the ports, labour costs and government incentives offered there.

This specialization of production confuses the statistics for European trade in automobiles. What is clear, however, is that an increasing proportion of car registrations in all European countries represent imports rather than domestic production. This is especially true for the UK and Italy. In 1968 imports accounted for only 8 per cent of UK new car registrations and 15 per cent in Italy. By 1988 these proportions had increased to 56 per cent and 39 per cent respectively. A decline in the proportion of production destined for export was also registered by these countries.

The precipitous decline of Britain as a major automobile producer since the late 1970s has been a particularly dramatic feature of the post-war European car industry. The response of the British government was to

---

The Effect of Integration on Industry – The European Automobile Industry (continued)

welcome American and Japanese direct investment in automobile assembly plants in the UK. Such inward investment offered jobs to this declining sector in the UK while allowing the Japanese to overcome European trade restrictions on the import of assembled vehicles. The result has been an increase in competition for continental European producers.

There is no doubt that trade policy in western Europe has influenced the geographical distribution of production in the region and encouraged investment from abroad. The reduction in trade barriers has also generated a regional rather than a national approach to production of many goods.

Payments Systems

European Payments Union

Alongside the initiatives to increase the trade of western European countries, came a succession of payments systems designed to facilitate this exchange. The European Payments Union was the first major post-war initiative. Launched in 1950 with American support, it created a forum for the reintroduction of multi-lateral settlements. The persistence of bilateral trade and payments until 1950 had inhibited the recovery and expansion of European economies, and it was deemed necessary to introduce a transitional regime on a regional basis in order to overcome these difficulties. Western European governments had pledged to eventually adhere to the global Bretton Woods system but this prospect faded into the future as the realities of the burdens of reconstruction were appreciated.

The EPU was essentially a clearing union in which participants agreed to accumulate each others' currency throughout each month in exchange for goods. At the end of the month, the accounts of each country against all other members as a whole were balanced and credits were available to those in overall deficit to overcome temporary imbalances and so avoid the need to restrict trade. As a country's deficit to the Union grew, it was required to settle an increasing pro-portion in gold and/or American dollars. Countries in surplus correspondingly offered credit for an initial proportion but then received gold and/or dollars for the remainder. By encouraging multilateral trade on a regional scale, and requiring the lowering of trade barriers among members, the EPU introduced discrimination in payments and trade against the rest of the world.

The freedom from bilateral settlements and the reduction of barriers to trade which the EPU provided, generated an almost immediate increase in intra-European trade. During the years in which it operated, the value of intra-European trade more than doubled from $10 billion in 1950 to $23 billion in 1959 and persistently outstripped the rate of growth of production. Other factors, such as the recovery of Germany, also fed the recovery of European trade but the

EPU facilitated this and allowed the German 'miracle' to fuel the growth of other European countries.

Currency Convertibility

Although the EPU was at first designed only to operate for two years, it persisted until the end of 1958 due to the delay in the reintroduction of formal external currency convertibility which would allow multilateral trade and payments. Only when all currencies are convertible is it possible to offset a trade deficit with one country using a surplus earned from another country. Convertibility therefore allows countries to buy in the cheapest market and to sell where their products can reap the highest price. It is this ability which allows international specialization and the most efficient allocation of resources that is essential to maximize all countries' growth prospects.

At the Bretton Woods conference in 1944, a return to convertibility at a fixed exchange rate was expected to take only perhaps five years. In the end, however, western European countries delayed this move for 14 years after the war. The danger of allowing premature convertibility had been shown dramatically in the UK experiment in 1947 when convertibility of the pound had to be suspended after only six weeks in order to forestall the bankruptcy of the British foreign exchange reserves. At a time of imbalance in international trade and payments, if one currency was convertible but its products were not in great demand in the international market, countries would merely present that currency to the monetary authorities to be converted, thus exhausting that country's foreign exchange reserves. Essentially, it was believed that the European economies could not 'afford' to have currency convertibility until their recovery was complete and their export competitiveness (against the USA in particular) was assured.

As early as 1955, western European governments had drawn up a plan to replace the EPU once convertibility was introduced. This was known as the European Monetary Agreement in which European governments pledged to maintain fixed exchange rates and to establish a European Fund to support convertibility. Throughout the 1950s payments were gradually liberalized but it was still nearly four years after signing the EMA that the move was made. After speculative pressures in the UK in 1956–57 had been resolved, and the US proposed to increase the funds available through the IMF, western European governments began to believe that the time for formal currency convertibility had finally come and in December 1958 most west European currencies were made convertible for trade purposes.

The terms of the EMA, however, did not suit the more unstable environment of the 1960s and it was gradually abandoned. Instead, short-term payments imbalances were dealt with through *ad hoc* arrangements, such as the Basle Agreements of 1961 which introduced mutual support among European and US central banks when there was a run on the foreign exchange reserves of a country. The UK was a main beneficiary of this scheme, borrowing $900 million in 1961. More generally, the European payments system merged with the global pegged exchange rate system designed at Bretton Woods. Initiatives to accelerate monetary integration on a regional basis were included in the Treaty of Rome which established the European Economic Community in 1957, but these provisions remained vague and unenforced through the 1960s while the commercial provisions of the Treaty were set in place. The 'European' focus of policy was to be revived, however, once the global system began to show its weaknesses.

Under the strain of supporting the inflexible Bretton Woods system in the 1960s, the world's policy-makers began to favour freer exchange rates. The pegged rate system, which allowed changes in exchange rates only in a crisis, generated speculation and seemed to create instability, especially as the US economy weakened and its balance of payments ran persistently in deficit. Under the pegged system, monetary authorities tended to be obliged to cling to inappropriate exchange rates for too long, which allowed speculative pressure to build. Under these circumstances, when the exchange rate was finally changed, the devaluation or revaluation often had to be greater than it would have been had the system allowed an earlier adjustment. The realization that pegged rates were too inflexible to cope with the changes in international competitiveness since 1945 was to culminate in the introduction of a freely floating exchange rate regime by 1973.

Western European governments, however, looked towards consolidating their own payments system through narrower margins for fluctuation. Within Europe there were infrequent but disruptive parity changes: in 1961 the Deutschmark and the Dutch guilder were revalued by 5 per cent, in 1967 sterling was devalued, in 1969 the French franc was devalued by 12.5 per cent while the Deutschmark was again revalued. It became evident in the EEC that parity changes were disruptive to trade and investment and that they jeopardized the working of the customs union. Only by tying their exchange rates and economic policies more closely together was it believed that they could preserve the integration which had so far been achieved. This pertained especially to the continuation of the Common Agricultural Policy since the principle of common agricultural prices across Europe required fixed exchange rates. From the late 1960s, therefore, western European payments policy moved in a different direction from that of the rest of the world. At the Hague Summit of the EEC in 1969 it was agreed in principle that monetary unification should be pursued. The Barre Report in 1969 marked out an approach to monetary cooperation based on tightly fixed exchange rates among European trading partners.

The Snake in (and out of) the Tunnel

World events overtook the European planners. Between 1969 and 1971 the US dollar came under increasing speculative pressure which finally drove President Nixon to suspend convertibility of the dollar into gold. This rupture of the basis of the Bretton Woods fixed exchange rate system brought the entire framework into jeopardy. A negotiated compromise was reached in Washington which made exchange rates more flexible and devalued the dollar against other currencies. This Smithsonian Agreement, which allowed greater margins for exchange rate

Plate 7.1. Troubled waters: cover of *The Economist*, 17 February 1973. Persistent exchange rate instability was a major problem of the international economy in the early 1970s. Here the yen rides high, though with little sense of permanence, in this satirical reworking of Hokusai's famous image of the breaking wave.

fluctuation, did not suit the EEC countries, which aspired to greater exchange rate stability among themselves. Their response was to establish bilateral parities of currencies within Europe which were allowed to fluctuate by only 2.25 per cent, while fluctuating against the US dollar by 4.5 per cent. This became known as the Snake in the Tunnel, the snake symbolizing the tight linking together of European currencies which 'wriggled' in a tunnel of wider fluctuations against the currencies of the rest of the world.

The Snake in the Tunnel was established in April 1972 and was to persist in some form until the end of the decade. In March 1973, when the global Smithsonian Agreements collapsed and the rest of the world turned to freely floating exchange rates, the Snake came out of the Tunnel and floated freely against other currencies while maintaining pegged rates within Europe. It never operated smoothly, however, and the membership of the Snake varied as currencies came under pressure and were unable to sustain their parity. The UK joined for only two months in May–June 1972, Italy left in 1973 and France in 1974. The Deutschmark was the only major currency which remained in the Snake throughout the decade. Largely due to the compensation payments necessary to offset changes in exchange rate parities, the cost of the CAP rose from 50 per cent of the EEC budget in 1965 to 80 per cent in 1978. The instability generated by frequent changes in parity inspired the European planners to press ahead with new plans to achieve monetary unification which culminated in the establishment of the European Monetary System in 1979 to be discussed in Chapter 9.

Capital Flows in Europe

Before the Treaty of Rome in 1957, the modest progress on liberalizing capital flows contrasted sharply with the alacrity with which European countries removed trade barriers. Capital movements, especially short-term capital flows, were deemed more dangerous to a nation's balance of payments since they could comprise speculative attacks on currencies or drain scarce investment resources away from domestic industry. When the European states made their currencies convertible in December 1958, therefore, this freedom was only extended to current account activities while controls on international investment were maintained. As part of the Treaty of Rome, the Six were committed to gradual liberalization of capital flows amongst themselves and technical relaxations on certain types of transactions began.

In 1960 and 1962 the European Commission issued directives on international capital flows which detailed the type of transactions that were to be liberalized and those on which controls could be maintained. Under these rules, direct investment, investment in real estate, investments on stock markets and several other more specific types of transfers were subject to unconditional liberalization. Members of the EEC were not obliged to allow short-term capital flows which might impinge on their monetary sovereignty. Further liberalization measures were introduced in 1985 and 1986 with the aim of achieving complete liberalization by 1992.

Table 7.5. Foreign direct investment of the UK ($ billion)

	Inward		Outward	
	EEC	**% of total**	**EEC**	**% of total**
1962	133.7	9.4	272.9	8.0
1965	178.4	8.9	392.2	9.3
1968	278.2	10.2	628.9	11.3
1971	472.9	12.4	985.2	14.8
1974	1,107.9	16.9	2,282.0	21.9
1978	2,034.7	18.3	4,570.2	23.9
1981[a]	6,502.0	22.6	8,254.8	18.8
1984	1,143.0	29.7	1,594.9	21.1

Note: [a]From 1981 includes oil, insurance and banking.

Source: United Nations, *From the Common Market to EC92; Regional Economic Integration in the European Community and Transnational Corporations* (New York, 1993), p. 45.

Where capital flows were demonstrated to be legitimately related to production and trade, European governments tended to be much more liberal than for possible speculative movements. For this reason, direct investment (by multinational companies) was much freer within Europe than portfolio investment. Within Europe, the spread of multinationals in response to economic integration is particularly striking. Most of this investment was prompted by firms from non-EEC countries opening production and distribution sites within the Community to avoid the common external tariff and to take advantage of the dynamic growth in the region. The 1960s and 1970s were also a period in which American firms, in particular, moved to a global approach to production. Within Europe, the reduction in trade barriers increased the tendency for firms to separate different stages of production, research and development to take advantage of geographical differences in labour costs or research expertise.

Information on intra-European direct investment is relatively sparse. What seems clear, however, is that investment by European firms in other European countries has been small relative to direct investment outside Europe. Between 1975 and 1983, 83 per cent of total outward foreign direct investment (FDI) from the 12 states of the EEC went outside the Community, mostly to the USA.[5] The major intra-European partnership is between the UK and continental Europe. Table 7.5 shows that UK FDI has been increasingly destined for western European countries. The fall in the share of the EEC from 1978 to 1981 was due to the increase in investment in the USA in these years.

The USA is also the main target for direct investment by other European countries. For the Netherlands, the USA took 8.7 per cent of FDI in manufacturing in 1973 and this rose to 27.3 per cent by 1984 at the expense of the share destined for other European states. The same pattern is apparent in West German

Table 7.6. Geographical distribution of US FDI stock (per cent of total US FDI)

	EEC(6)	**Other western Europe**
1950	5.4	9.3
1955	6.1	9.4
1957	6.6	9.7
1962	10.0	14.0
1967	14.4	17.9
1972	17.1	18.2
	EEC(9)	**Other western Europe**
1972	17.5	18.8
1977	33.7	9.2
1982	34.1	10.1
1985	35.4	10.5

Note: from 1982 EEC(9) includes Greece.

Source: United Nations, *From the Common Market to EC92*, p. 30.

FDI, with the USA receiving 14 per cent of total FDI in 1976 and 29 per cent 10 years later.

The United States was also the most important source of FDI for western Europe, which reflected its dominance of this type of firm organization. In the 1960s, the USA accounted for about 60 per cent of total outward FDI in the world. The impact that European integration had on US FDI is demonstrated by the relatively rapid increase in such investment in the EEC in the first decade after the Treaty of Rome, as is shown in Table 7.6. It must be remembered, however, that the relatively rapid growth in incomes on the Continent also attracted much of this investment. Despite not being in the EEC, nor exhibiting such attractive growth rates, the UK remained an important destination for American firms, absorbing 31 per cent of all new European investment of US firms between 1957 and 1967 while the EEC attracted 49 per cent. This reflected the close commercial and cultural ties between the UK and the USA.

In the 1970s American FDI grew more slowly in response to the international recession but the share destined for Western Europe continued to increase, so that by 1985, 46 per cent of US FDI stock was in Europe compared with 15 per cent in 1950.

The impact of accession to the EEC on the direction of US investment has been particularly marked for Spain and Portugal which joined the EEC in 1986. Between 1985 and 1988, US FDI in these countries increased by 90 per cent after falling 7 per cent in the previous three years. Political and economic instability in Greece seems to have inhibited a similar performance in that country after accession in 1981.

As the rate of American FDI declined in the 1970s, it was partly replaced by Japanese investment, the stock of which quadrupled between 1974 and 1984 from $2 billion to $8 billion. Most of this investment has been targeted at finance, insurance and other services, although car and electrical machinery manufacture are also important sectors. The late 1980s saw an extraordinary acceleration in such investment in Europe so that in 1987 and 1988 the flow of investment exceeded that of the entire post-war period up to 1986. In the late 1980s Japan became the third largest foreign investor in the UK (after the USA and West Germany), and the largest foreign investor in West Germany. These changes in flows of Japanese investment have much to do with developments in the Japanese economy itself, but also important are the attractions of the single European market and increasing hostility in Europe to Japanese exports.

Since 1950, then, western Europe has seen dynamic changes in the volume and direction of international capital which have affected its growth performance. These capital flows were due partly to the trade policy of the EEC but also to the attractive market generated by the growth in incomes during the Long Boom. While high levels of growth initially helped to attract such investment, the accumulation of capital in this way has no doubt helped to sustain growth in incomes through the 1970s and 1980s.

Historiographical Debate: The Effects of Customs Unions

In theory, a customs union can have two possible effects on the pattern of international trade. Trade 'creation' is the result of the specialization of production made possible by the reduction of trade barriers among members, and also the economies of scale made possible by exploiting a larger market. In the case of the EEC this would arise from the expansion of the 'domestic market' to include the territories of all members. Trade 'diversion' is caused by the common external tariff shifting imports from trading partners outside the customs union to those within the union. Trade diversion may represent a reduction in the efficiency of trade if the external tariff shifts trade to a less efficient producer within the union. In the case of the EEC, diversion of agricultural imports from low-cost developing country producers to higher-cost European producers would be an example of trade diversion. The problem with measuring these theoretical effects is the need to make assumptions about what would have been the pattern of trade without the EEC, and then to isolate the impact of membership from the other influences on the pattern of trade.

There is consensus in the literature that the creation of the EPU and the trade liberalization of the 1950s and 1960s contributed significantly to growth in these decades. In particular, most studies estimate that the trade creation effect has been considerably greater than trade diversion. This has been especially true of countries such as France and Italy, which entered the EEC with high tariffs at the outset. It must also be remembered, however, that this was a period of general trade liberalization, and that when growth slowed in all countries in the 1970s the effects were felt particularly strongly in western Europe. The slow-down in growth was manifested in sustained mass unemployment, inflation, and declines in the rate of investment, all of which hindered European enthusiasm for freer trade and payments, especially with respect to countries outside Europe.

One way of examining the impact of the reduction in trade barriers is to assess the implications of accession to the EEC by the UK in the troubled decade of the 1970s. There is no doubt that the pattern of British trade underwent significant changes in this period. The most obvious change in the geographical structure of imports and exports is the rapid increase in the share of the EEC(6) from 23 per cent of UK exports in 1973 to 30 per cent by 1978. The share of British imports from these countries increased just as fast from 26 per cent in 1973 to 34 per cent by 1978. This changing geographical distribution, however, was part of a longer term reorientation of trade away from the Commonwealth which stretched back to the 1950s. The acceleration of the trade with Europe began well before Britain joined the customs union.

During this period there was also a shift in the commodity distribution of British imports towards manufactures, which contributed to the larger share of imports coming from industrialized Europe. Imports of finished manufactures increased from 23.3 per cent of total British imports to 30.5 per cent between 1972 and 1981. This was accentuated by the sharp increase in British demand for consumer goods in the early 1970s brought on by expansionary domestic policy. The share of food, drink and tobacco, for which non-EEC markets were more important, fell from 15.5 per cent to 9.8 per cent over the same period. A shift of trade towards Europe would thus be expected even in the absence of a customs union because of this shift in the commodity distribution of British imports as well as the rapid growth of the European countries themselves. This commodity shift and its implications were also reflected in most other European states in the 1970s.

The impact of EEC membership on British trade becomes even more uncertain when the gradual nature of the reduction in tariff barriers is recognized. Most studies assume that 1973 marked a dramatic change in British tariff policy with respect to Europe. In fact, tariff barriers were reduced only gradually through a transition period established in the Treaty of Accession in 1972, and it was not until 1975 that the incidence of duty on imports from the Six fell below duties on goods from outside Europe. Moreover, the reduction in tariffs was from a fairly modest level. Under the auspices of the Kennedy Round of the GATT the incidence of duty on British imports had already fallen from 3.17 per cent in 1966/67 to 2.74 per cent in 1971/72.[6]

Despite the shifting geographical source of British imports, then, it must be remembered that tariff rates were relatively low to begin with. Combined with the longer-term shifts in British trade, this suggests that the impact of EEC membership in Britain's trade pattern in the 1970s was rather modest. Indeed, this has been the conclusion of most surveys of the topic. The House of Lords Select Committee on the European Communities, for example, concluded in 1983 that 'the effect of membership on the trade balance has probably been negligible'.[7]

In any case, by the end of the decade the rise in the sterling exchange rate in response to the exploitation of North Sea oil had reversed most of the positive effects of tariff reduction for British exporters.

The argument of this section is not that trade liberalization within Europe has had little impact on Europe's economic performance or trade pattern, but rather that the implications of the customs union alone must be assessed within the greater global economic context in which each member operated. Because of the difficulties of isolating the impact of the customs union, we still do not have a complete assessment of the role it has played in Europe's post-war economic growth.

Bibliographical Note

There is a broad range of literature on Europe's trade and payments since the war, although most work is focused exclusively on EEC countries. Kaplan and Schleiminger's volume on *The European Payments Union* (Oxford, 1989) traces the evolution of OEEC trade and payments before 1958. Dennis Swann's updated text on *The Economics of the Common Market* (London, 1995) details the intricacies of EEC relations with some historical perspective. R.C Hine's *The Political Economy of European Trade* (Brighton, 1985) covers most aspects of western European trade policy and has a good range of material on relations between Europe and the rest of the world.

Notes

1. 'Between 1951–53 and 1969–71 the volume of world trade in manufactures grew by 349 per cent whereas the volume of output grew by 194 per cent', P. Armstrong, A. Glyn and J. Harrison, *Capitalism since 1945* (Oxford, 1991), p. 153.

2. J.J. Kaplan and G. Schleiminger, *The European Payments Union; Financial Diplomacy in the 1950s* (Oxford, 1989), p. 343. 'Intra-European' refers to trade among OEEC countries.

3. For a more detailed analysis see A.S. Milward, *The European Rescue of the Nation-State* (London, 1992), pp. 134–67.

4. R.C. Hine, *The Political Economy of European Trade* (Brighton, 1985), p. 53.

5. United Nations, *From the Common Market to EC92; Regional Economic Integration in the European Community and Transnational Corporations* (New York, 1993), p. 50.

6. 'Incidence of duty' is the duty collected as a proportion of the value of total imports.

7. House of Lords, Select Committee on the European Communities, *Trade Patterns: The United Kingdom's Changing Trade Patterns Subsequent to Membership of the European Community: Minutes of Evidence*, 7th Report, 1983, p. xliii.

8 Welfare States

Paul Johnson

The provision of various forms of welfare service by public authorities has been a key aspect of economic and social development in Europe since 1945. Over the past 50 years social expenditure in European countries has more than doubled in scale, such that it now typically accounts for around 50 per cent of public expenditure and over 25 per cent of GDP. This reflects a massive increase both in the supply of services by government agencies and in the extent of public income transfer programmes. It means that European governments have acquired direct and powerful influence over the living conditions of all citizens. Everyone in Europe today is closely tied to the nation state in which they live by their liability to pay taxes and social security contributions, and by their entitlement to receive services such as education and health care, and cash benefits such as pensions.

Public involvement in the provision of welfare is not, of course, a creation of the post-war period. Bismarck inaugurated a contributory social insurance system in Germany in 1881, and over the following 40 years most European countries introduced some combination of sickness, unemployment, accident and old age insurance for groups within the manual working population. But the expansion of welfare provision since 1945 has been distinct from the earlier development, both quantitatively and qualitatively. Post-war welfare has been increasingly incorporationist, drawing in groups such as agricultural workers, shopkeepers, white-collar employees and the self-employed, so that it has become, in most countries, practically universal. It has also been increasingly expansive in its objectives, developing from piecemeal responses to particular social problems towards the comprehensive promotion of social security 'from the cradle to the grave'.

It is this comprehensiveness of coverage – in terms of both the population and the social circumstances included – that has led many commentators to describe post-war European welfare systems as 'welfare states'. Public welfare agencies of some description now account for such a large part of government activity, and for such a significant share of each citizen's interaction with the state, that the nature of the state appears to have been changed in a fundamental way. Instead of the European nation states playing their traditional role as guarantor, by means of army, police, and judiciary, of the physical security of the citizen, they have come to adopt a much more ambitious agenda that includes the provision of a guaranteed level of economic and social security.

Many consequences, both good and bad, have been attributed to this expansion of state activity in the social sector. For example, Milward identifies the post-1945 expansion of welfare spending, and the extension of welfare services to previously excluded groups, as an important element in the process of re-legitimizing the war-ravaged European nation states.[1] A different interpretation has been advanced by Baldwin, who argues that post-war governments have revised and adapted welfare systems to create supportive electoral alliances among groups subjected to common social risks and with similar welfare needs – groups that he describes as 'actuarial factions'.[2] But the post-war welfare states have also been blamed for inducing economic stagnation and inefficiency. At an individual level it has been argued that welfare benefits undermine the incentive to work and to save; at the macro-economic level, public welfare expenditure may 'crowd out' – or reduce – private investment.[3] This chapter will assess these positive and negative views of welfare state expansion. The first two sections examine different ways of defining and measuring welfare systems, since any analysis of outcomes will depend in part on exactly what is included within the umbrella term 'welfare state'. This is followed by a discussion of differences between countries in the pathways of welfare development, and an examination of alternative explanations for these differences. The chapter concludes with an assessment of the positive and negative results of welfare state growth in Europe since 1945.

Definitions

The term 'welfare state' is attractively comprehensive but annoyingly vague. Rudolph Klein has noted that 'it is a useful shorthand, but a dangerous abstraction. The welfare state is a bundle of institutions, policies and programmes which varies in its composition from country to country.'[4] This bundle can be unravelled into its constituent parts in a number of ways, each of which is valid, but none of which provides a complete description.

One way of defining welfare states is by categorizing and measuring the different elements of welfare state; we can call this the 'accounting' approach. Since the 1960s the Organisation for Economic Co-operation and Development (OECD) has produced comparative data on social expenditure in the major industrialized countries which cover public expenditure on education, health, pensions, unemployment compensation, and other social benefits such as sickness, maternity and disability benefits, family and child allowances, and minimum income support schemes. The International Labour Office (ILO) by contrast distinguishes between social insurance programmes (occupational injury, health, old age and unemployment insurance provided by the state in return for contributions –

mandatory or voluntary – made by members) and social assistance, which consists of non-contributory income-maintenance programmes, typically targeted on the poor and on families with dependent children. Meanwhile the statistical office of the European Commission (EC) broadly follows the OECD definition in its collection of data on social protection, but excludes education spending. As well as obvious differences in the accounting procedures adopted by these agencies over what is included or excluded, there are other variations which emerge because national governments adopt different procedures in classifying their systems of social protection.

These problems of data comparability are not simply trivial matters of detail. Two countries may *appear* to have very different levels of public expenditure in the area of, say, disability, yet they may offer very similar levels of financial support to the disabled person, but with one doing so through a designated disability insurance programme, the other through general unemployment benefit. Different institutional structures, which are reflected in different accounting practices, may therefore conceal similar welfare outcomes, and vice versa. This should caution us against drawing simplistic conclusions about welfare state performance from aggregate expenditure data.

An alternative to this 'accounting' approach is the 'functional' approach, in which welfare states are defined by reference to the type of social security they provide. We can, for instance, think of sickness or unemployment or homelessness as types of social risk to which all citizens are subject, to a greater or lesser extent. Welfare systems can respond to these risks in different ways. They may, for instance, respond to the risk of sickness by providing a public health care system, or by requiring individuals to subscribe to private sickness insurance schemes. They may respond to the risk of unemployment by organizing a public unemployment insurance scheme, or by offering retraining to redundant workers, or by creating jobs in public work schemes, or by some combination of all three. They may react to homelessness by encouraging the indigent to migrate somewhere else, or by building public housing, or by subsidizing rents, or by providing capital grants to the private housing market.

This functional interpretation of welfare states as combinations of specific policies designed to respond to specific social risks generates a more diversified and disaggregated view of welfare provision than does the 'accounting' approach. It recognizes that social risks may be ameliorated not only by direct public provision of services or via public mutual insurance schemes, but also through regulation of the private market (for instance by requiring employers to provide maternity leave) or by providing incentives for particular sorts of market-sector activity (for instance, giving employers tax relief on pension fund contributions). The functional approach explicitly embraces the concept of a 'mixed economy' of welfare in which protection for the individual against social risks arises from a combination of public and private sector activity. This in turn implies that a purely accounting-based assessment of public sector social expenditure may misrepresent the underlying level of social security or insecurity faced by the individual.

Table 8.1. Social expenditure as a percentage of GDP, 1949–93

	Denmark	France	Germany	Italy	Netherlands	Portugal	Spain	UK
(a) 1949–74								
1949	8	–	15	8	7	–	–	10
1954	10	13	14	11	8	–	–	10
1960	11	13	15	12	11	–	–	11
1965	12	16	17	15	16	–	–	12
1970	17	15	17	16	20	–	–	14
1974	21	22	21	21	24	–	–	15
(b) 1970–93 EC data								
1970	20	19	22	17	21	–	–	16
1980	29	25	29	19	30	13	18	21
1985	28	29	28	23	32	14	20	24
1990	30	28	27	24	32	15	21	22
1993	33	31	28/31	26	34	18	24	27

Note: German data for 1949 to 1990 relate to the former West Germany. For 1993 the first figure relates to the former West Germany, the second to the newly enlarged Germany incorporating the provinces formerly in East Germany.

Sources: 1949–74: P. Flora, *State, Economy and Society in Western Europe, 1815–1975*, Volume 1 (Frankfurt, 1983), p. 456; 1970–93: European Commission, *Social Protection in Europe* (Luxembourg, 1995), p. 61.

Measurement

The different accounting conventions of the international agencies make it difficult to assemble consistent data on welfare state expenditure since 1945. Table 8.1 presents a best guess at the evolution of social expenditure in eight European countries since the Second World War. Data in the upper part of the table (1949–74) are derived from ILO sources, whereas those in the lower part (1970–93) come from the EC. The definitions are slightly different – for 1970 the EC figures are consistently greater than those from ILO – but the trends are clear. In France, West Germany, Italy and the United Kingdom the proportion of GDP devoted to social expenditure doubled between the early 1950s and the early 1980s; in Denmark this proportion rose more than three-fold, and in the Netherlands it rose four-fold. Since the early to mid-1980s, however, the rate of expansion of social expenditure in these countries has been checked. Meanwhile Portugal and Spain, both relative late-comers to the establishment of comprehensive welfare provision, have experienced faster expenditure growth since 1985 than have the more mature welfare systems in the other countries.

Welfare states do not provide 'something for nothing', and this expansion of public social expenditure since the 1940s has inevitably necessitated an increase in the revenue of governments. Table 8.2 shows that total tax and social insur-

Table 8.2. Total tax and social insurance revenue of government as a percentage of GDP

	Denmark	France	Germany	Italy	Netherlands	Portugal	Spain	UK
1950	–	21	29	17	22	–	–	31
1955	23	–	31	31	26	15	–	30
1965	30	35	32	26	33	18	15	30
1975	41	39	39	27	43	27	20	36
1980	44	42	38	30	46	29	24	35
1985	46	45	38	34	46	32	29	38

Source: B. Guy Peters, *The Politics of Taxation* (Oxford, 1991), p. 27.

ance revenue for the same eight countries has followed a similar upward path over time, although there are some obvious differences between countries. Whereas in the Netherlands the increase in tax revenue as a percentage of GDP is almost fully explained by the expansion of social expenditure in the 35 years up to 1985, in the United Kingdom tax revenue has risen much more slowly than social expenditure. This is explained by significant proportional reductions since 1950 in the relative size of other areas of public expenditure in the UK, particularly defence spending, and it illustrates the fact that there is an opportunity cost to welfare state expansion, which comes in the form either of lower public expenditure in other areas or of a higher overall tax rate.

These aggregate data present a picture of fairly similar patterns of welfare state expansion within post-war Europe. However, once the aggregate statistics are pulled apart, they reveal a considerable degree of inter-country variance. For example, in both 1960 and 1993 Italy and the United Kingdom devoted similar proportions of GDP to social expenditure – about 12 per cent in 1960 and 27 per cent in 1993. But whereas in 1960 both countries allocated around 30 per cent of total social expenditure to old age benefits, by 1993 this proportion had doubled to 60 per cent in Italy, but increased to only 40 per cent in the UK. This demonstrates that similar overall rates of expenditure growth can conceal divergent trends in the distribution of social expenditure among different social welfare functions.

A low level of expenditure on any particular type of social protection does not necessarily mean that the degree of protection against that type of social risk is particularly poor. Luxembourg has consistently devoted a very small proportion of total social expenditure to unemployment benefit; in 1993 only 0.8 per cent of total social expenditure in Luxembourg was spent on unemployment benefit, compared to 6 per cent in France and 12 per cent in Denmark. However, the unemployment rate in Luxembourg was a trivial 1.7 per cent, compared with over 12 per cent in both France and Denmark. This demonstrates that variation in expenditure by type of benefit partly reflects the level of underlying demand. However, the different expenditure shares of France and Denmark, despite their similar unemployment rates, is evidence of different priorities in the distribution of social benefits.

Whereas the 'accounting' approach to social welfare expenditure reveals the financial inputs into the welfare state, the 'functional' approach can provide a better indication of the welfare outputs. Welfare may be defined according to many different criteria, but two that have been widely used in economic and social evaluation of social expenditure are the amount of poverty in any country and the degree of inequality in the distribution of income. There are many routes to poverty – for instance via unemployment, sickness, old age, or large families – and therefore the proportion of people living in poverty is a good composite measure of the overall effectiveness of a welfare system in protecting individuals and families from the many social risks that they may face.

The degree of income inequality in any society is an alternative, and in some respects a broader, indicator of performance of the welfare state. A European family may not be poor in an absolute sense of having inadequate income to purchase basic food, clothing and housing, and may not be poor relative to a family in a developing country, yet may have an income so far below the European average that they cannot adequately participate in social life. A highly unequal distribution of income, especially if the inequality is driven by large numbers with income significantly below average, suggests that the welfare state may not provide sufficient protection against social risks to prevent substantial social exclusion.

Measuring either poverty or income inequality in Europe is no easy task. Data are typically not strictly comparable between countries, and technical decisions about what income to include, how to define poverty, and whether to study families, households, or individuals, can all affect the conclusions. Atkinson has drawn together much of the evidence on income inequality in a comparative analysis for the 1980s and has concluded that the Scandinavian countries, Benelux and West Germany have apparently distinctly less inequality in disposable income; southern Europe and Ireland have distinctly higher inequality, with France and, to some degree, the UK and Italy occupying an intermediate position.[5]

When this finding is compared with the proportionate share of social expenditure shown in Table 8.1, it seems that lower levels of income inequality are associated with higher levels of social expenditure. This appears to indicate that a higher level of social protection, and the redistributive system of income taxation with which this is associated, is effective in reducing the level of social exclusion. However, a longer-run analysis demonstrates that the relationship between income inequality and the level of social expenditure is not so straightforward. In the 1970s, when social expenditure was rising rapidly in most European countries, income inequality was falling fairly consistently. In the 1980s, as the rate of growth of social expenditure fell, income inequality began to increase in most countries, but not in all. According to Atkinson, income inequality and the proportionate level of social expenditure were both virtually constant in Germany between 1980 and the early 1990s, whereas in the Netherlands and in the UK inequality rose over this period despite an expansion of the social sector. While it is clear that a well-developed welfare state has a general tendency to equalize incomes, it is also apparent that this relationship is not mechanistic. Some social expenditure may equalize incomes by transferring resources from

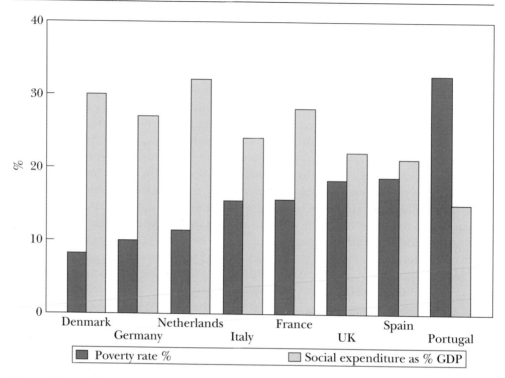

Figure 8.1. Poverty and social expenditure in Europe in 1990. *Source:* European Commission, *Social Protection in Europe* (Luxembourg, 1995).

rich taxpayers to poor beneficiaries, but the transfers can go in the opposite direction. For example, some services such as university education may be paid for out of general tax revenue but enjoyed disproportionately by people from families with above-average income.

Data on poverty show a similar pattern to that for income inequality. The EC defines people as living in poverty if they have an income of less than 50 per cent of the average income for their country. According to this definition, the proportion of the EC population living in poverty has grown from 12.6 per cent in 1975 to 13.7 per cent in 1988 and 14.7 per cent in 1992. This increase in poverty coincides with the general growth of income inequality in the 1980s, and in the slow-down in the rate of growth of social expenditure. Figure 8.1 shows, for 1991, the poverty rates across the same eight countries used in Tables 8.1 and 8.2. Again there is a clear, though not exact, relationship between high levels of social expenditure and low levels of poverty.

Development

The preceding discussion has shown that, within a general pattern of welfare state development in Europe since 1945, there has been considerable variation between countries in the timing and rate of expansion, and in the relative growth paths of different parts, of each national welfare state. These differences are a consequence both of the particular welfare inheritance of each country at the end of the Second World War, and of deliberate political choices that have been made since 1945 about how welfare systems should be developed.

No European welfare state emerged from the Second World War unchanged, but none was completely transformed. In Germany the institutional framework of the social insurance system inherited by the Nazi regime in the 1930s survived the war more or less intact, and the existing principles of contributory insurance were incorporated in the 1949 constitution of the Federal Republic. As part of the system of political checks and balances within this constitution, the administrative and financial responsibilities for the welfare system were divided between different agencies and levels of government. The Federal government became responsible for welfare state monitoring and regulation, for some aspects of capital finance, and for the administration of the unemployment insurance scheme; the provinces assumed responsibility for policy-making and planning, provision of some services and partial finance of social assistance; the communes undertook provision of some services and administration and partial finance of social assistance; and the voluntary sector was involved in the provision of many welfare and health services. In addition over 1,000 separate self-governing sickness insurance funds have been sustained or established to provide cover for different groups of workers organized by occupation or firm or locality, and separate pension insurance schemes have evolved at the regional level for manual workers and at the federal level for white-collar workers.

This complex network of local and national administration working in collaboration with a multiplicity of semi-autonomous insurance funds reflects the piecemeal growth and extension of the German welfare state since the introduction by Bismarck in 1881 of a contributory sickness and unemployment scheme for certain groups of manual workers. A similarly fragmented administrative structure exists in most European countries, but not all. In the UK the pre-war welfare system was fundamentally reformed between 1945 and 1948 according to the plan devised during the war by William Beveridge. Since 1948 most parts of the British welfare state, including unemployment and sickness insurance, pensions, family benefits and health care, have been administered and financed by departments of the central government.

Most European welfare states lie on a spectrum between the fragmented German model and the centralized British model, but even where the administrative structures are similar across countries, welfare finance and welfare outcomes can vary significantly because of the different priorities accorded to different social programmes. The EC has noted that systems of social protection within the member states 'appear to be very different: indeed so different that it may seem impossible to identify common traits and pointless to speak of the European welfare model. Each nation has followed a distinct path in the development of its social policy which has greatly influenced the precise characteristics of the present system.'[6] Nevertheless the Commission has identified some general patterns within this diversity, and suggests that EC welfare states cluster into four 'geo-social' groups.

The first group comprises the Scandinavian countries, where social protection is a citizen's right, and coverage against social risks is universal. Administration is centralized, and the system is financed primarily through general taxation. In Denmark, for example, taxes finance almost 90 per cent of social expenditure, with contributions from workers and employers covering the remainder.

The second group comprises the UK and Ireland. Again coverage is effectively universal, and administration is centralized, although the basic level of benefit is less than in Scandinavia and many benefits are means-tested. Health care is financed through general taxation, but contributions from workers and employers cover around 40 per cent of total social expenditure.

The third group includes Germany, France and the Benelux countries. These have all maintained some element of the 'Bismarckian' model of social protection, with coverage being derived from employment or family status rather than any more inclusive concept of citizenship. These welfare states continue to operate on insurance principles with benefits and contributions both related to the level of earnings, and with many quasi-autonomous insurance funds providing protection against different social risks for different groups of people. Because not all persons are covered by the social insurance system, these countries also have extensive social assistance schemes to act as a safety net for people who fall through the gaps between the multiplicity of separate insurance funds. These welfare states are financed primarily by contributions from employers and employees – these account for more than 80 per cent of social protection revenue in France, and for more than 70 per cent in Germany.

The final group is made up of the Mediterranean countries of Italy, Spain, Portugal and Greece. Here the distinction is more quantitative than qualitative; these countries also have inherited a mixture of 'Bismarckian' insurance schemes and separate social assistance provision for the uninsured, but the level of benefit is lower than in the third group, and the gaps in the safety net are much larger. It is these gaps that account for the high poverty rates and large degree of income inequality found in these countries.

This four-way categorization produced by the EC is useful in grouping welfare states according to their administrative structure. However, the welfare outcomes produced by different administrative systems may be more similar than this grouping implies. This is very apparent if we examine the single most costly form of social protection offered by all the European welfare states – the old age pension.

Interpretations

What accounts for the expansion of European welfare states since 1945? One view is that welfare state growth is just a natural concomitant of general economic growth. We can think of social protection as a luxury which people will wish to

In focus: The Evolution of Old Age Pensions in Italy and the United Kingdom

In 1989 old age pensions accounted for between 32 per cent (Ireland) and 60 per cent (Italy) of total social expenditure in European countries, and on average pensions made up just under half of total national welfare state expenditure. Pension expenditure has grown in all countries since the Second World War, but it has consistently been the single largest item in the welfare budget. There are, however, great differences between countries in the value of the public pension and in the way in which pension entitlements have been accumulated, and these differences are largely a consequence of distinct patterns of historical development. Consider the examples of the UK and Italy.

The first non-contributory old age pension was introduced in the UK in 1908; by the beginning of the Second World War all manual workers were covered by a contributory public pension system, and this was extended to cover the entire workforce in 1948. Since that date virtually all men from age 65 and women from age 60 have been eligible to receive a flat-rate pension. This was paid at a rate which fluctuated between 20 and 24 per cent of average earnings until 1980, since when its value has declined to 15 per cent of average earnings. Since 1975 workers who are not accumulating any additional pension have been required to pay into a supplementary public earnings-related pension scheme which can increase the total public pension to something over 30 per cent of average earnings.

Italy has had a compulsory pension scheme for manual workers since 1919 and for white-collar workers since 1939. Civil servants have been covered by a separate pension scheme since the nineteenth century, the self-employed have been provided for through their own pension scheme established in 1957, and specific occupational groups such as miners, electricity workers and professionals have additional pension schemes. In 1969 a 'social pension' was introduced to provide a minimum income for old people not covered by any other pension scheme.[1]

In both the Italian and UK systems the pensions are financed through contributions paid by workers and employers, but the benefits received are very different. Since 1948 the British public pension system has paid flat-rate benefits at a fairly low level – the objective has been to prevent pensioners slipping into poverty. The Italian pension system, on the other hand, has been designed with the primary intention of giving people an income in retirement which replaces the income they received in their former employment. After 40 years of contributions pensioners in the general scheme accumulate an entitlement to 80 per cent of their average annual

1. D. Franco and F. Frasca, 'Public pensions in an ageing society: the case of Italy', in J. Mortenson (ed.), *The Future of Pensions in the European Community* (London, 1992), pp. 69–95.

The Evolution of Old Age Pensions in Italy and the United Kingdom (continued)

earnings in the last five years of work, while civil servants can gain a pension equal to 100 per cent of their final salary.

Do these different systems mean all pensioners in Italy are rich while in Britain they are poor? Evidence on poverty rates suggests there is little difference between the two countries; in the late 1980s estimates of consumption expenditure indicated that the poverty rate of elderly persons was 33 per cent in Italy and 37 per cent in the UK.[2] There are two separate reasons for this surprising finding, and they both relate to the historical development of the two pension schemes. First, in the Italian scheme, although the full pension entitlement is 80 per cent or more of final salary, the actual amount of retirement benefit received by pensioners was only 27 per cent of average earnings in 1960 and 28 per cent in 1980, although it rose to 36 per cent by 1990. This low average pension level was a consequence of few pensioners having accumulated a full 40 years of contributions, and many pensioners being entitled to just the minimal 'social pension'. The rise in the average pension level in the 1980s reflects a growing proportion of new pensioners retiring with full pension entitlements.

Secondly, in the UK the consistently low value of the public pension has induced many people to make additional private provision for old age, mainly by means of contributions to an occupational pension fund managed by their employer. In the 1930s around one in ten British workers were members of an occupational pension scheme, but by 1956 more than a third, and by the mid 1960s around half of the total UK workforce was accumulating an additional pension entitlement through an employer-based pension scheme. As a consequence the contribution of occupational pensions to total pensioner income has risen sharply over time, from around 15 per cent in the early 1970s to over 25 per cent by the early 1990s.[3] In Italy, on the other hand, the generosity of the public pension system means that there has been little incentive to develop any additional form of old age saving, and private pension funds are practically non-existent.

Because the UK has never attempted to offer a public pension which replaces previous income, an alternative private pension system has emerged to service this need. The consequence is that although the Italian and UK pension systems have developed along very different administrative lines, the pension outcomes in the two countries are surprisingly similar.

2. P. Tsakloglou, Elderly and non-elderly in the European Union: a comparison of living standards', *Review of Income and Wealth*, vol. 42 (1996), pp. 271–91.
3. P. Johnson and J. Falkingham, *Ageing and Economic Welfare* (London, 1992), pp. 59, 115.

consume only when they have adequate supplies of the necessities of life. A common feature of luxury goods is that they have an income elasticity of demand greater than 1 – which means that as income rises, people will choose to devote a growing proportion of their income to purchase the luxury item. This is just what appears to have happened to social protection in Europe since the Second World War. During the 'golden age' of post-war European economic growth, from 1950 to the mid 1970s, all European countries had social expenditure elasticities greater than 1, with the Netherlands recording the highest rate of 1.63 (which means that for every 1 per cent increase in GDP, social expenditure rose by 1.63 per cent).[7] Although the rate of growth of social expenditure in general was lower in the 1980s than in the previous three decades, so too was the rate of growth of GDP, and this meant that the expenditure elasticity remained above 1 except in West Germany and Belgium, where social expenditure declined very slightly as a share of GDP.

The nature of the relationship between GDP per head and the proportion of GDP devoted to social expenditure in 1993 is shown in Figure 8.2. The positive relationship which is apparent here between the levels of income and social expenditure indicates that the association between higher incomes and higher social expenditure found for individual countries over time is also found in an analysis across countries at one point in time. Yet it would be inappropriate to conclude that welfare expenditure growth is a 'natural' outcome of economic growth, for two reasons. First, both the USA and Japan have higher levels of GDP per capita than European countries, yet they have consistently spent less on social protection (in 1990 the share of social expenditure in GDP was around 12 per cent in Japan and 14 per cent in the USA). Secondly, Figure 8.2 shows that there are large differences between the richer European countries in the proportionate size of the social sector. Italy and Denmark, for instance, have similar levels of per capita GDP, but very different social expenditure shares. Something other than 'natural' growth must account for these differences.

One way to analyse changes in welfare state activity is to decompose expenditure into three separate elements relating to the size of the population relevant to a particular social programme, the proportion of this population that is actually covered by the programme, and the level of the benefit received. An increase in any one of these elements will raise overall social expenditure, but whereas the first element is largely a function of demography (for example, more children will increase education expenditure) and so can be thought of as natural, the other two elements reflect a degree of political choice. Table 8.3 reports the results of a decomposition analysis of the change in social expenditure between 1960 and 1981 carried out by the OECD.

There are several points to take note of in this table. First, the rate of real social expenditure growth was, in all five countries, lower in 1975–81 than in 1960–75. This reflects the reining-in of welfare expenditure after the economic downturn of the mid-1970s. Secondly, there was consistent demographic pressure leading to higher welfare expenditure over the two decades covered by the table; this was mainly a consequence of population ageing which increased health care and pension costs. Thirdly, it is clear that the dominant reason for increased expenditure, particularly in the period 1960–75, was an increase in the real value of social benefits. Since most welfare state benefits are set by

Social protection expenditure (% GDP)

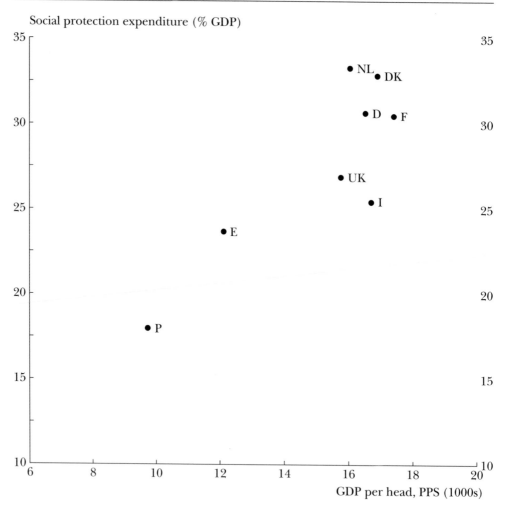

Figure 8.2. Social protection expenditure and GDP per head, 1993. *Source:* as Figure 8.1.

governments, this decomposition makes clear that the growth of social expenditure since 1960 has been driven by political pressures rather than any 'natural'
process of expansion.

A number of attempts have been made to identify the mechanism whereby
enthusiasm among some sections of the electorate for welfare state expansion is
translated into policies to widen coverage or increase benefits. Esping-Andersen
has interpreted broad differences in welfare regimes within Europe as a function
of underlying national politico-economic ideologies, while Korpi has used comparative quantitative data to argue that welfare provision is expanded most when
left-of-centre parties are in power.[8] However, these quantitative results are very
sensitive both to the way in which 'left power' is measured and to the time period
included; since the mid-1980s a curtailment of welfare state expenditure growth
has been a common policy objective throughout Europe, regardless of the polit-

Table 8.3. Decomposition of social expenditure growth, 1960–81

	Period	Annual average real expenditure growth (% p.a.)	Composition of % growth		
			Demography	Coverage	Benefit
France	1960–75	8.7	1.6	1.6	5.2
	1975–81	6.3	0.7	1.4	4.1
Germany	1960–75	6.6	2.3	0.2	4.0
	1975–81	2.1	0.4	0.5	1.2
Italy	1960–75	7.4	1.4	1.3	4.6
	1975–81	4.8	1.4	−1.2	4.7
Netherlands	1960–75	8.0	1.7	0.6	5.6
	1975–81	3.8	1.2	0.9	1.7
UK	1960–75	4.9	1.0	0.7	3.2
	1975–81	1.8	0.9	0.3	0.7

Note: The figures for demography, coverage and benefit do not sum exactly to the total for real expenditure growth, because of some minor omitted items.

Source: OECD, *Social Expenditure, 1960–1990* (Paris, 1985).

ical complexion of any particular national government. Moreover, Kohl has found that, for the 'golden age' period 1950–75, centrist governments tended to increase social expenditure more rapidly than 'pure' socialist or conservative governments.[9] While it seems clear, therefore, that electoral politics has affected both the speed of welfare state development in Europe since 1945 and the specific composition of each national system of social protection, it also appears to be the case that the commitment to public welfare provision has been embraced by parties of all political colours.

Assessment

Welfare states have undoubtedly been important elements of the political process in post-war Europe, but what impact have they had on economic behaviour and performance? Data discussed above show that, looking across the European economies, higher levels of social expenditure are associated with lower levels of poverty and a more equal distribution of income. Yet the substantial growth of social expenditure over time has not eradicated poverty – in fact the proportion of households in the EC living in poverty has risen by more than a fifth since the mid-1970s despite significant growth over this period in social expenditure. Does

Plate 8.1. 'Shrinking the welfare state'. Another *Economist* cover, this time from 2 May 1992. The long-term viability of public welfare provision 'from the cradle to the grave' has been the subject of continuous debate since the late 1970s.

this mean the ever-rising expenditure is going to waste, or even worse, that welfare state activity is actually exacerbating the problem of poverty and inequality? This is just what has been argued by opponents of the social chapter of the Maastricht treaty. The United Kingdom government of John Major successfully lobbied for an exemption from this part of the treaty on the grounds that further social benefits for workers would increase wage costs, make British business uncompetitive, and increase unemployment and poverty. These arguments are not new; similar concern about the negative consequences of welfare state expansion emerged during the debate about the welfare state 'crisis' in the 1970s.

The fact that earlier attempts to identify a negative link between welfare provision and economic performance produced inconclusive results need not mean that there is no negative relationship today. As unemployment rates throughout Europe have risen in the 1990s a greater awareness has developed of the way in which unemployment benefit may reduce the incentive to find work, or may even trap people in semi-impoverished unemployment because benefits exceed the available wage. However, when we remember that roughly half of social expenditure is received by retired people, and large parts of the remainder are directed towards health care, education and family benefits, it becomes less obvious how most of this social expenditure can significantly undermine worker effort and economic performance.

A recent British study has shown that the major function of the welfare state is to act, in effect, as a savings bank. Over the life course, the average individual receives back in benefits and services around 70 per cent of what they pay in contributions.[10] Any contraction of welfare state activity, therefore, would require a compensating increase in private provision against social risks. Private insurance may be more efficient than public insurance in some circumstances, but there is no necessary reason for it to be so. The private health care system in the USA consumes almost double the proportion of GDP compared with the public health systems common in Europe, but the American population fares no better than the European in standard measures of health and life expectancy.

Nevertheless, the fact that European poverty rates have risen despite an expansion of social expenditure does appear to indicate a clear failure of welfare states effectively to counter social risk. Yet in fact this rise in recorded poverty may be due not to incremental welfare state failure but rather to profound social and economic changes that have occurred in Europe since 1945. The four major causes of poverty in post-war Europe have been old age, unemployment, sickness and family breakdown. Since 1945 the incidence of three of these – old age, unemployment, and family breakdown – has risen sharply. In 1960, 10 per cent of the population in western Europe was aged 65 and above, compared with almost 16 per cent in 1994. Over the same period the unemployment rate has risen massively, for instance from the trivially low levels in 1960 of 1 per cent in West Germany and 0.7 per cent in France to 8.4 and 12.3 per cent respectively in 1994. The proportion of births occurring outside marriage has risen since 1960 from 5 to 18 per cent, and the divorce rate in the EC has increased almost fourfold over the same period. As a result single parents have become much more

---

In focus: When is a Crisis Not a Crisis?

In the late 1970s the welfare state appeared to be in crisis. More than two decades of unprecedented economic growth had been interrupted by the oil price rises of 1973–74, which ushered in a period of high inflation and rising unemployment. In 1981 the OECD produced a report on *The Welfare State in Crisis* in which it argued that the slow-down in economic growth was in part caused by the burgeoning welfare budgets in the developed economies. High tax and contribution rates needed to support large-scale welfare provision were blamed for reducing work incentives, and the expansion of public sector employment, particularly in education and health care, was criticized for drawing workers away from high-productivity manufacturing and into low-productivity services. Yet these negative conclusions were based more on rhetoric than on analysis. It was true that a speed-up of welfare expenditure in the 1970s coincided with a slow-down of economic growth, but there was no necessary connection between these two trends. It was equally true that 20 years of unprecedented welfare expansion from 1950 to 1970 had coincided with the most dynamic economic performance ever witnessed in western Europe. Furthermore, a subsequent quantitative analysis of social expenditure trends carried out by the OECD found that the presumed negative link between welfare expenditure and economic growth was difficult to locate. Among the developed economies the country with the worst economic performance over the period 1960–81, the UK, was also the country with the slowest growth rate of social expenditure, while Japan, the leading economic performer, also experienced the fastest expansion of social expenditure of any OECD member state. In addition, among the seven largest OECD economies, West Germany devoted the highest proportion of GDP to social protection over this period, yet had a better growth record than either the UK or the USA. Neither the level nor the rate of growth of social expenditure could be shown to have a consistently adverse impact on economic performance. The presumed welfare state crisis of the late 1970s was shown to be a myth.

---

common; over the five-year period from 1986 to 1991, for instance, the number of single parents in the EU rose by 20 per cent.[11]

These changes in demographic, economic and social circumstances have increased the size of the major welfare client groups several times over, while recorded poverty rates in the EC have risen by only about one-fifth since the mid-1970s. This indicates that the European welfare states continue to ameliorate many of the economic costs associated with major social risks. It also suggests, however, that there are limits to both the effectiveness of public welfare provision and the degree to which electorates will tolerate the higher social security taxes required by more comprehensive poverty-prevention programmes.

Bibliographical Note

There is relatively little comparative literature on European welfare states since 1945 that takes an historical approach. The European Commission's *Social Protection in Europe* (EC, Luxembourg, 1995) provides a very good survey of current systems of social protection, but says little about their evolution. A. Cochrane and J. Clarke (eds), *Comparing Welfare States: Britain in International Context* (London, 1993) is a good attempt to set current social policy in an historical context, although it is biased towards coverage of the UK system. There are a number of good essays on the period up to the late 1970s in P. Flora and A. Heidenheimer (eds), *The Development of Welfare States in Europe and America* (New Brunswick, 1981). Peter Flora (ed.), *Growth to Limits* (Berlin, 1986–87) is a four-volume study of welfare state development in a number of European countries which is packed with administrative and legalistic detail, but which says very little about welfare outcomes. There is a concise survey of the evolution of social protection in Europe since 1970 written in French by Daniel Lenoir, *L'Europe sociale* (Paris, 1994).

Notes

1. A. Milward, *The European Rescue of the Nation State* (London, 1992), chapter 2.

2. P. Baldwin, *The Politics of Social Solidarity* (Cambridge, 1990).

3. H. Glennerster and J. Midgley (eds), *The Radical Right and the Welfare State: an International Assessment* (Hemel Hempstead, 1991).

4. R. Klein, 'O'Goffe's tale', in C. Jones (ed.), *New Perspectives on the Welfare State in Europe* (London, 1993), p. 14.

5. A.B. Atkinson, *Incomes and the Welfare State* (Cambridge, 1995), p. 63.

6. European Commission, *Social Protection in Europe* (Luxembourg, 1995), p. 25.

7. J. Kohl, 'Trends and problems in postwar public expenditure development', in P. Flora and H. Heidenheimer (eds), *The Development of Welfare States in Europe and America* (New Brunswick, 1981), p. 317.

8. G. Esping-Andersen, *The Three Worlds of Welfare Capitalism* (Cambridge, 1990); W. Korpi, 'Power, politics, and state autonomy in the development of social citizenship', *American Sociological Review*, vol. 54 (1989), pp. 309–28.

9. Kohl, 'Trends and problems' (see Note 7), p. 324.

10. J. Falkingham and J. Hills, *The Dynamic of Welfare* (Hemel Hempstead, 1995).

11. Data in this paragraph drawn from: European Commission, *Social Protection in Europe* (Luxembourg, 1995); *European Economy*, no. 1 (1978) and no. 61 (1996); W. Dumon and T. Nuelant, *National Family Policies in the Member States of the European Union in 1992 and 1993* (European Commission, Directorate General V; Brussels, 1993).

9 The European Community – 1958 to the 1990s

Valerio Lintner

Introduction

One of the most significant aspects of post-war west European development has been the process of economic and political integration. During the first half of the twentieth century, the various European nation states that had emerged during the course of the previous century operated as largely discrete economic and political entities, each pursuing their own independent policies, at least to the extent that factors such as their size and economic power permitted.

It was very much as a 'Europe of nations' that western Europe had emerged from the Second World War. Yet by the early 1990s the same European countries had taken important steps towards establishing a common market among themselves, were on the verge of a monetary union, and were seriously considering forms of ever closer political integration and cooperation in a number of key areas. In addition, European societies have converged in very many areas, ranging from rates of inflation to fashions, architecture and eating habits. Moreover, the integration process has frequently dominated the political agenda, precipitating controversies and strong emotions between and within European nation states.

Thus European economic and political developments and policies have become increasingly conditioned by the process of integration in the continent. What is more, there is every prospect that over the coming years this process will continue, shifting the locus of policy-making away from the individual nation state and towards the supra-national level. It is with this process that this chapter is concerned. The chapter will first of all discuss the origins of the integration project, and will then proceed to analyse the progress that has been made in key policy areas. It will cover the development of the European Community (EC) from its inception in 1957 until the Maastricht Treaty on European Union (EU), which was signed in 1992 and came into operation in the course of the following year. However, the EC was not the sole organization promoting integration, the European Free Trade Area,[1] for example, being an important contributor to the process.

Origins and Structure of the European Community

A starting point in our analysis concerns the forces that have caused the EC to be set up in the first place and then conditioned its development into what it is now. Many of these are essentially political:

- a basic desire, in the immediate post-war period, to prevent another war in Europe;
- the desire, up to the late 1980s, to establish a capitalist bloc in western Europe as a bulwark against Soviet Communism, sometimes referred to as the 'cold war' approach to European integration;
- the possibility of the Continent collectively wielding greater power in international relations;
- the later wish of the newly established democracies in Greece, Spain and Portugal to anchor their political systems by linking them to established democratic states;
- the fundamental idea that cooperation, interchange, mobility and access on a Europe-wide scale was eminently desirable; and so on.

Others are more economic, for example:

- the desire to benefit from whatever rewards might be available from internal trade liberalization and access to a vast market (gains in economic welfare as a result of better allocation of resources, economies of scale, greater X-efficiency[2] resulting from increased competition, and so on);
- a wish to obtain any gains in efficiency that might result from increased intra-union labour and capital mobility;
- the benefits to be had from coordinating policies in various areas (despite the losses inherent in the Common Agricultural Policy, CAP – see below);
- the desire to protect the European economy from external challenges, for example from the Newly Industrialized Countries (NICs) in the Pacific Basin and elsewhere;
- the wish to follow 'best practice' (i.e. German practice) in macroeconomic management;
- latterly, the desire to recapture collectively some of the economic power and influence which has been lost by individual nation states as a result of increased economic interdependence, and in particular the vastly increased power of deregulated global capital markets (see below).

Be that as it may, the original European Economic Community set up by the six countries (West Germany, France, Italy, Belgium, the Netherlands and Luxembourg) which signed the Treaty of Rome of 1957, has grown, via the EC,

Plate 9.1. French President de Gaulle and German Chancellor Adenauer meet in Bonn in 1963. Activists call for the creation of a European *federal* state.

into the current EU of 15 countries. The United Kingdom, Ireland and Denmark joined in 1973, Greece in 1981, Spain and Portugal in 1986, and finally Finland, Sweden and Austria became members on 1 January 1995.

The original EEC had been preceded by the European Coal and Steel Community (ECSC). This was agreed in April 1951, largely on the instigation of the French federalists Jean Monnet and Robert Schuman. Ostensibly an economic arrangement, it also had the political objective of precluding another war between France and Germany by transferring an important element of war-related production to a supra-national body. The supra-national aspect is significant here, since it reflects Monnet's vision of a united Europe and is in contrast with other arrangements, such as the Western European Union military arrangement (WEU, formed in 1954) or EFTA, which were inter-governmental in nature. Thus the EEC can be seen as having developed directly from the ECSC.

The United Kingdom was not an original signatory of the Treaty of Rome, preferring to found EFTA instead. However, the success of the EC and the UK's own relative economic decline precipitated a UK application under Harold Macmillan in 1961. This was vetoed by de Gaulle in 1963, who was then instrumental in delaying UK entry until the early 1970s under Edward Heath. The UK's relationship with the Community has been a difficult one ever since, as is testified by two referenda, the antics of the Thatcher years, the opt-outs from EMU and the Social Chapter of Maastricht, and the recent emergence of the 'Eurosceptics'. An interesting point here is the crossover in the positions of the Conservative and Labour parties, the former from proponents to antagonists of integration, the latter from critics to supporters of the process.

The various enlargements of the Community have all been economically logical and largely successful, since, with the partial exception of the southern enlargement, they have all involved countries at similar stages of economic development. In future we may be looking at further expansion to include the east/central European states formerly under the control of the Soviet Union, and to an EU of 20 or more states. This expansion will pose more serious problems, since we are dealing with less developed economies.

During the period with which we are concerned, the European integration project has principally concerned economic arrangements, although political aspects have naturally always been present, and indeed have increased in importance in more recent years, especially in the context of the Maastricht Treaty. The institutional structure of the EC (and of the present EU) has been such that nation states have retained and continue to retain most of the power. The real decision-making power has always lain with the Councils of Ministers, which are inter-governmental bodies rather than supra-national ones. Of the supra-national bodies in the EC, the Commission has played a significant role in proposing and policing legislation, but as the 'civil service' of the Community it cannot take decisions. The European Parliament is not a legislative body, despite its name and the existence of some cooperation and co-decision procedures. The European Court of Justice interprets and enforces EC law (which, however, supersedes national law). Individual countries can still exercise a veto over fundamental developments, although decisions are being increasingly taken by (qualified) majorities. Enlargement and the need to reduce the EU's 'democratic deficit' will be strong forces for institutional reform in the future.

We now turn to an examination of the development of the EC in each of the main policy areas with which it has been concerned. The arrangements which form part of the 'acquis communautaire', the range of legislation and regulations contained in the Treaty of Rome and developed since then, can be conveniently divided into four categories: trade arrangements in the customs union, the free movement of labour and capital within the common market, the various common policies, and monetary integration.

Trade Arrangements[3]

We begin with the **customs union**, which is the most basic of the EC's economic arrangements. This involves establishing and policing internal free trade between members, that is EC members have to remove all tariff as well as substantial non-tariff barriers (NTBs) to intra-union trade in goods and services. Explicit tariffs on trade between EU members were removed relatively soon after the Treaty of Rome and the various accessions,[4] but in any case the importance of tariffs as sources of trade distortion has been greatly diminished on a global scale during the period with which we are concerned. NTBs have become more important impediments to trade, and some of these have been removed or reduced as a result of the EC's ambitious and reasonably successful '1992' programme.

The 1992 programme was established in 1986 at the instigation of the UK under Margaret Thatcher, with the Single European Act of the same year providing the enabling legislation, by amending the Treaty of Rome to remove the veto for Single Market measures. It is probably fair to say that the 1992 programme kick-started a period of rapid 'intensification' of the integration process, which eventually led to the Maastricht Treaty. It is also probably fair to say that this happened much to the surprise and horror of the principal UK actor involved.

Membership of the customs union also necessitates adopting a common external trade policy *vis-à-vis* the rest of the world. This involves both common external tariffs (CETs) and common NTBs, as well as adopting a common stance in trade negotiations such as the various rounds of the GATT. The introduction of the EC's CET was completed by 1968.

Largely as a result of the above and of the additional factors discussed in Chapter 7, the importance of intra-Community trade has increased substantially, as can be seen from Table 9.1.

This growth in intra-Community trade is particularly striking if one considers that in 1958 the share of intra-Community exports for the EC nine was a mere 34 per cent, and as low as 20 per cent for the UK.

Factor Mobility

In addition to the trade measures discussed above, membership of the EC **common market** also involves accepting the free movement of labour and capital within the union, while adopting common policies and stances towards inflows and outflows of labour and capital from and to the rest of the world. The freedom of movement clauses of the Treaty of Rome established legal rights in this area from the outset, but in practice intra-EC migration has been limited during most of the post-war period,[5] while exchange controls provided a barrier to capital mobility until the 1980s.

Efforts to increase mobility were intensified as part of the 1992 programme to complete the internal market. It is fair to say, however, that at present the mobility of capital within Europe and between Europe and the rest of the world is substantially greater that is the mobility of labour. In fact deregulated markets and advances in technology have rendered vast amounts of capital highly mobile throughout the world, rendering the delivery by governments of democratically expressed preference in economic policy very problematic (see the box on the 1992 ERM crisis later in this chapter). Figure 9.1 shows how, for example, portfolio investment increased between the principal EC countries during the 1980s.

Table 9.1. Share of intra-trade in total trade: imports and exports by member state (%)

	1980 Imports	1980 Exports	1985 Imports	1985 Exports	1990 Imports	1990 Exports	1992 Imports	1992 Exports
Original six member states								
Belgium/Luxembourg	61.6	73.2	68.6	70.2	70.7	75.1	71.2	74.8
France	52.0	55.4	59.4	53.7	64.9	62.7	65.7	63.1
Germany	49.4	51.1	53.1	49.7	54.3	54.3	54.7	54.1
Italy	46.2	51.6	47.1	48.2	57.4	58.2	58.8	57.7
Netherlands	54.7	73.5	55.8	74.7	59.9	76.5	58.8	75.4
First enlargement								
Denmark	50.3	51.6	50.7	44.8	53.8	52.1	55.4	54.5
Ireland	75.3	76.0	71.7	68.9	70.8	74.8	71.9	74.2
United Kingdom	40.9	45.0	47.3	48.8	51.0	52.6	50.7	55.5
Second and third enlargements								
Greece	40.9	48.2	48.1	54.2	64.1	64.0	62.8	64.2
Portugal	45.3	58.6	45.9	62.5	69.1	73.5	73.6	74.8
Spain	31.3	52.2	37.9	53.3	59.1	65.0	60.3	66.3
EC-12	49.2	55.7	53.4	54.9	58.8	61.0	59.3	61.3

Source: European Economy.

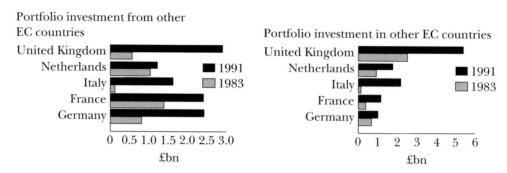

Figure 9.1. Intra-EC portfolio investment in selected European countries.
Source: European Economy.

While it is true that the actions of the EC (for example, the abolition of all foreign exchange controls) have contributed to the increased mobility of capital in Europe, it is also probably fair to say that this is something that would have happened even in the absence of the EC. On the other hand, the steps contained in the 1992 and subsequent programmes have concentrated on enhancing the mobility of people with substantial educational backgrounds and professional skills, rather than on mobility for the majority. At the same time, the control of immigration into the EC has been developed largely outside its official structures, as evidenced by the activities of the Trevi group of internal affairs ministers and by the Schengen Treaty, which removed passport controls between Belgium, France, Germany, Luxembourg, Spain, the Netherlands and Portugal.

Common Policies

By far the most significant of the EC's common policies has been the **Common Agricultural Policy** (CAP) which came into operation in 1964. The objective of the CAP was to provide a system of agricultural protection and subsidy designed to promote the development of an industry that was both strategic and very basic, particularly in the aftermath of the war when food was in short supply. This was to be done on a pan-European level by creating a single market in food, partly to promote integration and partly to mediate potential tensions between France and West Germany, both of which possessed large and influential farming sectors. The method chosen to achieve this was to operate directly through the price mechanism: minimum prices are set for most agricultural products above world market prices. These are maintained at the desired level by a tariff, the Variable Levy.

Prices are often set without much regard for what people actually want to buy, and so frequently they have been above the level required for intra-Community equilibrium between supply and demand. The result has been not only expensive food, but also surpluses, which have been mopped up by the EU's 'intervention buying'. These surpluses have sometimes been stored, generating the infamous 'butter mountains' and 'wine lakes' which scarred the public image of the EC for much of the 1970s and 1980s. Alternatively they have been 'dumped' (exported at below cost price) on world markets, to the detriment of food producers elsewhere. The CAP, it should furthermore be noted, has redistributed resources in a generally regressive fashion, i.e. the benefits have tended to be disproportionately skewed in favour of the better-off member countries and individuals. It has also arguably contributed to the continent's ecological degradation by promoting the indiscriminate use of chemical additives, since the subsidy system rewards quantity of production rather than the quality of what is produced.

The CAP has resulted in some benefits to European societies: Europe is now a substantial net exporter of food where once it was a net importer; food is plentiful, if you can afford it; agricultural incomes have been increased, however inefficiently and inequitably this may have been done; and there have been vast improvements in agricultural technologies and productivity, even at the cost of the environmental damage referred to above and of the threat to the purity and integrity of what we eat. The consumer has had to pay heavily and twice over for the policy, mainly through high food prices, but also via the EU budget, 60–70 per cent of which has typically been swallowed up by the CAP.

There have been numerous attempts to modify the excesses of the policy: for example production quotas, set-aside and price cuts during the 1980s, in 1989 in the wake of the budget reforms that doubled the size of the structural funds following the establishment of the 1992 programme, and through the McSharry Plan and the Uruguay GATT round. Reform from inside has proved to be difficult because of the numerous vested interests involved, and any change that has occurred has been precipitated by external forces. For example, the Community has agreed to cut agricultural subsidies to some extent under pressure from countries such as the USA, Australia and New Zealand during the Uruguay round of GATT negotiations. Over the last few years prices have fallen, surpluses have been reduced, and the budgetary cost of the CAP has been moderated to an extent. The fundamental problem lies, however, in the very nature of the policy which is based on millions of consumers paying to protect the interests of a minority of large farmers. Such regulation has been distinctly unavailable to other industries such as steel and coalmining, which, despite some national protection, have increasingly had to live (and die) in the free market.[6]

In examining the CAP, however, it is important to note that objections to what are undoubtedly its fundamental flaws are more strongly felt from a British perspective than they are in other member states. This is a policy which the UK did not help frame because of its refusal to join in 1957.

The CAP is of course not the only common policy to be pursued at EC level, although one could be forgiven for thinking that it is, given the adverse publicity that it has generated and the huge proportion of the budget that it has accounted for. Other major policies have been operated at EC level through the **'structural funds'**: the European Regional Development Fund (ERDF), which has become the main instrument of the EC's regional policy, and the European

Social Fund (ESF), the principal means of implementing the Community's social policy. In addition, important aspects of European industrial and competition policy, and fiscal, transport, environmental and fisheries policies have been increasingly conducted at EC/EU level, while the common regulatory frameworks established by the 1992 programme affect a wide range of aspects of economic and political life, from employment contracts to the quality of drinking water, from local economic development to industrial subsidies.

Despite its limited size (typically around 1–1.2 per cent of Community GDP), the **Budget** itself has frequently been an issue of contention, particularly for the UK, which has resented its position as a net contributor to the financing of the EC's policies and administration. It is financed from customs duties, agricultural levies, a proportion (currently 1.4 percentage points) of VAT receipts and a (limited) GNP-based 'fourth resource'. The 'British problem' has arisen from the fact that most of the budget has been spent on agriculture since the inception of the CAP, and the UK agricultural sector, although efficient, is relatively small in size (see Chapter 6). These imbalances were tackled with much posturing on a yearly basis, and frequently brought the Community to the verge of collapse, until they were stabilized on a longer-term basis in the late 1980s.

Monetary Integration

In recent years monetary integration has become the single most important issue facing the EC. It was not originally an explicit aim of the then EEC, and there was no mention of it in the Treaty of Rome. However, a single currency for Europe by the millennium is now envisaged in the Maastricht Treaty.

The limiting case of monetary integration is a complete **monetary union**. This is popularly conceived as consisting of a situation in which countries agree to replace their own national currencies with a single common currency, the European Currency Unit (ECU) or Euro. However, the important point about European Monetary Union (EMU) is that it necessitates substantial amounts of coordination or joint determination of economic policies at the supra-national level in order to function at an acceptable political cost. This has always been the case, but more so in the context of the greatly increased power of capital markets that has characterized the 1980s and 1990s. Amongst other things, a monetary union would involve substantial structural change in the European economy, especially as far as the weaker economies are concerned. Minimizing the costs of such change would require substantial convergence in economic objectives and outcomes among European countries. This requires formal policy coordination and cooperation at the supra-national level exercised through EC/EU organizations such as a European Central Bank. The critical point here is that this in turn inevitably involves some surrender of **economic sovereignty**, the ability of nation states to conduct their own independent economic policies. The economic and institutional arrangements implicit in a complete monetary union would mean the establishment of a *de facto* economic union. Since the surrender of economic sovereignty inevitably involves surrender of political sovereignty, some form of political union would probably follow, and thus in the long run the position of the nation state as we have come to know it may be called into question.

Specifically, a monetary union would necessitate some surrender of national control over important objectives of economic policy, as well as the tools required to implement these policy preferences. For example, a country involved in a monetary union cannot pursue a policy designed to reduce unemployment when its partners are involved in pursuing policies designed primarily to reduce the level of inflation. If a country wants to pursue its preferred policy stance it must first of all win the political argument in the union over the fundamental objectives of economic policy. The main policy areas affected would be exchange rates as a tool of economic management,[7] aspects of monetary policy,[8] and, since there is more to divergence than inflation, perhaps other aspects of economic policy such as fiscal policy and labour market policies as well.

The fundamental argument in favour of a monetary union is that it might increase the efficacy of European economic policy making. The grounds for believing this are twofold: that countries with a poor record of economic management would be able to adopt (German) best practice in the conduct of macroeconomic policy, and that the joint conduct of aspects of economic policy is necessary in order to attempt to recapture some of the economic sovereignty which has been lost as a result of increased international economic interdependence in general, and the vastly increased power of capital markets in particular. The arguments against monetary union essentially concern two areas: first, distribution, for any economic gains that result from the union are likely to be unevenly distributed, and the costs of structural change that are likely to result from a monetary union may be concentrated in some regions of the union;[9] and secondly, possible loss of national control over economic policy making and implementation. The key issue here is thus whether countries lose sovereignty by pooling it, or in fact enhance it through cooperation.[10]

In this context, we can now examine the EU's attempts at monetary integration over the last 30 or so years. These can be divided conveniently into three phases.

The Werner Plan

The issue of monetary integration first appeared on the European agenda at the Hague summit in 1969, partly as a strategy aimed at restoring stability after the political events of May 1968 (see also Chapter 7). The debate at the time centred on the extent to which Europe was in fact an 'optimum currency area' (an area in which it is possible and beneficial to have fixed exchange rates), and on the best strategy for constructing a monetary union. On the latter issue, there were two points of view, which came to be referred to as the 'economist' approach and the 'monetarist' position (not Milton Friedman's monetarism). The former, mainly supported by the Dutch and the Germans through the Schiller Plan, favoured a gradualist approach to EMU, concentrating on the promotion of harmonization and convergence necessary to prepare the ground for the single currency. The

latter position, canvassed by the Commission, France and Belgium through the
Barre Plan, may be regarded as a 'shock theory' approach, involving the introduction of fixed exchange rates as a *fait accompli*, leaving countries to adjust to
their effects *ex-post*.

The outcome was predictably a compromise between the two, in the shape of
the Werner Plan of 1970, most of which was adopted by the Council of Ministers
in March 1971 and which came into effect in March 1972. It provided for efforts
to harmonize economic policies, but also created the 'snake in the tunnel' system
of fixed exchange rates. The 'snake' consisted of fixing the exchange rates between the 10 participants (the original six plus the UK, Denmark and Ireland
which were in the process of joining the then EEC) within bands of ±2.25 per
cent. The 'tunnel' was the fixed parity of the snake currencies against the dollar
and other world currencies within the 4.5 per cent bands established in the
Smithsonian Agreements of December 1971. The overall objective was a 'monetary union by 1980', so it is easy to see that the plan failed, collapsing in the
wake of the economic disarray which followed the oil crisis (see also Chapter 7).
This placed national economies under severe strain, and EEC states responded
by pursuing policies designed to further their own perceived individual short-
term requirements. When it really mattered, European nation states showed themselves to be unwilling to subordinate their own interests to those of European
integration. Thus sterling left the snake in June 1972, Italy departed in February
1973, France in January 1974 and the project collapsed.

European Monetary System

The impetus towards monetary integration was revived in 1977 by Roy Jenkins
and Helmut Schmidt, and the EMS was set up at the Bremen Council of 1978,
coming into operation in March 1979. Its original objectives were somewhat
more modest than those of the Werner Plan, based on a return to more fixed
exchange rates as a means of stimulating intra-Community trade. The EMS basically
had two features:

(1) The European Currency Unit (ECU), which was the European 'parallel
    currency' and around which the Exchange Rate Mechanism (ERM) was
    structured. It was based on a 'weighted basket' of all the currencies involved.

(2) The ERM, which attempted to fix the exchange rates between the participat-
    ing countries and between these currencies and the ECU within a band of
    ±2.25 per cent (±6 per cent for weaker currencies such as the lira and
    sterling).[11] There was thus a 'snake', but this time no 'tunnel', since the ERM
    currencies could float *vis-à-vis* world currencies. The mechanism for main-
    taining exchange rates within the system of exchange consisted of agree-
    ments for supportive central bank intervention in foreign exchange markets,
    a limited reserve pooling obligation, and a largely redundant divergence indic-
    ator. This was backed up by some measures to promote policy convergence.

Prospects for the EMS did not seem particularly rosy at the time of its launch, and it encountered early instabilities. But to many people's surprise, from the mid-1980s it proved to be a considerable success. It promoted exchange stability in western Europe. There were only 11 realignments (12 if one includes the exit of sterling and the lira in late 1992) altogether, and none at all between January 1987 and the exit of sterling, while currencies outside the ERM experienced considerably greater instability. It furthermore contributed to lower and increasingly convergent rates of inflation in Europe, although it must be said that price stability was also facilitated by the neo-liberal consensus on economic policy in this period. Finally, it established an increasing role for the ECU as a private-sector currency in the course of the 1980s.

However, the EMS was weakened by the UK's refusal to join the ERM (although sterling was always part of the ECU basket) until 'the time was right' in October 1990,[12] and arguably by excessive reliance on German leadership. Its partial disintegration in 1992 represents a good example of the relative impotence of modern nation states in the face of powerful and deregulated capital markets (see the box below). Nevertheless, it paved the way for what was to follow.

Maastricht

The very success of the EMS provided the stimulus in the late 1980s for a debate on how the system should develop. The Commission's response was to set up the Delors Committee which produced the Delors Report in April 1989, advocating a full monetary union to be established in three stages. This spawned two Inter-Governmental Conferences (IGCs), one of which was on the subject of political union, which now came onto the agenda, and then the Maastricht Treaty, which was eventually ratified in EC member states after an often difficult process. It is important to note that the Maastricht Treaty deals with more than just monetary union, for it constitutes a wide-ranging reform of the Community and a significant step forward for European integration on a number of fronts. Its principal feature is the Treaty on European Union, which amends the Treaty of Rome.[13]

The Treaty envisages that EMU will be introduced in three stages. Stage One consists of the completion of the single market, increased coordination and cooperation in economic and monetary fields, strengthening the EMS, an extended role for the ECU and an enhanced role for the Committee of Governors of members' central banks. This stage began in July 1990 and was partially completed by January 1993, the ERM crisis, German unification and the European recession notwithstanding.

Stage Two essentially involves the groundwork for the single currency: all members were to be included in the narrow band of the ERM, and the European Monetary Institute (EMI) was set up to promote the coordination necessary for EMU. This stage began in January 1994, but has clearly been placed under severe

Plate 9.2. The European leaders in this cartoon by Nicholas Garland, which parodies the famous Victorian painting by Sir Luke Fildes (*Daily Telegraph*, 15 September 1992), seem very uncertain of the recovery prospects of the patient, 'Maastricht', during the course of the ERM crisis in September 1992.

pressure by the ERM crisis and the difficulties involved in meeting the convergence criteria (see below) in a recession.

Stage Three is then complete monetary union, with the introduction of the ECU (now the Euro) as the single currency for Europe.

A specific agenda has been prepared for this, with deadlines and convergence criteria to be met. The timetable involved introducing the ECU by December 1996, if a 'critical mass' of seven states (six if the UK opts out) met the convergence criteria. Failing that, December 1997 was to see the start of an automatic process leading to complete monetary union by 1999 among a minimum of five states. Additionally, 1998 should see the start of the creation of the European Central Bank (ECB, which takes over from the EMI, and is seen as the independent issuer of currency), and of the European System of Central Banks (ESCB, the independent conductor of monetary policy and foreign exchange operations). If these institutions are not yet in place, then national central banks are to become independent at this time.

The Maastricht convergence criteria consist of a maximum budget deficit of 3 per cent of GDP per annum, a maximum total public sector debt of 60 per cent of GDP, no realignments within the ERM, a rate of inflation a maximum of 1.5 per cent above the average rate in the three lowest-inflation EU countries

(4.7 per cent when the Treaty was signed), and long-term (government bond) interest rates a maximum of 2 per cent above the average of those in the three lowest-rate countries. The original timetable for EMU has now slipped somewhat, and many states are experiencing severe problems in meeting the convergence criteria. The ERM crisis has emphasized the relative impotence of the EU in face of international capital markets, and not least there has also been a considerable backlash to the whole idea of EMU, typified by the so-called 'Eurosceptics' in the UK Conservative Party. Nevertheless there remains a considerable impetus towards some kind of EMU at the beginning of the next century.

In focus: The 1992 ERM Crisis

A central theme of this chapter is the relationship between integration and the nation state in Europe, and the extent to which European integration is driven by the desire to recapture sovereignty that has been ceded to deregulated international capital markets. A good case study of the limits to the power of European nation states is provided by the ERM crisis of September 1992.

Before the crisis ERM membership had been a central feature of economic policy in most EU countries in the post-Maastricht attempts to prepare for EMU. In the UK this stance not only represented government policy, but was supported by the opposition Labour Party, the Liberal Democrat Party, the Confederation of British Industry and the Trades Union Congress. It was felt that exchange rate stability was needed to break the British experience of continuing devaluation and to force internal economic change.

At the same time, the 'judgement' of major operators in international currency markets was that some currencies such as the lira and sterling would find it problematic to stay within their ERM bands. They therefore started to sell lire and sterling, to drive their exchange rates down (and make speculative profits). Despite intervention by the Italian authorities, the lira was forced to devalue on 13 September. In the UK the Bank of England used its reserves to buy sterling (making huge losses in the process), and interest rates were increased (to 15 per cent on 16 September). In Germany, interest rates were cut to support the pound. Despite all this, sterling and the lira were forced to leave the ERM on 16 September.

The significance of this episode lies in the fact that international capital markets were effectively able to subvert the policies of democratically elected governments in major European countries, despite all the tools and resources available to national governments and despite the monetary cooperation between European countries that had been developed on an inter-governmental basis and through the EU. This would suggest that there are severe limits to the economic sovereignty of European nation states in the late twentieth century. It also provides a case for integration as an attempt to recapture some of this lost control.

Historiographical Debates and Conclusion

A central concern for students of integration has been whether the establishment and development of the EC/EU can be explained systematically by means of one or more over-arching theories. Some would argue that this is not possible, and that the events in the EC are a unique phenomenon which has been driven by particular national interests and particular historical circumstances. Nevertheless, a number of explanatory theories of integration have been developed, the most important of which are **federalism** and **neo-functionalism**.

Federalism consists in a belief that integration is driven by the desirability of a form of government in Europe in which power is divided between a central authority and several regional authorities, each exercising appropriate functions. It is fundamentally concerned with the achievement of political union within a supra-national organization. It is an overtly normative doctrine, and it is based on the belief that this is the best way of reconciling and mediating the variety of different ethnic, cultural, economic and regional groupings of which Europe is composed. The founding fathers of the EC (Jean Monnet, Robert Schuman, etc.) are considered to be **pragmatic federalists**, in that they believed that the objective of European federalism could be best achieved by incremental steps in areas where this was politically possible. Hence the establishment of the ECSC and then the EEC itself.

Neo-functionalism, on the other hand, builds on functionalist theories, according to which nation states will surrender control over certain policy areas if there is a net technical advantage in so doing. Neo-functionalism concentrates on the management of conflict in a pluralist society as the best means of achieving integration. Central to it is the concept of 'spillover', which is based on the idea that each part of the integration process creates the need for further integrative steps. These approaches to European integration do yield some interesting insights, but their usefulness as over-arching explanations of European integration is limited, since they have often been shown to be factually inaccurate, as well as of limited use in terms of their predictive powers. A recent and interesting addition to these theories, however, is what we might term the 'Milward hypothesis'.[14] This starts from the assumption that nation states have a number of purely domestic policy objectives that they wish to realize in the context of an increasingly open and interdependent world. States will attempt to use existing international arrangements to fulfil their objectives, and when appropriate structures are not available, they will construct new ones. Hence European integration in the post-war period. This debate is of considerable significance, not least for those interested in sovereignty, the future of the nation state and its relationship to the EU, as is discussed below.

Although it is probably not possible to explain its development by any single systematic theory, there are a number of features which one can highlight about it:

(1) It is a process that seems to be **cyclical** in its development. Since the signing of the Treaty of Rome in 1957, one can broadly identify phases of rapid

progress, followed by periods of stagnation or even reversal of the process. These cycles of development seem to be related to an extent to the economic cycle. Thus the period from the mid-1960s until the early 1980s were a period when little happened in the EC. Yet the mid- and late 1980s were a period of hectic development characterized by the implementation of the 1992 programme to complete the internal market and by the Maastricht Treaty. The early 1990s have been a period of slow-down, with the Maastricht process called into question by the deflationary nature of the convergence criteria during a recession, by German unification, by the power of capital markets and by uncertainty surrounding the democratic control of the institutions that are contemplated.

(2) The process of integration is essentially **cumulative** in nature, since each development provides the rationale and strengthens the case for further ones. Thus the completion of the internal market gave more weight to the arguments in favour of monetary union. It is also probably fair to say that there is a strong link between economic integration and political integration. Monetary union in particular is difficult to envisage without some development of integration in the political field.

(3) The process of economic integration is in some senses a **circular** one. Integration is to an extent a reaction to the growing openness and interdependence of the European economies, but at the same time it reinforces the processes that are making the European economies interdependent.

The key to the future of the European integration project in the immediate future is EMU. The prospects for this are uncertain, as has been discussed. However, a rump of the most economically advanced countries in the EU (Germany, France, Austria, Belgium, Luxembourg, the Netherlands, and perhaps Sweden and even the UK) seem both ready and willing to proceed within something like the conditions and timetable set out in the Maastricht Treaty. Various outcomes are possible, including a two-speed or even a 'variable geometry' Europe.[15] The view taken here is that it is by no means certain[16] that EMU will take place as envisaged in the Maastricht Treaty, but that in the long run such a development is likely. If and when this happens, we shall see a rapid increase in the pace of European integration.

Bibliographical Note

There are many books which deal with development of European integration in all its various aspects. The following provide additional reading on the themes of this chapter. F. Brouwer, V. Lintner and M. Newman (eds), *Economic Policy Making and the European Union* (London, 1994), deals with various aspects of the debate on economic sovereignty. C.H. Church and G. Hendriks, *Continuity and Change in Contemporary Europe* (London, 1995), discusses the recent history and future prospects of the development process. K.D. Dyson, *Elusive Union* (London, 1994), is a well-researched analysis of the process of monetary integration, while D. Edye and V. Lintner, *Contemporary Europe: Economics, Politics and Society* (Hemel Hempstead, 1996), provides a treatment of integration in the context of unity and diversity among European nation states. V. Lintner and S. Mazey, *The European Community: Economic and Political Aspects* (Maidenhead, 1991), is a useful introductory and interdisciplinary text on the EC. A.S. Milward, *The European Rescue of the Nation State* (London, 1992), and A.S. Milward, F.M. Lynch, F. Romero, R. Ranieri and V. Soerensen, *The Frontier of National Sovereignty* (London, 1993), are important works on the process and theory of integration and on the relationship between integration and the nation state in Europe. Further light on the politics of this is shed by M. Newman, *Democracy, Sovereignty and the European Union* (London, 1996).

Notes

1. EFTA was established in 1959, largely at the instigation of the UK, as a counterweight to the EEC. The original membership comprised the UK, Austria, Spain, Portugal, Sweden, Norway, Denmark, Finland, Switzerland, Ireland, Iceland and Liechtenstein. The UK, Ireland and Denmark left to join the EEC in 1973. Spain and Portugal became members of the EC in 1986, while Sweden, Austria and Finland acceded to the EU in 1995. Switzerland and Norway have both rejected membership of the EU.

2. According to the American economist Harvey Liebenstein, economic actors are faced with a trade-off between income and leisure, and competition forces people away from an X-inefficient position where they choose a quiet life and towards an X-efficient one in which they have to work harder to survive. This proposition is naturally impossible to test empirically, which is perhaps why it has proved so attractive to politicians.

3. See also Chapter 7.

4. The six had removed all intra-tariffs by the end of 1969, while new entrants were allowed transition periods of five years, and seven years for Spain and Portugal.

5. The main internal migration took place between the Italian Mezzogiorno (south) and Germany, France and northern Italy in the years immediately following the Treaty of Rome. Thereafter, labour shortages in northern Europe were tackled by importing extra-EC workers. In recent years, high unemployment has meant that intra-EC migration has been very limited in size – see also Chapter 11.

6. There is a shortage of alternatives available. The obvious other approach to agricultural protection is through some system of direct cash transfers on the model of the former UK 'deficiency payments' system, which would probably be politically unacceptable because of its tax implications and because of the transfer of direct spending power to the EU that it would involve.

7. This is potentially particularly serious if we consider the experience of, for example, the UK in the post-war period. Here we have the case of a country that has lost competitiveness steadily throughout the period, and to an extent has safeguarded its level of production, employment and wealth by a steady devaluation of sterling against the DM and other European currencies. Without the possibility of devaluation, future differentials in UK competitiveness would have to be borne at the cost of relative stagnation and/or outward migration.

8. The current ideological consensus is that inflation is the most important aspect of a country's economic performance, and that inflation can best be controlled by monetary policy.

9. This has led many people to consider some form of effective redistribution mechanism as essential within a European monetary union.

10. The key issue here boils down to how much power nation states really have at present. This is of course an issue that is not empirically verifiable. Based on the experience of recent years (for example the Mitterrand Presidency of 1981–83, sterling's ejection from the ERM in 1992, etc.), the author's view is that national economic sovereignty is limited in the modern world, and that there must be at least a good chance of some of it being recaptured through a process of pooling.

11. By the time of writing the bands had expanded to ±15 per cent, following the currency instability of the early 1990s.

12. Arguably the worst time imaginable, in the context of German unification and the coming recession.

13. This consists of five aspects:
    (a) a European Union, based on the EC and its institutions, a common inter-governmental foreign and security policy, a common home affairs and justice policy, again conducted on an inter-governmental basis, and a number of common policies in areas such as education, training, youth, public health, the labour market, industrial policy, communications, research and development, regional policy, environmental policy and development policy;
    (b) subsidiarity;
    (c) a Committee of the Regions, with solely advisory powers;
    (d) European citizenship; and
    (e) EMU.
    All this is to be supplemented by some limited institutional reform granting a little more power to the European Parliament, and some provisions for tackling fraud and ensuring financial rectitude (the Court of Auditors becomes a full EC institution). Finally there is the Social Chapter, a separate Protocol to which the UK did not initially adhere to, but which it has, since 1997, *de facto* signed up to. The UK and Denmark also have the right to 'opt out' of the provisions for EMU.

14. A.S. Milward, F.M. Lynch, F. Romero, R. Ranieri and V. Soerensen, *The Frontier of National Sovereignty* (London, 1993).

15. 'Variable geometry' refers to a situation with member countries being left, to an extent, free to opt in and out of various EU developments.

16. Under the prevailing conditions EMU may not even be desirable, given that (a) the convergence criteria are rigid and ideologically biased to the exclusion of real criteria such as unemployment and regional disparities; (b) the issue of the democratic accountability of EU institutions such as the ECB remains unresolved; and (c) there is a largely insufficient redistribution mechanism within the EU.

PART TWO: LONG-TERM FORCES IN ECONOMIC AND SOCIAL CHANGE

10 European Demographic Change since 1945

Dudley Baines

There was considerable demographic change in western Europe after 1945. This chapter discusses the causes and consequences of the fall in both mortality and fertility and the changes in the nature of the family. It will also discuss the degree to which the demographic behaviour of the different countries became similar, i.e. 'converged'. The causes and consequences of the important changes in migration patterns are discussed in Chapter 11.

Mortality

If fertility had remained constant, the population of western Europe would have grown at quite a fast rate. Mortality fell and net migration was positive. The main mortality changes are shown in Table 10.1 which shows life expectation at birth – a commonly used measure which discounts for the effects of age distribution. (See the box on measures of fertility later in this chapter.) By the 1990s, people in most of the western European countries could expect to live 8–10 years longer than they had only 40 years before. The main exceptions were Spain and Portugal where the fall in mortality had been very much greater.

Falling mortality was not new. It had started in some countries as early as the mid-nineteenth century and was well established in all western European countries before the Second World War. The main causes in the last 50 years were improvements in the environment (for example, better sanitation and drainage systems), better access to welfare and medical services, partly via their extension into the more remote areas, and improvements in diet and a reduction in dangerous occupations. Clearly, many of these changes were a consequence of the rapid rise in incomes in the period.

The greatest fall was in infant mortality. In the 1950s, between 20 and 40 of each thousand children born in the richer countries were failing to reach their

Table 10.1. Life expectancy at birth (years), western European countries, 1950–94

	Males			Females		
	1950	1970	1993–94	1950	1970	1993–94
Belgium	65.2	67.8	73.0	70.3	74.2	79.8
France	63.6	68.3	73.6	69.3	75.8	81.8
Germany (W)	64.6	67.4	73.1	68.5	73.8	79.4
Ireland	64.5	68.8	73.6	67.1	73.5	79.0
Italy	63.6	69.0	73.9	67.5	75.0	80.6
Netherlands	70.6	70.8	73.9	72.9	76.8	80.0
Portugal	56.3	63.7	71.2	61.5	70.3	78.2
Spain	59.8	69.7	73.4	64.3	75.0	80.5
Sweden	70.0	72.0	75.5	72.7	77.0	80.8
Switzerland	66.4	70.2	75.1	70.9	76.2	81.6
UK	66.2	68.7	73.6	71.2	75.0	78.9

Source: Council of Europe, *Recent Demographic Developments*, various issues.

Table 10.2. Infant mortality, western European countries, 1950–94 (deaths during the first year per 1,000 live births)

	1950	1970	1994
Belgium	40.8	17.6	7.6
France	34.2	12.7	6.1
Germany (W)	40.6	20.2	5.5
Ireland	36.0	16.6	5.9
Italy	56.6	25.8	7.3 (1993)
Netherlands	19.4	10.7	5.5
Portugal	87.4	48.7	7.9
Spain	59.1	17.2	6.9
Sweden	17.0	9.5	4.4
Switzerland	25.6	12.4	5.1
UK	23.8	18.5	6.3 (1993)

Source: see Table 10.1.

first birthday. By the 1990s, the rate had fallen to six or seven. Infant mortality (and also, to some extent, child mortality) was high compared with mortality at most other ages in the 1950s. It is not surprising, therefore, that it fell particularly far. For example, changes in the environment greatly reduced the incidence of diarrhoea and enteric infections. Nor is it surprising that the level of infant mortality fell more in the poorer southern countries, since the level was very high in these countries in the 1950s. By the 1990s, there was little difference between any of the western European countries in this regard (see Table 10.2).

In the mid-twentieth century, mortality rates of older people fell rather slowly. This was because the causes of death of older people, such as cancer and heart disease, were less susceptible to changes in medical knowledge and practice. Medical advances had more effect on infectious diseases – the main cause of death of younger people. But this changed in the later twentieth century when the mortality of older people began to fall relatively quickly. Life expectancy at age 65 in West Germany, France and Italy increased by about two years in not much more than 10 years after 1980, for example. In 1993, a 65-year-old Frenchman could expect to live until nearly 81 and a woman until 85. This relatively new demographic phenomenon had implications for pensions and welfare services, particularly since it was additional to the effect of the continuous fall in the number of births, which was already occurring. The economic effects of changes in the proportion of older people are discussed below.

Fertility

The fall in fertility was the most striking demographic phenomenon of post-war Europe. The most important features may be seen in Figure 10.1. They were a long-standing trend of falling fertility which was reversed in some countries during the Second World War, a brief post-war 'baby boom' in most countries, a steep fall in fertility starting in the mid-1960s and a slower rate of decline, starting in most countries in the 1970s and early 1980s, but only after fertility had fallen to exceptionally low levels.

Fertility change did not follow a common pattern during the Second World War. Fertility fell in Belgium and Italy, but rose in Britain, France and Scandinavia. It rose in Germany to 1943, then fell. We must remember, however, that in 1939 fertility was at exceptionally low levels in most western European countries. The reasons for rising fertility during the war are elusive but may be related to the reappearance of full employment in Europe. Illegitimate fertility also rose.

After the war, all countries, irrespective of the wartime pattern, experienced rising fertility. By 1950, total fertility rates in all western European countries were well above 2, and in several were above 3. Yet, by the mid-1970s, fertility was above the replacement level (of just over 2) in only three western European countries (Ireland, Spain and Portugal). And by the early 1990s, fertility had fallen to below replacement level in these countries as well. In other words, by the late twentieth century, all the western European countries were facing a long-term decline in the size of their populations. (The *total fertility rate*, a measure on which these calculations depend, is discussed in the box.)

The fact that the fall in fertility was universal should warn us against a simple explanation. Fertility fell in both Catholic and Protestant countries. It fell in most eastern European countries. It fell in countries whose governments had pro-natalist policies (e.g. France) and in those countries where the government had no such policies (e.g. West Germany). It fell in countries where the contraceptive

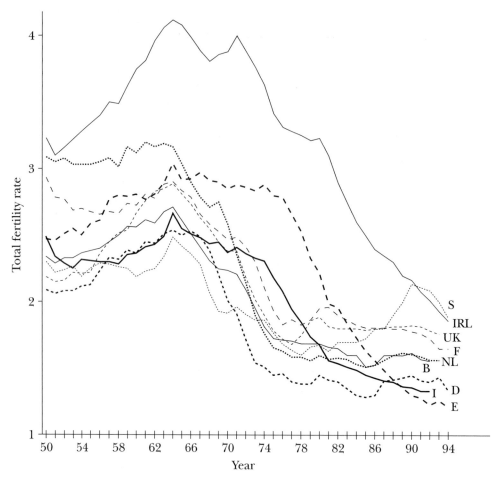

Figure 10.1. Total fertility rates in western Europe, 1950–94. *Sources:* G. Calot and
C. Blayo, 'Recent course of fertility in western Europe', *Population Studies,* 36 (1983),
pp. 349–72; Council of Europe, *Recent Demographic Developments in Europe* (Strasbourg,
1995).

pill was commonly used and where it was virtually unused. And, as we have
already noted, fertility had been falling in all western European countries before
the Second World War.

The Demographic Transition

The idea that countries pass through a demographic transition is commonplace in demography. Pre-industrial societies (such as Europe before the early
nineteenth century) experienced both high fertility and high mortality. In
consequence, population growth was low. Mortality was high because average

---

In focus: Period and Cohort Measures of Fertility

The simplest demographic measures are *birth and death rates.* They measure the number of births or deaths relative to the total population (usually shown as the number per thousand per year). They show what is happening to population growth in the short run. The problem is that *crude birth and death rates* may be insufficiently sensitive measures. A rising death rate, for example, could be caused by a falling birth rate rather than by factors affecting the number of deaths directly. If the crude birth rate fell, the number of children would fall, since each *cohort* (those born in a single year) would be smaller than the previous cohort. Hence, if there were no other changes, the population would become progressively older. In turn, the death rate would rise, since the proportion of the population in the older, more vulnerable, age groups would rise. Modern measures of *mortality* are corrected for age distribution effects. For example, the *expectation of life* (which could be at birth or at any other age) shows how much longer on average a person will live given the death rate that he or she would be subject to at each age. Similarly, the *total fertility rate* shows the number of births that would occur if the age structure of the women in the population remained constant and nothing else changed. These are called *period* measures. The total fertility rate (TFR) is often related to a *replacement rate.* For example, if the TFR is not above 2.0 the population will ultimately fall, since on average the population is not producing enough people to replace each woman and her partner.

Of course, period measures of mortality and fertility are abstractions. They do not predict, for example, how many children women will actually have in the future, only what will happen if the number of children women are having at each age remains the same. If women decided to have more children in the future, total fertility would rise. In contrast, *cohort* measures show, for example, the total number of children born to a particular birth cohort – e.g. to women born in 1950. Naturally, cohort fertility cannot be known until the women complete childbearing. In the 1930s, period fertility rates predicted that the population of many European countries would fall substantially by the early twenty-first century. This did not happen because cohort fertility rose – the 1910s and 1920s birth cohorts eventually had more children than they were predicted to in the 1930s. But women born in the 1940s, 1950s and 1960s had fewer children than period measures initially predicted, i.e. their cohort fertility fell.

---

income was low and resistance to disease was low. Fertility was at 'natural' levels, as demographers put it. This does not mean that there was no fertility control. There could be restrictions on the age at which people could marry, for example. Demographers mean that *within marriage* there was no *parity specific* birth control. Couples did not attempt to achieve a target number of children, avoiding births after the target had been achieved. Attempts to 'space' births, so that they occurred at more convenient times, were common, however. In other words, before the transition, most older couples were still having children.

As the rate of development increases, which in nearly all the western European economies occurred in the nineteenth century, the demographic transition entered its second stage. Mortality fell, but fertility fell only slowly, if at all. Fertility was still largely determined by a set of social attitudes, formed at a time when mortality was high, and when high fertility was necessary to avoid population decline. Hence, population growth rates were high in the early years of industrialization. In the final stage of the demographic transition, fertility adjusts, so that population reverts to a low growth rate. However, in this stage population growth is controlled largely by fertility – i.e. by individual behaviour.

The idea of 'modernization' lies behind the concept of the demographic transition. The causes of falling fertility are economic and social changes, and particularly those associated with industrialization in the long run – a rise in the proportion of the population living in urban areas, a rise in the economic status of women and a decline in the economic status of children. And most important, there are the effects of rising incomes, so that the opportunity cost of children in terms of consumer goods increases. ('A baby or a baby Austin', in British parlance of the 1930s, for example.)

On the other hand, it has proved difficult to apply the demographic transition model to the historical decline in European fertility. This was the reluctant conclusion of the most extensive research programme to date, the *Princeton European Population Project* in the 1970s and early 1980s. It is true that the technical reasons for the fertility fall may be identified in every western European country. But the timing and pace of the fall cannot operationally be related with a set of variables, corresponding to the features of the individual countries' rate of 'modernization'. Such variables might be average income, the proportion of the population that was urban or the proportion in agriculture, for example. The first country to achieve a substantial fall in fertility (France) did so long before successful 'modernization', defined in this way, had occurred. On the other hand, Britain was a highly developed country, with the most urbanized population in Europe, before there was any fall in fertility. In other words, different circumstances seem to have caused the same phenomenon.

A major difference in the fertility fall of the late twentieth century was the availability of reliable methods of birth control. They included intra-uterine devices (IUDs) such as the coil, voluntary sterilization, both of which came into use in the 1960s, and abortion, which was legalized in most western European countries in the 1970s. But it was the contraceptive pill, which became widely available in the 1960s, which has attracted the most interest. (In Germany, the decline was called *Der Pillenknick*, 'the Pill bend', referring to the change in the slope of the fertility curve.) In fact, the commonest birth control method was sterilization. But the availability of superior birth control cannot be a sufficient explanation. In the first place, the TFR had already fallen to not much more than 2 in several countries in the inter-war period, including Britain, without very much use of *any* contraceptive methods. This also seems to have been true of

Belgium in the 1970s, for example. Of course, modern methods of birth control allowed couples more easily to attain a target number of children. But efficient birth control seems to have had more effect on sexual behaviour than on fertility *per se*. In the past, many communities had successfully limited sexual activity among unmarried (and even among married) people. This control began to break down in many countries during the second half of the twentieth century. At the same time, modern contraception and access to abortion ensured that any increase in sexual activity, particularly among the young, was not accompanied by an equivalent increase in fertility. In turn, this phenomenon is related to changes in the structure and function of the family, which are examined below.

Fluctuations in Fertility

The basic pattern of western European fertility was a rise until the mid-1960s, then a fall. There was a post-war baby boom, but it was muted compared with changes in the United States, Canada, Australia and New Zealand (see box). A major change was that in most western European countries before the 1960s, there was considerable fluctuation in fertility rates. After the 1960s, most countries experienced a continuous decline. In the earlier period, the number of births in the short run was affected by economic conditions or political uncertainty. For example, fertility was inversely correlated with the trade cycle. But the fluctuations in fertility seem to have had little effect on the ultimate size of the completed fam-ily. Couples seem to have been aiming at a target number of children. Adverse circumstances postponed births but, ultimately, did not eliminate them.

Causes of the Fertility Fall

The main components of the fertility fall in western Europe give us some clues about its causes. First, there was no general increase in childless couples but families became smaller. For the majority of couples, desired family size seems to have been two, and by the 1990s, 80 per cent of all births were of first or second children. (Some simple arithmetic shows that if there are insufficient children in the large families to compensate for the single-child and childless families, population in the long run must fall.) The second component was that the proportion of the population that was married fell and the age at which people married rose. Thirdly, the average age at which mothers were bearing a first child rose. Around 1970, this was about 24 years in most countries. By the 1990s, it was 25–26. Moreover, those mothers who had a second child, had them very soon after the first, enabling them to complete their childbearing at a relatively young age. Older mothers were not, in general, having children, which was a fundamental contrast with earlier periods.

In focus: The Baby Boom

The post-war baby boom has attracted a great deal of scholarly attention. It relates to the increase in fertility that occurred immediately following the Second World War. In the United States, Canada, Australia and New Zealand fertility rose to the levels of 40 years before (see Figure 10.2). In the USA, for example, the TFR, which had been 2.2 in 1936, rose continuously from the end of the war to 1957, when the fertility rate was nearly 3.8, higher than it had been since the beginning of the First World War and only returning to its 1936 level in 1972. The effect on age distribution was considerable – the 'Baby Boom' generation. This meant, for example, that the teenage population in 1960s America was exceptionally large, with effects, for example, on popular culture and the demand for university places.

A famous explanation of this phenomenon was advanced by Richard Easterlin.[1] Easterlin argued that attitudes to family size were formed in

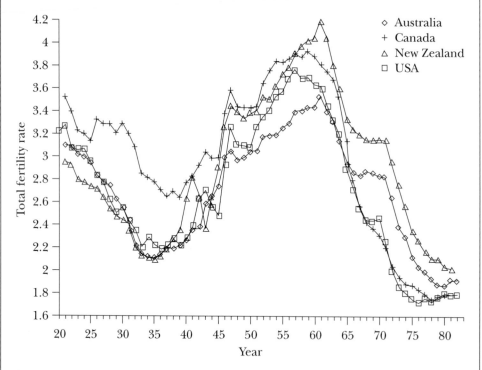

Figure 10.2. Total fertility rates in Australia, Canada, New Zealand and the USA, 1920–83. *Source:* M.S. Teitelbaum and J.M. Winter (eds), *The Fear of Population Decline* (New York, 1985).

1. R.A. Easterlin, *Population, Labour Force and Long Swings in Economic Growth. The American Experience.* Princeton University Press, 1968.

The Baby Boom (continued)

adolescence. He pointed out that the parents of the large post-war families had been brought up in small families in the inter-war period when children were relatively scarce and each child could expect a generous share of whatever resources were available and of affection. Hence, these children came to believe that large families were desirable. On the other hand, *their* children, who were born in the 1950s and 1960s, were brought up in large families where resources and affection per child were relatively scarcer. Hence, according to Easterlin, the small size of the 1920s and 1930s cohorts predicted the large cohorts of the 1950s and 1960s.

The Easterlin explanation does not fit European experience. Family size in Europe in the 1930s was low, as in the USA. But the post-war fertility rise was much less. Moreover, the main characteristic of the muted European baby boom, in contrast to the USA, was an increase in *nuptuality* (the number of people marrying). Hence, the European experience casts doubt on the accuracy of the Easterlin explanation for *all* countries. The European baby boom was most marked in France and the UK and least marked in West Germany. (It was actually more marked in eastern Europe.) The rise in nuptuality is relatively easy to explain. The post-war recovery in Europe led to rising family incomes. But there were few employment opportunities for women, particularly when compared with the experience of the war years. Hence, in the short run, the number of women who married increased. Contraception was less efficient than in the 1960s and fertility rose.

In short, the average woman was delaying marriage, but once married was bearing and rearing children in a very short time. On the other hand, there is no evidence that a large proportion of couples wished to remain childless. (In the 1990s, only about 20 per cent of married women in their late thirties were childless, some of whom were infertile or had infertile husbands.) The number of childless families did not increase as fast as the number of single-child families. In other words, we may assume that as late as the 1990s, most women wanted at least one child.

It is tempting to relate the fertility fall to changes in the quality and quantity of women's employment. With the decline of manual and the rise of service employment from the late 1960s, the employment structure for male and female workers became increasingly similar, at least for full-time workers. And, in many countries, the differential between the wages of full-time female and male workers was reduced. This was a striking comparison with the position in the 20 or so years after the Second World War, when women were routinely discriminated against in most European countries, by hiring practices and promotion policies. In other words, in the earlier period, when women expected to be discriminated against in employment, they would have to give up relatively little of their lifetime income if they decided to devote a large part of their adult lives to raising a family, even if the family consisted of only two or three children. But by the late twenti-eth century, the opportunity cost of raising a family was far higher. Hence, the optimal strategy for the majority of women who wanted children was to have a small family and to spend less time raising it. And the optimal strategy for women who were establishing a career was to begin childbearing relatively late.

Moreover, if there was a relationship between female participation in the paid labour force and fertility it was not a simple one, and it has proved difficult to establish statistically. For example, participation in many of the northern Euro-pean countries rose as fertility fell. But in the southern countries, where fertility fell faster, female participation remained relatively low. It is probably more accurate to consider trends in both female participation and fertility as only two components of a complex phenomenon.

The major changes in the economies of the western European countries since the end of the Second World War cannot fail to have affected fertility levels. The most important effect could be characterized as 'consumerism', but that would be an oversimplification. The underlying phenomenon was probably a desire among a very large number of people for individual fulfilment. The desire to have children, and for those children to prosper, was a very important part of that fulfilment, but it became only a part. (Families became less child centred and more couple centred – i.e. fewer 'King Children' and more 'King Pairs'.) Evidence for a change in beliefs in the late twentieth century may be seen in the decline of organized religion. Despite the extensive exposure of organized religion in the media, it largely lost the ability to control private behaviour. For example, many different forms of birth control are routinely used in all nomin-ally Catholic countries (including the most Catholic country in western Europe, the Irish Republic) despite Papal Encyclicals to the contrary. In fact, by the 1990s, fertility was on average *lower* in nominally Catholic countries than in nom-inally Protestant countries.

Convergence

A glance at Tables 10.1 and 10.2 shows that mortality differentials (including infant mortality) between the different countries narrowed. This is partly a con-sequence of improvements in diet, medical practice and welfare services – i.e. the convergence of GNP levels. There are also signs of convergence in fertility. The downturn in fertility rates occurred in a very short period (1965–75) in all coun-tries. That is, it occurred at roughly the same time in the high fertility (southern) countries and in the low fertility (northern) countries. However, fertility rates stabilized in most northern countries earlier than in the southern. By the 1990s, Italy, Spain and Portugal had relatively *low* fertility. These trends are summarized in Table 10.3.

Fertility convergence must have been partly the result of economic conver-gence, to the extent that fertility was related to economic changes. But conver-gence in behaviour and attitudes must also have occurred. This is not surprising.

Table 10.3. Total fertility rates, western European countries, 1950–94

	1950	1960	1970	1980	1990	1994
Belgium	2.24	2.52	2.25	1.69	1.62	–
France	2.93	2.73	2.48	1.95	1.78	1.65
Germany (W)	2.10	2.37	2.02	1.45	1.45	1.34
Ireland	3.23	3.75	3.87	3.23	2.12	1.86
Italy	2.49	2.41	2.43	1.68	1.36	–
Netherlands	3.09	3.12	2.57	1.60	1.62	–
Portugal	3.04	3.13	2.76	2.19	1.51	1.44
Spain	2.46	2.79	2.84	2.22	1.30	1.22
Sweden	2.30	2.17	1.94	1.68	2.14	1.88
Switzerland	2.40	2.44	2.10	1.55	1.59	1.49
UK	2.22	2.69	2.45	1.89	1.83	–

Note: see box for a definition of total fertility rates.

Source: see Table 10.1.

Information was freely disseminated across Europe by television and newspapers. Moreover, by the early 1990s, nearly 80 per cent of the population of western Europe lived in urban areas, although not necessarily in very large cities. Only 65 per cent had been urban in 1965.

The 'Europeanization' of fertility behaviour was only a late stage in a longer-standing phenomenon. In the nineteenth century, there were major regional differences in demographic behaviour, for example in the age and incidence of marriage, within the individual European countries. The differences were sometimes related to language differences, for example Occitan, Languedoc and Basque in France and Flemish and French in Belgium. Regional differences were greatly reduced by national educational systems, national taxation, transport developments and universal military service, among other factors. In 1870, differences in demographic behaviour were greater within countries than between them. By 1960, most regional differences within countries had been eradicated. The differences between countries were greater. After 1960, inter-country differences also fell markedly.

Changes in Family Structure

There were bewilderingly complex changes in the structure of the average western European household in the later twentieth century. In the 1950s, the typical household was much the same as it had been for many years. Many households were producing units, particularly in agriculture, which still employed some 20 per cent of the western European population. As late as the 1960s, marriage in most European countries coincided with the point at which children

Table 10.4. Illegitimate births per 1,000 births

	1970	1993
Belgium	2.8	11.6 (1990)
France	6.8	34.9
Germany (W)	5.5	11.9
Ireland	2.7	19.5
Italy	2.2	7.3
Netherlands	2.1	19.1
Portugal	7.3	16.9
Spain	1.4	10.5 (1992)
Sweden	18.4	50.4
Switzerland	3.8	6.3
UK	8.0	31.8

Source: see Table 10.1.

left the family home and set up households of their own. Most children were born within marriage, and the household usually included a male and a female partner.

By the 1980s, there was no typical western European family pattern. The proportion of single-person households had increased substantially. There were two main reasons: the increase in the number of older people and the increase in the divorce rate. By the 1990s, about a third of marriages in the western European countries were followed by divorce, each divorce creating about one and a half households. One effect of these changes was that, by the 1990s, only a third of all western European households contained children.

In addition, it became economically possible for young people to leave home at an earlier age than hitherto. In some countries, a high proportion of young adults in the 1990s lived in cohabiting (non-married) households. This was one area where there were still significant national differences, however. The proportion of births outside marriage increased, causing much soul-searching in some countries. More than 25 per cent of all births were illegitimate in Sweden, France and Britain by the early 1990s, although other countries had relatively low illegitimacy rates (Table 10.4). The significance of the growth in illegitimacy was often misunderstood, however. The stereotype teenage illegitimate births caused by promiscuity were, except in Britain, rather rare. Nor was the illegitimate birthrate necessarily related to the proportion of cohabiting couples in the population. Germany, Norway and Belgium all had high cohabitation rates in the 1990s but only a small proportion (around 10 per cent) of births were to cohabiting couples or single women. In general, in the countries where cohabitation was common, the fertility behaviour of cohabiting couples was similar to that of married couples – which is hardly surprising, since operationally, they were difficult to distinguish from married couples.

Table 10.5. Additional years of life expected for a person aged 65

	c. 1980		*c.* 1993	
	Males	**Females**	**Males**	**Females**
France	14.0	18.1	15.9	20.3
West Germany	13.1	16.8	14.6	18.3
Italy	13.4	17.1	15.3	19.1
UK	12.9	17.0	14.2	17.9

Source: see Table 10.1.

Table 10.6. Ratio of persons aged 15–64 to persons aged 65 or over

	c. 1960	**Predicted 2000**
France	5.32	4.24
Germany (West)	6.25	4.00
Italy	7.04	4.02
Spain	7.81	4.39
UK	5.56	4.24

Source: see Table 10.1.

Effects of Demographic Changes on European Economies

The most important effects of the demographic changes were a consequence of changes in age structure. A simple example demonstrates this effect. If fertility is falling, the *birth cohorts* become progressively smaller. For example, the number of school leavers in a particular year will be less than it was in the previous year. But in this particular year, the number of pensioners will not be substantially fewer than in the previous year, since they are the survivors of a large birth cohort. The effect of falling birth cohort size takes a long time to affect the number of old people. And in addition, the life expectancy of older people increased (Table 10.5). If, conventionally, we think of those aged 0–15 and over 64 as 'dependents', then in the later twentieth century, the proportion of producers decreased relative to the proportion of dependents. This could not fail to have economic consequences.

The most rapidly ageing population in the later twentieth century was in southern Europe (Table 10.6). The reason is easy to see. The fall in fertility rates in the southern European countries was more recent than in the northern. The older persons in the southern countries were drawn from larger birth cohorts than in the northern countries. Since mortality among older people had fallen to northern levels, the surviving older cohorts were exceptionally large.

On the other hand, the ageing of the western European populations did not *necessarily* mean that dependency was increasing. The health of a 70-year-old was very different in the 1990s than it had been in the 1950s, for example. The key problem was political, that is, finding a way of increasing the economic participation of the old, at a time when youth unemployment was high (see Chapter 5).

Other effects of changes in the age distribution of the populations were, in general, beneficial. Higher survival rates meant that the *human capital* embodied in education was amortized over a longer period than hitherto. (This effect was muted, however, because modern technical change implied that skills required continuous updating.) The fall in the proportion of children had, in principle, important implications for the provision of education. But, simultaneously, expectations about children changed, for example children had more access to tertiary education. Hence, the fall in the relative proportion of children in the population has led to an increase in education expenditure, public and private, rather than a decrease.

The most important effect of population ageing has been the increasing difficulty of financing state pensions. Most western European countries had instituted so-called 'pay as you go' pension schemes. Such schemes did not have a pension fund, although they used a vocabulary ('contributions' and 'benefits') that implied that they did. The contributions paid by employees and employers were, in effect, a tax. In return, individuals had a claim to a pension, the level of which depended on the number of years worked, and which was paid from future taxation. Since such pensions had minimal short-term costs, it is easy to see why the European governments from the 1950s were willing to introduce generous pension provisions. In France, for example, many workers could expect an index-linked pension equivalent to two-thirds of their average salaries. But the long-term problem became increasingly clear. The number of pensioners increased relative to the employed population. By the 1990s, 90 per cent of the European population could expect to reach pension age. The real value of pensions could only be maintained by increases in taxation, which would be politically very difficult to achieve. By the 1990s, many European governments were attempting to reduce their commitment by increasing the retirement age (Germany), reducing the payments (France and Italy) and partially privatizing the system (Britain). These reforms, although necessary, were politically very contentious.

Pro-Natalist Policies

Policies aimed at supporting families existed before fertility levels became an issue. They were initially part of the welfare consensus which developed in western Europe after the Second World War. The fertility decline alarmed some European governments because of the long-run effect on age structure. Hence they reinforced their pro-family with pro-natalist policies. Taxation measures, including tax deductions for children and child allowances, were widespread. State

Plate 10.1. 'It appears that I am a socio-cultural phenomenon'. Despite government campaigns such as this one which emphasised that 'France needs children', pro-natalist policies failed to make a significant impact in western Europe.

aid for nursery provision was increased in some northern countries, although private provision remained more common. In the southern countries family support was easier to obtain than in some of the northern countries, in particular in Britain, where there were massive changes in the conventional family. Alternatives included government information policies, of which one of the more famous was the French poster campaign showing a baby with the caption 'Il paraît que je suis un phénomène socio-culturel'.

Pro-natalist policies were largely unsuccessful. In the 1990s, for example, there were still large numbers of young adults in the European populations which should have predicted an increase in the number of births, but fertility rates continued to fall, that is, age-specific fertility fell. The reasons are not difficult to see. Most of the policies assumed that children and female employment were partial substitutes. Women were, understandably, not very impressed with campaigns that in some cases were aimed, however subtly, at sending them back to the kitchen. (In Germany, because of the recent history of population policies, such thoughts could not officially be articulated.) The cost of having two children in this period was estimated to be, on average, between a half and a quarter of a woman's lifetime income, depending on the cost of child care. Few governments offered compensating financial incentives. Moreover, labour shortages in some countries meant that some governments would not be in favour of policies that took more married women out of the labour force. In the mid-1990s, there seemed to be little prospect of reversing the fertility decline.

Bibliographical Note

The following references are relevant to this chapter.

G. Calot and C. Blayo, 'Recent course of fertility in western Europe', *Population Studies*, 36, 1983, pp. 349–72.

J.C. Chesnais, *La transition démographique. Etapes, formes, implications, économiques* (Paris, 1986). A major study of the demographic transition in almost every country in the world. Takes for granted the proposition that it was the pre-eminent demographic phenomenon of the last 200 years. An English translation was published in 1992.

D. Coleman (ed.), *Europe's Population in the 1990s* (Oxford, 1996). An excellent and sophisticated survey of recent changes in the main demographic characteristics of the European countries, written by several experts in the field. Includes much statistical material.

Council of Europe, *Recent Demographic Developments in Europe* (Strasbourg, 1995). The most accessible up-to-date collection of demographic statistical material. Contains some comparative historical data.

J.R. Gillis, L.A. Tilly and D. Levine (eds), *The European Experience of Declining Fertility, 1850–1970. The Quiet Revolution* (Oxford, 1992). Excellent collection of studies from a range of historical and sociological viewpoints. Good material on women.

D. Noin and R. Woods (eds), *The Changing Population of Europe* (Oxford, 1993). A general survey of the demographic characteristics of Europe, including the geographical dispersion of many phenomena – family, health, education, urbanization, position of women, etc.

M.S. Teitelbaum and J.M. Winter (eds), *The Fear of Population Decline* (New York, 1985). Short introduction to the fall in fertility since the First World War, and official reactions to it.

D.J. Van de Kaa, 'Europe's second population transition', *Population Bulletin*, 42, 1, March, 1987, pp. 1–59. A study of the fall in fertility since the Second World War which emphasizes non-material factors, such as attitudes to children, marriage, etc.

D.J. Van de Kaa, 'Anchored narratives: the story and findings of half a century of research into the determinants of fertility', *Population Studies*, 50, 1996, pp. 389–432. The best and most recent survey of research on the causes of falling fertility. Makes many difficult technical papers accessible to the non-specialist.

11 European Immigration since 1945

Dudley Baines

Since the end of the Second World War, very large numbers of immigrants have entered the western European countries. This chapter discusses the causes of the immigration, the changes in its character and the economic consequences to the receiving and sending countries.

Numbers

Strangely, it is not all that easy to measure the extent of European immigration since the Second World War. Table 11.1 shows the foreign populations living in the main western European countries as a first approximation. The table shows the number of 'foreigners' resident in the European countries at three dates. The total foreign-born population includes natives of other rich western European countries, who are rather few in number, but excludes illegal immigrants holding 'visitor' visas and also asylum seekers. But the main reason why it is difficult to be precise about the extent of immigration is that countries have defined 'immigrant' and 'foreigner' differently. For example, Table 11.1 does not include residents of former colonies who held the nationality of the mother country, as many did. In the early 1990s, the foreign population of France was about 6.3 per cent of the total population, while the proportion of the French population born abroad, including people with French nationality, was about 9 per cent. On the other hand, immigrants' children who were born in the country are sometimes considered to be 'foreigners', as in Germany or France, or as 'natives', as in the UK.

Table 11.1 shows that the foreign population (those born outside western Europe) grew significantly after the Second World War. In 1950, foreigners numbered about 5 million. By 1982 the number had risen to 15 million, and by 1992 to more than 18 million. This was 1.3 per cent of the population of western Europe in 1950 and 4.9 per cent in the early 1990s. By the early 1990s, Germany was the most important emigrant destination. Nearly seven million (8 per cent of the German population) were foreign-born. In addition there were at least

Table 11.1. Foreign resident population in selected western European countries (000s)

	1950	1970–71	1991–92
West Germany	568	2,976	6,800[b]
France	1,765	2,621	3,600
UK			1,930
Switzerland	285	1,080	1,190
Belgium	368	696	918
Netherlands	104	255	728
Total W. Europe[a]	5,100	10,900	18,400

Notes: [a]includes estimate for missing data; [b]includes ex-GDR in 1991–92 only.

Source: H. Fassmann and R. Munz, *European Migration in the late Twentieth Century. Historical Patterns, Actual Trends and Social Implications* (Aldershot, 1994).

Table 11.2. Foreign resident population (per cent of total population)

	1950	1970–71	1991–92
West Germany	1.1	4.9	8.4[b]
France	4.1	5.3	6.3
UK			3.3
Switzerland	6.1	17.2	17.6
Belgium	4.3	7.2	9.2
Netherlands	1.1	2.0	4.8
Total W. Europe[a]	1.3	2.3	4.9

Notes: see Table 11.1.

Source: see Table 11.1.

10 million ethnic 'Germans', many of whom had been displaced persons. France was the second most important destination with something under four million foreign-born by the 1990s (6.3 per cent). In fact, in most years, over a half of the total foreign-born population of western Europe was to be found in only two countries, West Germany and France.

Chronology

Chronological trends are less easy to see from point-of-time data, but we know that in the early 1960s some three-quarters of a million workers were entering the western European countries annually, and 300,000–400,000 were returning. By the early 1970s, immigration was between two and three million a year, with

Table 11.3. Foreign workers in main western European countries, 1973

	Millions	**Per cent of labour force**
West Germany	2.5	12
France	2.3	10
Switzerland	0.6	30
Belgium	0.2	7
Sweden	0.2	6
Total W. Europe	6.5[a]	

Note: [a]does not include illegal immigrants.

Source: OECD.

about 1.5 million returning. From the early 1970s to the later 1980s, immigration fell markedly, but return migration rates also fell (see below). This means that the foreign-born population of western European countries increased much faster before the early 1970s than subsequently, which illustrates another important difference. In the early 1970s, six million, or more than half of the foreign populations, were *migrant workers*, of whom 2.1 million were in West Germany and 1.6 million in France. By the early 1980s, only five million, or less than a third, were migrant workers, and far more of the immigrants were *dependents*, with all their attendant political implications. Immigration finally returned to a high level in the early 1990s. It was exceptionally 1.9 million in 1992, or 1.0 million *net of returns* in 1992.

Origins

The most important migration flows may be seen in Table 11.4. It demonstrates an important feature of almost all migration – the tendency for migrants to cluster together. We can see that three-quarters of Turkish and Yugoslav emigrants to all five countries were living in Germany. On the other hand three-quarters of the Portuguese emigrants and over 90 per cent of the emigrants from Algeria and Morocco were living in France. An important reason was historical – both Algeria and Morocco had been French colonies. In addition, particular nationalities were targeted by government recruitment agencies. In fact, immigrants were more closely clustered than is apparent in Table 11.4. This was because of the phenomenon of 'chain migration'. Immigrants need quality information to help them make the decision to move. Obviously, the experience of emigrants who have already left is a key source of unbiased information, which reduces the uncertainty that is inherent in migration. Consequently, emigrants tend to follow friends and relatives who have already moved. Chain migration means that it is possible that emigration from some villages and towns will be relatively higher than from others.

Table 11.4. Origins of foreign population in major receiving countries, *c.* 1990 (000s)

Born in	Living in					
	Belg.	France (1985)	W.Ger.	Neth.	Switz.	Total
Italy	242	253	550	16	385	1,448
Portugal	16	646	84	8	85	841
Spain	52	216	136	17	116	536
Turkey	85	202	1,677	203	64	2,228
Yugoslavia	5	51	650	13	140	864
Algeria	11	621	5	–	–	637
Morocco	142	585	68	157	–	951
Others	352	1,034	2,071	278	310	4,038

Source: various OECD publications.

The main changes in the nature of western European immigration in the 50 years since the end of the Second World War are as follows. Immigration was initially dominated by refugees. But economic motives began to dominate as the unprecedented growth of the western European economies led to labour shortages, which were met by immigration. Initially, the immigrants came from the poorer southern and eastern countries and worked in agriculture. But within a few years, more immigrants worked in industry. A second change was the shift from temporary to permanent immigration. Before the 1970s, a large number of the immigrants were temporary. The intention of many of the immigrants was to return home once they had reached a financial 'target' – that is, a certain level of savings. But in the 1970s, for reasons which are discussed below, the temporary immigrants became permanent. They formed families or their families joined them. At the same time, attitudes to immigration in western European countries hardened, and became even harder in the 1980s. The most recent change in the history of post-war immigration is that some of the countries which in the 1960s had high emigration rates, now have net immigration. This is because their income has risen, reducing emigration, and they now attract immigrants from poor countries to the south.

Labour Shortages

The fundamental reason for the immigration into the rich economies of western Europe was the rapid and sustained growth of their economies in the 1950s and 1960s (see Chapters 4 and 15–18). Growth created a high demand for labour that could not easily be satisfied. This was hardly surprising, given the heavy military and civilian losses during the war. There were four ways in which the wartime losses and the additional labour demand of the post-war period could be met: (a) by the natural increase of the labour force (more young adults entering the labour force than older workers who were retiring); (b) by an increase in the labour force participation rate, for example an increase in the number of married women taking paid employment; (c) by the movement of workers from less productive sectors of the economy, for example by moving out of the agricultural sector; and (d) by immigration.

The natural increase of the population was low. Fertility had been falling in almost every European country in the pre-war period – something which

---

In focus: The Economics of Emigration

In economic theory, emigration may be explained by the differences in the return to labour in the origin and destination countries. Consider a country with rapid population growth and a shortage of capital. Such a country would almost certainly have a high proportion of its population in agriculture, and would be relatively poor. Consider another country with a relatively large capital stock in, for example, infrastructure and industry. The latter country would have a higher return to labour than the first – i.e. wages would be higher. If emigration from the first to the second country were allowed, many people could significantly improve their incomes if they moved from one country to the other. In theoretical terms, we would also have to consider the relative abundance of resources. If a country had abundant resources, both labour and capital would be in short supply, so these countries would attract emigrants and there would also be inward investment. This is what happened in the later nineteenth century when both labour and capital were attracted from Europe to the so-called 'regions of recent settlement', for example, the United States, Argentina and Canada. But resources were not important determinants of emigration flows in the second half of the twentieth century. Modern industry and services are not very resource intensive. Hence, emigration tends to run along the lines of relative capital shortage.

This formulation, which is called 'factor price equalization', has an important implication for international trade, because migration of people and trade in goods are partial substitutes. If there were trade between the two countries, capital would tend to move to the poorer country where wages are lower, since the goods could then be made cheaper and exported to the rich country. Hence, trade would equalize the price of the goods. This would not occur without trade. But if immigration were allowed, it would reduce the price of the goods in the rich country. The prices would then be equalized through the migration. This means that, other things being equal, the greater the amount of trade between countries the lower the migration between them. (Remember, however, that it is easier to trade goods than services.) The increase in trade between western European countries is probably the most important reason why migration rates between the European Community countries have become relatively low.

had caused much concern among governments at the time. Moreover, in those countries where there had been a birth shortfall during the war, it had not properly been made up (see Chapter 10). This meant that the post-war cohort of labour market entrants was small. In other words, European populations were ageing. Nor could participation easily be increased. The number of women in the labour force had increased during the war and it would be fair to say that most women who wanted paid employment were already working. Labour *was* released by structural shifts in the western European economies, mainly from agriculture to industry. But, initially the labour released by agriculture was insufficient. Demand for home-grown foodstuffs was high and agricultural productivity could not be transformed overnight. In some countries, notably France and Germany, there were even labour shortages in agriculture, which in the 1950s were met by recruiting immigrants, only later did the bulk of immigrants go into industry. It was clear that immigration was essential if economic expansion was not to be accompanied by serious wage inflation.

East to West Emigration

As it turned out, the first large migrations into western Europe after the Second World War were politically motivated. About eight million people had been forced to move after the First World War, but this was nothing compared with the situation after the Second, when it has been estimated that some 25 million people were displaced. Not surprisingly, the largest number displaced were German, or ethnic Germans. The inflow into Germany was greatest immediately after the war, but continued under bilateral agreements between several east European countries and West Germany. Between 1945 and 1955, eight million people entered West Germany, and an additional four million moved from East to West Germany before the Berlin Wall was erected in 1961.

The flow of 'political' emigrants into West Germany meant that, despite the exceptional German growth rate, there was no need for the Germans to look for immigrants from other countries. Hence relatively few of the immigrants to West Germany in the 1950s came from the poor 'southern' countries. Their numbers started to grow quickly in the 1960s. Initially they came from Italy, Greece and Spain, then predominantly from Turkey, Yugoslavia and other eastern countries. By 1993 1.9 million of the immigrants in West Germany were Turkish nationals.

South to North Migration

In the late 1950s and early 1960s, European governments, and some private corporations, made bilateral agreements with some of the poorer countries of southern and eastern Europe (Turkey, Greece, Yugoslavia, Italy and Portugal). These countries had large undeveloped agricultural sectors and little industry. Average incomes were very low compared with those in western Europe. Bilateral

Plate 11.1. Southern Italian families in Bedford, 1955: an early case of post-war *intra*-European migration. These families from the impoverished rural south of Italy moved to Britain in the 1950s in search of work – which, here, they found in the Bedfordshire brickworks. Note the stylish Italian scooters, fashionable consumer accessories of the time.

agreements were critically important. In the 1950s, free entry of foreign workers – i.e. by non-Germans into West Germany – was very difficult. (Nor was there free movement *between* western European countries.) And some countries (such as Turkey) actively discouraged emigration. Hence, recruitment was essential because emigrants would leave the southern countries only if they were sure of obtaining employment and if they knew that a rich country was willing to accept them. These conditions were not difficult to meet in western Europe during the 1950s and 1960s.

As time went on, the European countries spread their net further. By 1974, France had bilateral agreements with Portugal, Spain, Morocco, Singapore, Senegal, Mauritania, Mali, Ivory Coast, Upper Volta, Togo, Dahomey and Niger. West Germany had agreements with Turkey, Yugoslavia, Greece, Spain, Portugal and Morocco.

German recruitment was minimal until the erection of the Berlin Wall in 1961. But by the late 1960s, West Germany was gaining 400,000 foreign workers a year, net of returns, the greater proportion of whom were Turkish. Twelve per cent of the West German labour force were foreign in 1973. And by this time, many of the immigrants had progressed from low-skilled jobs in agriculture and construction to arduous but more skilled jobs in industry. Five thousand of the 33,000 workers at the Ford factory in Cologne were Turkish in 1966, and 11,500 in 1973. At the same time, 11,000 out of 17,000 BMW workers were immigrants. By the early 1970s, a substantial proportion of the industrial labour force was composed of immigrants in every rich western European country.

Historical Associations

Not surprisingly, most of the emigrants from the colonies and ex-colonies went to the 'Mother Country'. Moreover, decolonization had a profound effect on migration. For example, most of the French citizens in Algeria, the so-called '*pieds noirs*', who numbered more than a million, returned to France after independence in 1962. A further million returned to France from the other colonies. And the non-European populations also began to move towards the old colonial power. The ex-colonies, French West Africa, for example, often remained within the sphere of influence of a European country. There were also practical reasons. Immigrants from ex-French, Dutch and British colonies spoke French, Dutch or English. Sixty per cent of the foreign residents in the UK in the 1990s were from former colonies or dominions. Even when post-colonial links were weak – as in parts of French North Africa – the language remained of great importance. French was, after all, the *lingua franca* of large parts of North and West Africa. There were also historical roots of German immigration. None of the main countries from which immigrants came had been formal German colonies, but they had certainly been within the German sphere of influence.

Periods

In the 1950s and 1960s western European governments (and their electorates) thought that immigration could be turned on and off, as if by a tap. They thought that when labour demand was high, workers would enter under short-term contracts and would leave when the domestic labour market weakened – that is, if unemployment rose. In other words, European countries were buying labour, not encouraging immigration. This belief turned out to be incorrect.

The End of the 'Gastarbeiter'

The First Oil Crisis in 1973 transformed the western European labour market. Immigrant recruitment stopped. Moreover, as unemployment in the western European countries rose, governments stopped issuing the work permits without which immigration was impossible. But the expected fall in the immigrant populations failed to occur.

In the late 1960s, when two to three million workers were entering the western European countries each year, about a half were returning. But changes in immigration policies meant that a second (or third) visit became problematic. Hence, most immigrants who were already living in western Europe decided to stay. It turned out that the western European governments lacked the political will to deport the immigrants, turning them into permanent immigrants. In turn, the immigrants would wish to be joined by their dependents. And from the government viewpoint, if the young male immigrants would not return home, family reunion programmes were desirable. It is now clear, however, that governments underestimated the numbers of 'dependents' who would enter. (There was another factor: governments were unwilling to enforce strict border controls because it would restrict the free movement of their own citizens, which was taken for granted.) The change in policy meant that by the 1980s, the composition of the immigrant populations had changed. There were more 'dependents', but many 'dependents' were working, leading to the 'feminization' of the immigrant labour force. The immigrants and their dependents could still find employment, of course, providing that they were willing to take relatively low-paid jobs. In other words, the interests of entrepreneurs and of governments did not necessarily coincide.

Permanent immigrant communities in western Europe were not new. For example, the Algerian community living in France (whose origins went back to the First World War) began to bring their families to join them when Algerian independence looked probable. In the UK, family immigration was the rule rather than the exception. But in the 1970s and early 1980s, the scale of family immigration into western Europe was unprecedented, leading to larger permanent immigrant communities and a new set of political problems. For example, until the mid-1970s, Swiss politicians had been able to argue that the country had 'no immigration'. This was a strange delusion, since Switzerland had had the highest proportion of foreign residents in western Europe since before the First World War. What the Swiss meant was that the immigrants only 'worked' there but did not 'settle'. What happened in the 1970s threatened the idea that Switzerland was a uni-cultural country with foreign temporary workers. There was a bitter anti-immigrant campaign, culminating in harsh immigration controls. By the 1980s, the number of foreign workers had fallen to only 180,000. In France, there was an attempt to deny French citizenship to the French-born children of immigrants. This proposal was aimed at the Arabs and led to an acrimonious debate on ethnicity. It was never enacted.

It was inevitable that immigration would fall in the 1980s. The number of dependents who could come via family reunion was finite. Moreover, despite reasonable GNP growth rates, western European economies had developed labour surpluses and immigration restrictions were further tightened. For example, a migration agreement between West Germany and Turkey made in 1964 had anticipated the free entry of Turkish workers by 1987. The agreement had to be renegotiated in the 1980s, to prevent more Turkish workers entering West Germany. The price was substantial compensation paid by the Federal government to the Turkish government. The Federal government also instituted a scheme to aid Turkish workers to return. Despite a promise that their German Social Security benefits would be honoured in Turkey, relatively few did so.

Inevitably, there was an increase in the number of refugees and asylum seekers. This phenomenon was not new, of course. The crises in Hungary (1956–57), Czechoslovakia (1968) and Poland (1980–81) had all led to a large number of asylum seekers, to which must be added the 4.6 million who crossed into West Germany before the erection of the Berlin Wall. But in the 1980s there had been a lull. The collapse of communism in the 1990s transformed the position. The number of asylum seekers entering western Europe rose from about 80,000 in 1983 to about 700,000 in 1992. (In 1992, about two-thirds went to eastern Germany.) Moreover, there were many more potential refugees from Africa and Asia, which created a new problem for the western European governments. By the mid-1990s Britain and France, for example, were routinely denying entry on the grounds that the refugees were in reality *economic* migrants (a nice distinction), and only Germany was accepting significant numbers of refugees. The attitude of the western European countries to refugees from the former Yugoslavia was a further sign that policy had changed. The bulk of the refugees were to be 'protected' in 'safe havens', not offered sanctuary in western Europe.

There were also changes in the provenance of immigrants in the 1980s. A fundamental change was the decline of migration *within* the EC. The first country to be affected was Italy. Italian emigration to Germany slowed in the 1960s – and, in consequence, immigration from Turkey and Yugoslavia rose. The newer (and poorer) entrants to the EC had to wait after their initial entry before they acquired free labour mobility within the EC – Greece, which joined in 1981, had to wait until 1988, and Spain and Portugal, which joined in 1986, until 1993. Recently, immigration from these countries has fallen and returns have risen. The reason is not difficult to seek. Income levels in the EC have converged, the southern countries becoming relatively less poor. By the 1990s Italy's income was above the EC average, and several of the once-poorer countries had net immigration, increasingly from Africa. In 1990, Italy probably had 1.5 million non-EU immigrants, many of whom were illegal.

Interestingly, the predicted (and politically worrying) mass immigration from eastern Europe, following the collapse of communism, failed to occur. In the early 1990s, immigration from the 'southern' non-European countries exceeded immigration from eastern European countries. Simple economics explains this. Growth rates were relatively high in many eastern European countries in the early 1990s, partly caused by inward investment from western Europe. Income differentials between east and west were, in general, much lower than, say, between west Africa and western Europe. Moreover, the poorest parts of eastern Europe, in the former Soviet Union, were very remote. On the other hand, western European governments are aware that the situation could change and that it would be difficult to deny entry to everyone. This has implications for future trade with eastern Europe and for investment policy. The implication of one recent change in the pattern of immigration is clear, however. European countries will never need another 'Gastarbeiter' programme.

Net migration within and between the EC countries has become relatively low, for the reasons discussed above. Regional income differentials have narrowed, the result of major structural changes accompanied by migration. For example, there were 30 million people working in agriculture in the Six in 1950 (29 per cent of the labour force). In 20 years the number had fallen to just over eight million (11 per cent of the labour force). In fact, the only large region within the Six with consistent net out-migration is the one that has remained relatively poor, the Italian South. By the 1990s movement across EC borders was higher than it had ever been, but *net* migration between EC countries was low. In fact, net migration rates between EC countries in the 1990s were lower than net immigration into the EC, when immigration was at its peak in the early 1970s. Low net migration was a major reason why it was possible to negotiate an open-border policy within much of the EC under the Schengen Agreement.

European Immigration in Long-Run Perspective

Before the First World War most European countries, with the exception of France, Germany and Switzerland, were characterized by emigration rather than immigration. Hence, for most countries, the immigration experience following the Second World War was a historical reversal. On the other hand, the greatest number of immigrants were going to the countries which had immigration before the First World War, rather than emigration. The reasons for this phenomenon are complex, but in the German case they stem from the long-standing dominance of the German economy in Europe, in both size and growth rate. In the French case the reason stems from the exceptionally low natural growth rate of the population, also of very long standing. The number of immigrants in the French labour force was the same in 1936 as in the early 1990s.

The Effects of Immigration

High levels of immigration affected the age structure of the western European countries. The immigrants had a far larger proportion of young adults than in the general population, which meant that the labour force was relatively larger and younger than it otherwise would have been. And since the immigrants' upbringing had occurred in another country, they were a free gift of capital to the European economies. They arrived at the peak of their producing and consuming power.

It was expected at one time that immigrants, once they started to settle and form families, would affect the population growth rate. This was an important consideration because the population of all the western European countries was ageing, raising among other problems the spectre that the state pension schemes could not be financed in the long run (see Chapter 10). Immigration could marginally increase the population growth rate, since fertility in most of the emigrant countries was higher than in western Europe. But the effect was limited. Immigrant fertility tended to fall to the native level in one generation, that is, to below the replacement rate. Hence, immigration would have a major effect on the age structure problem only if the rate increased. But in the 1980s and 1990s, even the *current* level of immigration was causing political problems, particularly in Germany, and there was no possibility of increasing that level of immigration.

Conversely, emigration reduced the population growth rate of the source countries and made their labour force older. But most of these countries had a labour force growing at nearly 2 per cent per annum. It is unlikely, therefore, that emigration harmed these economies, unless the emigrants were particularly well educated, with exceptional skills. There is little evidence that this was the case.

On the other hand, emigration was a major source of foreign exchange for many countries because of remittances. It is known that remittances were very large, but not how large. (The estimate that $2.5 billion, or about $400 for each worker, was remitted from western Europe in 1972 is probably an underestimate.) There has been some controversy about the effects of remittances. Obviously, remittances allowed the countries from which the emigrants came to import more than they otherwise would have done. In 1973, remittances were thought to be equivalent to 47 per cent of Turkish, 37 per cent of Portuguese and 24 per cent of Greek exports. Many villages in these countries depended on them. The long-run effect on the economy depended on whether the remittances were consumed or invested. There is evidence from several countries that much of the remittances were put into private housing. Housing provided local employment but not necessarily the industrial investment that the governments of these countries wanted. Attempts to persuade the emigrants to place their remittances in government savings banks were not very successful. Moreover, as immigration became more permanent, remittances fell (see box).

There is little doubt that wages would have been higher in western Europe if there had been no immigration. But, in the main, the immigrants took jobs in industry and services that the natives did not want. In other words, immigration allowed some of the natives to move into easier, more pleasant jobs. The precise

---

In focus: Return Migration and Remittances

A 1988 German study interviewed 721 Turkish families. It found that an expressed desire to return was correlated with remittances, with low savings in Germany and with property in Turkey. 'Staying' was correlated with higher savings and lower remittances. In other words, the study suggested that, as return migration to Turkey fell, the flow of remittances into the Turkish economy from Germany would also fall.

effect on individual incomes would depend on how far the labour market was segmented. Workers, say, the unskilled, who could not obtain higher paid jobs, would be in direct competition with immigrants and their wages would be squeezed. But the rest of the labour force would benefit because immigration would reduce the cost of the goods and services without threatening jobs.

This is roughly what happened in most European countries. It is not surprising that attacks on immigration by the less well-off, sometimes orchestrated by politicians, became commonplace when jobs became scarce in the 1980s. This is why prejudice against immigrants increased when returns fell and family reunion increased. (For example, single immigrants who returned had made virtually no demands on welfare services, but young families did.) The situation was not helped by the tendency for immigrants to cluster in particular localities – a consequence of chain migration. In addition, in some countries the local authorities tended to house the poorer immigrants in particular housing estates which made them more conspicuous and more likely to political attack, as 'welfare scroungers' – charges which several studies showed to be unjustified. But it is also clear that a second-generation problem developed among certain immigrant groups. Studies have quantified the alienation of second-generation Arabs in France and second-generation Turks in Germany. They show that these groups had relatively low school attendance, low skills and relatively high unemployment. On the other hand, other second- and third-generation immigrants have done as well or better than the native populations. An important factor in the success of some groups has been the ability to develop immigrant-owned enterprises.

Some countries, the Netherlands, for example, attempted to forestall political attacks on immigration through housing policies that distributed the immigrants (from the Antilles and Surinam) more evenly through the country. This policy failed, not least because the immigrants were drawn to areas where a high proportion of their compatriots were already settled.

Bibliographical Note

The following references are relevant to this chapter.

R. Cohen (ed.), *The Encyclopedia of Immigrant Groups* (Cambridge, 1995). An excellent collection of short authoritative chapters. The chapters concerning western European immigration are very informative.

Council of Europe, *Recent Demographic Development in Europe* (Strasbourg, 1995). The most recent and accessible collection of relevant data.

H. Fassmann and R. Munz, *European Migration in the Late Twentieth Century. Historical Patterns, Actual Trends and Social Implications* (Aldershot, 1994). A collection of chapters, giving an up-to-date non-technical description and analysis of the effects of recent east and west European migration patterns.

H. Giersch (ed.), *Economic Aspects of International Migration* (Berlin, 1994). A collection of articles on recent migration movements, not all about Europe. Some papers are very technical.

L.P. Moch, *Moving Europeans. Migration in Western Europe since 1650* (Bloomington, Indiana, 1992). A good introduction to the causes of the changes in migration patterns in the last 300 years.

J. Salt, *Migration and Population Change in Europe* (Geneva, 1993). A short general report written for a United Nations agency.

K.F. Zimmermann (ed.), *Migration and Economic Development* (Berlin, 1992). Another collection of articles concerning aspects of contemporary migration patterns. Some chapters are very technical.

12 Education

Martin McLean

Educational reform throughout western Europe in the 50 years after 1945 was a response to very similar demands for expanding provision to satisfy perceived labour market requirements and to meet social aspirations for educational opportunity. Much was promised by governments of the major countries of Europe at the end of the Second World War. Yet little happened until the 1960s. When change did come it reflected differing and often ancient national traditions and produced new structures with almost as much variation as those they had replaced. European educational systems diverged in the 1990s as much as they had done a century earlier.

This chapter will focus mainly on three countries – France, Germany and Britain – because each adopted a different approach to educational change and the reform project in each was mirrored in other European nations. France and Germany, in the years since 1945, have been at the centre of western European economic development. Broadly, French policy was typified by strong centralized state control and the orientation of education to the economic needs of the wider society as identified by the central government. In Germany, education was organized by individual states and maintained strong historical traits, while British localism, ostensibly with parallels to Germany, was associated with rather different traditions of secondary and higher education which were relatively untouched by the continental collectivist tradition which influenced Germany as well as France.

Post-War Issues of Educational Reform

State education throughout Europe was largely a nineteenth century innovation. While churches, in some cases aided by monarchs, had achieved widespread primary education in the seventeenth and eighteenth centuries in parts of Germany, Scandinavia, Switzerland and Scotland, in France, England and Wales and other European countries governments took the lead in laws and financial aid of the 1800s which permitted the achievement of universal, free and compulsory elementary schooling before the end of the century.

The question across the major countries of Europe after 1945 was how to provide *secondary* education for all. Universal and, indeed, common secondary education was not an invention of the second half of the twentieth century. It had begun in the United States in the nineteenth century and was close to completion by the first 10 years of the twentieth century. But in western Europe it was only in Sweden in 1948 that the common lower secondary year school was adopted as policy in the immediate post-war period.

The starting point was not the same. In most countries there had been some higher primary classes for those completing elementary school about the age of 12 since the late nineteenth century. In France and the UK, pressure had been placed on governments to introduce universal secondary schooling since the end of the First World War. This led to landmark policy statements at the end of the Second World War. The 1944 Education Act in England and Wales (with equivalents following in Scotland and Northern Ireland) led to secondary education for all – but in different kinds of schools – in the late 1940s. In France, the 1947 Langevin–Wallon Report was accepted in principle by the main political parties but its recommendation of universal secondary school was not translated into law until 1959. The debate in both countries from the early 1960s shifted from the desirability of universal secondary education to the ideal of common schools for students of all ranges of educational attainment and occupational futures.

The divide on this matter between France and the United Kingdom on the one side and Germany on the other involves other countries. The Netherlands, Austria, Switzerland and Luxembourg continue to maintain differentiated lower secondary schools similar to Germany. Almost all other western European countries have common lower secondary schooling. But while Britain adopted a pattern of 11–18 comprehensive schools, most other countries made a distinction between the common lower secondary school up to the age of 14, 15 or 16 and different kinds of upper secondary education – vocational as well as academic. This was the French pattern and the processes by which France reached this structure may have wider relevance.

In contrast, the main approaches to vocational education had been established in the nineteenth century. The apparent superiority of some historic national approaches was given prominence by some commentators in the 1970s and 1980s. But the main lines of French state-dominated training of young workers, employer control of on-the-job training in Germany and a rather less formal version of the German system in Britain changed little in the twentieth century. The issues were mainly about how to reconcile academic and vocational upper secondary education or, in Britain, how to resurrect an apprenticeship system which had begun to wither in the mid-twentieth century.

Higher education expansion occurred everywhere in the 1960s, though in Britain it took a second spurt from the late 1980s to reach the norm of 30–40 per cent of the age group in higher education institutions. Expansion raised similar issues as with secondary schooling. How could 30 per cent or more of the age group be given the same kind of education as had been enjoyed previously by only 5–10 per cent? The responses varied, reflecting differences in national traditions as much as in current functions of universities. As in other areas of education, nineteenth century national ghosts continued to haunt late twentieth century reformers.

France

Nineteenth-Century Origins

In France there was a significant difference from the European pattern of gradual involvement of the state in education. The élite sector of secondary schools and higher education was built on the radical reforms of the Revolutionary and Napoleonic period (1789–1815) and when universal primary schooling became a reality in the late nineteenth century the Catholic Church, unlike in other countries, was seen as a rival rather than a partner.

Governments of the post-1789 revolutionary period had proposed widespread schooling, and the Guizot Law of 1833 had attempted but failed to widen provision extensively. A series of elementary school laws of the 1880s were designed to install the authority of governments of the Third Republic across a diverse French countryside against the very real enemies of the Catholic Church and supporters of the monarchy. So state school consciously and effectively spread a republican and anti-clerical message.

France also undertook reform of academic secondary schools – the *lycées*. These were state institutions and also fee-paying schools which were socially restricted in access and, in the mid-nineteenth century, were classical in orientation. Yet the lycées, which had been established or at least nationalized by Napoleon, had had an original forward-looking function in educating future officers and bureaucrats and were given a more scientific, modernist orientation in the late nineteenth century. The impetus was the republican, secular, centralizing and reforming drive of French politics after 1870.[1] This gave a premium to the acquisition of rational, logical thinking which could be encouraged not only by philosophy, a central subject in the last years of the lycée, but also by mathematics and science.

Technical–vocational education for industrial workers lacked the vigour and vitality of that in Germany. Indeed government intervened in ways that presaged mid-twentieth century central planning. The state took over vocational education of young workers – including the provision of state certificates of competence which were a *sine qua non* of practising a craft – but instituted a levy from employers to pay for this provision. This system was completed by the Astier Law of 1917 which provided the framework for government-led expansion of vocational education in the later part of this century.

In contrast, higher education had changed very little in the nineteenth century so that when reform came in the 1960s it was dramatic and impelled by forces of popular unrest rather than effected by government-dominated initiatives.

Post-1945 Educational Change

The demand for universal secondary education up to the age of 18 was justified by appeal to principles of social justice. Yet labour market considerations continued to be a significant subordinate theme which can be perceived in the actual organization of mass secondary schooling.

The labour market justification for mass secondary schooling was provided by systems of economic planning which emerged from the Second World War (see Chapter 17). The Five Year National Plans included labour market targets expressed usually in the required numbers of workers with specific levels of skill and training. Forecasts of labour and skill requirements in the 1950s and 1960s gave force to the demands for increased secondary school provision.

Yet it was political change that created the circumstances in which major reform took place. De Gaulle, who had returned to power as president of the new Fifth Republic in 1958, and his governments were politically right of centre and nationalist. But they were also radical. The school reform plan initially was modest. The 1959 Debré Law mirrored the English reform of 1944 and the actual situation that had emerged in West Germany. *Collèges d'Enseignement Générale* were to provide for the majority of the primary school population who did not gain places in the lycée but offered only four years of schooling up to the age of 15 and gave no possibility of taking the examination for the state certificate of the *baccalauréat*. The lycées were undisturbed in their clientèle and functions.

Yet more genuinely common secondary education came quickly. The 1963 Fouchet decrees produced a major change in structure. All children leaving the primary school at the age of 11 were to enter the local *collèges d'enseignement secondaire* to follow a four-year course. The lycée was to become a three-grade academic upper secondary institution preparing students for the baccalauréat while the *collèges d'enseignement technique* were renamed *lycées techniques*, offering upper secondary vocational training.

The process of internal reorganization of the collèges and lycées took longer. At first the collèges had three streams – the top was very similar to the old lycée in teachers, curriculum and aspirations. The bottom had an emphasis on practical studies and was taught by former primary school teachers. The middle concentrated on the standard curriculum without extras like a second foreign or a classical language and additional classes where necessary in mathematics. These distinctions were removed in 1975 when the common lower secondary school was completed, in which the study of French, mathematics, science and a foreign language was central.

The collège from the 1960s to the 1990s was clearly designed to prepare students of 11 to 15 years of age for working life even if the study was general and academic. But a substantial proportion, perhaps 20–25 per cent, failed to achieve a standard of attainment for which a certificate could be issued. Many of these failures had repeated grades since the beginning of the primary school – and left the collège after only two years at the age of 16 to enter vocational courses from which they often failed to gain the necessary certificates for skilled employment.

Issues of social justice reappeared strongly in the early 1980s with Socialist governments in the first phase of the presidency of François Mitterand. Although France, unlike Britain with its socially élite independent schools, had a predominantly state system of education, there were still élite lycées which monopolized entry to the most prestigious branches of higher education, and these lycées were fed by students from collèges and primary schools within their geographical catchment areas. At the other end of the scale of student attainment, the percentage of failures was much higher than was widely accepted and among these failing students were high proportions from ethnic minorities (Portuguese as well as North Africans) and socially disadvantaged groups. Government advisers in the early 1980s indeed suggested a less centralized kind of instruction which would take some account of the cultures of the socially disadvantaged.

But by the mid-1980s, when the relationship between national industrial competitiveness and the standard of education of workers began to be accepted by governments in North America and the UK, the emphasis switched back to the national economic interest in France. National tests were introduced for primary and secondary schools in France in 1989 just as they were in Britain after 1988. The first function of the collège was seen to ensure that all students would reach high enough standards of learning to be able to become fully and formally qualified for participation in skilled work at upper secondary or higher education level. The historic role of French education to create citizens with a common and standard body of skill and knowledge was reasserted but with a more thorough-going economic dimension.

By the 1980s, a majority of collège leavers continued their studies. The extension of secondary education to all raised questions about whether traditional academic upper secondary education courses could be made available to all as happened, with only slight modifications, in most countries in the lower secondary school, and how extended secondary education could be linked to vocational training.

The response was unambiguous. The lycée was recreated as a general upper secondary three-grade school on the formation of the common lower secondary school. Technical and vocational courses were taught at first in separate vocational lycées which were then amalgamated with the general lycée. The aim from the 1970s was to produce equivalence between general and vocational courses.

Three conditions aided this simplicity of purpose. First, the prevalence of economic/manpower planning principles made it acceptable to direct upper secondary schooling to labour market imperatives as perceived by government. Second, élite higher education in France was concentrated in *grandes écoles* for which entry occurred two years *after* upper secondary schooling was completed, while universities were mass institutions which, at least after 1968, in most subject areas began with a two-year diploma course rather than intense specialization. The outcome was that the French lycée course was based on a broad national curriculum of 10 subjects or so. Students specialized by concentrating in depth on some of these subjects – there were four main branches: letters, social science, mathematics and physical science, mathematics and biological science. Of these, mathematics and physical science had the highest status because it gave best chances of entry to *grande école* preparatory courses. Third, the lycée emphasized the acquisition of capacities for logical–rational thought, traditionally through philosophy which was a compulsory subject in the last two years of the lycée course but increasingly from the 1960s through mathematics and physics. So depth of specialized knowledge was less important than more generalized intellectual skills.

This intellectual orientation of the lycée made easier the narrowing of the gap between academic and technical/vocational studies. So a technical *baccalauréat de technicien* which had specialisms in engineering studies could be included in the lycée because it was founded on the same basic intellectual learning as the general baccalauréat.

The major problems, however, lay in the vocational areas covered in the lycée technique which after 1963 concentrated on craft skill courses. These craft-orientated courses gave a status which was higher than the unsystematic training of apprentices in Britain and distinctly different from those of Germany. The *certificat d'aptitude professionel* (CAP) was a qualification awarded by the French state without which it was not legally possible for a skilled craft worker to practise a trade, whether in plumbing, hairdressing or in secretarial areas. Students had every incentive to acquire the certificate. Furthermore, the logical–rational encyclo-pedic rationale of French education extended to vocational areas. CAP studies began with general education – notably in mathematics and science – upon which vocational skill was to be based. The separation of general and vocational education was not as acute as in the UK and Germany.

However, the CAP was not without its problems. The failure rate in the three-year part-time course (two-year full-time) was high, often 60 per cent, which re-flected the origin of many students in the slow or repeater streams of the college. And despite the legal–occupational value of the CAP, most students and their families preferred to aim at something higher. The main issue then became the reconciliation of the principles of occupational preparation at an early age with maintenance of principles of equality of opportunity.

The solution was, first, to introduce higher technical qualifications such as a new *baccalauréat professionel* from 1985 (and earlier precursors) which subsequently became the means to meet the target of 80 per cent of the age group reaching higher education entry standards by the year 2000. And, secondly, to amalgam-ate the general and technical lycées.

Higher Education

Of all levels of education, it was in regard to universities and similar institutions that the governments of west European countries most specifically gave eco-nomic rationales for policy in the period after 1945. Yet by the 1990s the varia-tions of practice between higher education in the three countries considered here (and others across Europe) were greater than at any other level of educa-tion. Not only did many differences in 1945 between élite institutions in various countries survive but also there were markedly different approaches to reform.

Plate 12.1. Paris, 3 February 1961. Students take to the streets in protest against the overcrowding of universities, poor facilities and financial hardship.

Alone among west European countries, French higher education was reformed as a result of a political – or quasi-political – revolution of the student uprising of 1968. Yet the pattern of reform reflected the statist tradition which was much older and which had an impact on other elements of education and wider public life. Furthermore the pinnacles of higher education – the *grandes écoles* – were untouched by 1968 yet constrained the ways in which the rest of higher education was changed.

The *grandes écoles* were systematized by Napoleon I as institutions for the training of bureaucrats, engineers, officers and higher-level teachers. They remained ever since the institutions for selecting and training a state élite, even though by the 1960s their graduates followed careers in which they moved smoothly from government ministries to nationalized industries to private enterprise, but always in top positions. The institutions had a slight scientific/engineering emphasis, especially in the Ecole Polytechnique and Ecoles des Mines, but all provided a general, theoretical education, especially in the Ecole Normale Supérieure, while the Ecole Nationale d'Administration was created in 1946 and was postgraduate.

They were élite institutions not only in that they offered entry to highest managerial positions and provided their students with a state salary during the course, but entry was on the basis of competitive examinations taken two years after the baccalauréat, the normal means of entering universities. The *grandes écoles*, catering for around 5 per cent of higher education students, remained the unchanging core of the otherwise unstable world of higher French education.

Universities in contrast had been state institutions in every respect but peripheral to state economic planning because they prepared for traditional occupations – teaching, medicine, the law. Their focus was on teaching rather than research which was based more in specialized institutes.

Most of all they were chaotic in organization. All students with a baccalauréat had the right to enter any faculty of any university. As a consequence when enrolments rose in the 1960s there were vast numbers in the University of Paris, overcrowded lectures, little contact between students and staff, and dropout/failure rates of more than 50 per cent.

This type of university and its chaos was not unique to France. It typified the universities of Italy and Spain also. Yet in France reform came in response to the demonstrations, seizure of buildings and other activities of May 1968 which, when they extended to strikes and occupation of buildings in secondary schools and industrial companies, amounted to a mass insurrection.

The 'revolt' lost steam and died out almost as quickly as it had flared up, but it brought the reform of French higher education which linked it even more firmly to state economic planning.

The old mammoth universities (especially that of Paris) were broken up into smaller institutions (13 in Paris) and new subject centres replaced the old faculties so that a more relevant knowledge and training would have priority. The crucial change was that a preliminary two-year cycle was introduced for all university institutions. The intention was that many of the new cohorts of university students would be diverted into work after two rather than the three or four years of the older degrees. However, the new first cycle diplomas were regarded by employers with some distrust. The reform became a filter for failures and drop-outs. The disaffected repeaters of earlier years would be identified earlier.

The French approach was interesting because the non-university vocationally oriented institutions of other countries – including Britain and Germany – were not central to policy. Indeed, the two-year university technological institutes which seemed the equivalent of the polytechnics in Britain or the *Fachhochschulen* in Germany in effect remained small in number and indeed more prestigious than general university studies. By the 1980s, they successfully demanded higher entry qualifications than the general universities.

France retained its cultural perspective that education was a contribution to national economic and general development and that higher education was a means to prepare students for the labour market. Even in the late 1980s this rationale for expansion of higher education was central to government policy. Furthermore, built on a tradition going back to at least Napoleon I, scientific and technological studies maintained a high prestige. However, French higher educa-tion remained uniformly statist in ways that were not found in Britain or some other countries such as the Netherlands. The market forces ideology never cap-tured French higher education policy-making from the late 1980s. The role of universities with a retreating state has yet to be decided.

Germany

Nineteenth-Century Origins

German educational traditions did include some elements of French statism but in the post-1945 period it was localism and pluralism that were emphasized. Statism, expressed in government control of schools, curricula and teachers, had its origin in the absolutism of Frederick the Great in eighteenth-century Prussia as well as in the nationalist revival following defeat by Napoleon in 1806 which adopted many Napoleonic institutions. Primary education was not a major issue in the late nineteenth century. It had been almost universal in eighteenth cen-tury Prussia and other states. The whole of the country acquired universal pri-mary education in part by conquest. The Prussian military success which unified Germany in 1871 did spread some Prussian institutions to other states. Yet overall the history of education since the late nineteenth century was one of local diver-sity and of the influence of traditional sectional groups as much as state centralism.

The reform of secondary and technical education was not neglected. In Prussia, the decaying secondary schools (*Gymnasien*) and universities had been rein-vigorated by Wilhelm von Humboldt as part of the national revival after 1806. The ideal was to create a professional and bureaucrat class through an education in classical Greek and Roman languages, history, literature and philosophy. Yet later in the nineteenth century the classical monopoly was broken in secondary education when mathematics- and science-oriented Gymnasien were established and, indeed, those with a business or commercial bias. The universities remained classical ivory towers into the late twentieth century, even though their reputation as centres of scholarship was enhanced. But secondary schools, designed for and patronized by the higher social classes, aimed at providing a thorough, systematic grounding in a wide range of academic subjects.

Vocational education was thoroughly developed for young manual workers. Industrialization in Germany in the later nineteenth century had been subject to tight controls by a government of Bismarck which represented the Junker land-owners. One measure designed to limit the social impact of new industry was the preservation of the power of traditional craft guilds in the new factories. The consequence was a thorough and systematic training of apprentices – covering a wider range of occupations than in, for instance, Britain.

Post-1945 Reform

In Germany secondary schooling had been accessible to a higher proportion of the population since the late nineteenth century but in distinctly different kinds of school. The main emphasis in policy reform was to achieve universal part-time vocational education. Proposals for a common secondary school were resisted when made by American occupying forces after 1945 and still have applied to only about 5 per cent of pupils at present.

Germany between 1945 and the late 1980s enjoyed a system of lower secondary education which was the envy of much of the rest of the world in the standards of attainment of its pupils yet, unlike most of its west European partners, carried out no major reforms of structure and permitted considerable variations in practice between the 11 Länder (16 after reunification in 1990) which had legal autonomy in educational matters. The salient characteristic of German education in the 20 years after the Second World War up to the 1960s was 'non-reform'.

The most striking area of 'non-reform' was lower secondary education. Unlike most other west European countries, Germany kept a differentiated system which had been in place from the early twentieth century. The Gymnasium was the academic and selective state secondary school which had changed little since the late nineteenth century. It offered a nine-year course for pupils leaving primary schools at the age of 10 – one year more than in most other countries in Europe – and focused on an academic curriculum with a heavy emphasis on languages and literary study even in those schools with a scientific bias. Students in the classical Gymnasien might study Latin, Greek and two modern foreign languages. The aim was to provide the intellectual training needed for lengthy humanistic studies in the university following success in the leaving examination, the *Abitur*.

The two other kinds of school offered shorter courses with a somewhat more practical bias. The *Realschule* also selected pupils at the age of 10 but provided a seven-year course in general education with a commercial flavour to languages and mathematics. The *Hauptschule* had developed from the upper grades of the primary school and was unselective. Teaching concentrated on general education but there was concession to the manual worker futures of its students in subjects such as the *Arbeitslehre* from 1964, which provided not only manual craft training and work experience long before other European countries but offered courses in industrial relations and safety at work as well as projects in design, production and marketing.

This system was not very different from that which was proposed in the UK in 1944 and in France in 1959. The oddity was that it survived into the 1990s with little expectation of change. The only significant movement was in the proportions of children and young people attending the different types of schools. The Gymnasium in the 1940s had taken little more than 10 per cent of the age group. By the 1980s this proportion had risen to over 30 per cent, reflecting not only parental ambitions for their children but also the willingness of school authorities to widen their intake rather than face possible closure when birthrates fell in the 1970s. The Hauptschule obstinately refused to die and still enrolled almost 40 per cent of the age group into the 1990s.

Social Democrat politicians demanded the common secondary schooling which had been introduced in other countries. But they did not press too hard. The federal political system prevented national change. So, while comprehensive *Gesamtschulen* were founded in the 1960s, they were almost exclusively confined to Länder controlled by Social Democrats and even there they never enrolled more than a quarter of the age group. Ironically when the two Germanies were reunited in 1990 the eastern states which had the Soviet-inspired common secondary school in some cases reintroduced selective Gymnasien.

The Hauptschule survived largely because employers dictated that it provide a sound and thorough education and were willing to give apprenticeships and, at least until the 1990s, secure jobs to its graduates. The leaving examination was a rigorous test and was required by employers as the condition of awarding the apprenticeship. The effectiveness of learning in basic subjects (including a foreign language – usually English) was indicated by the results of international tests in mathematics in the early 1960s which were confirmed by other studies of the early 1980s. The relatively high standards of the Hauptschule, compared with equivalent schools or pupils in other countries, also permitted easier transfers of pupils to selective schools on completion of the course.

One problem of the Gymnasium was its duration. Students were 19, often 20, by the time they left. The traditional function of the Gymnasium in its final years was determined by the peculiar nature of the German universities. Students in the latter were supposed to have the maturity necessary to undertake very autonomous work (with much flexibility in the length of studies and where they would take place). The Gymnasium was to give breadth of study and depth in some areas to equip university students with high standards of general education. Indeed the main debates in West Germany after the 1960s, when the proportions of the age group participating grew rapidly, were between the maintenance of these traditional academic standards and the permissibility of greater individual choice of study of a more diverse school population. The immediate response to expansion came in 1972 when students were permitted to focus on advanced studies of their choice. After much debate in the 1980s this development was partly reversed by an insistence that students would need to perform well in basic elements of the course – including languages and mathematics as well as in the advanced personal choice areas. However, the terms of this debate made it difficult to achieve other aims such as reducing the length of the course or integrating vocational with general education.

Legally, Germany was the first country to achieve universal education for all to the age of 18, in 1938. But this target was reached by two very different routes – the traditional academic Gymnasium course and the 'Dual System' of apprenticeship and part-time study. The emphasis of France on coherence and on the articulation of general and vocational upper secondary education was replaced in Germany by rigid and deliberate separation.

The vocational sector had its own marked success, at least in the view of many in other countries, but also less frequently noted weaknesses. Vocational training for 15–18-year-olds was founded on the apprenticeship system which had origins in the medieval craft guilds. These had been incorporated by law into new industrial cartels in response to the policy of Bismarck in the 1880s. So training was regulated by local chambers of commerce or craft employer associations. A very high proportion of crafts required apprenticeships which had to be completed through formal examination before the worker could claim skilled status and the right to practise the trade. The largest proportion of this training occurred in the workplace and each apprentice was under the tutelage of a skilled worker – the Meister – who had also passed rigorous tests to achieve this position. Apprenticeship examinations, regulated largely by craft employer associations, not only had a legal standing but they tested largely skills and knowledge acquired in the workplace.

The 'Dual System' was in effect the addition of general education part-time onto this vocational workplace training. The provision of general education to young workers had been part of the Socialist/Social Democrat agenda at the end of the nineteenth century, and ministers made attempts to introduce federal legislation on this matter in the 1890s. However, it was in Bavaria where Georg Kerschensteiner, as Director of Education, at the turn of the century first introduced compulsory day release for apprentices following his own conception that 'Occupation was Citizenship' so that moral–civic courses would back up the civic–moral values learned informally in the workplace.

The Bavarian experiment was copied by other states and in 1938 became national law. Even after 1945 this federally enforced obligation to maintain the Dual System remained. The *Berufsschulen* in the state education system emphasized religious and community studies as well as the general–theoretical learning in areas such as mathematics and language to reinforce the practical learning of the workplace.

However, the 'Dual System' depended upon the willingness of employers to pay for industrial training in the workplace and to recruit large number of apprentices. This obligation had been supported by the broader 'Social Contract' consensus of government, employers and trade unions. By the 1990s the pressures

Plate 12.2. Berlin, 14 May 1968. A group of students burning the great seal of the Free University of Berlin. As elsewhere in western Europe, discontent with the conditions of academic study in the more traditional universities had grown into a much wider protest against the 'establishment' in what was perceived as a stagnant and repressive society.

on the competitiveness of German industry forced employers to be less generous and the 'Dual System' came under some threat.

Even despite these more recent developments there had been a movement towards full-time vocational training in *Berufsfachschulen* with two-year courses for school leavers preparing for occupations for which the traditional route was unsuitable. Furthermore there were increased numbers of students completing the full Gymnasium course who, instead of entering higher education, entered apprenticeships in occupations such as banking and financial services. Yet the tradition of separation between the work-orientated vocational sector and the very academic general part of education remained strong in the upper secondary level and indeed was transferred increasingly to higher education.

German universities, of all those of western European countries, have been the most remote from the concerns of economic enterprise. They have maintained their mission as identified by Wilhelm von Humboldt to carry out research which extends knowledge for its own sake. Professors may be appointed by the state but their academic autonomy gave them the right to devote themselves to scholarship without reference to its application to a wider society. Students learned by sitting at the professors' feet. Yet students themselves had independence to decide whether to move to another department or university in the course of their study and to decide when they were ready for examinations which usually culminated in the presentation of a thesis. The outcome was that German university students, even into the 1990s, were taking an average of seven years to complete their first degree and pursued studies without a clear vocational purpose.

The Federal German government was concerned to reform this condition to provide for labour market needs. Yet their proposals to reform universities lacked bite. Instead they focused on a very different type of institution – the *Fachhochschulen* – to provide trained technical workers in 1968. Not only are the subjects of study more vocational, but workplace experience is frequently part of the course, and crucially the students, more frequently taught in formal classes, are required to complete their studies in four years.

The Fachhochschulen were successful in attracting students and in winning employer approval. Yet there were still more students in traditional universities. The Fachhochschulen may by their success have diverted attention away from university reform which, even by the 1990s, had still not dealt with the old problems of the lengthy periods of time that students took to complete degrees, nor with newer pressures of being cost-efficient and entrepreneurial. In some ways the labour market reinforced this inefficiency with the continued preference of employers, especially in traditional occupations like the Civil Service or teaching, for new entrants in their late twenties or early thirties. It was indeed the students who responded more quickly to new conditions, with many more undertaking lower-level vocational training before embarking on university studies. They used this qualification to seek part-time employment during studies, so that full-time students became a rarity in the 1990s, and this previous qualification was a useful safety net as university graduation was more frequently accompanied by failure to get a job related to the university specialization.

Britain

Nineteenth-Century Origins

The British[2] had similar priorities as France and Germany but the outcomes were rather different. Socially élite secondary schools emerged from the mid-nineteenth century as certain of the ancient grammar schools were reformed into a network of Public Schools – that is, fee-paying and often boarding schools designed to produce 'Christian gentlemen'. The significant difference from other west European countries was not in their élitism or even in their classical curriculum but in the fact of the private or local nature of the institutions. English secondary education was not provided in institutions of the state which were held to meet state objectives.

In England, a fear of social unrest in new industrial cities persuaded government to aid the churches in the provision of schooling to civilize the masses. By 1870, with the extension of suffrage in 1867 for which Robert Lowe, Secretary of the Board of Education, suggested ironically that our future masters had better learn their lessons, government moved to fill the gaps left by church provision.

As in France and Germany, the English grammar schools that had not separated themselves off into private schools did begin to recruit a minority of pupils from public elementary schools from the late nineteenth century. These pupils were paid for by local education authorities, though it was not until 1945 that all their pupils came through this route and they could be seen as completely state schools. Even as they moved into the state sector, the grammar schools continued to share the classical, humanist ideals of their private school cousins.

There were concerns, as in France and Germany, about educational responses to pressures of economic–industrial competition. The Science and Art departments developed vocational qualifications such as City and Guilds which were taken in local technical colleges, but proposals to develop technical secondary education beyond elementary schooling were undermined by a legal ban on Higher Grade schools. Vocational education in England remained very much a responsibility of industry rather than of the education system. Most skilled manual workers acquired recognition through serving apprenticeships for the successful conclusion of which, unlike in France and Germany, a formal, examined qualification was not mandatory. In Britain, unlike France and Germany, there was no significant early twentieth century reform of vocational education. The reciprocal contempt of educationists and employers, while not absent in the other European countries, was at its most acute in Britain.

Post-1945 Reform

In some ways the movement to reform lower secondary education in Britain after 1945 seemed to occupy a middle position between France and Germany. There were thoroughgoing reform packages emerging in 1944, 1965 and 1988 which mirrored the French approach and contrasted with the stasis of Germany. Yet British change – at least until the 1980s – was initiated at local level, permitted diversity of institutions and lacked the subordination of educational planning to overall economic and labour market goals found in France. British reforms up to the 1980s lacked an articulation with the labour market which was produced by government fiat in France and by local arrangements in Germany.

As in the other two countries, universal secondary education had been proposed before the Second World War. The major change came in the 1944 Education Act which, however, did not take the bold step of introducing a common secondary school such as Sweden did in 1948. Instead three types of school were proposed – the existing selective and academic grammar schools, selective secondary technical schools and unselective secondary modern schools. The rationale had been provided in the 1943 Norwood Report which proposed three types of ability of children – 'academic', 'technical' and 'practical'. The prevailing justification was social justice rather than economic or labour market needs.

In practice, few technical schools were established – and they enrolled only about 2 per cent of the age group. Local Authorities found them expensive to provide with their necessarily extensive workshop facilities, while parents judged that if their children were capable of selective education then it should be in grammar schools.

The secondary modern schools were the problem. Pupils stayed only until the legal end of compulsory schooling at 15 in most cases, and took no examinations, unlike the grammar school students who prepared for the School Certificate (from 1951 the General Certificate of Education Ordinary Level) at 16 which gave access not only to upper secondary education but also to 'white collar' jobs in both public and private enterprises. Both social justice and economic value issues had been raised in an official report in 1957 (Crowther Report) which pointed to the large numbers of young people of high intelligence who had been educated in secondary modern schools and had few opportunities for future educational advancement.

The common or comprehensive school movement developed at local rather than national levels and was supported equally by Conservative and Labour Local Authorities. The arguments for comprehensive schools focused on social justice rather than economic needs, though in some cases it was costly to run two or three types of school in the same area and the 'successful' secondary moderns had tended to copy the grammar schools and enter their best pupils for GCE 'O' level. The Labour central government simply encouraged the process with a circular of 1965 detailing the different forms of comprehensive school arrange- ments which were desirable. It was only when five of the 104 LEAs in England and Wales refused to introduce comprehensive schools that the Labour central government in 1976 attempted to enforce compulsion by law. This was reversed by the Conservative administration in 1979, but by this time 83 per cent of children were in common schools which were lacking in only a tiny number of areas (though including the whole of Northern Ireland) but coexisted with a small number of grammar schools elsewhere.

What is interesting was the form the British (or specifically the English and Welsh) comprehensive school took. There was no tight articulation with the labour market as in France. Instead schools were seen by Local Authorities either as expanded grammar schools or as experiments in social integration in which community mattered more than individual differentiation. A similar move- ment had occurred in the primary schools which, when freed from pressures to prepare for the 11+ examination for grammar school entrance, adopted a more 'child-centred' approach with the support of the 1967 Plowden Report. In prac- tice, however, the comprehensive schools concentrated on the 20–25 per cent of pupils who equated with the old grammar school stream and prepared for 'O' levels. The rest had no recognized qualification to aim at since the Certificate of Secondary Education introduced after 1964 failed to win widespread support from employers. Comprehensive schools in poor areas, notably in inner cities, were in effect secondary modern schools with no 'grammar school' band.

The demand for economic relevance and efficiency, while having expression in other European countries, came earlier in Britain. In a 1976 landmark speech,

THE WORLD ACCORDING TO GRIFFIN

SELECTION BOARD

A LEVELS TOO EASY

'We're fully aware of your four A-level passes at Grade A. We'd just like to see you write your name.'

Plate 12.3. Charles Griffin's cartoon (*Daily Express*, 15 August 1995) amusingly characterises the debate about standards of literacy and numeracy achieved in British schools, and what should be done to increase them, which had intensified in the 1990s.

which set the tone for future legislation, Prime Minister James Callaghan stressed the need for higher standards of achievement among pupils and a greater uniformity of achievement among schools which he suggested could be achieved by a uniform national curriculum.

The implementation of this reform package came largely in the 1988 Education Reform Act which enforced not only a national curriculum but national testing of pupils at the ages of 7, 11 and 14 as well as the GCSE (which had come from the amalgamation of 'O' level and CSE in 1986) at 16. Pressure was put on schools by the requirement to provide information to parents from the mid-1970s which culminated in the 1990s in national league tables of school examination results.

While the ideology of reform in the late 1980s stressed competition between schools on 'market' principles (thus allowing parents freedom of choice of school and giving individual schools much more managerial autonomy), the twin motif behind both Labour and Conservative government reforms was parental dissatisfaction and the need of the economy for higher levels of skill among the workforce. The awareness of the threat to British industrial competitiveness of poor educational standards had become clear in government and among employers by the early 1980s and had been reinforced by the poor performance of English and Welsh children in international tests in the early 1980s which had shown other countries, especially in the Far East but also in Europe, performing much better.

The broadly common pattern of change in the three countries in the 50 years after 1945 was disrupted by particular surviving differences between them which had little to do with the kinds of political party in power. While these differences reflect varying national traditions in the valuation of different kinds and types of learning as well as in the residual power of national authorities or of interest groups such as teachers, one central difference was in the relationship between education, training and the labour market in the three countries. These variations can be illuminated in relation to upper secondary, vocational and higher education.

Vocational education at upper secondary level had developed quite apart from the mainstream school and higher education system. Unlike in France and Germany, successful completion of craft apprenticeships did not depend on the award of certificates following examinations or other assessment but simply on spending a fixed number of years on the job. Vocational qualifications did develop from the nineteenth century but were optional and additional for apprenticeships. It was only by the 1980s that this gap began to be filled and measures were taken to enforce formal training, certification and the equivalence between academic and vocational courses.

As in Germany, vocational qualifications had been accredited by employers' organizations in partnership increasingly with educational authorities. Craft apprenticeship-level courses were examined by the City and Guilds of London Institute from the nineteenth century and, through the Technical or, later, Further Education Colleges, part-time day release and evening classes were offered to prepare for them. Technician-level courses were examined by Ordinary and Higher National Certificates and Diplomas. These had no correspondence in level, below university degree standard, with academic qualifications such as GCSE, or GCE 'O' or 'A' level, just as further education or technical colleges were not equivalent strictly to any level of general educational institution.

The issue of lack of universal and mandatory vocational qualifications had been taken up in a range of official reports since the mid-nineteenth century, often pointing to the deficiencies of the British system compared with continental European counterparts. Attempts were made to harmonize and simplify vocational qualifications in the early 1980s but it was not until 1992 that equivalent structures of general and vocational qualifications were enforced.

Britain moved from a German style of separation of academic and vocational education, with emphasis on workplace experience and employer control of training, to a French-style state-dominated system with strict equivalences between general and vocational branches. But the rationale that the apprenticeship system decayed in Britain when it continued to prosper in Germany ignored the other main difference that formal vocational qualifications were essential for work in Germany but not in Britain. The British adoption of the French approach conveniently ignored the history of the latter as state-controlled mechanisms for entry into the labour market in a context of state domination of economic development.

British higher education experienced one wave of reform in the 1960s with parallels with France and Germany. This change was limited and a second phase occurred at the end of the 1980s which changed the direction again.

There was perhaps more ambivalence about the contribution of higher reform in the 1960s to the economy and labour market in Britain than in France or Germany. The Robbins Report of 1963 was the landmark document and proclaimed the ambiguous principle that higher education should be available to all who could benefit from it. The usual interpretation was that individual capacities and interests should predominate rather than collective economic needs. But Robbins was the justification for a policy of expanding higher education access and creating new universities. Soon the government endorsed non-university institutions, notably polytechnics, as a means to a more vocationally relevant preparation. As in Germany, the old university autonomy and often remoteness from labour market concerns produced a response of creating a new strand of institutions rather than reforming old ones.

There is debate about whether the polytechnics did meet vocational needs and suffered from 'academic' drift towards an older university ethos that a liberal education should not take the utilitarian requirements of wider society as its guide. But the binary system principle was effectively abandoned between 1990 and 1992 when American-style diversity of institutions and standards was accepted. From 1992 most institutions, except the small and specialized, were allowed to describe themselves as universities. In practice, though not in overt statement, a range of standards could be tolerated and, as in the USA, it was expected that the student would be the informed consumer. The reform was a response to a decision – taken largely on economic grounds – to expand the proportion of the age group in higher education from 15 per cent in 1985 to over 30 per cent in 1990.

Yet there was more than the rule of the market. Government intervened with a variety of quality assurance measures to maintain standards, including assessment of research achievement which was linked to funding. In effect, rather than the contribution of higher education to the labour market it was the cost-effectiveness of public education that was judged. Another indication was the gradual replacement of student maintenance grants by student loans after 1990.

A New Perception of Economic Relevance of Education

Throughout western Europe, the driving concerns between the 1940s and 1960s were economic relevance and social justice. The balance between the two was not always the same in every country, nor always fully separated. Economic concerns were overt in France but more subdued in Britain. Yet everywhere ancient traditions survived and the resulting systems of education continued to differ between each among the main countries even though they had each moved away from older patterns.

By the mid-1980s, concern was voiced about the dangers of creeping and uncontrollable public expenditure, especially in a global economy in which autarkic national economies could not insulate their currencies or their economies more generally from international pressures. State education, in every country, continued to expand to respond to the greater sophistication of occupations, but governments adopted new priorities of assessing outcomes of education, by national tests in France, Sweden, the UK and the Netherlands or by seeking the cost-efficiencies which Far Eastern competitors seemed to have achieved. Differences remained between Britain, with its old private tradition in education, and other continental countries still committed to state education. But no country could ignore these pressures.

Interpretations

Interpretations of the educational history of Europe from an economic standpoint are sometimes not so much conflictual as uncommunicative. That is educationists, economists and historians each have different perspectives rather than different interpretations within the same broad paradigms. This divergence is heightened by the comparative dimension. Conflicting views focus more often on developments within one country than on comparisons between them.

With these provisos two wider interpretative stances may be identified. One school of thought would see education as a subsidiary area dependent on economic developments. Yet exponents of this viewpoint may include Marxists Samuel Bowles and Herbert Gintis who argued that education simply 'reproduces' the labour market segmentation required by dominant interests, or supporters of Theodore Schultz's 'Human Capital Theory' who explored the contribution that education can bring to economic growth – for instance Arnold Anderson and Jean Bowman.[3]

Others, in looking at the development in education itself across countries, have focused on the common impact of certain agencies such as churches, political movements or sectional interests including teacher unions in thwarting economically necessary education reform.[4]

Other approaches, often drawing upon national typologies inspired by Max Weber, have emphasized the power of national cultural, political, indeed philosophical traditions in ensuring that educational reform never wholly breaks links with particular national histories so that new institutions differ as much between nations as those that they replaced.[5]

Of course, division is not as clear cut as the preceding paragraphs suggest. Some economists focus upon national political and cultural differences in explaining economic growth, and there may be differences even in interpretations of historic culture and economic relevance within countries, as in the debate between Weiner and Rubinstein about whether Britain is primarily an industrial or a commercial country.[6] Yet from a broader comparative perspective, decision is needed first about the extent to which education is the seed or flower of economic growth before the interpretations can be evaluated.

Bibliographical Note

The central works, in English, are histories of education in each country. For France, the period up to 1976 is best dealt with in W.D. Halls, *Education, Politics and Culture in Modern France* (Oxford, 1976) with the debates of the 1980s collected in A. Corbett and B. Moon (eds), *Education in France* (London, 1996). Education in Germany has been less fully treated by authors writing in English. A. Hearnden, *Education, Politics and Culture in West Germany* (Oxford, 1976), may be supplemented by the chapters in D. Phillips (ed.), *Education in Germany: Tradition and Reform in Historical Context* (London, 1995). The United Kingdom, understandably, has been covered more fully in English. B. Simon, *Education and the Social Order 1940–1990* (London, 1991) and S. Maclure, *Education Re-formed* (Sevenoaks, 1988) are among the more accessible works. General comparative studies include N. Hans, *Comparative Education* (London, 1958); I. Kandel, *Comparative Education* (New York, 1933) and M. McLean, *Educational Traditions Compared* (London, 1995).

Notes

1. E. Durkheim, *The Evolution of Educational Thought* (London, 1977).

2. More precisely, English and Welsh, since Scotland was not only legislatively separate but had a much more extensive secondary and university provision than England in the nineteenth century.

3. S. Bowles and H. Gintis, *Schooling in Capitalist America* (London, 1976); C.A. Anderson and M.J. Bowman, 'Education and economic modernization in historical perspective', in L. Stone (ed.), *Schooling and Society* (Baltimore, 1976).

4. M. Archer, *The Social Origins of Educational Systems* (London, 1979).

5. I. Kandel, *Comparative Education* (New York, 1933); N. Hans, *Comparative Education* (London, 1958).

6. G.C. Lodge and E.F. Vogel (eds), *Ideology and National Competitiveness* (Boston, MA, 1987); M. Weiner, *English Culture and the Decline of the Industrial Spirit* (Harmondsworth, 1985); W.D. Rubinstein, *Capitalism, Culture and Decline in Britain 1750–1990* (London, 1993).

13 Transport and Communications

John Armstrong

Transport and communications have seen huge advances in technology over the last half century. At the same time, on average, people in western Europe have become much better off. As their income rises people tend to spend a higher proportion on transport, travel and keeping in touch. For example, the proportion of national income spent on travel and transport alone in western European countries roughly doubled between 1946 and the late 1980s. This has meant radical changes in who uses such services and for what purposes, so much so that some commentators have suggested that manufacturing is of decreasing importance whereas services, which include transport and communications, are the growth sector. This chapter examines the changes in the demand for and technology affecting transport and communications, and analyses their social and economic impact.

The Main Developments in Transport

In this section we will explore some of the main developments that have oc-curred in transport since 1945, concentrating on the changes firstly in freight traffic and then in passenger transport. Many of these were not new, but rather were in the same direction as before the Second World War. One of the func-tions of transport is to save time. Higher travelling speeds are important not only for passenger transport, but also for freight transport in that less capital is tied up in goods in transit, and perishable and short-life products can expand their markets. Thus, since 1945 many modes of transport have increased both their top and average speeds.

Another continuing aim of transport providers is to reduce the real cost of transport, as this should widen the market for their services and so increase revenue and perhaps profits. A number of approaches to cost reduction have been evident since 1945. One method has been to decrease the labour content by replacing some workers by mechanical or automatic methods; another was to amalgamate a couple of jobs and require one employee to carry out both; yet a third has been to cut the capital cost of transport systems by using new construction methods or cheaper materials, or trying to achieve economies of scale by longer production runs. Another approach to cost reduction has been to increase the size of vehicle which is doing the transporting, as this is likely to give lower unit costs; for example, compare the 350-seater Boeing 747 with the Douglas DC4 with 42 passengers. Yet a further aspect of cost reduction has been to improve the efficiency of the power unit, the engine, and more importantly, output produced for any given fuel input.

The reliability and, even more crucially, the safety record of a transport mode are aspects likely to affect its appeal. Thus, in previous eras much work went into improving the reliability and safety of transport and that trend continued after 1945. Breakthroughs in technology were sometimes associated with increased risk and spectacular disasters and these then required further research to determine causation and remedy the specific weakness. Progress involved taking risks with the unknown, but mistakes were sorted out. There was also some trade-off between safety and the other objectives such as increased speed and scale or reduced cost, which meant risk rose as a result of the search for the other gains. It was the differing ability of various modes of transport to respond to these desires in the travelling public which determined whether their market share rose or fell and hence their relative importance in the economy. That and their ability to respond to an environment which was changing rapidly were important factors, and hence each type of transport had to anticipate and outflank competitor reactions.

Freight Transport

At the end of the Second World War the railways were the largest single carrier of goods in most western European countries, despite growing competition from road transport in the 1930s. By 1988 the roads were carrying many times more freight traffic than the railways (see Table 13.1). Air transport in 1945 or 1950 played a negligible part in goods movement and, although its share had increased by the 1980s, it was still a very minor player in this particular game. In part the rise to predominance of road haulage was a function of technical changes. The growth in lorry size and the greater power of engines allowed both larger loads and higher speeds. Improvements in road surfaces and layouts, especially bypasses and motorway quality roads (Table 13.2), allowed high speeds to be maintained over long distances, and the construction of road bridges over rivers and estuaries reduced unit transport costs. In addition, the growth of trade among European countries encouraged the use of lorry traffic which used 'roll-on-roll-off' ferries to undertake longer trans-European journeys.

The competition from road transport spurred the railways on to greater effort. In part they retreated from traffic they believed uneconomic – small loads or lightly travelled routes – leading to reductions in track mileage (Table 13.2) and a massive shedding of employees. In part they endeavoured to advance

Table 13.1. Freight traffic carried by rail, road and air (billion tonnes-kms)

	Rail				Road				Air			
	1955	1965	1975	1985	1955	1965	1975	1985	1955	1965	1975	1985
Belgium	6.6	6.8	6.8	8.2	na	8.5	16.5	22.1	0.02	0.06	0.3	0.6
France	46.9	64.6	64.0	55.8	18.6	45.8	84.9	89.1	0.07	0.19	1.0	2.9
West Germany	78.1	100.0	107.0	124.0	25.0	59.0	82.2	105.0	na	0.15	0.9	2.5
Italy	14.7	15.3	14.9	18.0	29.5	45.8	62.8	144.0	na	0.10	0.4	0.8
Spain	8.2	9.2	10.7	12.1	na	33.2	76.5	111.0	na	na	0.2	0.5
UK	34.9	25.2	23.5	15.4	31.9	66.0	89.0	99.1	0.07	0.30	0.8	2.3

Sources: B.R. Mitchell, *International Historical Statistics: Europe 1750–1988* (New York, 1992), pp. 671–6, 725–8; UN, *Annual Bulletin;* European Conference of Ministers of Transport, *Statistical Trends in Transport 1965–89* (Paris, 1993), pp. 68–9.

Table 13.2. Railway track and motorway open (km)

| | Rail track | | | | | Motorway | | | | |
	1950	1960	1970	1980	1988	1950	1960	1970	1980	1988
Austria	6,734	6,596	6,506	6,459	6,338	28	150	488	800	1,400
France	41,300	39,000	36,532	34,362	34,563	–	188	1,542	4,600	5,300
West Germany	49,819	52,193	47,668	45,745	44,153	2,116	2,408	4,110	7,400	8,580
Italy	21,550	21,277	20,212	19,814	19,700	na	na	3,913	5,800	6,044
Spain	18,071	18,033	16,507	15,743	12,550	–	na	185	1,800	2,290
UK	31,336	29,562	18,969	17,645	16,599	–	112	1,133	2,600	3,130

Sources: Mitchell, *International Historical Statistics: Europe 1750–1988*, pp. 655–63; UN, *Annual Bulletin of Transport Statistics for Europe* (Geneva, 1950, 1960, 1970, 1980, 1990).

technologically, switching from steam locomotion to diesel power, using larger and purpose-specific freight wagons, and installing automatic signalling systems and level-crossing barriers. As a result productivity per employee rose dramatically in most countries. Reductions in employment ranged from 14 per cent in Austria to 66 per cent in Britain between 1950 and 1980. This in part reflected the reduction in the track network (Table 13.2). This retrenchment was carried furthest in Britain where the rail network was virtually halved in 40 years. Most other countries were more moderate, cutting up to 30 per cent of the mileage. Cuts were also made in the maintenance and ancillary staff, raising some questions as to security and safety, and some were privatized, leading also to reduced staffing.

The railways found it increasingly difficult to compete for freight traffic, for their forte lay in moving large quantities of bulk goods such as coal or iron ore. Yet it was the heavy industries which were in sharpest decline. Lighter, high-value products needed the faster point-to-point transport of motor lorries and delivery in smaller consignments. Thus, the need for predictable arrival times to conform to just-in-time production requirements and to minimize stock levels and reduce capital tied up in transit, led to railways losing market share throughout the period.

As a result road freight traffic demonstrated startling growth throughout this period, as shown in Table 13.1. The average size of commercial vehicle rose as the legal maximum weight limit was increased and motorway-standard roads became more widely available (Table 13.2), allowing higher average speeds. These motorways, pioneered in Italy and Germany in the 1930s, limited access and departure points, banned very slow-moving traffic like mopeds and bicycles, and eliminated sharp bends, traffic lights, crossings and other obstructions to allow sustained high-speed motoring. Everywhere road haulage was increasing its share of freight traffic but the trend was furthest and fastest in Britain.

The great economic advantage of road transport was not so much cost, though that fell in real terms, as its trackability, flexibility and speed. Using lorries meant a journey with an 'unbroken seam', that is only one loading and unloading, whereas rail usually required double that number. Lorries and vans were also more suited to sequential deliveries of small quantities at a number of drop-off points, and it was easier to trace and monitor a particular consignment. Railways were particularly suited for punctiform traffic of bulk products, but increasingly it was smaller parcels of goods needing areal distribution that dominated the economy, and as value relative to bulk rose, it was important to deliver quickly and to track the parcel. For this, road haulage was more suitable.

Throughout this period air freight was a very minor proportion of total goods traffic. Even with the huge technical improvements to aircraft and air travel discussed later, it remained a very expensive mode of transport and air cargo in the 1980s and 1990s was restricted to perishable and high-value commodities which brooked no delay and carried a premium price. Air freight, however, demonstrated very fast rates of growth, over 10 per cent per annum in the late 1970s and early 1980s, suggesting it would be a more major player in the next century.

Inland waterways also played a small and decreasing part in total European freight transport. The navigable waterway network contracted in most countries.

Plate 13.1. A passenger lounge at Heathrow airport in 1946. Just after the war, Heathrow was a temporary tent village (complete with Elsan toilets), able to meet the requirements of what then was, compared to today, only a tiny number of air travellers.

Plate 13.2. A passenger lounge at Heathrow airport in 1994. Over the last half century, the size of airports and the range of facilities offered to air passengers have enormously expanded just as passenger numbers have risen and travel speeds increased.

Many canal systems had been built early in the process of industrialization and were often of low capacity, took tortuous routes or contained obstructions to easy navigability. As a result, speeds were low which was not suited to a society increasingly concerned with just-in-time delivery and rapid transit. Very few factories had direct access to a waterway, so transhipment was usually necessary, increasing the time taken and cost involved. The advantage of inland waterways was low unit cost based on large-scale units, where waterways had both depth and width sufficient to accommodate large barges and convoys of lighters. The wider continental rivers such as the Rhine and Rhône saw much traffic but the main growth on waterways was of pleasure craft and narrow-boat marinas.

Passenger Transport

In 1945 or 1950 the railways still carried the lion's share of passengers, but they were under a triple-headed threat, from private cars, motor buses and aeroplanes. As people became more affluent they appreciated the advantages and status of a motor car, with its door-to-door transport, convenience, privacy and, once the fixed costs were paid, low unit cost for family transport. Private motoring became more effective with the construction of bypasses, ring roads and motorway-style roads easing congestion and giving higher average speeds. As a result car ownership and fleet sizes soared, as Table 13.3 demonstrates. Growth rates were huge in the 1950s and 1960s, though they slowed down in the 1970s and 1980s as the market reached maturity. Motor buses benefited from the improvements to the road network, as well as technical changes in suspension and engine to make them more powerful and comfortable. In addition, long-distance buses became more passenger orientated by fitting toilets and providing refreshments, which allowed them to make longer, non-stop runs and hence reduce journey times.

Air transport has seen the most impressive growth rates of any mode of transport in the post-1945 period (see Table 13.4). For intercontinental traffic, planes killed off the prestigious passenger liner, relegating it to the role of cruise ship. For instance, in 1951 about 750,000 people crossed the Atlantic by sea and 300,000 by air. By 1957 both modes carried about one million passengers each, and in 1967 half a million travelled by sea and five and a half million by air. By 1975 Atlantic liners were dead.

The surge in air transport usage can be explained by factors on both the supply and demand side. The commercial exploitation of two wartime innovations played a part: the jet engine and radar. The advantage of jets was their superior speed to piston engines: whereas fast piston-engined aircraft achieved 200 mph, the early jets were reaching 400 mph. In addition the jets were much smoother in flight and avoided the turbulence of propeller-driven planes, which caused air sickness. The jet was also capable of much development in terms of power output so that ever larger planes could be built which lowered unit costs. The average speed of aeroplanes in 1952 was 300 kph, by 1962 it was over 450

Table 13.3. Motor vehicles in use (thousands)

	Cars					Commercials				
	1950	1960	1970	1980	1988	1950	1960	1970	1980	1988
Belgium	274	753	2,060	3,159	3,614	145	177	376	482	547
France	1,500	5,546	12,900	19,130	22,520	na	1,634	2,745	2,332	3,087
West Germany	516	4,489	13,941	23,192	28,878	372	703	1,038	1,277	1,322
Italy	342	1,995	10,181	17,686	na	229	456	904	1,338	na
UK	2,258	5,526	11,515	14,772	18,432	572	1,491	1,694	2,146	2,730

Source: Mitchell, International Historical Statistics: Europe 1750–1988, pp. 714–23.

Table 13.4. Passengers by rail and by air (billion passenger kms)

	Rail					Air				
	1950	1960	1970	1980	1988	1950	1960	1970	1980	1988
Belgium	7.0	8.6	8.3	7.0	7.0	0.24	1.26	2.45	4.8	6.5
France	26.4	32.0	41.0	54.7	62.6	1.12	5.23	13.6	34.1	32.0
West Germany	30.3	38.4	38.1	38.9	46.4	na	1.45	9.2	23.1	37.3
Italy	23.6	30.7	34.8	39.6	48.3	na	1.34	8.4	14.1	19.2
Spain	7.1	7.3	13.3	13.5	16.3	0.22	0.95	7.1	15.5	22.3
UK	32.5	34.7	30.4	30.3	31.7	1.28	7.29	18.9	56.7	83.0

Source: Mitchell, *International Historical Statistics: Europe 1750–1988*, pp. 683–8, 725–8.

and by 1972 exceeded 600. Average aircraft capacity rose from about 40 passengers in 1952 to 80 in 1962 and 120 in 1972. By the early 1990s it had doubled again to 230.

On the demand side, the growth of the aeroplane as a business tool was promoted by the globalization of industry and the large influx of foreign firms operating in Europe. This led to the growth of business and club class travel. At the other end of the plane, growing affluence and institution of the two-week annual holiday brought the growth of a mass tourism industry (see box). Thus, long-distance holiday travel came within the reach of most workers in affluent western Europe, which increased enormously the demand for air transport.

However, the railways fought back for passenger traffic. They had a safe clientèle for regular commuting into city centres from suburbs and dormitory towns. To compete against long-distance motor buses they introduced special discounted fares which were hedged around by restrictions. To respond to the airliners, the railways perceived speed as crucial and in most western European countries introduced high-speed trains, spurred on by the example of the Japanese bullet train introduced in 1964. France was the prime exponent of this, with the *train à grande vitesse* (TGV) achieving speeds of 170 mph in the early 1980s and exceeding 200 mph by the 1990s. Britain introduced Inter-City 125s in 1976 and a later generation capable of 150 mph in the early 1990s, but the failure of the Advanced Passenger Train and low levels of investment meant British railways failed to exploit the full potential of such high-speed trains. In many European countries which did adopt high-speed rail systems, passenger numbers grew in

In focus: The Package Holiday

In 1952 Spain welcomed $1\frac{1}{2}$ million foreign visitors; in 1984 the number had grown to 43 million. In 1950 international tourism receipts were running at about $2 billion; by 1984 this had risen to $70 billion. In the early 1950s there were about 30 million scheduled air passengers in the world; by the late 1980s there were nearly 900 million. These figures give some idea of the massive growth in the tourist industry, largely based on package holidays including cheap air travel. This case study explores the nature and causes of this growth.

The concept of an annual holiday from work began to gain currency in the inter-war period in a number of western European countries. Rising real incomes helped, as did the belief in the efficacy of getting completely away from the workplace, the benefit of sunbathing and sporting activities. Initially, funds permitted only relatively short-distance travel and there was a rapid growth of domestic seaside resorts, and holiday camps and villages. In many ways the holiday camp was a precursor to the package holiday, for after paying the standard charge, activities such as sports, shows and other entertainments were mostly free. Of course the middle and upper classes had

The Package Holiday (continued)

long travelled abroad and the development of tour operators, like Thomas Cook in Britain, helped by sorting out the technical problems of choosing and booking hotels, foreign exchange, tickets on a range of railway companies and countries, guides, etc. It also spawned a genre of publishing, namely the travel guide, in which (theoretically) experienced travellers provided itineraries, notes on history, topography, customs, language and cuisine and so made travel much less of a gamble.

In the post-war period rising real incomes, reductions in the hours of work and especially the growth of holiday entitlements, increased demand for the services of a holiday industry. In addition, holidays were often associated with sun, sea and sand and hence there began mass transit from northern Europe, where weather was unpredictable, or predictably cold and wet, to southern, especially around the shores of the Mediterranean. This mass migration was greatly aided by falling costs of air travel, as jet planes of increasing capacity reduced fuel and labour costs per seat. To achieve low unit costs, the plane needed to be full, and so there developed the idea of aggregating individuals into groups and filling planes. This gave rise to charter flights which departed full, rather than scheduled services which were committed to depart at set times with regular intervals, whether partly empty or not. The charter airlines usually commenced as independent firms, initially in troop carrying or in moving groups who had some affinity such as birdwatching or country music. The other reason for the formation of charter airlines was to avoid the strict International Air Transport Association (IATA) rules about fares. Air travel was a worldwide cartel in which scheduled air fares were set jointly and no discounts were allowed. Given that scheduled flights were normally working on 50 per cent load factors, charter flights which were guaranteed to be full could much reduce their price per seat and still make a profit.

Apart from their capacity, the other advantage of jet planes was their speed. Being much faster than propeller-driven planes meant that destinations which had been too distant became possible for mass tourism. Once people had become accustomed to a three- or four-hour flight, longer journeys, such as across the Atlantic, did not seem so daunting. Key components in this mass transhumance were the package holiday and the tour operator. The importance of the package holiday was that virtually all of the essential components of a holiday were known and made explicit at the time of booking. Thus, tour operators put together air fares, transfers, accommodation, meals, tips, local trips and even entertainment, and the holidaymaker knew the total cost. The package holiday made holidaymaking easy, for the customer needed no skills in choosing an itinerary or coordinating transport and hotels. All the difficult work was done by the tour operator. The secret of this profession's success was to ensure all the capacity – hotels, flights, etc. – was fully utilized, and so keep unit costs down, and to ensure local hotels were up to the standards expected. Their expatriate

The Package Holiday (continued)

labour costs – made up by representatives in the resorts – were kept low as mostly young people, and a majority of women, accepted low cash wages in return for food and accommodation and some free time in resorts which others had paid to visit. Tour operators also needed to be good bargainers to keep local costs down and standards up. A further strength of tour operators was their ability to make money by investing their spare cash. They had a particularly advantageous cash-flow, as at the minimum a deposit was paid at the time of booking and sometimes the whole cost. Given that tour operators tended to promote their products many months in advance, this left them with cash up front whereas many of their costs were paid well after the holiday had taken place. So the tour operators were often holding substantial sums for several months and these could be profitably lent on the money market to provide additional returns to the tour operator.

Although there were various moves towards integration in the tourism industry, for instance tour operators linking with charter airline companies, and forwards into high street travel agencies, it remained a competitive market, with discounts, special offers and limited availability quite normal. In part this was because of the extreme perishability of the product. If a particular seat on an aeroplane and a room in a hotel were not filled they became valueless. Hence it behove the tour operator to discount the price if it looked as though there were going to be spare places. To some extent the customer became more sophisticated in the 1980s, knowing that such discounting would occur and holding back a purchase until then. In part, too, costs of entry to the industry were relatively low, since most bills were settled *post hoc* and there was room for niche companies serving particular groups. From this base some branched out into full line companies.

The effects of the mass tourist industry were a mixed blessing to the recipient countries. There were benefits, including large foreign exchange earnings and the creation of employment. However, adverse effects also ensued. The employment was perceived as low-wage and of poor status; development of hotels and resort complexes could be tasteless and despoil local scenery and at worst exclude local people from their own territory. Dependence on tourism earnings was also seen as unhealthy because of the fickle nature of the trade and, as a non-essential, it was disproportionately affected by the cycle of economic booms and busts. There was also the problem of long-term sustainability. Tourists destroyed historic and beauty spots by their sheer numbers and made huge demands on infrastructural systems as well as creating problems of pollution, litter and rubbish disposal which, if not adequately tackled, created conditions which deterred future inflows of tourists. Hence, in the late 1980s the idea of long-term sustainability began to develop. This was likely to increase the cost of the package holiday and restrict the numbers available at particular resorts, but it was essential to ensure the longer-term future of the industry.

the 1970s and 1980s (see Table 13.4). By the 1990s the French had a large high-speed network and many other European countries followed their lead, such as Germany, Spain and Italy. This offered real competition to the airlines.

Shipping

At the beginning of the period marine transport was the most important means of international travel for both passengers and goods. A large merchant fleet was seen as essential for overseas trade and hence Britain, as a major exporter and importer, had the largest fleet in Europe (see Table 13.5), contributing to invisible earnings. Although the regular passenger trade was killed off by large-capacity jet aircraft, and air freight grew very strongly, maritime traffic remained important for goods transport. Its relative importance declined for a number of reasons. The loss of colonies and the formation and extension of the European Community caused a diversion from intercontinental to intra-European trade so that more was moved by lorry and on short sea crossings by ferry. In addition some of the heavier raw material importing industries went into a long slow decline, thus obviating the need for such bulky imports.

The trend in western European merchant fleets was expansion to the 1970s and decline thereafter. The UK's relative decline was the most precipitate, falling from first place in 1976 in Table 13.5 to third in 1985 and fifth in 1995. The Greek merchant fleet, on the other hand, was the most successful in western Europe, expanding when others were shrinking in the 1980s and taking first place. It was a tight international maritime network based on kinship and social ties. The general decline of the 1980s was a function of the rise of fleets registered outside Europe, especially in Asia, aided in part by European companies registering their ships under flags of convenience, such as Liberia or Panama, where wage levels and other cost-incurring regulations were less onerous.

Table 13.5. Merchant fleet sizes (thousands of gross tonnes)

	1950	1965	1976	1985	1995
France	3,207	5,198	11,278	8,237	4,055
West Germany	670	5,279	9,265	6,177	5,398
Greece	1,304	7,137	25,035	31,032	29,212
Italy	2,809	5,701	11,078	8,843	6,305
Netherlands	2,958	4,891	5,920	4,301	3,755
Norway	5,679	15,641	27,944	15,339	20,475
Spain	1,175	2,132	6,028	6,256	1,619
UK	11,103	21,530	32,923	14,344	5,299

Sources: UN, *Annual Bulletin of Transport Statistics for Europe* (Geneva, 1966, 1978, 1988); Mitchell, *International Historical Statistics: Europe 1750–1988*, pp. 701–6; Institute of Shipping, *Shipping Statistics Yearbook* (Bremen, 1995), pp. 23–8; Lloyds Register of Shipping, *World Fleet Statistics 1995* (London, 1996), pp. 11–13.

Changes took place on the supply side which drastically altered the pattern of maritime trade. Ships became larger and more specialized as this gave them lower unit costs; but this made it increasingly difficult for them to use existing docks and harbours where water depth or lock sizes were too restrictive. As a result, a number of port cities constructed new deep-water terminals which moved the centre of gravity down-river and out of the city centres. The critical trend was the growth of containerization. Although pioneer container services can be traced to the later 1950s, it was the 1960s which saw their rapid growth on a number of routes. The concept spread rapidly so that it became the norm. This required a massive re-equipment and hence vast investment in ships and land-based facilities. Special ships were built to maximize their container-carrying capacity and speed loading and discharging. In addition, large container parks were needed on shore to store containers awaiting embarkation or onward rail or road delivery. To load, discharge, sort and reassemble these large boxes, specialist handling equipment was needed, ranging from large fork-lift trucks to massive overhead gantries and travelling cranes. These changes required space and deep water, hence downstream terminals were preferred.

As well as containerization the other major trend in freight handling was to 'roll-on-roll-off' or 'ro-ro'. This was where lorries drove straight on to ships with their cargo rather than the goods being unloaded and then loaded into the holds of conventional ships. The big advantages of this were greater speed and reduction in costs of handling, for unloading from lorry to ship was time-consuming and labour-intensive. The ro-ro principle was particularly suitable for short sea crossings, such as between Britain and the mainland of Europe or across the Baltic. It was not suitable for long oceanic hauls such as from Europe to America or Australia where containers were more efficient. The shift to ro-ro and containers meant a drastic reduction in the need for labour. Previously dock work had been very labour-intensive, involving men in shifting sacks, barrels and crates of goods with the aid of cranes, winches and derricks. The geographical shift of the centre of maritime activity and the massive reduction in labour decimated the dock workers as an industrial force and caused a collapse in employment in some dockside communities, especially from the 1970s.

The growth of ro-ro traffic and the increasing numbers of holiday makers travelling by car meant an increasing demand for car and lorry ferries. To maximize available space and speed up loading and unloading, a design evolved of large open car decks with no watertight bulkheads or other means of division. This was a fundamentally flawed design because once water got onto the car deck its progress was unimpeded and it could act to destabilize, as was demonstrated in one or two high publicity failures with large-scale loss of life, such as the Zeebrugge disaster of 1987.

Urban Transport

The main theme in urban transport was increasing congestion invoking a range of responses to try to reduce it. Most western European countries by 1945 were mature in terms of the shift of rural population to urban areas, but as cities grew in population size they also grew in extent. Hence there was a continual shift of population to ever more far-flung suburbs and dormitories. City centres became deserted residentially and concentrated on commercial purposes, thus exacerbating the need for commuter transport. Rising real wages and slight reductions in nominal hours worked facilitated longer distance commuting. Increasingly this became motor transport, especially in some countries like Britain, where car costs were often met by employers. This put pressure on existing road networks and led to plans for urban motorways and ring roads combined with pedestrianization of shopping centres. Another tack was to put fast urban transport underground, by building or extending subway and metro systems. These construction activities were extremely costly and were difficult to justify on pure cost/revenue grounds, so a wider cost/benefit analysis was used to quantify other gains from such improvements. Various methods were tried to reduce the usage of motor cars in city centres. These included encouraging the pedal cycle by introducing dedicated cycle lanes, 'park and ride' schemes, encouraging motorists to use the bus, and even banning cars from city roads on alternate days, depending on their registration number.

Initially the post-war years saw a decline in trolley bus and tram mileage in some cities and even their demise, for motor buses were cheaper in terms of capital costs and more flexible. However, as congestion increased, dedicated bus lanes were introduced in some cities to speed up their often appallingly slow rate of progress. These were seen as being not much different from tram routes, and electric trams were perceived as environmentally friendly compared to the motor bus. In the effort to reduce total costs, urban transport sought to reduce the amount of labour employed. Methods included one-person operation on buses by doing away with the employee who collected fares and requiring the driver to do this as well. On underground systems the mechanical issuing and collecting of tickets drastically reduced the labour required and so total costs. To cut labour numbers further, closed-circuit television and video monitoring were introduced in the 1980s to allow drivers to check when passengers had alighted and boarded, and to allow station security to be centrally monitored. These moves brought complaints about the safety of stations, especially when incidents occurred such as the King's Cross fire.

Communications

In 1945 the methods of communication, by the standards of 1998, seem few and slow. Mail, of course, existed and was recovering from wartime interruptions, as did the telephone. The latter, however, required personal connection, was expensive for long-distance and overseas calls, and few people owned their own receivers, the telephone being mostly a tool for business and the better-off consumer. Radio broadcasting was an accepted form of information, education and entertainment, but television was still little more than an experimental laboratory toy and the number of radio stations and channels was very limited. There were radical changes in the means of communication in the next 50 years. Radio stations and channels proliferated, allowing a range of minority and local interests to have their own channels. This expansion in the number of broadcasting outlets was a function of developments in technology, which allowed greater segmentation of the air waves, and a growing belief that radio was not such a threat to public order and security that it needed to be strictly monitored.

Perhaps the largest single change came in the commercialization of television. An experimental method in 1945, television broadcasting began in the early 1950s in most western European countries, and by the 1960s had evolved into a boom industry in producing the television sets themselves and also in programming. Initially there were very few channels and limited broadcast hours. Over the long run a number of trends are apparent. The hours of broadcasting expanded until in the 1980s some channels were virtually 24-hour broadcasters. In Europe the number of channels expanded slowly in the 1960s and 1970s to proliferate in the 1980s when satellite and cable brought dozens of channels into homes. Whereas many of the early television services were financed by licence fees or from advertising revenue, in the 1980s the principle of paying for specific channels became accepted and even 'pay per view' for specific programmes, especially world-class sporting events. Television was taken up avidly as a cheap form of home entertainment, and its consumer value was enhanced by the advent of colour broadcasts, better definition, and stereo sound. The introduction of the video recorder from the 1970s was a mixed blessing to television. On the one hand it allowed a 'time shift' whereby programmes could be recorded when the viewer was otherwise engaged and watched later. On the other hand it allowed the viewing of pre-recorded films which competed for viewing time with regular broadcasting. By the mid-1990s television was ubiquitous and the future looked to be concerned with integrating it with other means of communication like the telephone and computers.

The telephone, too, became a boom industry after the Second World War, as Table 13.6 demonstrates. In 1945 it was largely confined to business use and the middle and upper income groups, with a wide range of take-up in different countries. Like television and car ownership, there was a positive correlation between phone ownership and standard of living, so that as real incomes rose so did both the number of people with telephones and the number of calls made. Technological change was as important in the telephone industry as in television, in terms of enhancing its value to the customer and reducing operating costs via automation and greater reliability of systems. The introduction of subscriber trunk dialling in the 1960s, cutting out the operator, made long distance calls easier and cheaper and the advent of satellites multiplied the number of international lines enormously and reduced the cost of international calls in the 1970s. The use of fibre optics and digital exchanges increased reliability and hence reduced maintenance costs significantly. In addition, these innovations allowed the phone firms to enhance the services they offered customers. Services like call tracing, itemized bills, automatic recording of incoming calls and memorizing of regularly used numbers were normal by the later 1980s. Document transmission by phone, which had been pioneered by Rank Xerox in the mid-1970s, became known as fax and really took off in the later 1980s. The other big change was the innovation of mobile phones, which allowed people to stay in contact at all times and in all places. These became the status symbol of the 1980s and commonplace by the mid-1990s. They were a clever device on the part of telecom companies to charge much higher rates for phone calls, and so avoid the trend of declining real prices for terrestrial lines.

During the 1980s the future seemed to lie in integrating these various network systems, so that shopping and banking by television and phone, accessing videos remotely, and video conferencing, all became practical possibilities. By 1995 e-mail and the Internet were threatening to curb the growth in direct telephone calls, being both cheaper and more convenient. The period between 1945 and 1995 saw many fundamental, technologically driven changes, but perhaps the most marked were in the field of communications. Despite this revolution the oldest form of communication, the letter, did not go into a steep decline. Quite the contrary. As Table 13.6 shows, the trend in western European countries was for the volume of mail to increase steadily. Despite premature predictions of the paperless society, in fact communication by letter grew, partially because 'mail shots' and 'junk mail' were seen as a cheap and moderately effective means of promoting products and services, being based on computerized databases of target consumers. Perhaps the advent of the mass use of faxes will change this in the late 1990s. By contrast to the growth in mail, the use of telegrams declined in all western European countries from the 1960s, if not before. The telephone was a more perfect substitute for the telegram and as phone ownership spread so telegram usage declined. It is no coincidence that Britain, with the most rapid take-up of telephone ownership, saw the greatest decline in the use of telegrams.

Debates and Interpretations

Transport was deeply involved in a number of key debates about the nature of the economy. In the 1940s and 1950s many types of transport in many western European countries were nationalized and in addition there was strict regulation of most aspects of their operation. For example, most western European countries had national flag-carrying airlines which were wholly owned by the state or received generous subsidies from it. Moreover most railway networks were owned by the state and operated at a significant loss, which was met out of taxation. The market was not being allowed to determine the type and level of services, prices or frequencies but rather it was determined by quango, cartel or civil servant. This was not a contentious issue, even in the 1960s. The argument for the International Air Traffic Association and the collusion on fares, frequencies and slots was complex. In part it was accepted that aircraft could not operate commercially as their capacities were too low and costs too high. Thus, it made sense to collude to keep prices up to minimize the loss. In part it was also a matter of national

Table 13.6. Communications (mail in billions, telegrams in thousands, and telephone calls in billions)

	Mail					Telegrams					Telephone calls				
	1945	1955	1965	1975	1985	1945	1955	1965	1975	1985	1945	1955	1965	1975	1985
Belgium	na	2.1	2.6	2.3	2.7	5.6	8.8	7.1	3.7	1.2	0.3	0.6	1.0	1.1	1.4
France	3.7	5.0	7.4	9.6	11.8	56	26	25	20	13	1.3	2.3	6.8	29.2[a]	81.6[a]
West Germany	na	6.2	9.7	10.5	12.6	na	29	31	15	6	na	4.0	7.4	15.7	29.7
Italy	na	3.9	5.6	5.9	6.4	19	34	37	23	23	na	0.2	0.9	2.4	na
Spain	0.8	1.4	3.0	4.5	4.2	38	41	50	35	24	0.1	0.8	0.2	1.1	2.9
UK	6.5	9.7	11.3	9.9	11.7	74	43	31	21	na	2.4	4.2	6.9	15.2	na

Note: [a]from 1966 on, numbers of units charged rather than calls made.

Source: Mitchell, International Historical Statistics: Europe 1750–1988, pp. 736–7, 748–53.

pride and prestige. Governments saw their air space as an extension of their national territory and thus felt empowered to negotiate who could cross it, land on and start from it, and the extent of such activities.

Railways too were finding it difficult to cover costs. This was partially because they had been so used and abused in the war that they needed massive investment to restore and renew their extensive fixed capital. In addition competition from road vehicles had creamed off much of the short-distance traffic in the inter-war period, and the growing efficiency and capacity of road transport in the 1950s and 1960s made further inroads into this revenue. Thus, virtually all western European governments accepted the financial burden that was required to keep the railways running. The idea that railways were important socially in linking otherwise remote communities and providing mobility for the less privileged groups in society helped to justify the subsidies.

Throughout the period there was a group of economists and politicians, usually on the right, who advocated market forces for such transport services and condemned subsidies and government intervention as distortions of the market. This view was associated with the Austrian School but while Keynesian policies held sway it was a minority who supported it, and it was largely ignored in policy terms. In the 1970s, however, when western Europe encountered two great economic shocks from the oil price rises caused by the Arab–Israeli War and the fall of the Shah, the belief in the impossibility of resisting market forces began to grow. Governments might delay the inevitable but not prevent it. The switch to monetarism, demonstrated by the Thatcher government in the UK and the Reagan administration in the USA, brought with it a commitment to freeing market forces, by privatization, deregulation and the encouragement of competition and thus the reduction of government intervention, subsidy and ownership. The policy debate shifted from seeing transport problems as essentially a matter of organization to seeing them as primarily a matter of economics.

In the air the Americans led the way in deregulation, allowing open competition, ease of entry to routes, freedom to discount fares and determine frequencies. The impact of these changes was much debated. Some old-established airlines went bankrupt. Initially there was a spate of fare reductions and increased frequencies, but these tended to evaporate as mergers occurred and new informal cartels came into being. In Europe there was much greater reluctance to take such drastic steps. European airlines remained largely a regulated cartel, despite European policy on competition and despite some airlines, such as British Airways, being privatized and slimmed down and becoming more profitable enterprises. A significant concern before the air market was freed was that airlines in their drive to be competitive would cut down on maintenance and repairs and so safety standards would slip. A similar argument was advanced for road passenger vehicles when they too became de-municipalized and deregulated. In practice the safety record of both modes of transport did not significantly worsen. This was aided by greater component reliability, the continuation of strict routine maintenance and replacement of key parts after a set number of hours' use. Human error continued to be the largest single cause of aircraft or bus crashes.

One common feature of the ending of cartels and central and local government monopolies was an attack on labour costs. This took the form of reducing staffing levels, so that the number of crew in the cockpit was reduced, increasing duty rosters and introducing more complex split shifts, and a reduction in rates of pay and other non-wage benefits. This reduced the costs of the transport operators but there is little convincing evidence of sustained reductions in real price to the customers. Rather, enterprises which were operating at a loss or barely making a surplus became profitable. Where the organization had been in the public sector this had the benefit of reducing government outlay, which contributed to a common governmental objective of reducing the public sector borrowing requirement (PSBR) and direct taxation, in line with monetarist thinking and the guidelines on entering a common European currency union. By the 1990s the balance had changed drastically compared to the 1950s. Privatization, deregulation, free markets, minimal government subsidies and intervention were the flavour in most western European countries.

Another marked change over time was to be seen in attitudes to the environmental aspects of transport. Although there have always been mixed feelings about the siting of airports, with resistance to the establishment of an airport evident in the 1930s and with some writers, such as J.B. Priestley, complaining of the ribbon development that took place alongside Britain's arterial roads, the overall feeling was of a need for better roads and airports as a visible sign of progress, for bypasses to reduce congestion and pollution in city centres, and for purpose-built motor roads to reduce accidents and speed up traffic flows. There was an element of competition between countries and also of emulation. The autobahnen and autostrade of pre-war Germany and Italy made Britain look old-fashioned in motoring terms, and hence encouraged the motorway programme. In airport terms Heathrow, which started commercial operations only in 1946, was the largest airport in Europe. Retaining its crown was not easy as others on the mainland of Europe, such as Schiphol (Amsterdam), Charles de Gaulle (Paris) and Frankfurt vied for the position. There were increasing complaints about aircraft noise, as the number of aircraft movements increased and more powerful engines were introduced. This reached a peak in the mid-1970s just before Concorde came into service, when its noisy engines and the furore over the sonic boom caused more racket than the thing itself. From the 1970s onwards aircraft manufacturers aimed to produce quieter engines and retrofitted hush kits on existing aircraft. This and the huge employment created by airports which supported the local economy seemed to reduce the resistance to adding terminals and runways and extending airport size.

Road construction was in part a political issue, with conservative governments favouring road building and espousing road transport as a free-enterprise sector of the economy, whereas socialist and liberal governments were more inclined towards the railways as a public sector. There was always some resistance to new road building from various bodies looking after the countryside and those supporting nature reserves and endangered plants and animals, but in general resistance was relatively muted in the 1960s and 1970s. However, as the traffic-creating capabilities of new roads were appreciated, and the general climate became more ecologically orientated, so the resistance to road-building programmes increased. This, combined with their cost when governments were looking for ways of reducing expenditure, led to cuts in some road-building programmes, notably in Britain. Where such roads were not provided as toll roads, which was normal for motorway-style roads in many mainland European countries, there was consideration of having parallel roads built by contractors who would levy charges and so provide fast tracks. This would effectively free government of substantial capital expenditure. This form of road pricing was also contemplated for urban congestion. It was feasible because of advances in electronic tagging and monitoring whereby road vehicles could be fitted with equipment which would log an entry in the road operator's computer every time the vehicle used the motorway and which would be the basis of charging. Similar devices were contemplated for city centre traffic, as a way of raising revenue, restricting use by price and hence reducing congestion and pollution and speeding up traffic speeds. In 1996 such measures were still in the future.

Bibliographical Note

The broad geographical and modal scope of the topic and its contemporaneity mean that there is not a great deal of historical literature available in books or journal articles. Rather, high quality newspapers and magazines, such as the *Financial Times* and *The Economist* often carry reports or special supplements on recent developments in transport and communications. Large quantities of statistical material are available; for instance, Brian R. Mitchell, *International Historical Statistics: Europe 1750–1988* (New York, 1992) has a large section on transport statistics, and the United Nations publishes an *Annual Bulletin of Transport Statistics for Europe* (Geneva, annually) and the European Conference of Ministers of Transport published *Statistical Trends in Transport* (Paris, 1993). In addition there are various agencies, such as the Union Internationale de Chemins de Fer (railways) and the Institute of Shipping, which issue statistics on one mode of transport.

A useful introduction is to be found in Derek H. Aldcroft, *British Transport since 1914: An Economic History* (Newton Abbot, 1975) which although mainly about Britain contains some foreign comparisons and deals with general issues. Despite its title, the vast majority is on the post-1945 period. The same author's article 'A new chapter in transport history: the twentieth century revolution' in *The Journal of Transport History*, volume III (1976), is also a good, if brief, statement of the main changes and issues, and less UK orientated. A more British orientation is to be found in Philip Bagwell's *The Transport Revolution 1770–1985* (London, 1988) of which the last two chapters are good on government policy and the debate over private versus public transport.

On particular forms of transport, T.R. Gourvish's *British Railways 1948–1973: A Business History* (Cambridge, 1986) is a vast and masterly exegesis of the changes in one country's railway industry, with some comparisons and contrasts to other countries, and Philip Bagwell's *The Railwaymen*, Volume 2 (London, 1982) is excellent on the shifts in working practices and what these meant for labour force size and conditions of work. On shipping Alan Jamieson's article 'Facing the rising tide: British attitudes to Asian national shipping lines, 1959–64' in the *International Journal of Maritime History*, volume VII (1995) outlines the growth of Asian fleets which impinged on European shipping; and Gelina Harlaftis in *A History of Greek-owned Shipping* (London, 1995) traces and explains the growth of Greek shipping to European dominance. An article by Jesus M. Valdaliso, 'The diffusion of technological change in the Spanish merchant fleet during the twentieth century: available alternatives and conditioning factors' in *The Journal of Transport History*, volume XVIII (1996) is particularly good on technological change in the Spanish merchant marine and some of his ideas have a European-wide importance. Colin Simmons and Viv Caruana have written a pioneering article on the impact of an airport on its local population, 'Neighbourhood issues in the development of Manchester airport, 1934–82', in *The Journal of Transport History*, volume XV (1994); and Peter J. Lyth and Marc L.J. Dierikx have explained the growth of the mass air transport market in 'From privilege to popularity: the growth of leisure air travel since 1945' in the same volume of the same journal.

Acknowledgements

I wish to thank Julie Stevenson for collecting the statistics which underpin this chapter, a small proportion of which appear in the tables; Terry Gourvish for reading an early draft and making numerous suggestions on how to improve it; Philip Bagwell for much sage and diplomatic advice over more years than either of us care to remember, and Giuliana Taborelli and team for accuracy and more patience than duty required.

14 Urbanization

William Lever

Introduction

Changes in the economic structures of the nations of western Europe have been paralleled by changes in the spatial structure of the towns and cities which house these economic structures. At the simplest level we can trace the transitions at national level from economies which are based on primary activities (farming, fishing, forestry, mining), in which populations of workers are usually located in rural settlements administered and serviced by a spatially regular pattern of central market places, to economies in which manufacturing is the dominant activity. In these latter economies, the labour force becomes increasingly concentrated in urban centres located in response to the availability of raw materials, sources of energy and transport routes.

The American economist W.W. Rostow described this transition from a rural-based agricultural economy to a town-based manufacturing economy and then went on to describe 'late industrialization' as a subsequent stage in which the demand for manual labour falls but in which more workers find employment in services, and urban growth continues.[1] In this so-called 'stages of economic growth' model, industrialization and urbanization occur concurrently as cities grow in order to accommodate the workforce of the manufacturing enterprises which grow in size in order to take advantage of scale economies. These growing cities provide an increasing range of agglomeration economies, both for their resident populations (education, health care, leisure facilities) and for the business located within them (financial services, legal services, information processing, other business services). This distinction is now characterized by using the terms consumer (or wealth-consuming) services for the former and producer (or wealth-creating) services for the latter.

By the 1960s it was being argued that these agglomeration economies conferred such an advantage on the largest cities that they would continue to grow at a faster rate than smaller urban centres, unless there was some form of planning policy intervention (population overspill agreements, New Towns, green belts) to limit their growth or to divert it to smaller or new settlements.[2] By the 1970s, in the more developed parts of western Europe, the manufacturing sector was declining, in employment terms at least, and the service sector was providing replacement jobs, although not always for the workers made redundant by the manufacturing sector (see Chapter 6). At the same time, families were moving away from the inner areas of the largest cities, adopting a suburban lifestyle, although the price to be paid was often a long daily journey to work by private or public transport. At this stage, jobs, especially in services, were moving to the suburbs more slowly than residential accommodation. Some families continued to move even further from the largest cities, preferring the lifestyle of small villages and towns, and gradually with the development of industrial parks, out-of-town shopping centres and commercial office construction away from the central business districts, a fear developed that cities would hollow out, creating what Garreau called the 'edge city'.[3] Over the past decade there has been a debate whether European cities would follow this American model or whether lower levels of car ownership, stronger planning laws and more concern for the environment will keep European cities denser and more urbanized.[4]

Within the nations of western Europe, it is possible to identify three types of urbanization. The first occurs in north-west Europe where the levels of, first, industrialization and subsequently of service employment are highest and where urbanization has progressed furthest. The second occurs in central Europe where industrialization has been slower as has been the shift to service employment and where urbanization is lower. Lastly in southern Europe, industrialization came significantly later as did the subsequent development of services, and levels of urbanization are lowest. Whilst this looks like a chronological sequence in which the centre follows the north-west and in which the south follows the centre, this would be overly simplistic. There are several reasons why industrialization and service sector development, and urbanization, in Greece or Portugal or southern Italy have not and will not exactly match that of Germany or France in the centre, or of Britain, the Netherlands or Scandinavia in the north-west. Southern Europe, for example, lacks the energy resources (coal, oil) which fostered industrial growth in the north. The economic integration of Europe has led to greater economic specialization. New sectors such as mass tourism have developed to shape the economies of southern Europe.

Urban Concentration

The shift from employment in spatially diffused activities such as agriculture, forestry, fishing and mining to employment in spatially concentrated activities such as manufacturing in Europe, and elsewhere, has only been possible by population migration from rural areas to rapidly growing towns and cities. Several preconditions were necessary for this migration – an excess of labour in rural areas, more efficient agriculture to supply food to the cities, together with an effective transport system, a rapid increase in the demand for industrial, manual labour, and an urban technology capable of supplying shelter, water, transport

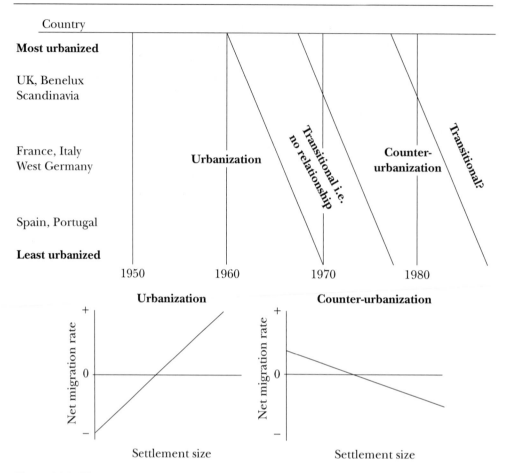

Figure 14.1. The transition from urbanization to counter-urbanization, 1950–90. *Source:* A.G. Champion, 'The stages of urban growth model applied to the British urban system', *Area* 18 (1986).

and other urban infrastructure (sewage, power). Within the cities of western Europe, urbanization and industrialization proceeded in parallel, although in its earliest phase in the nineteenth century often the physical environment of the rapidly growing cities was very poor. Unlike the current situation in many Third World cities, the demand for labour and the supply of labour remained roughly equal and the problems of 'overurbanization' (lack of employment, shanty town development, poor standards of health and hygiene) did not occur.

The first stage of urban change in post-war Europe is a continuation of the trend which began in the nineteenth century, namely centralization. As Figure 14.1 shows, however, this is a phenomenon of the periphery of western Europe, especially its southern Mediterranean periphery. By 1945–50, north-west Europe had already reached the stage where the core regions, usually the capital city regions, whilst growing by net immigration, were doing so at a declining rate.[5] The rate of growth of the core regions in north-west Europe fell from about 10 per cent in

1945–50 to zero in 1960. The rate of population loss from the periphery fell from 10 per cent in 1945–50 to zero in 1960 in north-west Europe.

As can be seen from Table 14.1, countries such as Belgium, the Netherlands and the United Kingdom had already reached their manufacturing peak in the 1960s, whereas countries such as France and West Germany were continuing to find their share of total employment in manufacturing rising until about 1970, and the countries of the southern periphery (Spain, Portugal, Greece) and Ireland continued to see their agricultural labour force decline and their manufacturing labour force rise into the 1980s. The growth of the manufacturing sector is therefore associated with the movement of rural workers from the rural–agricultural south of Italy to the industrial towns of the north such as Turin and Milan. Eventually the supply of potential manufacturing workers in rural areas diminishes and employers are forced to look elsewhere. Britain, for example, was forced to recruit textile workers from the Indian subcontinent and service workers from the West Indies in the 1950s and early 1960s, and somewhat later France found migrants from north Africa, and West Germany absorbed workers from Turkey and Yugoslavia in the 1970s (see Chapter 11).

Figure 14.1 shows that the countries of the west European periphery continued to experience centralization, defined as a positive correlation between population density and population change due to migration flows, until the mid-1960s. Thereafter the rate of population gain from migration in the core regions fell from about 10 per cent to about 2 per cent around 1980, and the rate of population loss from the periphery from net migration fell from −10 per cent to −2 per cent.

Counter-urbanization

Demographers examining the key trends in urban population distribution in post-war western Europe place the greatest importance on the 'turning point' at which centralization and urbanization turn into counter-urbanization. Berry, in the context of the United States, defines counter-urbanization as 'a process of population deconcentration; it implies a movement from a state of more concentration to a state of less concentration'. This gives the impression that the changeover occurs at one point in time and is irreversible. In the European context, however, Champion points out that there are several elements within counter-urbanization.[6] The first of these is simply 'spill-over' in which population growth leads to the physical expansion of a city's built-up area so that it extends beyond the spatial limits of its administrative area. In population terms the relative decline of the core city and the relative growth of the periphery, albeit that it is physically a continuation of the core city, look statistically like counter-urbanization but do not imply either a cultural change (in the form of a rejection of city lifestyle) or a relocation of employment. A second variant of counter-urbanization is better termed 'suburbanization'. In this process people choose to live at the periphery of the large urban centres, enjoying a suburban lifestyle (lower density housing, better public services) but remaining dependent upon the core city for much of their

Table 14.1. Proportions (per cent) of national labour force in agriculture, manufacturing and services

	1959			1969			1979			1989			1995		
	A	M	S	A	M	S	A	M	S	A	M	S	A	M	S
Belgium	9	45	46	5	43	52	3	36	61	2	30	68	2	29	69
Denmark	19	37	44	12	38	50	7	33	60	6	27	67	5	27	68
France	24	38	38	15	40	46	9	36	55	6	30	64	5	26	69
Germany	14	47	39	9	48	43	6	44	50	4	40	57	3	38	59
Greece	58	17	25	43	24	33	31	30	39	22	33	45	20	27	53
Ireland	38	23	39	28	30	42	20	32	48	13	27	60	na	na	na
Italy	34	33	33	22	39	39	15	38	47	9	32	58	8	32	60
Netherlands	10	40	50	6	39	54	5	33	62	4	24	72	4	21	75
Norway	22	35	43	14	37	49	9	30	61	6	26	68	5	23	72
Portugal	45	30	25	31	33	36	31	35	35	20	35	46	11	32	56
Spain	38	30	32	28	35	37	19	36	44	13	33	54	9	30	61
Sweden	16	40	44	9	41	51	6	33	62	4	29	67	2	24	71
UK	5	47	48	3	45	51	3	39	59	2	29	69	2	24	73
OECD Europe	27	37	36	19	39	42	15	36	49	8	28	64	6	26	68

Sources: OECD, Labour Force Statistics, 1962–82; ILO, Yearbook of Labour Statistics.

employment and higher-order services, such as higher education, advanced health care and some leisure facilities (theatres, concert halls, etc.).

A more profound form of counter-urbanization occurs where people choose to live in small urban places – towns and villages – accepting a different lifestyle from that of suburbia, although they may still be dependent upon the bigger urban centres for employment and for services. This process, often termed exurbanization, represents a rejection of urban values, which are often equated with social pathologies such as crime and deprivation, and is often seen as an attempt to recreate a new sense of community felt to have been lacking in suburbia. Lastly, the exurbanization process is extended to include employment and services where employers are driven from the inner areas of large cities by rising costs (of labour and land), by local taxation and by urban agglomerative diseconomies such as traffic congestion, pollution and problems such as crime and arson. In much of western Europe urban–rural shift has been seen both as a market-driven process as first manufacturing and then services moved away from the largest cities where costs were highest and profits lowest, and as an outcome of land-use planning which favoured industrial estates on greenfield sites, out-of-town shopping centres, office and science parks at motorway intersections, and the construction of speculatively built housing on estates attached to smaller urban centres.

These processes, aggregated in the term counter-urbanization, continued until the early to mid-1970s in north-west Europe and to about 1980 in central Europe. Statistically the process is described as a negative correlation between population density and population growth through migration: in other words the densest (and largest) population centres and regions had the smallest growth (or larger losses) in population. Table 14.2 shows that in the 1970s in the 14 countries of western Europe, only in five was centralization still occurring, marked by a positive correlation between density and migration gain. Of these five, three were underdeveloped peripheral (Ireland, Spain and Portugal) and two were mountainous and sparsely populated (Austria and Norway) with a primate population distribution (i.e. dominated by their over-large capital cities, Vienna and Oslo).

By the end of the 1980s, demographers were extending their explanations for counter-urbanization to encompass variables other than changes in the location of employment and lifestyle preferences. These additional factors included the growth in the number of people and households who did not depend upon a job for their living (such as the retired and students) and who were thus not tied to big city–core region employment. In addition, more households were becoming the owners of two (or more) residences: this would permit the family to live in small urban places whilst the main breadwinner could spend weekdays in a small apartment in the large city. Economically, regional policy in many European countries was having the effect of decentralizing employment away from overcongested core regions. Moreover, improved educational systems outside the large cities meant that the supply of qualified labour increased away from the core region, and whilst some young people would continue to migrate from the periphery because of a lack of adequate jobs, greater balance would occur and more investment would move to the periphery, in countries such as Italy, Spain,

Table 14.2. Net migration trends

Country (number of regions)	1970s tendency		1980s tendency		Direction of shift
	Period	*r*	**Period**	*r*	
Austria (16)	1971–81	+0.38	na		?
Belgium (9)	1971–81	−0.36	1981–83	−0.41	−
Denmark (11)	1975–78	−0.79	1981–83	+0.16	+
France (22)	1968–75	−0.26	na		?
Ireland (9)	1971–75	+0.50	1979–81	−0.07	−
Italy (69)	1978	−0.01	1981–83	−0.27	−
Netherlands (12)	1976–78	−0.83	1981–83	−0.12	+
Norway (8)	1976–79	+0.21	1981–83	+0.53	+
Portugal (18)	1970–71	+0.36	1981–83	+0.53	+
Spain (46)	1970–81	+0.53	1979–81		?
Sweden (12)	1976–79	−0.26	1981–83	+0.37	+
Switzerland (11)	1970–80	−0.49	1981–83	−0.51	−
United Kingdom[a]	1971–81[a]	−0.65	na		?
West Germany (30)	1978	−0.29	1981–83	−0.45	−

Note: [a]Number of regions unspecified and based on total population change.

Source: A.G. Champion, 'Introduction: counterurbanization experience', in A.G. Champion (ed.), *Counterurbanization: The Changing Pace and Nature of Population Deconcentration* (London, 1989), Table 1.4, p. 16.

Portugal and France. Lastly, in many European countries owner-occupied housing was becoming increasingly attractive when compared with private rental or social rental housing, and owner-occupancy is proportionately more common in smaller places and under-represented in large cities.[7]

We now examine the process of counter-urbanization in a little more detail in three west European countries, Denmark, West Germany and Italy. In Denmark, there was a dramatic change in migration patterns between the 1960s and the 1970s. The 1960s showed that Copenhagen continued to experience a net migration gain of 2.8 per thousand per annum, whereas marginal areas such as north Jutland were experiencing net losses in excess of 4.0 per thousand per annum as people moved to city employment in the new service sectors. By the 1970s the Copenhagen region was losing 3.9 persons per thousand per annum whilst north Jutland was gaining 1.7 per thousand per annum. Denmark's urban structure is dominated by Copenhagen but the same transition was experienced by the second-order city regions such as Aarhus and Odense. Data on migration by age show that it was largely those under 15 or over 25 who rejected Copenhagen, whilst the 15–24-year-olds were still drawn to the capital in the 1980s, although in significantly smaller numbers than in the 1970s. The transition largely reflects the changing distribution of jobs. Although the numbers employed in manufacturing fell nationally in Denmark, the rural periphery experienced growth.

Table 14.3. Federal Republic of Germany: population change

Urban size (millions)	Total population change (% p.a.)		Population change by migration (% p.a.)	
	1970–80	1980–85	1970–80	1980–85
2.0 and above	+0.21	−0.27	+0.05	−0.09
1.2–1.99	+0.02	−0.16	−0.19	+0.05
1.0–1.19	+0.02	−0.13	−0.16	+0.07
0.5–0.99	+0.29	+0.11	+0.27	+0.17
Below 0.5	+0.10	+0.06	+0.01	+0.19

Source: T. Kontuly and R. Vogelsang, 'Federal Republic of Germany: the intensification of the migration turnaround', in Champion (ed.), *Counterurbanization*, Table 8.2, p. 152.

Whilst Copenhagen lost almost 50,000 manufacturing jobs (40 per cent) between 1972 and 1982, the rural periphery experienced a gain of 10,000 (10 per cent), a fact which has been attributed to much higher levels of entrepreneurialism in the periphery. Even in the much larger service sector the much slower rate of growth in Copenhagen (28 per cent, 1970–80) contrasts sharply with the much faster growth in peripheral Jutland (51 per cent).

West Germany was one of the first west European countries to undergo industrialization and has, unlike Denmark, a wide range of industrial cities. Industrialization was accompanied by urbanization which continued until the 1970s, but there was a distinction between the north, characterized by the coal, steel and heavy engineering development of the North Sea coast and the Ruhr, and the south, characterized by much lighter industry. Population growth moved to the large urban regions of the centre and the north in the 1950s, but in the 1960s it was the large cities of the south (Frankfurt, Stuttgart, Munich) which were growing whilst the northern cities had already begun to decline. During the 1970s these patterns were reinforced but by the 1980s the north–south regional effect had been submerged by the urban size effect as Table 14.3 shows, in which population change due to migration was smoothly negatively correlated with urban size. Newer, large urban centres with modern employment bases (cars, chemicals, electronics) which had expanded rapidly in the 1960s and 1970s stopped growing, whereas some of the smaller and more peripheral urban centres gained population.

As in Denmark these trends affect different age groups in different ways. The young (below 16 years of age) and those over 30 began to move away from the large cities around 1970 and those of retirement age began to move to small urban places around 1960. Those aged between 16 and 29 continued to move to large cities until the mid-1980s, although not in sufficient numbers to offset the losses in other age groups. The German economy was heavily dependent upon immigrant workers. In the 1970s foreign workers moved into the largest cities, especially into cities with a population exceeding one million, to take up new jobs in manufacturing and low-skill services; by the 1980s the foreign workers were leaving the large cities, some to return home but some to move into the smaller urban centres.

Whereas West Germany may be divided into a north and a south with the north experiencing both urbanization and counter-urbanization earlier than the south, the contrast is nowhere near as extreme as that between northern and southern Italy. In the period 1951–61 several of the northern provinces were experiencing rapid industrialization and urbanization, Turin and Milan, for example, growing by more than a quarter in the decade. Rome too was growing rapidly. These gains were largely at the expense of the surrounding agricultural areas, not the far south. This pattern continued in the period 1961–71 except that the regions of Calabria and Sicily in the south became major sources of migrants to the industrial towns of the north in search of 'the three ms' – mestiere, a job; moglie, a wife; and macchina, a car. The period 1971–81 showed considerable differences from the earlier decades. The growth by migration of the cities of the north had stopped, but the south was still experiencing rural to urban migration. This migration, however, no longer consisted only of males seeking urban work in a new milieu but was now more likely to be male or female singles, more highly educated and with a marketable skill. By the 1980s, net outmigration was occurring from the northern cities such as Turin, Venice and Genoa, and the medium-sized cities of middle Italy (Modena, Reggio Emilia, Bologna) became the new industrial destinations.

Reconcentration

Whilst the patterns of concentration and subsequent counter-urbanization in western Europe are clear enough, the 1980s brought a more confused picture to light. As Table 14.2 shows, some countries such as Belgium, Ireland, Italy, Switzerland and West Germany continued to decentralize, but others such as Denmark, the Netherlands, Norway, Portugal and Sweden had begun to reconcentrate. In the case of Portugal this may be seen as continued and accelerated movement to the largest cities as the first wave of industrialization continues, together with the return to Portugal of expatriates from former colonies such as Mozambique and Angola, such return migrants tending to concentrate in Lisbon. However, in the Scandinavian countries and the Netherlands (and possibly the United Kingdom and France) this trend can be seen as a further turning point or reversal of the counter-urbanization process.[8]

There are several reasons why reconcentration should have come about. First, the new jobs which have been created since the early 1980s are of two types, but both tend to be located in the most concentrated regions of the most developed economies. High level services for business, including financial and legal services, together with corporate head offices, are growing in employment terms and these activities tend to locate in the largest cities. They do so because of the range of external economies available there, including a well-connected airport and the presence of major nodes on the global telecommunication system, be-

Plate 14.1. Canary Wharf, London in 1984. The decline of the London docks since the 1950s, partly as a result of containerisation of sea freight and the subsequent shift of port facilities further downstream, meant that by the 1970s there were large derelict or under-used waterfront areas near to the centre of London.

Plate 14.2. Canary Wharf, London in 1991. The re-development of Docklands in the 1980s led to the rapid construction of office space on 'brownfield' sites and the conversion of former warehouses for residential purposes.

cause of access to a large supply of highly qualified staff, and because of the easy opportunities for interaction with other knowledgeable people, especially for unprogrammed 'orientation contacts'. The second group of jobs which are expanding in number are the personal services and leisure industry jobs. These are often poor quality jobs (part-time, poorly paid, antisocial hours) but they too tend to be located in the large cities and core regions.

Secondly, there are demographic and 'lifestyle' factors at work. More households in western Europe now take the form of single young adults, childless couples, and the elderly, and fewer are parents with children at home. The former are less eager for the suburban lifestyle and are more likely to prefer the attributes of large cities and core regions such as shorter journeys to work, better access to cultural facilities, and better access to services such as health care. The suburban ideal may persist in some west European countries such as the UK, but elsewhere in most of continental western Europe urbanization has always been more preferred.

Thirdly, changes in the housing market, both political and economic, have switched emphasis from the production of one-family houses, often in small towns and suburbs, to the production of denser housing and the refurbishment of older multi-family structures in larger cities. Changes in the housing market have also been associated with changes in land-use planning policies which have

---

In focus: Randstad, Netherlands

In a small, densely populated country such as the Netherlands, where much of the land has had to be expensively reclaimed from the sea, there is inevitably a high level of land use and settlement planning. As European governments have become increasingly concerned about issues such as environmental sustainability, countries such as the Netherlands have been quick to use their extensive planning powers to stop suburban sprawl and concentrate population and investment within existing centres. At the heart of the Dutch urban system is the Randstad or 'rim city' which comprises an almost circular settlement with its major nodes at Amsterdam, Rotterdam, the Hague and Utrecht. Inside the circle is the 'green heart', an area of virtually unsettled land; outside the circle is the remainder of the Netherlands. The Randstad contains 16 per cent of the area of the Netherlands, 47 per cent of the employment, 46 per cent of the GDP and just 50 per cent of the population.

The Randstad's share of the Dutch population and economy has gradually increased with the move away from agriculture to manufacturing and subsequently to services. The economic development of the Randstad has been planned to allow each of the four major centres to specialize, Amsterdam in tourism and office development, Rotterdam in port-related manufacturing activities, the Hague in administration and Utrecht in office

Randstad, Netherlands (continued)

activities. This specialization has been possible because of the well-developed road and rail transport system.

By the 1960s, suburbanization was beginning to occur around the four cities of the Randstad and a major effort was made to restrict development within the Green Heart where Gouda remained the only town of any size. Restrictions on development on the outer edge of the Randstad in the 1970s created a population movement towards Dutch towns well away from the Randstad such as Groningen in the north-east and Maastricht in the south-east. By the 1980s increasing concern for environmental issues led Dutch planners to try to reduce dependence upon the private car and make greater use of public transport, and the Fourth Physical Planning Memorandum, in 1988, sought to restrict all major urban development to so-called A-class land close to intersections between national railway routes and other forms of high quality public transport. Smaller-scale development is permitted at B-class land where there is intersection between public transport and motorways. Development is very restricted on C-class land which has access only to road transport. The objective of restricting development in this way within the Randstad has had the effect of displacing population and industrial–commercial development to towns away from south-west Holland to areas where planning rules are less stringent. The national planning authority, however, is determined to continue the ecological allocation of land, and the Work Plan of the Fourth Memorandum, published in 1991, has emphasized the redensification of the four Randstad cities. Of the 14 key projects specified, nine are situated in the Randstad: these include the redevelopment of harbour land in both Rotterdam and Amsterdam, new commercial–residential centres for the Hague and Utrecht, and waterfront developments on the IJssel and Rhine within existing built-up areas. By contrast only 15,000 additional houses will be permitted in the period 1995–2005 within the Green Heart of the Randstad.

The consequences for population distribution of these planning policies may offer a model for what has become known as 'compact city' development. The rate of suburbanization is sharply reduced in the cities of the Randstad, except where it lies along corridors or 'fingers' of high quality public transport. The inner city areas, although still losing population, are henceforth likely to redensify as new housing developments are completed and more households exhibit a preference for an urban, rather than suburban lifestyle, and smaller towns will remain attractive to industry and some commercial development, away from the largest cities.[1]

1. The best accounts of population change and planning policy in the Randstad are to be found in F.M. Dieleman and S. Musterd, *The Randstad: a Research and Policy Laboratory* (Dordrecht, 1992), and in the Special Issue of *Urban Studies*, 31 (1994), no. 3, devoted to the Randstad, especially the contribution by H. Priemus on 'Planning the Randstad: between economic growth and sustainability'.

sought to redensify large cities and have developed innovative techniques for the urban revitalization of industrial and waterfront sites.

Lastly, concern about ecological issues such as pollution, the wasteful consumption of energy, especially petroleum, and the extensive use of suburban land for non-productive purposes, has led a number of west European countries such as the Netherlands to use strict land-use planning controls to restrict or prevent suburban and exurban development.

The Urban Life Cycle

While our discussion this far has focused on the concentration and deconcentration of population at the regional level in west European nations, there is a parallel set of trends at the urban scale. The urban life cycle model is portrayed in Table 14.4 which shows how urban centres move through a series of stages defined by the relative rates of population change in the central city and the urban periphery. In Stage 1 the periphery loses population as the core grows when rural labour is drawn to the industrializing workforce. In subsequent stages there is further urbanization although the core steadily becomes more congested. By Stage 4 the peripheral ring is growing faster and by Stage 5 the core is losing population as suburbanization occurs. Stages 6 and 7 form the process of exurbanization as the city in total loses population, although it is significant that the core city's rate of loss is slowing down. The forecast final stage to complete the model is reurbanization in which the core city begins to grow in population again.

As we have already indicated, the processes of urbanization do not act simultaneously across the whole of Europe. Thus, the cities of northern Europe moved from Stage 3, core city growing faster than hinterland in 1951–61, to Stage 5, core city declining but hinterland growing in 1981–91. The cities of southern Europe, however, moved from Stage 2, core city growing but hinterland declining in 1951–61, to Stage 4, core city growing more slowly than hinterland.[9]

At the leading edge of this process are the small group of cities, all located in north-west Europe, which by 1991 seemed to be reurbanizing. Reurbanization is defined as either (i) core city growing, hinterland declining, (ii) both core city and hinterland growing but the core city experiencing a faster rate of growth, or (iii) both the core city and the hinterland declining but the core city experiencing a slower rate of decline. A study of 241 cities in the 15 nations of the EU and Switzerland and Norway identified 15 such recentralizing cities. As Table 14.5 shows, these are all clustered in Germany, the Benelux nations, the UK and Denmark. Almost all are medium-sized (total population exceeds 300,000, but core city less than 200,000). Most are architecturally distinguished with well-preserved historic cores, there is a strong bias towards ancient university cities, and most are characterized by a highly educated and skilled population. Most have pleasant inner city environments offering attractive lifestyles. The two cities which do not conform to this stereotype are Glasgow and Krefeld – they are larger, post-industrial and lack an historic core of any significance.

Table 14.4. Stages of economic growth and decline

Development phase	Stage	Population change			
		Core	**Ring**	**Agglomeration**	
I. Urbanization	1. Absolute centralization	++	−	+	⎫
	2. Relative centralization	++	+	+++	⎬ Growth
II. Suburbanization	3. Relative decentralization	+	++	+++	
	4. Absolute decentralization	−	++	+	⎭
III. Disurbanization	5. Absolute decentralization	− −	+	−	⎫
	6. Relative decentralization	− −	−	− − −	⎬ Decline
IV. Reurbanization	7. Relative centralization	−	− −	− − −	
	8. Absolute centralization	+	− −	−	⎭

Source: L. van den Berg and L.H. Klaassen, 'The contagiousness of urban decline', in L. van den Berg, L.S. Burns and L.H. Klaassen (eds), *Spatial Cycles* (Aldershot, 1997), pp. 84–99.

Table 14.5. Cities undergoing recentralization, 1981–91

	Percentage change in population				
	Whole city	Core (C)	Hinterland (H)	H – C	Type
Germany (West)					
Ulm	8.37	12.67	7.60	−5.07	ii
Krefeld	7.38	10.34	6.10	−4.24	ii
Freiburg	8.89	11.29	8.41	−2.88	ii
Benelux					
Maastricht	2.79	16.57	−2.90	−19.47	i
Brugge	−6.80	−1.10	−9.45	−8.35	iii
Zwolle	8.36	14.17	7.01	−7.16	ii
Groningen	0.08	3.53	−1.89	−5.42	i
Apeldoorn	3.54	4.90	2.35	−2.55	ii
UK					
Glasgow	−9.83	−4.83	−17.20	−12.37	iii
Canterbury	3.39	8.24	2.84	−5.40	i
Oxford	7.21	10.64	6.35	−4.29	i
Cambridge	9.87	11.68	9.34	−2.34	i
Denmark					
Odense	2.72	6.09	0.52	−5.57	ii
Aarhus	6.60	9.08	4.18	−4.90	ii
Alborg	0.61	1.44	0.20	−1.24	ii

Source: P.C. Cheshire, 'A new phase of urban development in Western Europe? The evidence for the 1980s', *Urban Studies*, 32 (1995), no. 7, pp. 1045–64.

Urbanization: Debates

The countries and cities of Europe exhibit a diversity of patterns of urbanization in the 1990s. In much of western and northern Europe the major concern will be whether an increasing share of the population will return to the inner areas of towns and cities, or whether the suburbs and smaller settlements will attract the majority of households. The balance appears to be swinging towards the former as fewer households will be at the child-rearing stage which has preferred suburban living. Young singles, young childless couples and elderly singles and couples will make up an increasing proportion of the future households and they are more likely to prefer inner city locations with smaller houses and fewer gardens. The growing sectors of employment in professional services and personal services favour inner city-centre locations and their employees place a premium on short journeys to work. Increasingly, environmental concerns will force planners to make decisions to redensify cities such as increasing limits on private car use, through road pricing

In focus: Glasgow

Glasgow is often regarded as the classic case of a post-industrial city. An economy based on shipbuilding, steel and heavy engineering reached its greatest extent in 1910 and declined thereafter. Attempts to provide replacement employment in lighter industries such as electrical goods and motor vehicles in the 1960s provided only temporary relief and by the 1980s Glasgow had become a city whose economy and employment were dominated by services. The rapid growth of the city in the period 1880–1910 left a legacy of extremely dense, poor quality housing and a shortage of vacant land by 1950. In consequence there was massive outmigration, some people driven by the major slum clearance programmes of the 1960s and 1970s to the New Towns and elsewhere, some attracted by the new, speculatively built housing for owner-occupancy in the suburbs and beyond. The core city's population fell from 1.14 million out of a total conurbation population of 1.93 million in 1961 to 768,000 out of a total of 1.72 million in 1981. However, at some point in the mid-1980s Glasgow's share of the conurbation's total population began to rise. In 1981 it was 44.5 per cent, in 1988 it was 45.6 per cent, in 1991 it was 46.2 per cent and by 1995 it was 47.1 per cent.

This reurbanization, in proportionate if not absolute terms, has several causes, some of which reflect positive attributes in Glasgow, some of which reflect negative attributes in the surrounding 'ring'. Residential population has been attracted back to Glasgow by the new owner-occupied housing which has located on the cleared sites, and by prestigious residential conversions of older buildings. The changing demography of the city in which a higher proportion of households are young singles, elderly singles and couples, and childless couples, has meant less demand for suburban lifestyles and more demand for city centre accommodation. There have been employment shifts within the service sector within the last 10 years with net job creation in professional–graduate services (finance, law, health, higher education) and in personal services (leisure, entertainment). Both of these sectors have chosen locations within the inner city which by 1995 housed 59 per cent of the conurbation's jobs compared with 55 per cent in 1984. When the journey to work by public or private transport is becoming increasingly stressful, many people are choosing to live closer to work and thus shifting towards the inner city where the new jobs are.

The outer city ring has seen a declining share of the conurbation's population although the impact of population change has been heterogeneous. The suburban dormitory towns continue to offer an attractive lifestyle, particularly to families with children, and there remains a steady flow of planning permission applications for speculative housing developments. The ring also contains two New Towns, East Kilbride and Cumbernauld, whose planned population growth encompassed some 140,000 people by 1981 but whose population has now begun to fall as a result of descheduling. The

Glasgow (continued)

ring also includes a number of older industrial towns whose economies were based on shipbuilding, engineering, steel and textiles but whose attempts to attract or to retain modern industry have not been successful, and in consequence their populations have fallen.

These population shifts in response to demographic, lifestyle and economic changes have been accompanied by growing social polarization. Up to the mid-1980s there appeared to be a growing differential between the poor inner city and the more affluent suburbs and New Towns. The regeneration of the inner city of Glasgow due to physical improvement, the arrival of new employment and the skilful urban marketing of Glasgow as a place of culture and leisure have diminished the inner city problems of unemployment, poor quality of life and physical dereliction, and the most deprived populations are now to be found at the edge of the city on large public sector housing estates constructed in the 1950s. Indices of economic well-being such as unemployment rates, income per household, and access to services, all show a widening differential between the poor and the relatively affluent.[1]

1. A fuller version of the deindustrialization and reurbanization of Glasgow is to be found in W.F. Lever, 'Deindustrialisation and the reality of the post-industrial city', *Urban Studies*, 28 (1991), no. 6, pp. 983–99, and W.F. Lever, 'Reurbanisation: the policy implications', *Urban Studies*, 30 (1993), no. 2, pp. 267–84.

for example, and by emphasizing the reuse of 'brownfield' land for residential and commercial uses. All these trends suggest that suburban and exurban development will slow but medium-sized towns which contain the major advantages of large cities (access to employment, leisure facilities, quality of life, lower taxes) without the disadvantages (congestion, antisocial behaviour) will continue to remain popular.

In southern and east-central Europe, the movement of rural workers to urban centres will continue as the demand for agricultural labour declines and urban life appears attractive. The major cities will continue to grow and small and medium-sized cities and rural areas will experience outmigration. The growth of the largest cities is accelerated by foreign immigrants from north Africa, the Middle East, eastern Europe and south-east Asia. These movements are likely to cause friction, particularly where the immigrants are perceived, rightly or wrongly, to offer unfair competition within the labour and housing markets. The counterargument that such migratory streams may be viewed as a source of urban strength through multiculturalism is less often heard in contemporary Europe.

Economic changes brought about in European cities by globalization are thought to increase social polarization. The workforce in cities is increasingly divided between professional, managerial and graduate workers in services, and low-paid personal service sector workers and the unemployed. The middle ground of skilled manual workers and clerical workers has been systematically eroded by imports from the Newly Industrializing Countries and by the increased use of machinery and computers. The 'rich' and the 'poor' are moving further apart in income terms, but also they are moving further apart geographically through the operation of housing markets. In the United States these processes have been described as creating an underclass, a group without employment or in very poorly paid uncertain employment, often African-American, with little access to services such as good education or health care, and with little prospect of improving their position. There remains some debate within Europe as to whether such an underclass exists, given more effective welfare systems, but it does seem likely that such a group has emerged and will continue to exist focused on ethnic minorities, the long-term unemployed, the residents of public housing, the unskilled and those in poor health.

Within the last 10 years a debate has emerged in western Europe, as elsewhere, concerning sustainable urban development. The long period of suburbanization and exurbanization has been dependent on increasing levels of car ownership. As concerns with global warming and atmospheric pollution have grown, a range of policies – carbon taxes, road pricing, legal bans, etc. – have been developed whose impact is likely to be more emphasis on inner city development. Improvements to public transport and renewed emphasis on the redevelopment of brownfield sites also seem likely to encourage the redensification of cities.

Bibliographical Note

The most comprehensive study of urban population change in post-war Europe is to be found in A.G. Champion (ed.), *Counterurbanization: the Changing Pace and Nature of Population Deconcentration* (London, 1989). This describes the transition from urbanization to counter-urbanization in general terms but also contains separate studies of the United Kingdom, Norway, Denmark, Germany, France and Italy by specialist authors. This volume concludes by asking the key question – will suburbanization continue as the dominant trend, or will people begin to return to the cities? The round of Censuses in 1990–91 provided mixed evidence but work by Cheshire, reported in *Urban Studies*, commissioned by the European Union, incorporated data to suggest that ecological, economic and demographic factors may cause reurbanization. In the early 1990s, demographers expanded their work to incorporate east–central Europe, Scandinavia and Alpine Europe. The volume edited by H.H. Blotevogel and A.J. Fielding, *People, Jobs and Mobility in New Europe* (Chichester, 1997), is able to move the debate into the mid-1990s with access to the 1990–91 Censuses, confirming some reurbanization. The debate is extended to cover the role of international migrants to western Europe, the situation in the marketized economies of east–central Europe, and age-specific migration. The concluding chapter by Fielding – the effects of economic restructuring on the populations of western Europe's cities and regions – is the most comprehensive and up-to-date account of the relationship between economic change and population movement available. The material emanating from the European Science Foundation's Regional and Urban Restructuring in Europe (RURE) programme is the largest single body of research work on urban change and is available in the Blotevogel and Fielding volume, in C. Jensen-Butler, A. Shachar and J.U. Weesep (eds), *European Cities in Competition* (Aldershot, 1997), and in W.F. Lever and A. Bailly (eds), *The Spatial Impact of Economic Change in Europe* (Aldershot, 1996).

Notes

1. W.W. Rostow, *The Stages of Economic Growth* (Cambridge, MA, 1960).

2. W. Thompson, *A Preface to Urban Economics* (Baltimore, MD, 1965).

3. J. Garreau, *Edge City: Life on the Frontier* (New York, 1991).

4. W.F. Lever and A.G. Champion, 'The urban development cycle and the economic system', in W.F. Lever and A. Bailly (eds), *The Spatial Impact of Economic Change in Europe* (Aldershot, 1996), pp. 204–24.

5. S.G. Cochrane and D.R. Vining, *Recent Trends in Migration Between Core and Peripheral Regions in Developed and Advanced Developing Countries*, Working Papers in Regional Science, no. 108 (1986), Regional Science Department, University of Pennsylvania, Philadelphia.

6. B.J.L. Berry, 'The counterurbanization process: urban America since 1970', in B.J.L. Berry (ed.), *Urbanization and Counterurbanization* (Beverly Hills, 1976), pp. 111–43; A.G. Champion, 'Counterurbanization: the conceptual and methodological challenge', in A.G. Champion (ed.), *Counterurbanization: The Changing Pace and Nature of Population Deconcentration* (London, 1989), pp. 19–33.

7. Much of the comparative study of European urbanization is to be found in P.C. Cheshire, *Economic Factors in Urban Change: European Prospects*, Discussion Paper no. 3 (1987), Department of Economics, University of Reading, where a major EU-funded research programme is under way, and more extensively in Champion (ed.), *Counterurbanization*.

8. One of the best summaries of the trend of reurbanization is to be found in S. Illeris, 'Counterurbanization revisited in Central and North Western Europe', in M.J. Bannon, L.S. Bourne and R. Sinclair (eds), *Urbanization and Regional Development* (Dublin, 1991), pp. 1–16.

9. The urban life cycle model of northern and western European cities was first developed by L. van den Berg, R. Drewett, L.H. Klaassen, A. Rossi and C.H.T. Vijverberg, *Urban Europe: A Study of Growth and Decline* (Oxford, 1982), and has most recently been extended to include data from the 1990–91 round of Census by P.C. Cheshire, 'A new phase of urban development in Western Europe? The evidence for the 1980s', *Urban Studies*, 32 (1995), no. 7, pp. 1045–64.

PART THREE: NATIONAL ECONOMIC POLICIES

15 The Benelux Countries[1]

Peter M. Solar

The three small countries of north-west Europe – Belgium, the Netherlands and Luxembourg – have been pioneers of European economic integration. Belgium and Luxembourg have shared the same money and tariffs since the 1920s. Even before the Second World War had ended, these two countries, together with the Netherlands, launched plans for the Benelux customs union, though this arrangement only came fully into force in the late 1950s. By then all three had become founder-members of the European Union (then the European Communities), and they have remained to this day the most 'European' of its members. Brussels, the Belgian and European capital, has become both shorthand and scapegoat for EU decisions and bureaucracy.

As small nations sandwiched among powerful neighbours, the Benelux countries have had strong political reasons for pursuing peace and cooperation in Europe. Their economic reasons have been no less compelling. Before the First World War their economies were very open to trade and their industries heavily oriented towards foreign markets, especially those of their neighbours. Among Europe's wealthiest countries, their excess savings went to finance infrastructure development and industry around the world. The disruptions of trade and investment during and between the two world wars hurt these small countries severely. Markets were closed to their industries and many of their foreign assets were lost. During the 1930s they were forced to fall back on their small domestic markets and on colonial markets, Indonesia for the Netherlands and the Congo for Belgium. Over the wars and the inter-war period economic growth in the Benelux countries was slower than elsewhere in north-west Europe.

In the more open world of post-war Europe the Benelux countries have, in general, done well. Unlike the UK, they have remained consistently near the top of the European league table of incomes. Strong growth has supported the establishment of elaborate welfare states, though to pay for these and other services their governments have taken more of incomes in taxes than have governments anywhere else, except in Scandinavia. As in other European countries, unemployment was very low in the 1960s but rose markedly in the 1970s and 1980s. Yet despite broad similarity to what was happening elsewhere in western Europe, the experience of the Benelux countries displays some distinctive features which serve to sharpen understanding of post-war economic and social development.

In the Beginning

What did the Benelux economies look like in 1945, when the Second World War ended? Belgium had survived the war with relatively little damage, though low levels of investment during the depression and the war meant that its industrial apparatus had aged significantly. In Wallonia, the French-speaking south of the country, there was a complex of heavy industry – steel, non-ferrous metals, chemicals, glass, cement – built upon the deposits of coal that stretched across the region. The large holding companies which controlled much of this industry faced two major problems. First, most Belgian products were standard items with low value-added and highly variable demand. Second, domestic coal was becoming more expensive as seams became depleted. The fate of the coal industry, with its 150,000 miners organized in powerful trade unions, would dominate much of the early post-war period.

In the northern part of Belgium, in Dutch-speaking Flanders, the economic structure was rather different. Here light industry and agriculture were more important, though employment in agriculture, only 12 per cent of the workforce in Belgium as a whole, was quite low by European standards. The main industry was textiles, in which most firms were small and family-owned. Yet within Flanders there were pockets of larger-scale industry, notably around the port of Antwerp, where non-ferrous metal refining, automobile assembly and telephone equipment manufacture took place. Nonetheless, Flanders remained the poorer relative of Wallonia. Its cultural, economic and political ascendance since the war would transform Belgium, and will perhaps one day tear it apart.

The Netherlands in 1945 was also marked by regional contrasts. The economic heart of the country was in the densely populated Randstad, roughly the area dominated by the cities of Amsterdam, Rotterdam and Utrecht. This region had a specialized, highly productive agriculture, typified perhaps by the production of bulbs and flowers for export. But its real vocation was international: banking and insurance, shipping, the transformation of colonial and other raw materials in its tobacco, sugar-refining and other entrepôt industries. Income and wealth were concentrated in this region, though its people and its economy had suffered grievously in the last years of the war. The Dutch industrial fabric had also aged from lack of investment during the depression and the war.

The rest of the Netherlands was more dependent on agriculture, though again it should be noted that the share of employment in this sector was much lower than elsewhere in Europe. Textile production, mainly for the domestic and Indonesian markets, was important in parts of the east and south. Elsewhere there were signs of change in the industrial structure. During the inter-war years chemical industries had grown up around the newly developed coal mines in Dutch Limburg. In nearby Eindhoven the electrical equipment manufacturer

Philips was the major employer. One peculiarity of the Netherlands, and especially its eastern and southern provinces, was its persistently high rate of population growth. Whereas in most other European countries, including Belgium, fertility had dropped markedly from the late nineteenth century, much of this fall was delayed in the Netherlands until after the Second World War. Another, related Dutch peculiarity has been very low participation by married women in the labour force.

The fate of Luxembourg, with fewer than 400,000 inhabitants today, has been ignored in most studies. In 1945 its economy depended on agriculture and on a strong steel industry based on rich indigenous iron ore deposits. During the post-war period, and especially after 1970, financial services and services to Europe became increasingly important. Luxembourg banks and branches of banks from other European countries have been active in the development of international capital markets, in large part because of the country's role as a tax haven for people from neighbouring countries. Its recycling of Belgian savings has also helped sustain the value of the Belgian–Luxembourg franc. More generally, the financial sector has contributed to making the Belgian–Luxembourg commercial union one of the world's leading exporters of services. Luxembourg has benefited from the presence of many European institutions, including the European parliament's secretariat, the court of justice, the court of auditors, and the European Investment Bank. Overall, Luxembourg's economy has been a picture of health, with low unemployment, relatively rapid growth, sound public finances, and per capita income at the top of the European league table.

Planning for the Future . . . or the Past

After the war the Dutch put together and executed a reasonably coherent strategy for economic development. Their relatively high rate of population growth meant that employment opportunities would have to be expanded rapidly in the late 1940s and 1950s. In traditional sectors the resurrection of the other European economies, especially Germany's, would be crucial. The Dutch depended far more on the German market than did the Belgians, due primarily to their river links with the German industrial heartland. They also saw in Germany a major market for agricultural products. Dutch diplomacy thus focused on the rebuilding of Germany and on securing access for Dutch agricultural products in the German and other European markets.

But the Dutch foresaw that their traditional industries would not be sufficient. Ambitious plans for industrial development were put forward after the war. These were supported by quotas on the imports of many manufactured goods, though quotas also owed a great deal to a severe shortage of dollars in the late 1940s. These quotas, along with Belgium's non-tariff exclusion of Dutch agricultural products, greatly hindered the implementation of the Benelux customs union, with the result that its effects were more symbolic than real. They also made the Dutch wary of early French initiatives towards European integration that focused more on the reduction of quotas than on lowering tariffs, which in the Netherlands were relatively low to start with.

Import quotas were only one feature of a highly centralized and interventionist reconstruction policy. Prices were also controlled, and raw materials and finished goods were rationed until 1949. Low interest rates encouraged rebuilding but this credit was rationed by the Ministry of Economic Affairs. Industrial investment was aided by Marshall Plan assistance, of which the Dutch were major recipients.

But the centrepiece of Dutch policy in the late 1940s and the 1950s was low wages. After the war wages were already low by European standards and the government sought to keep them low in order to make Dutch goods competitive on export markets and to keep profits high and so encourage investment. This wage policy was remarkable for the consensus with which it was adopted and implemented. Dutch wages remained low by the standards of neighbouring countries during the 1950s, though the gap narrowed. This narrowing gap implies that 'wage moderation' still left room for more rapid wage increases than in other countries, a feature which may have helped sustain the consensus. Wage rises were also moderate given that Dutch unemployment in the 1950s was very low, only a few per cent.

Dutch economic performance in the 1950s was quite good in other respects. Thanks to high rates of investment, the industrial sector was modernized and expanded. Labour productivity rose more rapidly than elsewhere in north-west Europe. On foreign markets Dutch goods increased their market share.

As everything went right in the Netherlands, everything seemed to go wrong in Belgium. During the 1950s Belgian goods lost out on world markets. Labour productivity rose relatively slowly. Profits and investment were low, and many Belgian industries faced difficulties, with unemployment remaining stubbornly at 6–8 per cent. While it must be remembered that Belgian economic performance in the 1950s was still much better than it had been before the war, by the end of the decade there was an increasing sense that the country was in a malaise.

Dismal performance during the 1950s is all the more surprising since the years immediately after the war appeared so promising. There was even talk of a 'Belgian miracle' when the country recovered so quickly. It was mostly good luck. War damage to industry had been relatively light. Unlike everywhere else in Europe, foreign exchange was not in short supply since the Belgians had managed to recover their gold reserve after the war and had earned dollars during the war by selling minerals from the Congo, including the uranium for the first atomic bombs. Further dollars came in from American forces based in Belgium and from the port of Antwerp, the only major port still usable at the end of the war. Belgian industry could thus be put back to work right away, and its products – steel, cement, glass – were in great demand during European reconstruction. The major problem was that other countries did not have the goods or dollars that the Belgians wanted.

The 'miracle' was short-lived and illusory. As other European countries reconstructed and modernized their industrial fabric, Belgian industry appeared antiquated. The lack of investment since the late 1920s was not corrected after the war. Too much of the proceeds of the 'miracle' went into higher wages and into consumption. The strength of the economy was persistently overestimated. Belgium was very late in asking for Marshall aid, and in the end received very little. In 1949, when the UK and several other countries, including the Netherlands, devalued their currencies by 30.5 per cent against the dollar, the Belgians chose to devalue by only 12.3 per cent.

Wages in Belgium had recovered rapidly, thanks to the immediate post-war boom, and were high by comparison with neighbouring countries. This was a major change. Before the war Belgium had been a country with relatively low wages and labour costs. High post-war wages and the new social security system were seen as the key to social peace. One reason that the 1949 devaluation was so limited was to prevent cost of living increases that would erode real wages. A persistent concern of Belgian diplomats was that freer trade in Europe, without the harmonization of social security and labour laws, would put downward pressures on Belgian wages. Despite these efforts to buy social peace, industrial relations in the 1940s and 1950s turned out to be no less troubled than they had been in the 1920s and 1930s. The contrast with the Dutch consensus on wage moderation is striking.

High wages were but one factor squeezing firms' profits in the 1950s. Energy costs had also become high by European standards. Belgian coal was expensive and in order to keep the mines running electricity generators were allowed to pass the higher costs on to consumers. The British and Dutch devaluations put downward pressure on export prices. This squeeze on profits reduced the internal funds available to firms for investment. External sources of finance were

---

In focus: The Political Economy of Coal

Everywhere in western Europe coal has given way to oil and other sources of energy since the war. Mine closures have been resisted by militant trade unions and powerful industrial interests, and the state has often been drawn into the industry. The ways in which the Belgian and Dutch coal industries were run down show remarkable contrasts in policy making.

The Belgian coal industry had two geologically, historically and politically distinct basins. Across the south of the country, in French-speaking Wallonia, were the mines that had been developed from the late eighteenth century and that had powered Belgium's early industrialization. By the inter-war period many of these mines were becoming expensive to work. The other basin, which had been developed mainly between the wars and was more susceptible to mechanization, lay in the Dutch-speaking province of Limburg.

After the war Belgium's prime minister launched a 'battle for coal'. Investment and workers were certainly needed to restore production for the post-war recovery, but throughout the late 1940s and 1950s the Belgian state poured resources into the mines, largely in order to keep up employment in what had become a high wage industry employing, at its peak, 175,000 workers.

The Political Economy of Coal (continued)

The industry was able to obtain such favourable treatment through the tacit alliance of the socialist trade unions and the powerful holding companies which dominated Belgian heavy industry and had substantial mining interests. Belgian government subsidies were initially augmented by much of the Marshall aid the country received, then were essentially replaced by funds from Belgium's partners in the new European Coal and Steel Community (ECSC). All of this aid did little to rationalize production or raise productivity, and Belgian mines, especially those in Wallonia, remained uncompetitive.

When ECSC funds dried up and coal prices turned down in the late 1950s, the Belgian government had no choice but to run down most of the southern mines, which were still producing almost 20 million tonnes of coal a year. The mining companies were bought out on fairly generous terms and further aid for reconversion was extracted from the ECSC, aid which has been seen as marking the beginning of European Union regional policy. The fact that aid is still being funnelled into these mining regions today shows the difficulties of industrial renewal.

The remaining Belgian mines, concentrated in Flemish Limburg and with annual production of around 9 million tonnes, also faced difficulties in the 1960s. In the face of strong union resistance to closures, the government bought out the mining companies, again on fairly generous terms, in 1967. These mines were kept going into the 1980s by direct subsidies and by indirect subsidies from electricity consumers. The survival of the northern coal field became one element in the complex regional compromises arising from political conflict between French and Dutch speakers. It is notable that when industrial policy became a regional responsibility in 1983, the closure of the northern mines was accelerated.

The Dutch coal industry, concentrated in the province of Limburg, just across the border from Belgium's northern field, was also developed in the 1910s and 1920s. The Dutch mines were relatively productive and after being restored to working order in 1945 and 1946, produced about 12 million tonnes per year until the early 1960s. Then, as coal prices came under pressure, the Dutch government, which itself owned several of the mines, decided that they had no future. It subsidized their closure and helped reorient activity towards chemical production, laying the basis for DSM, which has become a major chemical company.

As in many other instances of industrial and economic policy, the Dutch government was able to set out and execute a coherent policy of mine closures and reconversion. The Belgian political system, by contrast, was susceptible to manipulation by powerful producer interests, at a significant cost in public resources. Whereas the Dutch saw little purpose in subsidizing hard, dangerous jobs that few northern Europeans wanted to do, the Belgians ended up maintaining mining employment, which increasingly depended on immigrant labour for the dirty jobs below ground.

limited by the very small market for shares and by constraints on bank lending. The results were a relatively low rate of industrial investment and investments directed more at marginal improvements in the efficiency of existing facilities than at any major renewal of industry.

Boom

The 1960s and early 1970s were the best years of the post-war period for both Belgium and the Netherlands. Unemployment was very low in both countries. Whilst economic growth accelerated slightly in the Netherlands, there was a striking turnabout in Belgium. After being one of Europe's laggards in the 1950s, it outpaced almost all other countries in the 1960s. Both countries underwent an investment boom, though with significantly different effects.

In the Netherlands capital-intensive industries were already absorbing large funds from the late 1950s. Capacity was expanded and modernized at Rotterdam, Europe's largest port. Around the port major investments were made in oil refining, chemicals and distribution during the 1960s. The development of the natural gas fields near Groningen, from 1963, required huge amounts of capital, and the initially low price of gas led to the expansion of energy- and capital-intensive activities like hothouse farming, metallurgy and chemicals.

Increased investment was also undertaken to save on labour as Dutch wages rose faster than elsewhere in north-west Europe during the 1960s. Unions obtained large increases in sectors with high productivity growth and through the centralized bargaining system were able to impose them throughout the economy. Some labour-intensive industries, like textiles and coalmining, contracted as a result. Employment in manufacturing reached its peak in the mid-1960s, hence all the growth in employment during the late 1960s and early 1970s went into services.

Whereas rapid growth in the Netherlands was sustained by the application of more and more capital per worker, the marked acceleration in Belgian growth came about more from the improved efficiency with which capital was used. Productivity growth in Belgium during the 1960s was exceptionally rapid, especially in manufacturing. The investment rate did increase, for which credit is often given to the incentives embodied in the so-called Expansion Laws of 1959. These laws were part of a more general opening up of the Belgian economy, itself in part a reaction to the dismal performance of the 1950s and in part an outcome of the nascent European Community.

The new dynamism of the Belgian economy in the 1960s owed a great deal to foreign direct investment, which accounted for more than a third of all investment in manufacturing. Foreign firms, mainly American at the start, were conduits for new technologies and new forms of organization. Much of this investment took place in Flanders and helped this hitherto impoverished region to overtake Wallonia in output and incomes.

Rapid economic growth brought industrial peace, consecrated in the system of 'social programming' which brought together trade unions and employers'

Plate 15.1. Container facilities in Rotterdam, Europe's largest port. The Dutch economy has long relied on shipping and related services, and to the present day much of western Europe's foreign trade is channelled through Rotterdam.

organizations at national and sectoral levels from around 1960. Government did not sit at the table but was expected to legislate in accordance with agreements. The system produced significant extensions of the social security system and tighter employment protection laws, measures that would later prove costly.

As tax revenues rose with rapid growth in the late 1960s and early 1970s, the national government, as well as regional and local governments in Belgium, went on a capital spending spree. There were many questionable investments in infrastructure, often as the result of complex regional compromises. The government also missed a window of opportunity, when unemployment was low, to raise productivity in the public sector and in the nationalized industries.

Bust

The sharp deceleration in world economic growth and trade from 1973 was a body blow to the Benelux countries. Their export industries, which had already

In focus: Multinational Companies

Global companies are a fact of economic life today. Many started before the war, including the Dutch giants Shell, Unilever and Philips. But the great increase in foreign direct investment – companies building factories and sales and distribution networks in other countries – has taken place since the war. In the 1950s and 1960s most direct investment was undertaken by American firms setting up in Europe (and elsewhere in the world); in the 1970s, 1980s and 1990s European firms have also become major players. Multinationalization has had important economic and political implications for both Belgium and the Netherlands.

Belgium has attracted a disproportionate share of foreign direct investment in Europe, with the result that foreign firms today account for more than half of its industrial value-added. Belgian companies have been much less active abroad – an important question in Belgian economic history is why the holding companies which controlled much of industry never developed the managerial capabilities for expansion abroad – so there has been a persistent net inflow of direct investment. The Netherlands has also had high levels of inward investment, though these have generally been more than counterbalanced by large outward flows. Far less of Dutch industry is in foreign hands.

In western Europe foreign direct investment has not been particularly important as a source of capital. Much of American investment in Belgium, for example, was financed locally. The economic impact of multinational operations lies elsewhere. Multinationals are generally very large firms with the resources and incentives to make significant investments in research and managerial development. These investments benefit their branches in different countries, both by diffusion through the organization and by the movements of managers and other key personnel across borders. Firms in Belgium, for instance, do relatively little research and development but as most are controlled by foreign firms, Belgian industry reaps the benefits of work done elsewhere. Dutch research and development spending, as a share of national income, is much higher than in Belgium but the difference is almost entirely accounted for by the activities of a half-dozen large Dutch multinationals.

After the war American firms setting up in Belgium and the Netherlands were a vehicle for the diffusion of new methods of management. Training and work experience at IBM, Ford and other big firms substituted for formal education, as business schools were still rare in Europe. Here is where the implantation of foreign firms had spillovers for the rest of the economy, as natives who had worked in these firms left to start their own businesses. The local firms which supplied parts and services to the multinationals were also influenced by managerial innovations.

Whatever its economic benefits, foreign control of industry has often been regarded with suspicion in Europe, though this has been remarkably rare in

Multinational Companies (continued)

Belgium and the Netherlands, the major exception being Flemish concerns about recent French investments. Closures of plants owned by foreign firms, especially during the 1970s and 1980s, were targets of criticism but employment in multinational firms generally held up better than it did in domestic firms during this period. The benefits of multinational ownership, as well as the external discipline to remain competitive, has probably accounted for the relatively strong productivity performance of Belgian industry during the past two decades.

seen margins falling from the late 1960s, were severely squeezed between stagnant demand and rising costs. Wages continued to rise rapidly in both countries, initially on the basis of previous agreements, then as unions sought to catch up with inflation. Other costs rose as more sheltered industries, like utilities and financial services, were able to pass their higher labour costs on to consumers in the form of higher prices. The large rise in energy prices after the first oil shock also hit Belgian and Dutch industry hard as both were particularly heavy users of energy.

Poor prospects led firms, especially those in manufacturing, to cut back on investment, and what investment they did make was often geared to saving on increasingly expensive labour. Although manufacturing output continued to increase during the 1970s and early 1980s, manufacturing employment collapsed and contributed to the rise of mass unemployment. The other side of these developments was that productivity in manufacturing continued to grow rapidly during this period, especially in Belgium. In the face of foreign competition, inefficient firms closed and surviving firms cut costs and improved efficiency. This was in marked contrast to more sheltered industries where productivity growth was very slow, again especially in Belgium.

Governments tried desperately to stem the tide. At first it was not obvious that the deceleration in growth was permanent. Both the Belgian and Dutch governments pursued expansionary monetary policies in the mid-1970s. Low real interest rates helped keep firms in business, stimulated other sectors such as house building, and made it possible to finance the rising government deficits. Higher unemployment put great strains on the public finances as tax revenues fell and expenditures on benefits increased. Both governments, but especially the Belgian government, also increased spending to keep up employment by hiring more workers in the public sector and in nationalized industries and by subsidizing private firms. In the late 1970s and early 1980s state aid to enterprises in Belgium grew by around 10 per cent per annum.

But slow growth persisted and by the late 1970s the policy of buying employment on credit became untenable. As their balances of payments deteriorated, tighter monetary policies and higher interest rates were necessary to keep the Dutch guilder and the Belgian franc in line with the Deutschmark. Interest rates rose further as world interest rates increased from 1979. Higher interest rates brought the frightening prospect that large public debts could snowball out of control. Without severe budgetary restrictions governments would have to borrow simply to pay the interest on their debts. By the early 1980s both Belgium and the Netherlands were in crisis.

Planning for the Future . . . or the Past

The measures taken by the two countries in the 1980s and early 1990s to deal with the structural imbalances that had developed during the 1970s have an eerie resemblance to their policies in the 1950s. In addition to the major chore of getting the public finances in order, both governments recognized the need to restrain wage growth in order to restore business profits and, it was hoped, investment. The Belgian government intervened repeatedly but intermittently in the labour market, temporarily suspending indexation in the early 1980s and imposing a real wage freeze in the mid-1990s. As a result, wages have been kept in line with those in neighbouring countries, though there has been a tendency to relax when the economy improved, as it did in the late 1980s and early 1990s.

In the Netherlands wage moderation has not only been more consistently pursued; it has significantly lowered Dutch wages relative to those in Belgium and other European countries. It has taken a remarkable degree of consensus between trade unions and employers' associations to keep real wage growth at less than 1 per cent per annum from 1982 to 1997. The slow growth of Dutch labour costs has paid off in the creation of jobs and in falling unemployment during the 1990s.

Both Belgium and the Netherlands have made exchange rate stability a central policy goal. The Dutch guilder has effectively been linked to the Deutschmark since the early 1980s, the Belgian franc since the late 1980s. Both countries have regarded stable currencies as crucial to European integration but each has had other reasons. For the Dutch, Germany has simply been their major trading partner. For the Belgians, domestic reasons have been paramount. As in the 1950s, exchange rate stability has been a guard against inflation: given the system of wage indexation, currency depreciations feed through too rapidly to wages. In addition, a credible link to the Deutschmark has reduced inflationary expectations and hence interest rates, making it easier to finance the large public debt.

The paradox of the 1980s and 1990s is that despite the Netherlands' sounder, more coherent policies, the Belgian economy has grown somewhat faster. While the Dutch have slipped down the league table of per capita income, the Belgians have remained closer to the top. The reasons for these movements are not clear. Perhaps the reductions in working hours and the rise of part-time employment that have been a feature of falling unemployment in the Netherlands have reduced the incentives for training and lowered the quality of the labour force. Or Belgium's relative dynamism may owe something to the continuing transfusions of capital and expertise from the foreign enterprises that dominate its industrial sector. Its large 'black economy' may be another motor for growth.

Both countries have stored up problems for the future. Public investment in training and infrastructure has been very low since the fiscal crisis of the early 1980s. Labour force participation is also low by European standards: in the Netherlands because fewer married women work; in Belgium because of high youth unemployment and lavish use of early retirement. In 1994 only 17 per cent of Belgians over 50 were working, as against 25 per cent in the Netherlands and 31 per cent in the UK. Low participation means that those in jobs have to put aside more and more to pay the social benefits of an underemployed population.

Two Traditional Societies

Much social change in post-war Europe has been closely related to rapid economic growth. Unprecedented increases in income and significant reductions in working hours have shifted consumption patterns away from food and other necessities to household furnishings, cars, holidays and leisure activities. More people have been able to finish secondary school and attend university. Service occupations have displaced those in farming and manufacturing. But other social changes, such as the fall in fertility, the rise of cohabitation and divorce, the increased labour force participation of married women, and the decline in religious observance, have much more complex relations to economic change. The variations across Europe are still large, which leaves room for the influence of national social structures and institutions.

Post-war social change in Belgium and the Netherlands has in many respects been less marked than elsewhere in western Europe. One reason is that much of what was to happen elsewhere had already taken place in these countries. Both countries were already heavily urbanized and relatively wealthy in 1945. Their agricultural sectors were relatively small and efficient, so there was little room for the massive migration from the countryside into the towns that took place elsewhere. Moreover, the short distances and the dense transportation network had long made it possible for industrial workers to live in their native villages and commute to work, a pattern which continued after the war.

There are other ways in which Belgium and the Netherlands changed relatively little. Family and locality have continued to play strong roles. Illegitimacy and divorce have been low by European standards. Although cohabitation has increased in recent decades, marriage still predominates. Both countries, but especially the Netherlands, have had relatively low participation by married women in the labour force. Individuals and families retain strong ties to their place of origin. Often they continue to live there; if they do move away, the small distances involved make possible frequent contacts. It is remarkable that in the universities regional societies are vibrant and that Belgian universities are deserted at weekends by students going home.

The strength of these family and local loyalties may have made it difficult to integrate immigrants fully into Belgian and Dutch societies. Immigration to both countries has been unusually high, though it has fallen off sharply since the early

1970s. The Netherlands received many migrants from Indonesia and Surinam. Belgium had two waves of migrants: one after the war from southern Europe; the other in the 1960s from north Africa and Turkey. The migrants worked mainly at unskilled jobs. Their children and grandchildren, many of whom have been born and educated in Belgium and the Netherlands, have found it difficult to move into skilled and middle-class occupations. Racial or ethnic discrimination has probably played some part, but in small societies where jobs are often found through personal contacts, immigrants start with a major disadvantage. Intermarriage between immigrants and natives has been limited, with religious differences often being a barrier.

Institutional Pillars[2]

Older religious differences have left their mark on Belgian and Dutch societies. Although the Netherlands is often regarded as an archetypal Calvinist country, it has always had a significant Roman Catholic minority concentrated in its southern provinces. During the twentieth century higher fertility among Catholics has made this minority more important. In Belgium, which is overwhelmingly Catholic, religious differences have appeared as conflicts between proponents and opponents of the authority and influence of the church hierarchy. The church has been strongest in Flanders; anti-clericalism in Brussels and Wallonia.

During the late nineteenth and twentieth centuries these religious differences interacted with ideological differences between socialists and liberals to produce distinctive institutional structures. Starting with their own schools, political parties and trade unions, groups developed entire sets of interlocking organizations, including social welfare agencies, insurance companies, youth movements, newspapers and cultural societies. In the Netherlands there arose Protestant, Catholic, socialist and liberal institutional 'pillars'. In Belgium the Catholic, socialist and liberal pillars during the second half of the twentieth century have increasingly been further split into Dutch- and French-speaking components. Quite small societies were thus broken down into even smaller entities, among which contact among individuals was often limited to the workplace. Not surprisingly, intermarriage across pillars has been quite rare.

The 'pillarization' of Dutch and Belgian societies has produced political systems characterized by stable parties and coalition governments. It has been a way for people with major religious and ideological differences to 'live-apart-together', and both countries have remained solidly democratic during the entire century. In practice the system has worked better in the Netherlands than in Belgium, probably because the Dutch have a much stronger national identity. In Belgium the Flemish movement for linguistic and cultural parity has had an increasingly prominent separatist element. As a result, where the Dutch are inclined to view their politics as based on consensus, the Belgians emphasize compromise. This distinction is nicely illustrated by the differences in wage policies during the 1950s and 1980s mentioned above. Industrial relations have also been more turbulent in Belgium than in the Netherlands.

Whatever the successes of pillarization in the Netherlands, the pillars started to come tumbling down from the late 1960s. This coincided with the European-wide social explosion but this only precipitated changes with longer-term causes. A major force was increasing secularization, which ultimately led Protestant and Catholic political parties to join forces. Socialists were also becoming less doctrinaire. Other factors were economic growth and the rise of the welfare state, which reduced individual and household reliance on support from pillarized organizations.

Although the same long-term forces were at work in Belgium, institutional pillarization has survived. The key factor has been the greater extent to which the pillarized institutions in Belgium have had access to the public purse. Where the Dutch created one welfare state after the war, the Belgians set up several. Unemployment compensation was paid through the different trade unions. Reimbursement for medical care was distributed through intermediaries linked to the various pillars. Jobs in the Belgian civil service and public funds for cultural and other activities have been allocated by complex formulas reflecting group interests and influence. The large increase in public spending and employment since the Second World War probably strengthened pillarization in Belgium. So, too, did the growing cleavage between Dutch and French speakers, which further fragmented the political scene and made each group more tenacious in defending its institutional base.

The persistence of pillarization contributed to the creation of Belgium's huge national debt and made it much harder to take difficult decisions about public spending in the 1980s and 1990s. The erosion of the pillars' ideological foundations has also increased public cynicism about the institutions and the people who run them. Such social differences between Belgium and the Netherlands further deepen the mystery of Belgium's relatively good economic performance in the 1980s and 1990s. They also suggest that the Dutch may be better placed to face the challenges of the future.

Bibliographical Note

The economic and social history of the post-war period is only beginning to be written in Belgium and the Netherlands, and most of the literature is in Dutch or French. There are few good overviews in any language. André Mommen, *The Belgian Economy in the Twentieth Century* (London, 1994) surveys economic development in Belgium and has an excellent bibliography. Jan Luiten van Zanden, *The Economic History of the Netherlands in the Twentieth Century* (London, 1997) is particularly stimulating on the Dutch economy. The long chapters by Cassiers, De Villé and Solar on Belgium, and by van Ark, de Haan and de Jong on the Netherlands in Nicholas Crafts and Gianni Toniolo (eds), *Economic Growth in Europe since 1945* (Cambridge, 1996) provide more advanced discussions of economic growth and structural change, as does the chapter on Benelux by Van Rijkeghem in Andrea Boltho (ed.), *The European Economy* (Oxford, 1982). Richard T. Griffiths (ed.), *The*

Economy and Politics of the Netherlands (The Hague, 1980) deals with several aspects of Dutch economic and political behaviour, while the complexities of Belgian society and politics are discussed in A. Lijphart (ed.), *Conflict and Coexistence in Belgium* (Berkeley, 1981). E.H. Bax, *Modernization and Cleavage in Dutch Society* (Aldershot, 1990) is a stimulating interpretation of post-war social change. No good overview of post-war Belgian social history exists in any language; a highly personal vision can be found in Renée C. Fox, *In the Belgian Château* (Chicago, 1994).

Notes

1. This chapter, especially those parts dealing with economic change, draws on my longer pieces on Belgium (Isabelle Cassiers, Philippe De Villé and Peter Solar, 'Economic growth in postwar Belgium', in Nicholas Crafts and Gianni Toniolo (eds), *Economic Growth in Europe since 1945* (Cambridge, 1996), pp. 173–209) and on Benelux (Peter Solar and Herman de Jong, 'The Benelux countries', in Bernard Foley (ed.), *The European Economies since the Second World War* (London, 1998), pp. 102–23. Fuller references may be found in these studies.

2. This discussion of pillarization draws on Bax (see bibliographical note).

16 Britain

Jim Tomlinson

In the 50 years after the Second World War the average standard of living in Britain, measured by GDP per head, more than doubled. This rise in the standard of living was faster than in any previous period, and brought a degree of affluence to the mass of the population unimaginable at the end of the war. Yet most accounts of Britain post-war economic history approach their topic asking the question 'what went wrong?'. This apparent paradox is explained by the clear slide in the Britain's *relative* economic strength, from almost the richest country in Europe in 1945 (behind only Switzerland in income per head) to one of the 'also-rans', lagging behind the major economies of Germany, Italy and France.[1] The average British citizen, it should be emphasized, remains exceedingly rich by world standards, but most perceptions of the British economy have been shaped by the affluence of West Germany rather more than the poverty of Bangladesh.

This sense of failure has led to intensive debates about almost every feature of the British economy. At one time or another almost every characteristic of British life has been accused of having 'caused' this lagging development. Included in

Table 16.1. Growth rates of real GDP per head, 1950–95 (per cent p.a.)

	1950–73	1973–89	1989–95
UK	2.5	1.8	1.3[a]
France	4.0	1.8	1.8
(West) Germany	4.9	2.1	4.1[b]
USA	2.2	1.6	1.9
Japan	8.0	3.1	2.3

Notes: [a]1989 was the last cyclical peak in the level of activity in the British economy, so this figure is not a trend rate of growth as the economy was still in a cyclical upswing in 1995; [b]this figure is distorted by German reunification.

Sources: A. Maddison, *Dynamic Forces in Capitalist Development* (Oxford, 1991), p. 49; *National Institute Economic Review* (various issues).

this long list of suspects have been a number of aspects of British economic policy, and it is those policies which form the focus of this chapter. Over the post-war period Britain has become an increasingly open economy (though this, it should be noted, was in many respects a return to the pre-1914 situation rather than wholly new).[2] Trade and international capital flows have become more and more important to the British economy, and policy has responded by being crucially concerned with international issues. The first part of this chapter therefore begins with an account of the development of the international policy regime, before going on to consider domestic economic policies.

The International Regime

During the Second World War the United States government became convinced that the future political stability and economic prosperity of the US and the world would be best secured by an open international economy, one which would encourage international trade and stabilize exchange rates. This was aimed at preventing a recurrence of the damaging 'beggar-my-neighbour' policies of the 1930s, when most countries tried to limit trade flows and gain economic advantage by competitive devaluation of their currency. Such policies were widely believed to have contributed to the economic and political problems of that decade. The British approach to this issue was complex. On the one hand British economists, especially John Maynard Keynes and James Meade, were closely involved in the design of this new regime, and this reflected the view of much opinion in Britain that in the long run an open international economy would be to Britain's advantage. On the other hand, Britain ended the war with desperate balance of payments problems coupled to a commitment to full employment, and together these made a *rapid* move to free trade and currency convertibility too dangerous to contemplate.

In the event Britain moved down the road of liberalization, but very slowly. Britain was a key participant in the Bretton Woods negotiations of 1944 which led to the foundation of the International Monetary Fund (see Chapter 3). She adopted a fixed exchange rate, but this was too vulnerable to downward pressure to allow people to freely convert their pounds into other currencies. Under American pressure free conversion was permitted briefly in 1947, but led to a disastrous run on the pound. Controls were then put back on, and only slowly eased in the 1950s. Only towards the end of that decade could it be said that Britain approached closely to the ideals of currency liberalization, and some residual controls remained in place until 1979. Britain stuck with a fixed exchange rate until the Bretton Woods system ended in the early 1970s, though that system allowed the weakness of the pound to be reflected in devaluations in 1949 and 1967.

From 1972 the pound floated, and although the timing of this decision reflected specifically British concerns, it was part of an overall break-up of the Bretton Woods system, which proved incapable of surviving the divergent inflation

Plate 16.1. 'Pigs for porcelain': Prepared by the Economic Information Unit of the British Ministry of Food, this poster from August 1949 offers a stark reminder of the need to earn dollars for essential food imports at a time of severely curtailed export opportunities.

rates of the major countries and the weakening of the international position of the US economy. The period of floating in the 1970s and 1980s saw the pound (along with most currencies) go through large fluctuations in its value, though the long-term trend to decline has continued. Britain cooperated in international efforts in these decades to try and stabilize currency values, but not until the entry to the European Monetary System in 1990 was there an attempt to go back to a fixed exchange rate. This policy aimed to provide an anti-inflationary anchor for the British economy by tying the currency to the strength of the Deutschmark. Unfortunately for this policy, it coincided with the reunification of Germany, and high interest rates in that country, which put enormous downward pressures on the pound, pressures which eventually proved irresistible. From 1992 the floating pound continued to sink.

In different ways both the fixed exchange rate regime before 1972 and the largely floating regime since have encouraged an enormous increase in capital flows between countries, with Britain as a major participant. Some of this capital takes the form of direct investment by foreigners in production facilities in Britain, such as Japanese car firms. But the majority takes the form of investment in financial assets and sterling bank accounts, and such money is extremely volatile, moving in and out of Britain very quickly in response not only to rates of return on the assets involved, but also to much more subjective judgements about the likely prospects of the British economy. Post-war currency liberalization under both fixed and floating regimes has unintentionally unleashed a torrent of movement of money between currencies and countries. In turn this has left governments of those countries, especially where the economy is perceived as having fundamental weaknesses, as extremely vulnerable to losses of 'confidence'. Such losses of confidence lead to capital outflows, falls in the value of the currency, and usually the necessity to pursue policies more congenial to international financial opinion. A particularly striking episode of this kind occurred in Britain in the mid-1970s, and this is looked at in detail in the case study later in this chapter.

The movement towards a more liberal trade regime was slower than for currency transactions. The first stage of this liberalization, the removal of quantitative controls over trade, was achieved quite quickly once it became apparent that the slump that had been expected to follow the war, as after 1918, failed to occur. But Britain remained a high-tariff country until the late 1960s. After the conclusion of the 'Kennedy Round' of GATT tariff negotiations (see Chapter 3) in 1968, Britain moved close to free trade in manufactured goods, though not in agricultural products. In the difficult years of the 1970s there were some pressures to revert to more trade controls, and tight limits continue on specific products such as cars from Japan and clothing and textiles from poorer countries, but overall free trade seems to have become accepted as the best regime by all the major political forces in Britain.

Britain's accession to the EC in 1972 may be seen as a deviation from this process of liberalization, but in fact by the time Britain joined, the common external tariff of the EC on manufactured goods was minimal. As a result, Britain's tendency to trade more and more with other EC countries was not mainly

Table 16.2. Sources of British imports in 1994

	Amount (£bn)	
EU	83.5	
Other west European countries	9.5	
North America	19.9	
Other OECD countries	10.6	
Oil exporting countries	3.2	
Rest of the world	22.8	
of which: the six 'Asian Tigers'		(9.8)
China		(1.7)
Total	149.5	

Source: Monthly Digest of Statistics.

the result of EC membership. It began in the 1950s, and seems to be best explained by the tendency of most of the growth in trade in the post-war period to take the form of swapping broadly similar goods (especially manufactures) between regional groups of countries of broadly similar incomes and tastes. This pattern has meant that in the post-war years Britain has imported a strikingly small proportion of its imports from poorer, low-wage countries. In the case of textiles and clothing, where low wage costs can confer a major competitive advantage, this has been at least in part the result of import controls, as noted above. But generally this pattern reflects the fact that other rich countries produce for their home markets the kind of goods British consumers want to buy, and similarly British producers can gain scale economies by selling their products in the broadly similar markets of other rich countries. This immunity from most low-wage import competition may be beginning to erode, especially as some Asian countries are now producing sophisticated goods which appeal to European consumers at lower cost than they can be produced at home. On the other hand, as Table 16.2 suggests, this is more a future threat than a current reality.

Domestic Policy

At the end of the Second World War there was a consensus between the major political parties that full employment should be given a much greater priority than was the case in the 1930s. This is demonstrated by the wartime coalition's 1944 white paper on *Employment Policy* which committed governments to try to secure a 'high and stable level of employment'. This political commitment was not, however, tested until the 1970s, because prior to that the boom in investment and international trade meant that governments did not need to take action to deal with a major threat of unemployment. In the 1970s the increase in unemployment, apparent from the late 1960s, accelerated, but governments proved

Table 16.3. Macroeconomic performance, 1945–95

	Inflation (annual change in GDP deflator)	Unemployment (% of labour force)	Balance of payments (current account balance as % GDP)
1945–50	4.3	1.4	−0.8
1951–67	3.8	2.5	0.5
1968–73	7.5	3.4	0.4
1974–79	15.5	4.0	−1.1
1980–89	7.2	10.4	−0.4
1990–95	4.5	7.7	−1.8

Sources: OECD, *Historical Statistics 1960–90* (Paris, 1992); OECD, *National Accounts of OECD Countries, 1950–1968* (Paris, 1970); Economic Trends, *Annual Supplement.*

unwilling or incapable of reducing it to previous levels. Between 1979 and 1981 unemployment doubled and it continued to increase until 1986. Initially the Conservative Thatcher government was extremely concerned that this return of mass unemployment would be disastrous for their electoral support. But this proved not to be the case, and whilst unemployment fluctuated sharply in the 1980s and 1990s, the average level remained well above those deemed wholly unacceptable in the 1950s and 1960s. But the issue proved less crucial to political support than had been assumed in those earlier decades, so the urgency of finding a policy response diminished.

The retreat from the full-employment goal was accompanied by a rising emphasis on reducing inflation as a policy objective. Like unemployment, inflation began to turn upwards from the late 1960s, and by 1970 was competing with unemployment as a policy concern. The 1970s may be characterized as a period when these two issues fluctuated in significance. Concern with inflation unsurprisingly peaked with the rise in the inflation rate to an unprecedented 25 per cent in 1974/75. The sharp reduction in this rate in the later 1970s saw the Labour government reassert its traditional concern with reducing unemployment. However, the Conservatives after 1979 put beating inflation at the centre of their economic policy agenda, and although the actual rate fluctuated sharply over the next 20 years, it became the one measure of economic performance the government was willing to target explicitly.

From the middle 1950s the achievement of more rapid economic growth began to figure in the pronouncements of politicians about desirable economic policy aims. In 1954 R.A. Butler, the Chancellor of the Exchequer, held out the prospect of a 'doubling in the standard of living in 25 years' if current trends continued. At that time the growth of the British economy was seen as broadly acceptable, but towards the end of the 1950s the fact that Britain was lagging behind the growth performance of other western European economies became a matter of considerable public concern. By the early 1960s both of the main political parties based much of their claim for electoral support on the claim that they, and only they, could deliver faster economic growth. This debate, predicated on a belief that given the right policies Britain could grow as fast as other western European economies, became fiercer in the 1970s as growth slowed down. The popularity of the view that Britain was suffering from a serious but reversible economic decline led to no agreement about the causes of the problem, and economic debate lurched from the advocacy of state-led planning to the neo-liberal radicalism of the Thatcher programme in 1979. The latter claimed that only by a sharp reversal of post-war trends in relation to taxation, public spending and borrowing, the role of trade unions and the control of inflation, would Britain be able to enjoy greater prosperity. By the mid-1990s Labour was claiming that this neo-liberal project had failed, evidenced by Britain's continued slipping down the world league table of income per head.

Assessment of the impact of post-1979 policies on growth is especially difficult because of the sharpness of the cyclical fluctuations in economic activity since that date. The years 1980–81 saw the biggest fall in output in the post-war years (concentrated in manufactures, where it reached 15 per cent), whilst the recession of 1990–92, though shallower, was more prolonged. To discuss growth we need to distinguish cycles from trends, but so far there has been only one complete cycle since 1979, that from 1979 to 1989 (see Table 16.1). As far as that period is concerned, what seems clear is that British growth recovered from the very low levels of 1973–79, at the same time as growth in other major industrial countries, especially Germany, was faltering. Hence Britain's relative position improved, though how far this was sustainable remains unclear. The cycles in economic activity in western European economies were not well synchronized in the early and mid-1990s, so it is impossible to determine whether Britain's recovery phase after 1992 signalled any change in its relative performance.

Promises of faster economic growth remained the staple of economic policy debate from the early 1960s through to the mid-1990s. Parties sought to differentiate themselves by different rhetorics about how this goal could be achieved. However, behind the rhetoric, policy proposals to achieve this objective notably converged in the 1990s on anodyne proposals such as those for more education and training.

Of all policy objectives in post-war Britain none have been more widely debated than those relating to the balance of payments. Many economists would argue that it is helpful to see the balance of payments not as an objective in its own right, but as a constraint on achieving other policy objectives. Thus, for example, it can be argued that the balance of payments is satisfactory when a country obtains enough foreign exchange (without having to borrow) to pay for the level of imports demanded by a fully employed economy. Whatever the logic of this argument, policy debate in Britain has generally been conducted as if the balance of payments were an object in its own right. This was reasonably straight-forward when the pound had a fixed rate of exchange, because an unsatisfactory balance of payments was one that threatened the current rate of exchange, though it was rarely explained why a given rate of exchange should in economic terms be regarded as particularly desirable.[3] After the pound was floated in 1972 less attention was paid to the balance of payments, but the trend deterioration in the current account (the total of imports and exports of goods and services taken together), and especially the balance on manufacturing trade over much of the next 25 years, meant that many commentators regarded the balance of payments figures as another sign of the relative decline of the economy.

In pursuing their policy goals, governments have had a limited range of policy instruments at their disposal. The wartime physical controls (rationing, and allocation of resources by government bodies) were not abolished immediately after the war, but the trend towards replacing them with macroeconomic instruments, especially fiscal policy (the manipulation of the balance between government spending and taxation), is in evidence from 1947. In the 1950s fiscal policy assumed pride of place in the policy repertoire, with monetary policy having a decidedly secondary role. Fiscal policy became extremely active, responding with frequent changes in direction to balance of payments difficulties (reduction of demand) and rising unemployment (increasing demand). From these alternating concerns was born the 'stop–go' cycle, with governments proving adept at timing the 'go' phase to coincide with a run-up to a general election. By the end of the 1950s this pattern of policy was under growing attack, as the concern with increasing economic growth led to charges that stop–go was inhibiting investment and hence slowing the expansion of the economy. This view became a popular criticism of post-war policy, though its accuracy can be doubted. Investment in this period was notably higher than pre-war, and though this cannot be decisive in the argument, it suggests that stop–go might have *increased* investment because it reassured investors that the government was going to stick with full-employment policies. Also it should be noted that the fluctuations in British economic activity associated with stop–go were no greater than in other western European countries where investment expanded substantially faster.[4]

These criticisms of stop–go were responded to by governments trying to refocus policy on long-term growth and away from what was portrayed as the short-termism inherent in the frequent attempts to change the pressure of demand in the economy. The Conservatives created the National Economic Development Council (Neddy) in 1962 to bring together government, employers and trade unions to assess the conditions for faster economic growth and to coordinate action in pursuit of that objective. This activity was commonly called planning, but this was misleading if taken to imply a significant increase in government control of the economy. No such increase took place, and 'planning' meant little more than a desire to give more attention to future economic prospects, and to try and talk-up those prospects by sharing ideas and opinions amongst the leaders of industry and the unions.

Under Labour after 1964 the rhetoric of planning became more popular, and in principle the government was more willing to get involved directly in the affairs of industry. But in practice little was done, as the government gave priority to solving the balance of payments problems. The government ended up by replacing stop–go not with a smoother expansion but with an almost complete stop.

Monetary policy found little favour with governments before the 1970s. The Conservatives in 1951 ended the policy of cheap money (low interest rates) of the previous 20 years and were willing to manipulate interest rates in managing the economy, but only in a subordinate role to fiscal policy. To deal with inflation in the period up to the 1970s, governments mainly attempted to use incomes policy, usually by striking a deal with the trade union movement. Such deals were easier to make with Labour governments, because of the shared views between Labour and the unions about the broad thrust of policy. The most successful such policy was in 1948–50, when the Attlee government was able to gain support for a tough incomes restraint by delivering full employment and welfare provision very much desired by the union movement. No later policy was anywhere near as successful, the policies usually breaking down after, at best, a short period of effectiveness. This failure reflected the fact that, except in time of crisis, both governments and unions were strongly attached to a system of free collective bargaining over wages, with the state relegated to a minor role in the process. Free collective bargaining fitted in both with the long-term union attachment to steering clear of government involvement in their affairs, and with government fears that if they were to become entangled in the wage bargaining process that process would become politicized, with great dangers to order and tranquillity in industry.

From the late 1960s inflation began to edge up, and at the same time the previous neglect of monetary policy in managing the economy was subject to increasing criticism. Monetarists, most notably Milton Friedman, argued that inflation was a monetary phenomenon caused by excessive growth of the money supply, and that governments should focus policy on restraining that growth. Such arguments became more influential in the crisis years of the 1970s as inflation and unemployment grew together, creating 'stagflation'. These views were increasingly advocated by participants in financial markets and influential figures in bodies like the International Monetary Fund. Governments, whatever their own views, were forced to take note of policies advocated by such powerful bodies of opinion. Labour governments in both the 1960s and 1970s paid lip-service to ideas of monetary targeting as a condition for borrowing from the IMF. After 1979 this reluctant monetarism was replaced by the full-blooded enthusiasm of the Thatcher government. Targets for money supply growth were central to the Medium Term Financial Strategy of 1980 (along with a targeted reduction in public borrowing), but were not achieved. For all their enthusiasm the Conservative governments of the 1980s could not find a monetary target they could properly control, and though 'control of the money supply' remained central to the stated objectives of policy, the idea of straightforward, quantifiable links between something called money and the rate of inflation proved a snare and a delusion.

Coupled to 'monetarism' after 1979, a programme of 'rolling back the state' aimed to improve incentives, encourage entrepreneurship and increase growth. Rolling back the state in some areas proved much more difficult than envisaged, and the government soon gave up its stated intention to cut the absolute size of public spending in favour of aiming to reduce the ratio of public spending to national income. As a result it also proved impossible for the Thatcher government to cut taxes, and they had to content themselves with switching the burden from direct to indirect sources, and to a substantial extent from the rich to the poor. Whilst in some areas the state was reined back in these years, the most striking change in the economy in the 1980s (alongside the squeezing of the incomes of the poor and the reversal of the long-term trend to greater income equality) was the weakening of the trade union movement. By 1979 the unions had emerged as the favourite scapegoat for Britain's perceived economic failings, and provided a ready target for reforms conducted in the name of labour market liberalization.

By the mid-1990s policy had returned to the 'fine-tuning' of demand of the stop–go period, but with a primary target of low inflation and monetary policy as the main policy weapon. However, fiscal policy had not been abandoned, and in the recession of the early 1990s, and in striking contrast to the recession of the early 1980s, the government was quite happy to see the fiscal stabilizers operate, declining tax revenues and increased public spending generating a level of public borrowing only previously exceeded in the mid-1970s. Towards the end of the twentieth century British economic policy looks as far as ever from producing the magic combination of low inflation, low unemployment, fast growth and healthy balance of payments. In particular, mass unemployment seems in practice to have become accepted as inescapable, despite its corrosive effects on both public finances and the social order.

In focus: The Crisis of the Mid-1970s

All industrial countries suffered a slow-down in economic growth, higher inflation and higher unemployment in the mid-1970s as a result of OPEC I, the quadrupling of oil prices in 1973–74. This rise in prices was both inflationary, because of the widespread use of oil, and deflationary, in the sense that resources used in other sectors had to be reduced in order to put them into exports to pay for the higher-priced oil. But Britain seems to have suffered the worst deterioration in economic performance of any major country as a result of this shock.

The crisis of the mid-1970s in Britain was particularly acute because she was already a slow-growing country with a weak balance of payments before OPEC erupted. But were these weaknesses compounded by policy errors in the British response to OPEC I? The crisis focused on two issues, the decline in the value of the pound and the level of public spending and borrowing. These two became intertwined because in order to support the value of the pound the government had to borrow foreign exchange from overseas, but potential lenders would not provide the funds unless the government changed policies on public spending and borrowing.

The decline in the value of the pound which began in early 1976 was initially welcomed by the authorities in Britain because it would restore British competitiveness after the rapid inflation of the previous 18 months. However, soon the pound appeared to be in free fall, and this was when

The Crisis of the Mid-1970s (continued)

Table 16.4. Percentage increase in British and west European economic performance during 1973–76

	GNP	Unemployment	Prices	Hourly earnings in manufacturing
UK	0.3	3.2	66.9	78.9
West Germany	2.7	3.1	18.5	26.9
Italy	5.4	0.2	63.1	87.2
France	6.8	1.4	39.1	60.6

Source: K. Burk and A. Cairncross, *Goodbye Great Britain: the 1976 IMF Crisis* (London, 1992), p. 221.

attention focused on public spending and borrowing. As Table 16.5 suggests, Britain was not a particularly large public spender by European standards, and though the growth in expenditure between 1972 and 1976 was certainly fast, it was not out of line with that in other countries. Probably more damning in the eyes of international financial opinion was the argument that this growth was out of control, resulting from slack procedures for determining expenditure rather than deliberate policy choices. The truth of such allegations was much debated in Britain in 1975–76, but the government rapidly brought in a system which led to a remarkable turnaround in the trend of public spending. This system was called 'cash limits', and meant that rather than the Treasury finding the money for whatever objectives had been agreed upon (e.g to build 100 miles of motorway or 10 hospitals), programmes would be allocated a specific cash sum which could not be exceeded. If inflation was faster than allowed for in this cash sum then the programme would have to be cut back, with fewer miles of road or fewer hospitals built.

Cash limits were introduced for most programmes in the budget of spring 1976. Their effects, coupled to planned reductions in programmes decided by the government, were much greater than anticipated, and public spending fell by 6.9 per cent in 1976/77 to 1977/78, the greatest ever peacetime cut in public spending. Yet because the scale of this reduction was not known even by the Treasury, the crises of the summer and autumn of 1976 were played out on the assumption that public spending and borrowing were still rising rather than already falling. In that summer the Labour government came close to breaking up over the scale of public expenditure cuts called for by international financial opinion. In the autumn a further crisis over the balance of payments, and a fall in the international value of the pound, accompanied increased cuts demanded by the International Monetary Fund in return for a loan to Britain.

The Crisis of the Mid-1970s (continued)

Table 16.5. Fiscal policy in Britain and western Europe, 1972–78

	Government expenditure as % GDP			Fiscal deficit as % GDP		
	1972	1976	1978	1972	1976	1978
UK	39.3	46.3	43.3	1.3	5.0	4.4
West Germany	40.8	47.9	47.8	0.5	3.4	2.4
Italy	38.6	42.2	46.1	8.6	9.8	10.4
France	38.3	43.9	44.6	0.8[a]	0.6	2.1

Note: [a]Surplus.

Source: OECD, *Economic Outlook*, 47 (1990), Tables R14, R15.

That these crises were based on quite mistaken information about the economy, and that big cuts were in place long before the IMF mission arrived to demand their pound of flesh, is itself interesting and even amusing, but it should not conceal the important point. What the crisis of 1976 showed in extreme form was that the British government's capacity to pursue economic policy was now heavily constrained by international financial opinion. The need to appease such opinion led to a famous speech by the Prime Minister, James Callaghan, at the Labour Party conference in September 1976, when he attacked the Keynesian assumptions of post-war economic policy, and seemed to accept that governments should focus their attention on controlling inflation by controlling the money supply, rather than using fiscal policy to try to reduce unemployment. However, once the crisis of 1976 was over, the policy of the government showed little sign of the revolutionary shift implied by Callaghan. Fiscal policy was still seen as crucial to unemployment, and the government still relied heavily on its 'social contract' (incomes policy) to contain inflation. Thus the Callaghan speech looks in retrospect like a short-term attempt to placate financial opinion, rather than suggesting a major change of heart in the Labour Party about how to manage the economy most effectively.

Debate and Interpretations: Was Policy to Blame for Britain's Slow Growth?

Britain's economic growth over the whole post-war period has been significantly slower than that of her western European neighbours, though there is evidence of some narrowing of the gap in the 1980s. How far has this been the result of economic policy? As suggested at the beginning of this chapter, various aspects of policy have often been blamed for this lagging performance, including the 'stop–go' cycle which was an especially favourite culprit in the 1960s. The most radical denunciation of previous policy has come from Thatcherite and New Right critics, who increasingly from the 1970s blamed the whole shape of post-war policy for slow growth. For them post-war Britain had excessive concern with employment compared with inflation; too much government spending, especially on welfare; too much public ownership of industry; trade unions that were too powerful; and generally governments that gave too little scope for the operation of market forces.[5] It was this kind of view which informed the shift to 'monetarism' and pro-free market policies after 1979.

In looking at these allegations it is useful to compare Britain with her continental neighbours, as for most of the post-war period these have been seen as the countries whose economic performance Britain should seek to emulate. On the question of priorities, it is probably correct to say that in the early post-war years British politicians put more emphasis on sustaining full employment than was the case elsewhere in Europe. This may have reflected the fact that mass unemployment in inter-war Britain, whilst not as extensive in the 1930s slump as in countries like the USA and Germany, continued for a much longer period in Britain than elsewhere in the industrial world. But whether this commitment harmed British performance is doubtful. As noted above, it was linked to the 'stop–go' cycle, but the contribution of this to post-war performance was, at most, small. Second, the commitment to full employment did *not* lead to indifference to inflation. Britain's inflation rate in the boom years was around the west European average, and notably below that in France, for example.

Public spending rose sharply in Britain in the 1960s and early 1970s, and much of this increase was fuelled by the increased scale of welfare spending. However, this was a pattern common across Europe, reflecting the impact of an ageing population and increased expectations about the quality of welfare provision (especially in health and education) in more affluent societies. By the 1960s Britain had become a relatively small spender on welfare in a European context, and this *ranking* remained broadly the same despite the increase in absolute expenditure.[6]

Similarly, the scale of the British nationalized industries was not notably different from that in other western European countries. Coal, iron and steel, gas and electricity were commonly in some form of public sector ownership, whilst manufacturing industry commonly remained almost entirely in private hands. In comparative perspective, the most striking feature of the scope of British public ownership was its almost complete *absence* from the financial sector. The performance of the nationalized industries was also more complex than commonplace denunciations would suggest. Whilst their financial performance was poor, and deteriorated notably in the 1970s, this reflected the worldwide problems of such 'smoke-stack' and utility companies as much as particularly British issues. In terms of productivity, British nationalized industries performed as well as the average of British manufacturing.[7] To a considerable extent this reflected massive labour-shedding as the demand for the industries' products declined, and perhaps it is not unreasonable to suggest that nationalization, rather than being a major burden, provided a quite efficient institutional form to manage the decline of industries which were contracting all over the industrialized world.

Of all the alleged culprits for Britain's post-war retardation, none has been so frequently blamed as the trade unions. Unions, it has been asserted, have obstructed technical change and resisted reform of working practices that would have brought about higher productivity. In comparative perspective British unions have been relatively strong if we measure the share of the workforce they organize, and this impression of strength is reinforced by the unification of the movement in the TUC, whilst in many countries the union movement has been divided on political and religious grounds. However, the notion of 'strength' is difficult to apply to trade unions. British unions have long been characterized by strong *local* organization, often craft-based, with relatively weak national leadership and a TUC which has little capacity to act separately from individual unions. The TUC and union leadership have usually been publicly committed to productivity-enhancing policies, but a common allegation is that their fragmented structure has given power to local groups who have often been obstructive and negative in their attitude to efficiency issues. Certainly examples can be found of such obstruction, such as in printing and the docks. But clear evidence for their general prevalence, especially in manufacturing, is lacking. Much of the criticism of unions is based on either 'saloon-bar' anecdotes or, in academic circles, theoretical models of economic behaviour with little evidence to support them. Criticism of trade unions represents the worst case of the regrettable process whereby the post-war obsession with slow growth has led to a demonizing of particular groups, rather than a cool analysis of remediable problems.

Bibliographical Note

Until recently books dealing with the whole of British post-war economic history were few and far between, but that is now being remedied. Some older books dealing with sub-periods remain very useful, such as J.C.R. Dow, *The Management of the British Economy 1945–60* (Cambridge, 1965), and there are newer books which are also central to detailed studies of specific periods and episodes, the most outstanding being A. Cairncross, *Years of Recovery: British Economic Policy 1945–51* (London, 1986). The Attlee government, because of the availability of the archives, has been particularly extensively studied, and to complement Cairncross's focus on macroeconomic policy there is the wider-ranging book by J. Tomlinson, *Democratic Socialism and Economic Policy: the Attlee Years* (Cambridge, 1997).

Of books dealing with the whole post-war period, A. Cairncross, *The British Economy Since 1945* (London, 1992) is very accessible. N. Crafts and N. Woodward (eds), *The British Economy Since 1945* (Oxford, 1991) is also a major work, though it requires some background in economics to be fully appreciated. The second edition of *The Economic History of Britain Since 1770, Vol. 3, 1939–1992*, edited by R. Floud and D. McCloskey (Cambridge, 1995), contains a range of essays, several of them dealing with aspects of economic policy and the economic decline. A. Booth, *British Economic Development Since 1945* (Manchester, 1995) offers extracts from key documents from the period, accompanied by a very helpful overview. R. Middleton, *Government Versus the Market: the Growth of the Public Sector, Economic Management and British Economic Performance, c.1890–1979* (Cheltenham, 1996), though not covering the whole period, is an extremely useful work, especially rich in a wide range of statistical material.

The 'declinist' approach to post-war British economic policy is well summarized in S. Pollard, *The Wasting of the British Economy: British Economic Policy 1945 to the Present* (London, 1982). The best critical discussion of the decline issue is K. Williams, J. Williams and D. Thomas, *Why are the British Bad at Manufacturing?* (London, 1983).

Notes

1. The relatively slow growth of the United States has led many commentators to emphasize the 'catching-up' aspect of fast expansion in western Europe, with those countries able to borrow techniques from the US. This still leaves open the question why Britain did not catch up more, though until the 1960s her lag behind the US was smaller than elsewhere in Europe.

2. Before the First World War Britain was an exceptionally open economy, with a policy of almost complete free trade, and a massive supplier of capital and short-term finance to the rest of the world. See M. Kirby 'Britain in the world economy', in P. Johnson (ed.), *Twentieth Century Britain: Economic, Cultural and Social Change* (London, 1994).

3. The attempt (ultimately unsuccessful) to prevent devaluation of the pound in the period 1964–67 seems to have had little economic logic, but to have been based on the belief that devaluation would be a political defeat for the government.

4. A. Cairncross, *The British Economy Since 1945* (London, 1992), p. 14.

5. For example, G. Maynard, *The Economy Under Mrs Thatcher* (Oxford, 1988), Ch. 1.

6. D. Heald, *Public Expenditure: its Defence and Reform* (London, 1982), Ch. 2.

7. R. Millward, 'The nationalised industries', in M. Artis and D. Cobham (eds), *Labour's Economic Policies 1974–79* (Manchester, 1991), p. 144.

17 France

Alain Guyomarch

A first glance at French statistics since 1945 might lead to the conclusion that the mid-1970s mark a watershed. Fourastié called the period from 1945 to 1975 'Les Trentes Glorieuses', asserting that those 'golden years' had witnessed greater changes in France than the preceding three centuries. Since then, however, the performance of the French economy has failed to match those achievements, as national income growth slowed down and unemployment rose markedly (Table 17.1). It would, however, be oversimplified to periodize post-war economic history in only two phases, since a closer look at economic policies and performance reveals five phases, which are analysed in the main part of the chapter. This discussion is complemented by a case study of innovations in economic policy making, brought about by the Monnet Plan in the immediate post-war years. In the concluding section it will be argued that the most useful insights about France's complex

Table 17.1. Growth, inflation and unemployment in France, 1945–94

Period	Average annual change, per cent			Unemployment[b] (per cent rate)
	GDP	GDP per head	Prices[a]	
1945–52	13.0	11.9	30.6	2.2[c]
1952–58	4.5	3.6	3.3	2.1
1958–73	5.3	4.3	4.6	1.9
1973–83	2.2	1.7	11.2	5.7[d]
1983–94	2.0	1.4	3.6[e]	10.0[f]
1950–73	5.0	4.0	5.0	2.0
1973–94	2.1	1.6	7.3[g]	7.9[h]

Notes: [a]Consumer price index; [b]period average of annual unemployment rates (per cent of labour force); [c]1950–52; [d]1974–83; [e]1983–93; [f]1984–93; [g]1973–94; [h]1974–93.

Sources: A. Maddison, *Dynamic Forces in Capitalist Development* (Oxford, 1991); A. Maddison, *Monitoring the World Economy, 1820–1992* (Paris, 1995).

economic development are provided by theories of internationalization and the new institutionalism.

Economic Development in Five Phases

1945 to 1952: Painful Reconstruction

The Liberation took a heavy toll on an economy weakened by poor pre-war performance and exploitation during the German occupation. Taking 1929 as a base, the index of industrial production had, by 1938, attained 116 in the UK and 124 in Germany, whereas in France, after a huge drop in the early 1930s, the index had reached only 79. After 1940, the German administration overexploited the mines of the Nord and Pas-de-Calais, before flooding them when forced to retreat out of France – a cruel blow for a coal-dependent economy. Transport infrastructure was also wrecked, not only by the retreating Germans, but also by the advancing Allies and by the French Resistance. In 1945, industrial output reached a mere 42 per cent of its already low 1938 level, and agricultural production only 60 per cent. Destruction and lack of renewal during the war meant that, in 1945, the capital stock was well below its pre-war level.

The early post-war period was marked by pronounced political and economic instability. Reconstruction from the effects of war and 10 years of pre-war depression had to take place in an environment of persistently high rates of inflation, permanent budgetary problems and balance of payments and foreign exchange crises. Rationing, which had been in force since 1940, was continued after the Liberation when rations fell to almost famine levels. Wage and price controls remained in force. Moreover, there were severe socio-political tensions: 'collaborators' were purged, and all who had profited from the German occupation, including company owners, farmers and small shopkeepers, were criticized. In politics, the temporary unity at the Liberation between Communists, Socialists, Christian Democrats and Gaullists soon gave way to bitter conflicts over economic policies.

Nonetheless, there were positive features of the situation. One of them was foreign aid, mainly from the United States, first through the extension of the Lend–Lease agreement, then by the Blum–Byrnes deal of May 1946 ($650 million), and finally by the $2.6 billion of Marshall Aid between 1947 and 1952 (see Chapter 3). A second positive factor was the 'baby boom' after 1945, with an increase in birth rates. A third factor was the ease of re-establishing trading links with colonies within the 'French Union', which grouped most of the former empire in a single monetary system, the franc zone. By 1949, franc zone countries were providing a quarter of French imports and consuming 40 per cent of exports. A fourth advantage was the renewal of politico-economic élites and ideas. After the Liberation purges, new men took leadership positions in politics, and in major companies, both public and private. Kindleberger sees this élite renewal as essential for the adoption of new ideas and institutions. Indeed, some widespread

Plate 17.1. A French peasant family taking delivery of a tractor provided by Marshall Aid. A rise in output levels and the modernization of production practices not only in industry but also in agriculture became major policy objectives in the late 1940s and 1950s.

agreement emerged about both 'reconstruction' and 'modernization' to transform France into a dynamic industrial economy on a par with other European countries. There was also consensus that this goal could best be achieved by state direction of the economy, with public ownership, regulation, credit allocation, subsidies and planning.

The political coalition for nationalization included, for nationalist reasons, de Gaulle, most Gaullists and many Christian Democrats. The nationalization programme covered most energy industries (including coal, electricity and gas), but also the main banks and insurance companies. The Renault car group was confiscated as a punishment for collaboration. These nationalizations, when added to pre-war acquisitions (the railways, Air France, the tobacco monopoly and the Bank of France), created a significant public sector. The extension of war-time regulatory powers over imports, exports, prices, rents and wages provided a second mechanism for state interventionism. Finally, a system of economic planning was institutionalized by de Gaulle in 1946 (see the box below). The post-war consensus also concerned the redistribution of incomes and the welfare of the population. A statutory minimum income was introduced (the SMIG) and *la Sécurité Sociale*, the core of the French welfare state, was established.

However, even with rationing and widespread controls over wages and prices inflation was endemic. This was a legacy of the war. There was a large monetary overhang as a result of wartime supply shortages. Moreover, the new post-Liberation government inherited a high stock of public debt which was accumulated as a result of the Vichy governments' obligation to pay for the German occupation. Inflation was one way of eroding the real value of this debt after the war. In addition, the new government faced enormous difficulties in financing its budget deficits by means other than the printing press. Given the need to fund the reconstruction effort, there was little room for reducing public expenditure. New public debt in the form of government bonds was difficult to issue. Eventually, it was Marshall Aid that allowed the government to get out of the dilemma.

Consumer prices rose at annual rates of up to 60 per cent during 1946–48 and this also fed unrest in the labour market. In the winter of 1947 there were a number of strikes for higher wages. In spring 1948, however, a strike at the Renault plant precipitated the dismissal of the five Communist ministers who broke ranks with the Government to support the strike. In November 1948 a further wave of strikes followed. The powerful Communist-led CGT unions, which had hitherto restrained the workers' demands, now encouraged them and supported the strikes. Despite blockages of the railways, the Government remained firm. The CGT split and the pro-Socialist minority, with American encouragement and funds, created *Force Ouvrière*.

Between 1946 and 1948, the level of French imports was on average more than twice that of French exports which, ultimately, led to an erosion of foreign exchange reserves, an increase in France's external debt and a balance of payments crisis in early 1948. In response, the franc was devalued by 50 per cent. Though this initially fuelled inflation (through an increase in import prices), it was sufficient to restore the balance of payments by making French exports competitive. A further 40 per cent devaluation of the franc followed in September 1949, after sterling had been devalued.

The arrival of Marshall Aid from early 1948 had a stabilizing influence on the French economy. US aid proved crucial not so much in giving France access to imports needed for investment-driven reconstruction: the most essential goods had been imported before the inflow of Marshall Aid and imports did not display a sharp increase after Marshall funds became available. In contrast, it was exports that were growing. Rather, Marshall Aid allowed the government to reduce its budget deficits, to replenish foreign exchange reserves and to stabilize the rise in external debt. One outcome was a dramatic fall in the rate of inflation from mid-1948.[1]

The outbreak of the Korean War caused a sharp increase in military expenditure which fed into a renewed surge of inflation to almost 20 per cent in 1951 and a subsequent balance of payments crisis. One outcome was the temporary suspension of the programme of exchange liberalization that France was implementing. However, the crisis was fairly quickly overcome under the new prime minister Pinay who came into office in 1952 and reduced public investment expenditure. As growth slowed down in 1952 and 1953, inflationary pressures dissipated.

It is interesting to note that the use of a large part of US aid primarily for the purpose of financial recovery does not appear to have had seriously adverse effects on the pace of reconstruction. By 1952, when the Monnet Plan and Marshall Aid both came to an end, not only was real GDP over 13 per cent higher than in the record year of 1929 but the population was growing, the transport infrastructure was largely rebuilt, the modernization of agriculture had begun and productivity was rising in most sectors.

In focus: Economic Planning

In January 1946 de Gaulle established a small Planning Commissariat, with the task of drafting a five-year Plan for reconstruction and modernization. Both the location of the Commissariat in the Prime Minister's office (rather than within the Ministry for the National Economy) and the choice of its head, Jean Monnet (then chairing the Import Committee and well experienced in international affairs), symbolized that the Plan was conceived in an international context. Indeed, Monnet's Plan won wide and continuing support, including that of the Foreign Affairs Ministry, precisely because it focused on increasing the strength of the French economy relative to that of Germany, and emphasized French dependence on the coal resources of the Ruhr. Thus it incorporated the foreign policy goal of internationalizing control of the Ruhr. A second specific feature of the Monnet Plan was that it set a number of national priorities about which there was to be little political debate: hence, it targeted only six leading sectors – coal, steel, electricity, cement, agricultural machines and the railways – leaving the rest of the economy to follow and adjust to changes in these sectors.

A third feature was that the main targets were set by the officials of the Planning Commissariat, and the consultative 'planning commissions' for each sector, which included representatives of both sides of industry, as well as experts and planners, met only to examine how the targets were to be met, but not to discuss the targets. In fact, the Commissariat decided that the goal should be to exceed the 1929 level of output by 1950, and in practice there was relatively little preliminary research. A fourth feature of the first Plan, launched in March 1946, was that its financing was treated as an implementation problem. After great debates about the rate of inflation and the desirability of encouraging exports to pay for essential imports, the problem was largely resolved by Marshall Aid. Paradoxically, a Plan which had been intended to demonstrate the need for an international body to ensure coal exports from the Ruhr to France, showed the American administration that France would make very efficient use of that aid. In practice, the Plan

Economic Planning (continued)

was extended by two years to cover the period of Marshall Aid. Although the USA helped to establish the International Authority of the Ruhr, in response to French demands, it proved so weak that Monnet and Schuman devised an alternative approach to achieve the goal of ensuring French influence over the energy resources of the Ruhr – the European Coal and Steel Community.

The institutionalization of planning since Monnet involved comprehensive, five-year Plans for the whole economy, and the 'indicative' planning method. There were three linked processes: forecasting studies, 'concerted' decision-making and implementation. A statistical 'total market study' of interrelationships and trends of the whole economy and its sectors led to the 'construction' of both long- and short-term 'scenarios'. Next followed an attempt to coordinate individual forecasting by key private actors (major firms and unions) in collective, economy-wide planning. This 'concertation' of social partners, involving information exchange between 'private' and 'public' actors in the planning 'commissions', was theorized as a dynamic process for replacing uncertainties, reducing intransigence, and building collective consensus to avoid the wastes of pure market competition and coercive Soviet-style planning.

In theory, implementation meant matching medium-term targets at a macroeconomic level by short-term micro-level decisions in individual firms and government ministries. Ideally, implementation was a consequence of 'concertation': by coming together for coordinated decision making, firms and state agencies were drawn into common ways of thinking and loyalty towards macroeconomic targets decided together. The state was expected to lead in implementation, both by using its power to determine public investment and bank lending priorities and by use of its regulatory powers, soft loan and subsidy facilities, public procurement policies and ownership rights in public sector industry.

Practices of planning, however, never matched the ideal. If in theory, each 'Plan' was the result of concertation, in practice priorities were set by governments. Whilst targets enumerated in the Plan were supposed to be firm commitments, in a dynamic and interdependent world no government could make firm promises even about its own budget for years ahead, so planning targets became increasingly adjustable. The first Plan set economic targets for only six sectors, but later Plans addressed economy-wide 'horizontal' problems, so that their content was as much social and regional as economic. Targets became less and less precise. At the same time, industrial strategy – a major part of governmental policy – was made with very little reference to planning. Even Mitterrand's Socialists, who in 1981 tried to make planning the core of macroeconomic decision making, had difficulty linking industrial policies to the Plan. Since the 1970s, industrial policy increasingly involved reactive measures, or 'fire-fighting', or opportunist decisions to create or refloat national champions.

Economic Planning (continued)

Did later Plans have the success of the Monnet Plan? Certainly some
targets were achieved. However, chronological coincidence does not
necessarily reflect causation: as Rueff warned de Gaulle: 'planners are like the
rooster who believes his crowing causes the sun to rise'. It is also important
to identify how economic planning influenced performance, and to measure
wider effects of planning on governmental activities, on centre–periphery and
firm–state linkages. Since 1947, there have been eleven such Plans, but the
last four have either been aborted or have contained few real targets. Estrin
and Holmes show Gross Domestic Product targets of the 2nd, 3rd, 4th and
5th Plans were achieved or exceeded, but not those of the 6th or 7th Plans,
where the target–result gaps exceeded 10 per cent.[1] For imports and exports,
outcomes were rarely close to targets, and for the 4th and 5th Plans, imports
exceeded the targets by over 30 per cent. Nor is there clear evidence that the
impact of the Plans on business expectations and hence resource allocation
explains why between 1958 and 1973, French growth was higher and more
stable than elsewhere. Estrin and Holmes attempted to quantify the impact
of the Plans by calculating 'alternative forecasts' and long-run trends: their
findings show only that the 3rd and 4th Plan targets were closer to the
outcomes than the predictions of businesses would have been had they been
made without the planning process. For the 5th and 6th Plans, however, firms
might have forecasted more accurately without the Plan.

In the late 1970s, a survey for the Planning Commissariat showed that the
Plan had little credibility amongst businessmen: only 9 per cent thought the
Plan was 'very important', over 60 per cent saw the Plan targets as the results
of government decisions, rather than of concertation, and 57 per cent said
the government was not committed to its own targets. Whilst this survey
revealed that many businessmen wanted more information, especially
independent forecasts relevant to their firms, under 10 per cent had ever
used the Plan for professional purposes, and over 60 per cent had never
consulted any documentation of the Plan.

The long experience of planning has had an impact on French
government by prioritizing public spending, normalizing rational forecasting,
forward studies and pluri-annual financing contracts. Since the 6th Plan,
a distinction has been made between ordinary targets and 'priority
programmes' of public spending. The 9th Plan introduced 'planning
contracts' between the state and public sector corporations, or between the
state and regions. In 1995, when Chirac finally abolished the fiction of a
national Plan whilst maintaining the Planning Commissariat, the practice of
formulating 'contracts' with the regions was continued. A survey of these
programmes and contracts shows a complex picture: most, but not all, these
targets were substantially achieved. Most ministries now undertake long- and

1. S. Estrin and P. Holmes, *French Planning in Theory and Practice* (London, 1983).

Economic Planning (continued)

medium-term analyses, usually by in-house planning services, whilst 'planning contracts' with central government give the regions a stable basis for infrastructure development. A second effect has been the creation of a talented network of planners. Finally, introducing concertation was a big achievement of the post-Monnet planners. In the 1950s planning 'commissions' were real innovations, but by the 1980s consultations with the social partners were part of the ordinary policy-making process in most ministries and local governments.

Paradoxically, the success of the first four Plans in reconstruction and modernization opened the economy to competition in European and world markets, and by the mid-1960s the French economy was well internationalized. French trade grew consistently faster than the planners foresaw, and the economy grew by the success of French firms in international trade. This extensive internationalization is both an indicator of the success of the early Plans and a marker of the end of a type of planning which its own success had made redundant.

1953 to 1958: Limits to Modernization

This period was marked by low levels of unemployment and continued economic growth, although unsurprisingly at a slower rate than that achieved during the reconstruction process in the immediate post-war years (Table 17.1). Initially inflation was halted, in 1953 prices even fell, and the programme of exchange liberalization was resumed. However, in 1957/58 inflation was again becoming a major difficulty as an outcome of the Suez crisis and the costs of the independence wars in Indochina and Algeria. The country faced a balance of payments crisis, the process of exchange liberalization was halted again, and the franc was unofficially devalued by 20 per cent in August 1957.

French leaders initiated the creation of the European Coal and Steel Community in 1952 and supported the Treaty of Rome in 1957, but maintained many import quotas and limited the convertibility of the franc (see Chapter 9). The Treaty of Rome was a challenge since high inflation and a weak franc made the phased reductions of quotas and tariffs seem impractical. Although overseas trade grew, the pattern of trade changed little: in 1958, as in 1949, a quarter of imports came from the franc zone and 40 per cent of exports went there. However, the costs of the independence wars were enormous. The Algerian imbroglio led to the Mollet government's initiative (with the UK) to invade the Suez Canal Zone, with dramatic repercussions: when the expeditionary force was withdrawn, oil prices soared, and in the subsequent financial crisis the government had to accept an International Monetary Fund (IMF) plan for financial restructuring to obtain a loan.

Throughout this period, the population growth of the late 1940s continued and large numbers left rural areas to take jobs in the growing industries (see Table 17.2). There was not only full employment, but even labour shortages, and firms began to recruit in the colonies and to encourage immigration. However, in growing towns housing shortages remained acute despite large public projects. There was also considerable overcrowding in schools. Paradoxically, the continuing economic success was not perceived by many citizens and did little to legitimize the political system of the Fourth Republic. In 1956 both the Communists and the Far Right won votes by arguing that modernization was ruining France. When in May 1958 de Gaulle took power to solve the Algerian problem, his condition that the Fourth Republic be replaced met little opposition.

1959 to 1973: The Golden Age?

The 1960s were a period of sustained expansion marked by high rates of economic growth, low levels of unemployment (see Table 17.1), a rapid international opening-up of the economy, massive structural transformations (see Table 17.2), and continuing support for Centre-Right governments of the Fifth Republic.

Following the recommendations of the Rueff committee, de Gaulle pushed through a number of reforms: the currency was devalued in December 1958 by 17.5 per cent and linked to the value of gold; exchange controls were suppressed; a 'new Franc' (worth 100 old francs) was introduced; and protectionist quotas and tariffs were reduced to implement the Treaty of Rome. If de Gaulle opposed supranational political elements of the EEC, he supported the economic aspects. Under de Gaulle and Pompidou, the planned development of public infrastructure was given a high priority. During the first years, public housing was greatly expanded, and subsequent years saw rapid building programmes for motorways, hospitals and schools.

De Gaulle's governments undertook other courageous, but initially unpopular, reforms. In the energy sector, they accepted the logic of cheap oil, and in 1959 planned the shut-down of a coal industry still supplying 74 per cent of the

Table 17.2. Employment structure (percentage share in total labour force) in France, 1950–91

	Agriculture	**Industry**	**Services**
1950	28.3	34.9	36.8
1960	21.4	36.2	42.4
1970	13.9	38.5	47.6
1981	8.5	35.2	56.3
1991	5.8	29.5	64.7

Sources: D. Coates (ed.), *Economic and Industrial Performance in Europe* (Aldershot, 1995); I. Lateson and J.W. Wheeler (eds), *Western Economies in Transition: Structural Change and Adjustment Policies in Industrial Countries* (London, 1980).

Plate 17.2. The Red Flag flies over the Renault works at Boulogne-Billancourt, Paris. In May 1968, widespread industrial unrest and factory occupations brought the French economy close to standstill.

economy's needs. This policy met considerable hostility, and in 1963, after major strikes by the miners, which won great public sympathy, funds were diverted to encourage new industries to locate in the coalfields and to retrain former miners. At the same time a new public-sector oil company, Elf, was established to compete in the growing oil industry. By 1973 France was dependent on oil and gas imports for much of its energy supply.

The reforms in agriculture were equally controversial. As governments were negotiating the European Common Agricultural Policy (CAP) to provide great opportunities for French farmers, they were also encouraging farmers to become more efficient. The abolition of the indexation of farm prices, followed by structural reforms aimed to transform peasant farming into modern agriculture, precipitated waves of protest. De Gaulle responded by appointing a new Agriculture Minister, Pisani, who took the reforms even further, by restructuring land tenure and farm sizes (by state land agencies), massively expanding agricultural training and research, and creating incentives for the establishment of cooperatives for marketing and production, pensions to encourage retirement, retraining schemes for those wishing to leave farming, and set-up grants for well-trained young farmers. At the same time, Crédit Agricole, the state-run bank, provided subsidized loans for capital equipment. CAP and the Pisani reforms changed farming dramatically: the agricultural labour force declined rapidly both in abolute terms and as a proportion of the total labour force (see Table 17.2), productivity increased and by 1973 highly profitable exports were growing.

Steel and armaments were other sectors in which decisive governmental action was taken. Soft loans and subsidies were poured into the steel companies both to introduce new technologies in existing plants, and to build large, on-shore, Japanese-style, integrated steel complexes at Dunkerque and Fos-sur-Mer (near Marseille). Not only was steel capacity expanded but the new technology also brought great productivity increases. Governments also carefully fostered the production and exporting of armaments. Major manufacturers, both private and public, were encouraged to expand by research grants, soft loans, cost-plus contracts to equip French forces, and special credits for exports. Under de Gaulle French spending on defence (as a proportion of GDP) was surpassed only by the USA and the UK in NATO. Unlike other governments, those in France placed very few restrictions on arms exports: indeed, before the 1967 war, French exporters had managed to sell arms to both the Egyptians and the Israelis. By 1970 France was a well-established military supplier.

If governments were often financing changes, they were not always leading them. In dealing with steel and armaments, governments were responding to initiatives from firms as often as they were initiating their own projects. In contrast, some sectors experienced little direct governmental intervention. The car industry was one such case, despite the public ownership of Renault. Peugeot, Citroën and Michelin all expanded rapidly with good products, competitive prices and a strong domestic market. Another example was distribution, where Leclerc discount supermarkets and Carrefour hypermarkets transformed a sector hitherto dominated by small, family-owned shops.

Despite the strong growth and many structural changes, there were numerous problems, some of which were increasingly visible. One was the growth of immigration, the first signs of racial tensions, and the development of shanty-towns around major industrial centres (see Chapter 11). Another was that in the early 1970s, France started to experience rising unemployment – for the first time since reconstruction. Indeed the social security system, which originally had no provision for the unemployed, had to be extended. Unemployment partly reflected the arrival on the labour market of the 'baby boom generation', although the full impact of the post-1946 increase in births was delayed by massive expansion in higher education (see Chapters 10 and 12). Universities, however, were greatly overcrowded. At the same time, the proportion of young women seeking to enter the labour market on a long-term basis started to rise.

There were many protests about economic difficulties – by impoverished small shopkeepers opposed to supermarkets, by disgruntled farmers, who blocked motorways with fruit and vegetables, and by underemployed rural youths, demanding more effective regional policies. A major explosion, however, came in May 1968, when student riots and occupations inspired large-scale industrial strikes. Half the country stopped work, many believing the government would fall. After a few days of hesitation, however, the government responded with a package of university reforms, an emergency building programme, a 10 per cent wage rise for all and increased workers' rights on the shop floor. The crisis inspired a run on the franc, but de Gaulle refused to devalue and reintroduced strict exchange controls. He also dissolved parliament and his party won an overwhelming majority in the new Assembly. Within a year, however, de Gaulle's proposal for a further reform, to regionalize the centralized administrative machine, had been rejected in a referendum, he had resigned and Pompidou had been elected in his place. The Pompidou presidency began with a 10 per cent devaluation and a package of reforms allowing economic growth and low inflation to be maintained. That presidency closed by adopting an ambitious nuclear energy programme, as a direct response to the OPEC oil price rises of 1973.

1974 to 1983: A Decade of Economic Instability

This period is characterized by a sharp fall in the rate of economic growth, a steep rise in unemployment and a return to high levels of inflation (see Table 17.1). Irrespective of governmental policies, whether liberally inspired under Giscard d'Estaing or Socialist, in Mitterrand's first years, these trends seemed irreversible. In 1974, the rate of unemployment stood at 2.7 per cent; by 1983, it had risen to more than 8 per cent. Whereas unemployment of 300,000 had caused great anxiety in 1967, the political result of the growing mass unemployment in the late 1970s was dramatic: in 1981, the Left won the presidency and a parliamentary majority. Then in local and European elections in 1983 and 1984, when the Left had failed to reduce unemployment, the right-wing extremism of the National Front showed its appeal.

During 1973 to 1983, consumer prices increased at an average rate of more than 11 per cent per annum. Whilst the initial sharp increase in the rate of inflation to nearly 14 per cent in 1974 and 12 per cent in 1975 can be explained by the short-run impact of the first oil-price shock, the persistence of high rates of inflation into the early 1980s had more to do with economic policy choices. These differed between different countries (see Chapter 5). By the early 1980s, inflation was growing faster in France than in most competing economies.

Part of the inflationary difficulty resulted from Pompidou's vast nuclear power-station programme, which was implemented with determination under Giscard d'Estaing, mostly by borrowing, often from abroad. Furthermore, the attempt to reflate a sluggish economy in 1974 and 1975 created a large budget deficit. A reduction of that deficit was made under Barre, as Prime Minister, in 1976, but public spending increased again in 1977 in preparation for the 1978 general elections, and yet again in 1980 and early 1981, before the presidential election. Mitterrand's first measures as president included further stimulation of the economy, intended to create jobs, but the effects were to increase inflation and public debt. Exchange-rate uncertainties were another source of anxiety for economists and business decision makers. The devaluation of 1969 did not lead to a new period of stability. In 1971 the convertibility of the dollar for gold was abolished and fluctuating exchange rates became the norm. The exchange-rate stabilization system within the EEC (known as the 'snake in the tunnel') included France, but pressures against the franc caused its withdrawal, three times. When the more structured scheme, the EMS (European Monetary System), was set up in 1979, the franc entered its Exchange Rate Mechanism (ERM) at an unsustainable high level. Three devaluations followed in 1981, 1982 and 1983 (see Chapter 9).

In such a climate, the shortage of private investment was hardly surprising. In general, the few firms which were investing were doing so outside France, in line with internationalization strategies. A particular problem was the steel industry, which, aided by huge state subsidies and soft loans for new plants, had such excess capacity that it was technically bankrupt by the mid-1970s. To save that industry the Barre government found no other option than nationalization. In contrast, the public sector continued to invest during this very difficult period. One success was Elf-Aquitaine, formed in 1976 by the merger of two smaller state companies, with activities in petrol, oil and petrochemicals. By 1983 Elf had become a major international player and one of France's largest and most profitable companies. A similar public-sector success was the DGT, then part of the state administration (it became France Télécom in 1990). In 1973, business complained bitterly about the backwardness of the French telephone system, but a decade of investment brought a huge transformation, plus public procurement contracts which greatly encouraged domestic electronics firms. Another public investment success was the railways with the replacement of rolling stock and the building of the high-speed line (TGV) from Paris to Lyon.

Hence, one Socialist argument for nationalizations in 1982 was that the public, rather than the private, sector was leading investment. This was a self-fulfilling prophecy: the more the Socialists looked likely to win power and carry out their programme, the less incentive private-sector firms had to invest. In 1982, the nationalization programme included Rhône-Poulenc, Pechiney, Thomson, CGE, Saint Gobain, Matra, Dassault and Bull, and Paribas, Suez, Rothschild, CIC and Worms amongst the banks, giving France one of the largest public sectors in Europe.

This period was marked by increases in budget deficits, public debt, and the fiscal burden. Whereas between 1965 and 1975 the fiscal burden, as a percentage of GDP, only increased from 35 to 37 per cent, in the next eight years it rose to 44 per cent in 1983. Most of the additional payments took the form of social security contributions.

1984 to 1997: Liberalization and Persistent Unemployment

Although Mitterrand was the first president to serve two successive seven-year mandates, the last two years of each presidency (1986–88 and 1993–95) were periods of 'cohabitation' when Centre–Right majorities in parliament supported the governments of Chirac and Balladur respectively. In 1995 Chirac was elected to the presidency, but in 1997 an early dissolution of parliament led to a third period of cohabitation, with a Left majority and Jospin as Prime Minister. In spite of these changes of government, there has been surprising continuity of many economic policies. Inflation has been cut and stabilized at very low levels. Efforts to stimulate economic growth continued, with some success between 1988 and 1991, but the hoped-for return to high growth did not occur. Despite constant attempts to create jobs, unemployment remained high, albeit with slight reductions between 1988 and 1991.

The crisis decision by Mitterrand in March 1983 to devalue the franc within the EMS marked the start of commitment to the 'strong franc' doctrine, implying tight control on money supply growth, public borrowing and public expenditure to fight inflation and maintain the Deutschmark value of the franc. Since 1986, 'competitive deflation' has replaced the 'competitive devaluations' of earlier decades. In 1994, the Bank of France was given a statute of autonomy, in preparation for the Euro. Although in 1997 France was not yet meeting the convergence criteria of the Maastricht Treaty, policies to reduce public borrowing and increase revenue were tough, although Jospin increased the job-creation programme.

Equally dramatic was the change in industrial and competition policies which followed the Delors 'rigour plan' of 1983–84 and the Single European Act in 1986. If the Socialists never renounced counter-cyclical public investment and continued to fund the steel industry and Renault, their 'managerial' approach became increasingly pronounced, especially when Fabius became prime minister in 1984. With few possibilities of increasing taxation or borrowing to finance investments, public sector managers were forced to 'restructure', which implied increasing productivity and shedding non-essential labour. Initially redundancy payments increased public spending, and restructuring was widely criticized by trade unionists and Communists.

By applying private-management principles to the public sector, the Socialists were tacitly accepting market economics. Furthermore, they increasingly turned to financial markets for investment in the public sector, sold off minor subsidiaries of public-sector firms and issued non-voting quasi-shares in nationalized firms. The Centre–Right government of 1986, however, enacted a massive privatization programme, including not only Socialist acquisitions of 1982 but also banks and insurance companies nationalized in 1945. After initial successes, this privatization programme slowed down after the stock-market slump of 1987 and the Socialists, back in government in 1988, interrupted it. In 1993, however, the Balladur government resumed the programme and both Chirac since 1995, and Jospin since 1997, have continued privatizations.

The Single European Act caused little controversy in France as it was supported by the Centre–Right and the Socialists. Nonetheless, its implications, by abolishing non-tariff barriers, in the Internal Market Programme, were dramatic. On the one hand, by explicitly accepting majority voting, political leaders abandoned de Gaulle's 'national-interest veto'. On the other hand, the abolition of non-tariff barriers involved destroying many tools of *dirigisme*. A first change came even before the Act was operational: in December 1986, the Chirac government abolished price controls. Measures which followed included the removal of remaining exchange controls, notably on capital movement, and the opening of banking and insurance to foreign competition.

Equally important were the rules against state subsidies and soft loans for national industries: henceforth, government subsidies were allowed only in exceptional circumstances, within limits fixed by the European Commission. In the cases of Renault and Air France, this led to protracted public haggling between successive governments and the Commission; in the first case, Renault was obliged to repay most of a subsidy, and in the second, the government had to reduce its aid to the airline. Similar conflicts arose out of the transfer of responsibility for controlling anti-competitive behaviour including mergers and acquisitions to the Commission. In the long run, the public procurement Directives may reduce French government use of public contracts to support domestic firms, although in 1997 over 90 per cent of all government purchases were made from French firms.

Since the Internal Market Programme, the mutual recognition of diplomas and qualifications prevents French employers from discrimination against those with other European qualifications. The French government has also opened recruitment to all public-sector and civil-service posts, except those directly concerned with 'sovereignty functions'. The immediate effect has been limited, but the effectiveness of public employment as a policy tool has been reduced.

If the defence industry remains outside the scope of the Treaties, the shortage of public resources in the late 1980s and the reduced security threat after the ending of the Cold War has meant that the pressures to reduce costs and improve productivity felt in other industries have also been imposed here.

Even agriculture has been subject to pressures for cost-cutting. The escalating cost of CAP led to cost-reduction packages in 1984 and 1988. As their impact on costs was less than anticipated and as international partners in the Uruguay Round refused any agreement which did not massively reduce farming subsidies, a further package of reforms was introduced by commissioner MacSharry in 1992 and extended in the World Trade Organization (WTO) agreement. Although French farmers warned that reducing subsidies and putting arable land into set-aside would ruin thousands and damage exports, neither the Socialists nor the Centre–Right was willing to risk the WTO deal, although some dramatic posturing was made to placate the farmers.

Since the 1980s, the economy has become increasingly Europeanized. Most international trade by French firms takes place with other EU countries. Many French companies are involved in production and distribution in other member states. Some French firms have formed European groups so that French corporate identities are being lost. At the same time, however, the ability of governments to control economic activity in France has been greatly reduced as increasingly policies are made jointly in Brussels and implemented under the supervision of the Commission.

As early attempts to reduce unemployment proved fruitless, attention has increasingly focused on labour-market policies including reductions of the working week, part-time employment, more flexible contracts of employment and lower employers' costs. Although some politicians argue that high exchange rates prevent growth rates high enough to reduce unemployment, many are concerned with rigidities of the labour market and costs of employment. However, all attempts to reduce workers' rights in employment contracts have met fierce resistance from trade unions. In late 1995, measures to improve efficiency in the social security system and to reduce worker privileges in the massively indebted SNCF provoked a wave of strikes and won widespread public sympathy. Although most citizens wanted more growth and full employment, many remained unwilling to accept any sacrifices to achieve those goals.

Explaining the Changes

Many writers admit the importance of state intervention but do not argue that *dirigisme* explains everything or that public policies have been coherent between sectors and over time. Fourastié and Carre, Dubois and Malinvaud draw attention to the many and varied forms of state interventionism and point out that many public policies are highly specific to sectors, circumstances and periods. Carre, Dubois and Malinvaud, for example, stress the importance of campaigns to increase productivity in the 1950s and note that two-thirds of economic growth up to 1972 can be directly attributed to productivity gains.

Two problems of theories which emphasize state interventionism, however, are that they are not comparative and neglect micro-economic behaviour. If the French growth rates were high, they were often exceeded by those of West Germany and Italy, neither of which had state interventionism on the French scale. Much French growth resulted from independent decisions of private-sector firms, and when public financing was involved, state agencies were largely responsive to private initiatives. Equally, the dynamism of many small and medium-sized enterprises is underrated.

Kindleberger, and Cohen and Bauer, stress the importance of social factors in explaining economic developments.[2] For Kindleberger, the renewal of élites at the Liberation played a key role in changing economic behaviour. Cohen and Bauer, in contrast, argue that post-1970 stagnation of top business élites partly explains the poor adaptation to the increasingly difficult competitive conditions.

Adams analyses the internationalism of the economy as a crucial factor in its development. If internationalization was a goal of the immediate post-war years, its achievement had policy implications of profound significance. France got richer by trading more abroad in both goods and services, and by encouraging tourism. To encourage trade and facilitate exchanges, French governments participated fully in the GATT rounds and the process of creating the EU Internal Market. The consequences were that the many methods of state interventionism had to be abandoned. However, policies which created opportunities for French companies abroad also opened the domestic markets to foreign competition.

Hall's 'new institutional' approach (1986) emphasizes the institutionalization of patterns of expectations and behaviour, and the costs and benefits of different types of institutional behaviour in different economic contexts. The advantage of this approach is that it does not take technocratic or *dirigiste* explanations at face value; rather it underlines the importance of decisions by non-state actors taken on reliable assumptions about public policies. The importance of formal rules is also underlined: even in the early years of the European Community, French governments retained enormous regulatory power and encouraged firms to use the courts to challenge decisions they thought unfair. Hall also shows that whatever the formal powers of French governments, their scope for policy changes became increasingly constrained as existing policies became institutionalized. The perennial problems of changing the basic features of a generous social security system, designed for a youthful population and full employment, typify this difficulty. Another case is that of employment protection. Most labour-market economists agree that employers are reluctant to create new jobs because both the rules and culture of employment are retained from a period of shortages, when employers offered 'jobs for life' to retain the services of workers. This rule-and-culture linkage has considerable explanatory value for economic developments since 1945.

Bibliographical Note

There is now a large body of works on French economic development since the Second World War. An important text, covering also the first half of the twentieth century, is J.-J. Carre, P. Dubois and E. Malinvaud, *French Economic Growth* (London, 1976). Useful survey articles are C. Sautter, 'France', in A. Boltho (ed.), *The European Economy – Growth and Crisis* (Oxford, 1988), and F. Lynch, 'France', in A. Graham and A. Seldon (eds), *Government and Economies in the Post War World* (London, 1991). G. Saint-Paul, 'Economic reconstruction in France: 1945–1958', in R. Dornbusch, W. Nölling and R. Layard (eds), *Post War Reconstruction and Lessons for the East Today* (Cambridge, MA/London, 1993) focuses on the process of post-war reconstruction. A detailed analysis of French economic development and policy in its international context is F. Lynch, *France and the International Economy: From Vichy to the Treaty of Rome* (London, 1997). Jean Fourastié, *Les Trentes Glorieuses ou la révolution indivisible de 1946 à 1975* (Paris, 1979) examines not only the nature and sources of the boom but also the social and political impact of economic growth. W.J. Adams, *Restructuring the French Economy* (Washington, 1989) is concise and covers much of the post-boom period. H. Machin and V. Wright, *Economic Policy and Policy-Making under the Mitterrand Presidency* (London, 1985) is also useful on more recent policies and results. H. Dumez and A. Jeunemaitre, *Diriger l'économie: l'Etat et les prix en France, 1936–1986* (Paris, 1989) covers the attempts at price control. On economic planning, there are many books in French (often by planners and generous in their praise for planning) but the most impressive analysis is by S. Estrin and P. Holmes, *French Planning in Theory and Practice* (London, 1983). Peter Hall, *Governing the Economy* (London, 1986) makes a useful comparison with the UK whilst strongly arguing the case of 'new institutionalism'. R. Kuisel, *Capitalism and the State in Modern France* (New York, 1981) covers the main ideological debates about the economy. On the Europeanization of the economy, see A. Guyomarch, H. Machin and E. Ritchie, *France in the EU, Politics and Policy* (Basingstoke, 1998).

Notes

1. See G. Saint-Paul, 'Economic reconstruction in France: 1945–1958', in R. Dornbusch, W. Nölling and R. Layard (eds), *Post War Reconstruction and Lessons for the East Today* (Cambridge, MA/London, 1993).

2. C. Kindleberger, 'The postwar resurgence of the French economy', in *In Search of France* (Cambridge, MA, 1963); E. Cohen and M. Bauer, *Les Grandes Manoeuvres Industrielles* (Paris, 1985).

18 Germany

Christoph Buchheim

Introduction: Post-War Economic Growth in Long-Run Perspective

The economic growth of West Germany between 1945 and the early 1970s was outstanding. It was the period of the so-called economic miracle, because the public, after a rather gloomy outlook in the second half of the forties, was much surprised by the quick rise in welfare and living standards. The index of real weekly wages in industry (1962 = 100), for example, rose from 40 to 54 between 1925 and 1939, an increase of 2.2 per cent per annum. From 1950 onwards, however, real wages grew by more than 5 per cent on annual average from an index level of 53 to 145 in 1970.[1]

The period before the First World War showed a steady trend of growth with an average annual rate of 1.5 per cent, and, at least from the 1890s on, a normal pattern of the trade cycle, i.e. a pattern in which output fluctuated moderately around its long-term trend. In contrast, the inter-war years were characterized by a heavily fluctuating growth trend with an irregular deep downswing in the Great Depression of the early thirties, after real product per head had only just re-covered to its pre-war level, and a rather artificial boom in the Nazi period fuelled by state demand with hardly any rise in the living standards of the population. The time after the Second World War, on the other hand, saw a very steep, albeit flattening trend of growth. Its average annual rate between 1948 and 1973 was about 6.5 per cent. There was a long period with not a single year of negative growth, implying that the normal trade cycle had disappeared. However, after 1973 the situation became again comparable to the decades before 1914. The trend of growth was more or less linear, the average rate until 1995 was 1.6 per cent and thus much lower than in the preceding period, and the normal trade cycle recurred, including years of recession. Thus, Figure 18.1 suggests an inter-pretation that distinguishes four periods of growth in Germany during the last one and a half centuries: two of a normal growth pattern, namely the time before 1914 and after 1973, and two of an exceptional pattern, i.e. the inter-war years and the period after the Second World War until about 1973.

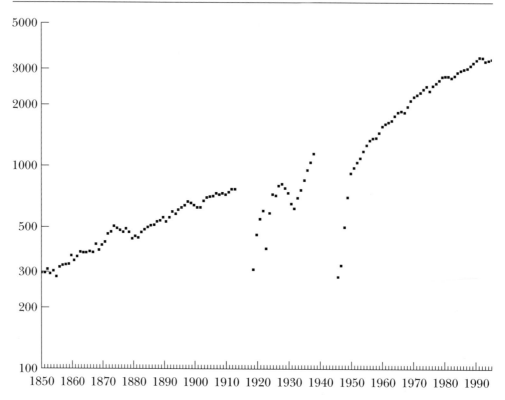

Figure 18.1. Long-run growth of real GNP per head in (West) Germany, 1850–1995 (1913 prices, Mark). *Sources:* W.G. Hoffmann, *Das Wachstum der deutschen Wirtschaft seit der Mitte des 19. Jahrhunderts* (Berlin, 1965), pp. 172–4, 827–8 (Germany 1850–1913, 1925–38; FRG 1950–59); *Statistisches Jahrbuch für die Bundesrepublik Deutschland,* various issues (FRG from 1960 onwards; estimates drawing on GNP growth rates); D. Petzina, W. Abelshauser and A. Faust, *Sozialgeschichtliches Arbeitsbuch III. Materialien zur Statistik des Deutschen Reiches 1914–1945* (Munich, 1978), p. 61 (GNP 1919–24 estimated with industrial production as a proxy); A. Ritschl, 'Die Währungsreform von 1948 und der Wiederaufstieg der westdeutschen Industrie', *Vierteljahrshefte für Zeitgeschichte,* 33 (1985), p. 164 (GNP of West Germany 1946–49 estimated with industrial production as a proxy).

With regard to growth in post-war West Germany it is therefore not so much its lower rate since the beginning of the 1970s which has to be explained, but its exceptional height in the time before. Two plausible concepts might be used to account for the super-growth. One is the reconstruction hypothesis, the other productivity gap growth.[2] The former says that in periods of deep economic crises, as for example wars, per capita levels of production and physical capital decline severely, whereas human capital continues to grow at least at its normal rate. The developmental discrepancy leads to a surplus of human capital in the post-crisis period relative to production and thus to a potential for extra-growth.

The reasoning presupposes that growth is ultimately limited by the speed of human capital accumulation. But when there is a surplus of human capital, the limiting factor for growth becomes physical capital which, contrary to human capital, can be accumulated rather quickly. Thus, higher growth will be realized until the human capital surplus has disappeared.

In fact, this scenario seems quite plausible in the case of West Germany. The qualification of the workforce was good enough for far higher production levels than those achieved in the second half of the forties, as is shown by the war-time production maximum. In addition, demobilization released many qualified workers, and a lot of skilled persons immigrated from the former Eastern provinces of the German Reich. Through the whole decade of the fifties there was an influx of thousands of qualified people from the GDR. At first many of the expellees and refugees settled in rural areas where they could be fed and housed more easily, but where there were hardly any opportunities to employ them according to their skills. Only the building boom of the fifties eventually enabled them to move to the cities where they could find adequate work. This example illustrates how rapid accumulation of physical capital made possible the use of a surplus of human capital. The formation of physical capital was indeed higher in the fifties and sixties than afterwards. In addition, even capital productivity increased in the beginning, because comparably small (repair) investments permitted the reutilization of a large stock of already existing physical plant.

Productivity gap growth, on the other hand, occurs if more productive technologies existing in other parts of the world can be imitated and if the social capability for the effective use of these technologies is given. In fact, already in the inter-war years there was a technological gap between the United States and Germany as well as other European countries, which had widened markedly by the end of the Second World War. After the war, however, it began to narrow, indicating that productivity gap growth really took place.[3] In a sense, the deeper causes for this type of growth are similar to those of reconstruction growth. One has to ask why the productivity gap developed in the first place. As in the reconstruction hypothesis, the occurrence of a productivity gap can be explained by the fact that the physical capital stock of a country does not reflect the more advanced state of the level of human capital, which should be more or less the same among industrialized nations. This discrepancy could be the result of either too low investment or isolation from the world market. The consequence of both is that the technology incorporated in the mass of capital goods is not up to date. In Germany both reasons certainly played a role, as investment in the inter-war years was rather low and autarkic policies led to partial isolation from the world market in the Nazi period.

To sum up so far, one can say that in post-war Germany there was a shortage of appropriate physical capital relative to the prevailing level of human capital. A potential for accelerated growth therefore existed. Since one of the conditions of its realization was high investment, one needs to examine the incentive climate for investment. In this context the currency and economic reform played a crucial role.

Figure 18.2. West German monthly industrial production, 1946–49 (1936 = 100).
Sources: W. Abelshauser, *Wirtschaft in Westdeutschland 1945–1948* (Stuttgart, 1975);
A. Ritschl, 'Die Währungsreform von 1948 und der Wiederaufstieg der westdeutschen
Industrie', *Vierteljahrshefte für Zeitgeschichte*, 33 (1985), p. 164.

The Establishment of a Market Economy

Before the currency reform of June 1948 there was a huge monetary overhang in
West Germany. This had been the result of inflationary war financing and the
official price stop instituted in 1936 and kept in force by the Allied occupation
authorities after the war. Sales of goods in return for money at official prices were
heavily discriminated against, because in view of repressed inflation they represented huge losses of substance. Black markets developed where goods were
exchanged at a multiple of official prices, and a large portion of transactions
among firms was realized through barter trade. The ratios at which goods were
exchanged in compensation trade showed that official prices were not only much
too low, but also that the structure of official prices was completely distorted.
Thus, even after inflating official prices by a common factor they could not be
used for ascertaining true costs and profits. This meant that normal calculation
was impractical altogether, because there was no alternative medium of exchange
ready at hand – the possession of foreign currencies being forbidden at the time
– and because it was impossible to know all relevant ratios in barter trade. With
no possibility of calculating profits, private entrepreneurs had little incentive to
invest and even to produce for markets. This then was the most fundamental

Plate 18.1. German citizens receiving their initial allowance of 40 D-Marks on 20 June 1948. Overnight, the previously empty shop windows filled with goods again, as the incentives to hoard and engage in barter were removed. In the eyes of many contemporaries, the currency reform of 1948 marked the start of the postwar German *Wirtschaftswunder.*

reason for the low industrial production in West Germany, which still amounted to less than half the pre-war level in mid-1948, when most other European countries had almost reached or even surpassed that level.

In addition, transaction costs in Germany were high because of barter trade and productivity of workers was insufficient, since low real wages provided no incentive to perform. In this situation entrepreneurs were guided not by the profit motive but by the desire for survival, and they tried to prepare their firms in the best way possible for the time after the expected currency reform. The production which was undertaken largely served that purpose, i.e. to provide products for barter with which to obtain goods for the repair of plant or for payment in kind to the core workforce, for getting hold of inputs, and qualifying for official allocations of raw materials.

In focus: The Currency Reform

Inter-allied negotiations on a currency reform for the whole of Potsdam Germany started in earnest in 1946 on the basis of the American Colm–Dodge–Goldsmith Plan. At first there was good progress towards this aim, but then the talks foundered upon the insistence of the Soviets to print the new banknotes in their zone as well. The Americans would not agree to that. As time went on, the political atmosphere between the Allies changed, too. The USA designed the Marshall Plan, and the creation of a West German state was contemplated. In the spring of 1948 the Americans finally abandoned the idea of a currency reform for the four zones of Germany. At about the same time preparations for a West German currency reform were intensified. The Bank deutscher Länder was created with the functions of a central bank, a unified conversion rate of the Mark was fixed at 0.30 US dollars, and the essentials of the planned reform were presented to German experts.

The currency reform itself consisted of four basic acts. The first two came into force on Sunday, 20 June 1948. One was the Issue Law which governed the issue of banknotes by the Bank deutscher Länder. The other was the Currency Law which introduced the Deutschmark or D-Mark as the West German currency. It was decreed that for current payments, such as wages, taxes or rents, one Reichsmark should be equivalent to one D-Mark. On the same day a per capita allowance of 40 Reichsmarks was exchanged against 40 D-Marks, later to be increased by another 20 D-Marks. One week later the Conversion Law regulated in detail the treatment of Reichsmark balances and debts. Principally, these were converted into D-Marks at a ratio of 10:1. However, half of the resulting D-Mark balances were put into blocked accounts. State debt held by financial institutions was altogether cancelled. Instead, new public debt instruments, the so-called *Ausgleichsforderungen*, were individually allocated to them in such a way as to cover the gap between assets and liabilities resulting from the conversion. Finally, in October 1948

The Currency Reform (continued)

the Blocked Accounts Law was issued annulling seven-tenths of the amounts in blocked accounts. Thus, larger Reichsmark balances were in fact converted into D-Marks not at a ratio of 10:1, but only at 100:6.5.

Whereas the currency reform took place under the responsibility of the Allies, the economic reform, which was undertaken at the same time, was mainly the work of Ludwig Erhard, then Director of the Bizonal Economic Administration, which jointly governed the economic affairs of the American and the British occupied zones. Its core was the Law on Principles for Rationing and Price Policy after the Currency Reform which promoted the abolishment of rationing and price controls. Thus, it reflected the view of Erhard and most of his advisors that the new currency had to be complemented by liberalized markets, in order to provide the greatest possible stimulus to production. As early as the beginning of July 1948, some food and most manufactured products had been freed from controls.

The consequences of the currency and economic reform were astonishing. Almost overnight markets were re-established, barter trade disappeared and the profit motive was restored. Whereas an index of industrial production (1936 = 100) stood at 54 in June 1948, it reached 80 at the end of 1948 and 100 one year later (Figure 18.2). Labour productivity increased by a good 30 per cent in the Bizone between June 1948 and March 1949. In the second half of 1948 industrial gross fixed investment grew to more than double the amount of the first half.[1] Although rising consumer prices initially triggered considerable public unrest, including a general strike, people soon considered the currency reform as the beginning of the so-called economic miracle. Thus, 20 June 1948 became more important in historical memory than 23 May 1949, the day when the Federal Republic's Basic Law was issued.

1. R. Krengel, 'Die langfristige Entwicklung der Brutto- Anlage-Investitionen der westdeutschen Industrie von 1924 bis 1955/56', *Vierteljahrshefte zur Wirtschaftsforschung* (1957), pp. 170–1.

The currency and economic reform restored strong incentives for investment, especially as consumption and exports were rising quickly. Therefore, it seems appropriate to describe the reform as the catalyst which made possible the actual use of the existing human capital surplus for the achievement of super-growth. In addition, the state encouraged private capital formation through tax concessions. In this respect special depreciation allowances were very important. Moreover, the legal possibility of higher valuation of existing plant was widely used, thus creating a huge potential for future depreciation. It is, therefore, not astonishing that most industrial investment was done by self-financing. In fact, until 1955, self-financing was almost the only way of financing private long-term investment, as the capital market was ineffective because strict regulation kept interest rates below their market level. As a result capital for general purposes was in short supply on the market. The reason for this outcome was that, according to the government, house-building should be favoured. Consequently, the state channelled cheap public funds through the capital market exclusively into house-building, where rationing and rent control offered little incentive to unsubsidized private investment.

Besides the capital market and housing, there were still other sectors where price controls were not abolished with the currency and economic reform. Above all, the basic industries – coal, steel and electricity – have to be mentioned in this context. With prices kept too low they were not able to make profits or even earn their depreciations, so they were not favoured by the tax concessions and could not rely on self-financing for necessary investments. To avoid major bottlenecks in the availability of their products, which were important inputs to the whole of the economy, public funds had to be given for this purpose. At first, a large part of counterpart funds was used for capital formation in these industries.[4] When these funds dried up after the end of the Marshall Plan, the Investment Aid Law was enacted in 1952 demanding a forced loan of one billion D-Mark from the rest of industry to these branches. However, this alone would have been insufficient a device. Therefore two more clauses were written into the law, one permitting extraordinary depreciation in basic industries which at this time was no longer allowed in other sectors, the other practically liberalizing prices in the coal, steel and electricity branches. Thus, the mechanism of a free market was finally established here, too, and as a result investment rose and the danger of bottlenecks disappeared. This suggests a general conclusion: if free markets are established in a large part of an economy, pressures develop in the still controlled sectors (for instance in the form of bottlenecks), which lead again either to greater interventionism (e.g. far-reaching investment control) or to the extension of liberalization to these sectors.[5]

From the beginning, West German industrial policy put great stress on safeguarding competition. Ludwig Erhard was convinced that competition was the most powerful instrument with which to secure high productivity, high levels of output and a high living standard for the population. Such an approach, however, ran completely against tradition in German industry which since imperial times had been characterized by a very high degree of cartelization. The Allies instituted a ban on cartels because they viewed this aspect of German economic life as one of the reasons for the country's aggressiveness. Fortunately, this ban was not lifted afterwards. Instead Erhard succeeded, against great resistance of industry, in issuing the Law Against Restrictions of Competition in 1957 which maintained the ban on cartels, albeit with exceptions. This law has repeatedly been strengthened since then, including the establishment of a control of concentration. The German state therefore felt responsible for the preservation of liberal markets and competition. This is an important aspect of the Social Market Economy: the state is not permitted to show a *laissez-faire* attitude towards business, because, as experience has shown, that leads to private restrictions of competition.

Integration into the World Market

The liberalization of imports was, in Erhard's view, at least as effective in preserving competition as control of cartelization and concentration. In that he totally agreed with American demands on Europe. West Germany mostly supported the endeavours by the USA to further liberal and multilateral trade as well as convertibility of currencies by using Marshall Plan money and the mechanism of the Organisation of European Economic Cooperation (OEEC) as a means to secure compliance of West European countries. An initial step in this direction was undertaken in 1949 when West Germany, still under the authority of the Allied Joint Export Import Agency (JEIA), concluded trade agreements with neighbouring countries, thus freeing many imports from quantitative restrictions. In the same year, the Federal Republic participated in the first round of OEEC-wide trade liberalization, as it did in the further steps during the following years. As a member of the European Payments Union (EPU) it also took part in the process of making currencies internationally transferable. However, the Korean crisis proved to be a major setback for the country. Rapidly rising domestic consumption and rising prices for raw material imports led to growing trade deficits. After repeatedly running into deficits with the EPU not covered by its quota, West Germany had to suspend liberalization measures completely in the spring of 1951. In that situation the solidarity of the other EPU members proved very valuable. By not withdrawing their liberalization measures towards German exports they enabled a quick recovery of the balance of payments of West Germany and the reliberalization of its import regime in 1952. From then on the Federal Republic became the country with by far the biggest surplus in the EPU, which greatly facilitated all further moves towards liberalization, including several unilateral reductions of customs duties. In 1958 the D-Mark, together with many other European currencies, became fully convertible, also against the dollar. By that time, the international exchange of services and capital transactions had largely been liberalized, too.

In cartel as well as trade policy Germany started afresh after the Second World War. At the same time, outside Germany, a similar policy shift was taking place. Whereas the inter-war period was characterized by high and mounting protectionism worldwide, after the war the opposite tendency prevailed, not least because the United States changed from Saulus to Paulus in this respect. In fact, the establishment of a new, rather liberal international economic system can be regarded as the greatest progress in economic respects over the inter-war years and the main reason for the achievement of far higher growth in almost all developed countries. This observation certainly holds for West Germany. Between 1960 and 1990 the volume of exports increased with an average rate of 6.8 per cent per annum, whereas real GDP rose with a rate of 3.1 per cent. Thus, exports became more and more important as a part of overall demand. Moreover they were decisive for the investment goods industry, in which the Federal Republic achieved a leading position worldwide. In 1990, this sector sold 40 per cent of its output abroad.

Plate 18.2. 'Aren't you ashamed of yourselves? – Naah!' Depicting Chancellor Adenauer and Economics Minister Erhard as the old couple, this 1961 cartoon by Horst Haitzinger comments on the rapid rise in material welfare and its consequences. By the early 1960s, prosperity and growth were increasingly taken for granted.

In the 1950s and 1960s and again in the 1980s upswings of the trade cycle were frequently initiated by an increase of orders from abroad. These improved profit expectations and the inclination to invest. High average levels of investment led to a quick realization of incorporated technical progress. Growing demand for investment goods at home and abroad stimulated investment and innovation in this sector, too, raising the rate of technical progress and further improving possibilities to export for German industry. Exports and investment were thus interdependent. Together they represented a complex which was largely responsible for the actual growth dynamics of the Federal Republic, given the respective human capital situation.

Table 18.1. Foreign trade of the Federal Republic of Germany (billion DM)

	1950	1960	1970	1980	1990
(a) Exports (fob)					
Sum	8.3	47.9	125.3	350.3	642.8
Manufactures	6.1	42.5	112.2	303.2	584.1
of which:					
Chemicals	0.9	5.3	15.0	44.1	81.7
Metals	1.2	6.2	11.9	29.8	36.3
Machines/vehicles	2.0	20.8	58.2	155.3	317.2
(b) Imports (cif)					
Sum	11.4	42.7	109.6	341.4	550.6
Foodstaffs	5.0	10.4	19.0	38.1	53.3
Raw materials/energy	4.1	12.8	23.4	102.7	75.0
Manufactures	2.2	18.7	63.7	188.3	409.2
of which:					
Machines/vehicles	0.4	4.0	20.7	63.7	178.1

Sources: OEEC, *Statistical Bulletins, Foreign Trade, IV. Series, Germany 1952* (Paris, 1953); *Statistisches Jahrbuch für die Bundesrepublik Deutschland,* various issues.

Macroeconomic Policy

Through demand for its exports West Germany profited from Keynesian full employment policies in other countries. The Federal Republic itself largely refrained from such policies in the 1950s, although at the beginning of the decade the unemployment rate was still about 10 per cent. However, this was structural unemployment. Consequently it disappeared step by step throughout the 1950s when expellees and refugees were integrated into the production process. From about 1960 on there was full, even over-employment with an unemployment rate of less than 1 per cent. Labour shortages encouraged the immigration of so-called guest workers from foreign countries, whose number counted more than two million in 1972.

In the 1960s Keynesian policies were slowly adopted in the Federal Republic. The first step in that direction was the appointment of a Council of Economic Experts in 1963. One of the aims of the new council was to address the causes of 'imbalances between overall demand and overall supply', thus alluding to a typical Keynesian concept. In 1967, when Karl Schiller was Minister of Economics, the Law for the Promotion of Economic Stability and Growth was passed. Federal and Länder governments were now called upon to take account of the need for an overall economic equilibrium in their economic and fiscal measures. These measures were to be chosen in such a way 'that in the framework of the market economy they simultaneously contribute to stability of the price level, to high employment and to balance-of-payments equilibrium with continuous and sufficient economic growth'. The instruments foreseen to achieve this so-called magic quadrangle of aims were of a fiscal nature, i.e. flexibility of government expenditures, short-term increases of tax rates, and credit restrictions.

It is rather ironical that West Germany changed over to full-fledged Keynesianism near the end of the international post-war boom period, which some observers mistakenly attribute to the successful implementation of such policies in many countries. Initially, however, the Stability Law appeared to be doing very well. By coincidence 1967 was the first year since 1950 with slightly negative growth and an increase in unemployment. Consequently, under Karl Schiller two expansionary fiscal programmes were adopted in that year. The recession was quickly overcome, and in 1968 the economy was in a vigorous upswing again. The general public credited demand management for the recovery. In reality, however, rapidly rising exports played a greater role in the upswing, as was generally the case in these years.

The next recession occurred in 1974/75 after a big wage push and concurrent inflation, the breakdown of the fixed exchange rate system and the oil price shock. The unemployment rate rose to a startling 4.7 per cent. The government again resorted to expansionary fiscal measures. However, this time the upswing was short-lived, and unemployment persisted, while inflation remained relatively high (see Figure 18.3). Fiscal stimuli towards the end of the seventies had the same unsatisfying results. In the meantime a large budget deficit had become structural, which itself proved to be more and more a menace to growth. Gradually, disillusion about Keynesian demand management developed and the eighties saw, after a change of government from one dominated by Social Democrats to one led by the Christian Democrats in 1982, a shift to supply-side policies. Their implementation, though, proved much less radical than in the United Kingdom under Margaret Thatcher or in the United States under Ronald Reagan.

Price stability has been a constant policy priority in West Germany. Its pursuit, however, has not been left to the government's discretion. Rather, price stability became the *raison d'être* of the Bundesbank. The German central bank was set up as a powerful institution independent from the government and charged with 'safeguarding the currency'. Its instruments are the fixing of the discount rate and of minimal reserve requirements for banks as well as the regulation of the stock of central bank money by purchases and sales of bonds. Already at the end of the forties and in the fifties the German central bank repeatedly applied restrictive measures in order to put a brake on price level increases, as, for example, in the autumn of 1948 and during the Korean crisis 1950/51. In the course of the fifties, however, the dilemma of stability-oriented monetary policy under fixed exchange rates became apparent: tight monetary policy could be undermined by inflows of foreign capital, which had to be exchanged at given rates. Foreign capital inflow increased the money supply and put downward pressure on interest rates, thus offsetting the central bank's attempts to restrict the money supply. Under these conditions, increases in the level of domestic

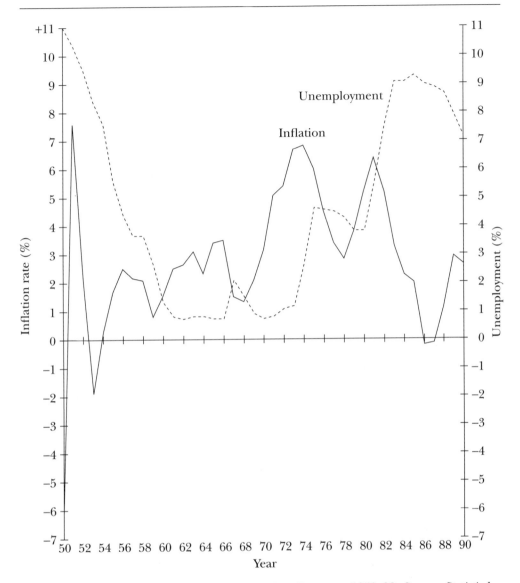

Figure 18.3. Inflation and unemployment in West Germany, 1950–90. *Sources: Statistisches Jahrbuch für das vereinte Deutschland 1991*, pp. 130, 608; Deutsche Bundesbank (ed.), *40 Jahre Deutsche Mark: Monetäre Statistiken 1948–1987* (Frankfurt/M., 1988), p. 4.

interest proved to be counterproductive. Thus, after October 1960, the Bundesbank changed its monetary stance by lowering the discount rate and the minimum reserve requirements, although a boom had developed. This was done under the pressure of speculative foreign capital inflows, and it was the admission of the Bundesbank that it was unable to fight inflationary tendencies. Only the first post-war revaluation of the D-Mark by 5 per cent in March 1961 relieved the situation.

In the boom of 1965 the case was different, as price increases coincided with a balance of payments deficit. Now restrictive monetary policy measures proved to be successful and largely contributed to the recession of 1966/67. But already in 1968 the old dilemma resurfaced. A second revaluation was undertaken after long discussions, federal elections and a change of government in the autumn of 1969. This time, there was only a respite from foreign exchange speculation. Huge amounts of speculative capital were imported into West Germany in the course of a sharpening dollar crisis. As a result, for the first time, the D-Mark was floated from May to December 1971. This phase ended with the so-called Smithsonian Realignment, which included another revaluation of the D-Mark. Afterwards new and even greater tensions quickly developed, until in March 1973 floating was finally adopted as the new dominant international exchange rate regime.

In the meantime inflation accelerated to a rate of about 7 per cent. Now the Bundesbank immediately applied sharp restrictive measures, which were largely responsible for the depression in 1975. Inflation, however, slowly diminished, and, in the middle of the 1980s it was nearly zero. From about 1975 onwards the Bundesbank also changed the philosophy of its monetary policy, announcing in advance yearly targets for the growth in central bank money. Experience therefore showed that price stability was an attainable goal under conditions of floating exchange rates. Monetary policy appears to have been effective in this respect, whereas fiscal policy did not achieve its goal of stabilizing the trade cycle.

Economic Problems of German Unification

The Federal Republic's currency union with the German Democratic Republic (1 July 1990) posed a major challenge for the Bundesbank. The technical substitution of the Mark of the GDR by the D-Mark, however, was organized perfectly. For current payments the conversion rate was 1:1 as was the case in the currency reform of 1948, although the Bundesbank itself had favoured a rate of 2:1. Balances and debts were mainly converted at 2:1. As in 1948 with the currency union went an economic reform in East Germany. The socialist economic system was liquidated and the market economy of the Federal Republic was introduced, including a liberal capital market and foreign trade regime. Thus the reform of 1990 was even more radical than the one of 1948, raising expectations that as in 1948 a quick and vigorous upswing of economic activity in East Germany would result.

However, this was not the case. Unemployment soared, while occupation in East Germany shrank from 9.6 million in 1989 to 6.6 million in 1992. Industrial production plummeted from 200 billion marks in 1989 to a low of 70 billion in 1991. About a third of this decline was accounted for by prices reflecting the rather bad quality of products.[6] Overall, three main reasons appear to be responsible for this very deep crisis in East Germany after its reunification with the West:

(1) Whereas in West Germany in 1948 there existed mainly private firms that had been very well prepared for the market economy, East Germany had a

socialist economic system with huge enterprises in the property of the state. To privatize and divide them into smaller units proved to be a complicated and lengthy task. Until it had been accomplished the old management had little incentive to restructure the firms according to the demands of the market. In addition, the East German economy was lacking a broad stratum of dynamic medium-sized enterprises.

(2) In contrast to the West where full convertibility of the D-Mark was achieved only after a longer transitional period, the East German economy suddenly had to face the full competition of the world market from day one. Making the situation worse, however, the conversion rate of 1:1 in fact meant an enormous revaluation. With productivity in manufacturing of about a third of the level in West Germany, which was the clear result of a very inefficient and undynamic economic system in the East, East German products were heavily overpriced after the currency union.[7]

(3) East Germans expected a quick rise in their living standard from reunification, and West German politicians supported them in this expectation. Thus, neither trade unions nor employers showed much restraint when driving forward a process of fast wage increases towards the West German level. Therefore wages literally jumped up. Between 1989 and 1991 alone, hourly-based wage rates grew by about 100 per cent. Since then they have risen further, aggravating the cost situation of East German industry, because productivity is increasing at a much slower pace.

The consequence of the East German economic crisis was that reunification placed a big burden on West Germany. Monetary transfers of 150 billion D-Mark and more a year were necessary, mainly because, along with the currency union, the West German welfare system had to be established in the East. A new structural budget deficit has thus occurred. Nevertheless, in the medium run, prospects for growth look promising in the East, as there is again a large human capital surplus, which is probably the most valuable inheritance from the socialist system.

Debates and Interpretation

In 1975 Werner Abelshauser challenged the widely accepted opinion that the currency and economic reform together with the Marshall Plan had initiated the West German economic miracle.[8] Abelshauser argued that the conditions for reconstruction were long given in the form of a surplus of qualified labour and physical capital. Therefore, growth would have occurred anyway. To prove his case he recalculated the official statistics of industrial production on the basis of electricity consumption assuming constant productivity of electricity. He showed that industrial production before the currency reform had apparently been underestimated because of secret hoarding by firms. Vigorous growth had thus begun before the reform or the Marshall Plan were implemented. Therefore, they could not have initiated it.

Provoked by Abelshauser's book, a debate developed in the eighties about the role of the currency and economic reform. Albrecht Ritschl criticized Abelshauser's revision of the official output statistics on the grounds that the productivity of electricity was actually higher after the reform than before. Rainer Klump argued that Abelshauser had failed to take into account the incentives provided by a market economy. According to Christoph Buchheim, secret hoarding could hardly have been an important reason for the underestimation of industrial production, because what was hoarded were mainly inputs and semi-finished goods rather than finished manufactures.[9] All in all it seems fair to conclude, though, that the potential growth conditions of the West German economy after the war were indeed positive, which Abelshauser emphasized. However, that alone was not enough to really get the economy growing. Rather, the currency and economic reform was necessary as a catalyst.

Abelshauser belittled the direct effects of Marshall Aid. But he stressed the role of the European Recovery Programme in substituting American deliveries for West German reparations. The first of these points is seen somewhat differently by Knut Borchardt and Christoph Buchheim who demonstrated that Marshall Aid played a role in safeguarding the liberal economic order after mid-1948 by easing severe bottlenecks in key industrial branches. In addition, it seems that Abelshauser largely overestimated the impact of reparations by counting almost all exports as such. Both sides, however, seem to agree that the most important effect of the Marshall Plan was its indispensable contribution to liberalizing foreign trade and payments in western Europe.[10]

Regarding the interpretation of the history of overall growth in West Germany, there is a split between a group of neoliberal economists and more historically minded people. The former explain the high rates of growth in the fifties and sixties primarily as the consequence of a liberal economic system and the retardation of growth afterwards in the tradition of Mancur Olson as a sign of bureaucratization, ossification and increasing dominance of interest groups.[11] The latter, however, interpret, as we have done here, the period of the economic miracle as exceptional and the seventies and eighties as characterized by more normal growth, after the potential for super-growth had been depleted.[12] This seems more appropriate, not least because the boom period also knew quite a lot of interventionism and, in that sense, was not purely 'liberal'. So far nobody has really undertaken the task of comparing in detail the illiberal traits of both phases. It certainly is not obvious which one was more interventionist, even though one need not agree with Abelshauser's opinion that already in the early fifties a new corporatism began to develop in the Federal Republic.

Bibliographical Note

The following references are relevant to this chapter.

Werner Abelshauser, *Wirtschaftsgeschichte der Bundesrepublik Deutschland 1945–1980* (Frankfurt/M., 1983). Abelshauser provides a standard account of West German economic history.

Volker R. Berghahn, *The Americanisation of West German Industry 1945–1973* (Leamington Spa/New York 1986). Berghahn deals with American influences on entrepreneurs and industry as well as with industrial pressure groups.

Christoph Buchheim, 'The currency reform in West Germany in 1948', *German Yearbook on Business History 1989–92* (Munich, 1993), pp. 85–120.

The problem of West Germany's reintegration into the international economy is examined in Christoph Buchheim, *Die Wiedereingliederung Westdeutschlands in die Weltwirtschaft 1945–1958* (Munich, 1990).

Herbert Giersch, Karl-Heinz Paqué and Holger Schmieding, *The Fading Miracle: Four Decades of Market Economy in Germany* (Cambridge, 1992). Giersch, Paqué and Schmieding provide an economist's account of the economic development of West Germany.

Alan Kramer, *The West German Economy, 1945–1955* (New York/Oxford, 1991). Kramer's book belongs to the Abelshauser tradition.

Charles S. Maier and Günter Bischof (eds), *The Marshall Plan and Germany: West German Development within the Framework of the European Recovery Program* (New York/Oxford, 1991) is an important collection of essays, covering a broad range of questions.

Gerlinde Sinn and Hans-Werner Sinn, *Jumpstart: Economic Unification of Germany* (London, 1993). An early influential look by economists at the economic aspects of reunification and offering policy recommendations.

Notes

1. Statistisches Bundesamt, *Bevölkerung und Wirtschaft 1872–1972* (Stuttgart, 1972), pp. 250, 254.

2. R.H. Dumke, 'Reassessing the Wirtschaftswunder: reconstruction and postwar growth in West Germany in an international context', *Oxford Bulletin of Economics and Statistics*, 52 (1990), pp. 459–91.

3. S.N. Broadberry and N.F.R. Crafts, 'European productivity in the twentieth century: introduction', *Oxford Bulletin of Economics and Statistics*, 52 (1990), pp. 331–41.

4. One of the conditions of US financial aid was that German importers deposited in special accounts the DM equivalent of the value of imports financed under the European Recovery Programme (ERP), the so-called counterpart funds.

5. C. Buchheim, 'Attempts at controlling the capitalist economy in Western Germany (1945–1961)', in E. Aerts and A.S. Milward (eds), *Economic Planning in the Post-1945 Period*, 10th International Economic History Congress (Leuven, 1990), pp. 24–33.

6. Statistisches Bundesamt, *Zur wirtschaftlichen und sozialen Lage in den neuen Bundesländern*, January 1992, p. 76; August 1994, pp. *168, *170.

7. B. van Ark, 'The manufacturing sector in East Germany: a reassessment of comparative productivity performance, 1950–1988', in *Jahrbuch für Wirtschaftsgeschichte* (1995/2), pp. 75–100; C. Buchheim, 'Die Wirtschaftsordnung als Barriere des gesamtwirtschaftlichen Wachstums in der DDR', *Vierteljahrschrift für Sozial- und Wirtschaftsgeschichte*, 82 (1995), pp. 194–210.

8. W. Abelshauser, *Wirtschaft in Westdeutschland 1945–1948. Rekonstruktion und Wachstumsbedingungen in der amerikanischen und britischen Zone* (Stuttgart, 1975).

9. A. Ritschl, 'Währungsreform von 1948 und der Wiederanfstieg der Westdeutschen Industrie', *Vierteljahrschefte für Zeitgeschichte*, 33 (1985); R. Klump, *Wirtschaftsgeschichte der Bundesrepublik Deutschland: Zur Kritik neuerer wirtschaftshistorischer Interpretationen aus ordnungspolitischer Sicht* (Stuttgart, 1985); and C. Buchheim, 'The currency reform in West Germany in 1948', *German Yearbook on Business History 1989–92* (Munich, 1993), pp. 85–120.

10. W. Abelshauser, 'American aid and West German economic recovery: a macroeconomic perspective', in C.S. Maier and G. Bischof (eds), *The Marshall Plan and Germany: West German Development within the Framework of the European Recovery Program* (New York/Oxford, 1991), pp. 364–409; in the same volume, K. Borchardt and C. Buchheim, 'The Marshall Plan and key economic sectors: a microeconomic perspective', pp. 410–51. See also C. Buchheim, *Die Wiedereingliederung Westdeutschlands in die Weltwirtschaft 1945–1958* (Munich, 1990), pp. 93–5.

11. M. Olson, *The Rise and Decline of Nations: Economic Growth, Stagflation, and Social Rigidities* (New Haven, 1982); Klump, *Wirtschaftsgeschichte*; H. Giersch, K.-H. Paqué and H. Schmieding, *The Fading Miracle: Four Decades of Market Economy in Germany* (Cambridge, 1992).

12. W. Abelshauser, *Wirtschaftsgeschichte der Bundesrepublik Deutschland 1945–1980* (Frankfurt/M., 1983); Dumke, 'Reassessing the Wirtschaftswunder'; F. Jánossy, *Das Ende der Wirtschaftswunder: Erscheinung und Wesen der wirtschaftlichen Entwicklung* (Frankfurt/M., 1969).

19 Italy

Vera Zamagni

The Performance of the Italian Economy over the Past Fifty Years

The end of the Second World War marked a radical turnaround of the Italian economy. The inward-looking, autarkic policies followed in the 1930s were abandoned and the economy was opened up to the process of integration into Europe and to the intense adoption of American technology and management principles. Reconstruction was achieved swiftly and Marshall Aid was used to expand industry, especially in its modern branches. The legacy of the past put Italy in a rather low position compared to other European economies, but the 'social capabilities'[1] on which to base a process of catching up with the most advanced leaders were not missing: well established, though still too small, firms in the crucial fields; widespread basic education, with flourishing technical and commercial secondary and higher level institutions; a high propensity to invest; a government willing to support industrialization. A period of sustained economic growth started at the end of the 1940s, driving Italy through a profound structural change into the club of the wealthiest countries in Europe.

At the beginning, this period was marked by very rapid growth, with an annual rate around 6 per cent up until 1963 and with low rates of inflation. Such an expansion contrasted markedly with the years of sacrifice and misery during the war that had seen a drastic squeeze in consumption and for this reason it earned the title of 'economic miracle', although it was certainly the result of much toil and ingenuity. Industry, construction, exports and investment all grew at rates of between 9 and 11 per cent per annum, thus enlarging the industrial base of the country and allowing more industrial exports. Companies started to grow bigger and reached a more efficient size, something that so far had been only a dream. The Italian design of durable goods such as lamps, fridges and motorcycles was appreciated in the world markets and engineering became the leading sector of industry.

The year 1963 marked a standstill in this tumultuous process. It was the year of the first round of excessive wage claims, of an inflationary price rise, and of a loss in competitiveness of Italian exports which had serious repercussions on the

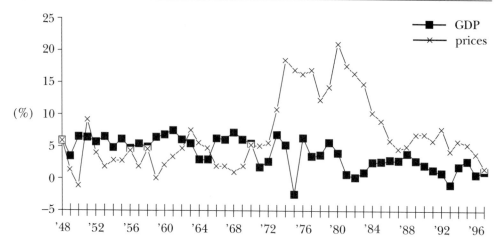

Figure 19.1. Rates of growth of GDP and consumer prices in Italy, 1948–96. *Sources:* N. Rossi, A. Sorgato and G. Toniolo, 'I conti economici italiani: una ricostruzione statistica, 1890–1990', *Rivista di Storia Economica,* 10 (1993); *Annuario Statistico Italiano,* various years.

country's balance of payments. Difficulties were, however, mild and temporary, as can be seen in Figure 19.1. Two years later sustained growth was resumed with particular emphasis placed on export markets.[2] A much stronger outburst of social discontent took place in 1969, in the so-called 'hot autumn', leading to an improvement in work conditions, a change in industrial relations towards greater job security and an enlargement of social services. A new workers' statute was approved in March 1970; pensions were increased; the unemployed got a better deal; maternity allowances were improved and a reform of health insurance was started, leading towards a National Health Service that was finally introduced in 1978. All this produced another temporary drop in growth rates in 1971–72, overcome in 1973 and 1974.

However, the international oil crisis of 1973 did not spare Italy. It marked the beginning of an era of much greater macroeconomic fluctuations, with deep crises and an ever-diminishing strength of recoveries, as shown in Figure 19.1. In 1975, Italian national income fell by 3.6 per cent and a process of persistent inflation was unleashed. Fortunately, a rather strong recovery followed, in which small and medium-sized enterprises took the lead, especially in winning new export markets, while big industry was undergoing a far-reaching process of reorganization, with the diffusion of automation, the thinning-out of the workforce and a drastic increase in productivity. These were the years in which 'Third Italy', namely the provinces of the north-east and centre of the country, definitively caught up with the original core of Italian industrialization, i.e. the industrial triangle (the provinces of the north-west), and developed a strong network of small to medium-sized firms organized in industrial districts.[3] The balance of payments was redressed, but another severe crisis (called the 'second oil shock') hit the Italian economy in the years 1981–83. This was followed by a less strong

Table 19.1. Percentage sectoral composition of GNP, Italy, 1951–94

	Agriculture	Industry	Private services	Public services
1951	19.8	37.1	31.9	11.2
1974	7.3	39.8	41.4	11.5
1994	3.4	29.6	53.0	14.0

Source: N. Rossi, A. Sorgato and G. Toniolo, 'I conti economici italiani: una ricostruzione statistica, 1890–1990', *Rivista di Storia Economica*, 10, 1993.

but substantial recovery that fared well by international standards and, lasting up to 1990, was achieved in the presence of diminishing inflation (see Figure 19.1) – an outcome largely due to policy measures that will be reviewed below. The years 1991–93 witnessed the third recession of the troubled years after 1974, followed by an uneven recovery still under way at the time of writing (autumn 1997).

Overall, the average rate of growth in the years 1948–74 was 5.4 per cent, and 2.2 per cent subsequently, a record that puts Italy among the best-performing industrial countries in both periods. The structure of the Italian economy has changed remarkably over time (Table 19.1), and the country has reached today a level of income per capita that is above the average of the European Union, slightly higher than the UK and close to the French and German level. This success story is, however, not without its bleak points: the south of the country is still lagging behind the centre-north, some of the institutions are inadequate to a modern society and the performance of public administration is much less than satisfactory; the budget deficit and public debt have climbed to fantastic peaks and the effectiveness of governments has been obstructed by the convulsive political life experienced in the last 5–6 years.

This process of modernization of the Italian economy has been the result of steady and widespread entrepreneurship[4] and of policy measures that are now being reviewed.

Monetary Stability and Supply Side Policies (1940s–1960s)

It fell on Luigi Einaudi when he was Minister of the Treasury in 1947 to stop the rapid inflationary process that had been unfolding after the end of the war. He was so effective in his stabilization policies enacted in the summer–autumn of that year that monetary stability was to last up to 1972, with the temporary exceptions of 1951 (the Korean war) and 1963 (wage push). The exchange rate, fixed in 1947 and slightly devalued in 1949 in connection with the devaluation of the pound sterling and of most other currencies against the dollar, remained stable up to 1973. The budget deficit was gradually reduced in size, with the help of the counterpart funds of the Marshall Plan, and then maintained at a very low level.

Plate 19.1. The rich North: the rapidly expanding business district of central Milan, seen from the Pirelli skyscraper, in 1963, during Italy's 'economic miracle'.

The public debt accumulated during the war and the immediate post-war years was swept away by the pre-1947 inflation and then remained small for about 25 years.

These orthodox monetary and fiscal policies[5] that conceded nothing to any Keynesian inspiration were the basis for a strong process of government intervention on the supply side. First of all, Italy had inherited from the fascist period a large body of public enterprises, mostly administered by the holding company IRI (Istituto per la Ricostruzione Industriale). This had been created in 1933 upon the bailing out of Italy's three large universal banks (the Banca Commerciale Italiana, the Credito Italiano and the Banco di Roma, that were turned into short-term banks). IRI, which was not privatized after the war and was given a new statute in 1948, started major projects of capacity expansion in basic industrial sectors and in infrastructures, especially steel (in connection with the ECSC), shipbuilding, telecommunications and motorways.

The government, under the pressure of the Americans, had instead planned to dissolve another public enterprise inherited from fascism, AGIP (Azienda Generale Italiana Petroli) created in 1926 for oil prospections and distribution. But its liquidator Enrico Mattei became convinced that oil and methane gas were strategic for development and the country should not wholly depend on foreign suppliers. He therefore managed to persuade the government of the desirability

Plate 19.2. The poor South: an animal market at San Marcellino in rural Calabria, 1955. The income-gap between the industrialised North and the largely agricultural South, and the policy attempts to narrow it, have been a central issue in Italy's post-war history.

of having a public enterprise in the field of oil, so that a new public holding was created in 1953, ENI (Ente Nazionale Idrocarburi), administering AGIP and other petrochemical companies. This public holding too was very expansionary and entered into joint ventures with Middle East oil countries and even with the Soviet Union, providing the country with an elastic supply of energy.

In 1947 Einaudi had also set up a fund to help engineering firms to restructure from war to peace production, FIM (Fondo Industrie Meccaniche). This fund worked as a long-term financial institution for some time, but slowly it came to administer a number of engineering firms and in 1962 it was turned into the third public holding company, EFIM Finally, in 1963 there was the nationalization of electricity sponsored by the Socialist Party, which was keen to break the power of the private electrical companies, and the public electricity company ENEL was created.

These public enterprises were instrumental in supplying energy, infrastructures, transportation and basic products to the expansionary drive that Italy experienced during the 'economic miracle' and were supported by the government, which created a Ministry of State Holdings in 1957 and supplied the necessary capital. Their performance in these prosperous years was satisfactory, in terms of both investments and returns. Difficulties emerged subsequently, in the troubled years of crises, mainly as a result of bad projecting that caused heavy losses and also because of the perverse effects of a political system that was becoming ever more corrupt.

Another line of public intervention on the supply side was directed towards the improvement of conditions in depressed and backward areas. An Agrarian Reform was enacted in 1949, aimed at breaking up the *latifundia*, and in 1951 a special agency was created to foster investments in the south ('Mezzogiorno') of Italy, called the Cassa per il Mezzogiorno. The Cassa devoted its attention first to agriculture and infrastructures and turned to industry only in the 1960s, with the help especially of public enterprises, bound by law to set up 60 per cent of their new plants in the south, and of new long-term financial institutions set up in 1953 to finance industry in the south. The results of this new policy are explored in the case study (see box).

The Italian government was also at the forefront of the process of European integration, participating in the negotiations from the very beginning, when the ECSC was founded in 1951, and then helping to set up the Common Market in 1957 and the CAP (Common Agricultural Policy) at the beginning of the 1960s. This proved to be highly beneficial for the country, that not only saw its international trade prosper, but tied domestic economic policies to decisions taken at the European level, pushing the economy towards modernization, as would also be seen in later years.[6]

Finally, there were attempts at planning development, at first during the years of the Marshall Plan, when the lists of goods to be acquired from the United States had to be set up, and then in the 1950s and 1960s, with the Vanoni 'Scheme', and the La Malfa 'Note', two successive documents aimed at fixing the medium-term growth targets of the country. These plans were never rigid or quantitatively detailed, but witnessed the effort by governments to move in line with the great leap forward that the Italian private enterprises were making.

In focus: The 'Mezzogiorno' Question

The Italian south was already in a condition of inferiority with regard to the rest of the country at unification, as a result of the much lower provision of infrastructures and education that the pre-unification governments had granted to the area. It took many years after unification before the central government decided to intervene with some special law in support of southern development, but the two world wars discontinued the attention to the south substantially. In the meantime the gap from the rest of the country had grown to intolerable levels. It was only during reconstruction after the

The 'Mezzogiorno' Question (continued)

Second World War that the parliament decided a range of measures for the south, of which the Cassa per il Mezzogiorno was the most important one.

Can we say that such measures have produced positive results? What has immediately to be pointed out is that the post-war period has been a period of exceptionally fast growth for the south if we look at it over the long run. For the first time since unification, the south has grown at rates that are at least equal (with the exception of the 1990s) to the average for the country, with a near stabilization of the relative gap. And we have to remember that for most of the period substantial rates of growth were prevailing, changing the south from being a backward area in absolute terms to being an area that is indeed lagging behind the north–centre, but has reached almost the same average level of income as Spain.

Dissatisfaction still remains, first of not having been able to produce even more positive results that would allow the closing of the gap, and secondly of having induced a kind of development that in many ways is weak and lacking an autonomous drive. Indeed, most of the industry that localized in the south has been of the capital intensive type – sometimes referred to as 'cathedrals in the desert' – to reap the benefits of the capital incentives granted by the central government. This has produced very weak backward and forward linkages within the region, as producers there were primarily connected to northern industry and northern markets. Such an outcome was inevitable, given that northern corporations owned most of the new southern plants. Few local small firms were opened up or strengthened by government subsidies, partly because of weak southern entrepreneurship, partly because of disadvantages in the field of credit, infrastructures and services, that increased costs for southern entrepreneurs, and also as a consequence of criminal acts, that were directed more easily against local small businesses. Another problem of southern industry is that it is not well positioned in the international markets, where it exports very little.

What makes the present situation worse is the realization that public spending in support of southern development had been turned into a highly 'clientelistic' exercise with little economic effectiveness, something that has produced a public revolt issuing in the abolition by referendum in 1993 of the Ministry for the South and of the agency that had replaced the Cassa per il Mezzogiorno in the second half of the 1980s. These measures drastically reduced the economic support for the south formerly granted by the central government, leaving much of the present support to the European Union regional schemes. It might be a coincidence, but the economic performance of the south has worsened in the last 4–5 years with reference to the rest of the country, which is a clear indicator of the need to invent some new way of solving the 'Mezzogiorno' question, a way that has to take into serious consideration the social, cultural and legal factors beside the economic ones.

The Conversion to Keynesianism and the Rise of Public Debt (1970s–1990s)

It was a domestic event, the already mentioned 'hot autumn' of 1969, that triggered eventually a steep increase in public spending for welfare purposes, unmatched by a parallel increase in public revenues. This gave rise to the first important deficit in the state budget in 1971 (7.4 per cent of GNP). The 'oil crises' of 1975 and 1981 superimposed their negative impact upon this deficit, enlarging it further. What has happened ever since has been a persistent incapability and unwillingness by governments to redress the situation of the state budget, that continuously remained in substantial deficit, with some improvement since 1992. The preoccupation to support income during crises and not to kill recoveries that were considered badly needed by public opinion and turned out not be as strong as desired, was constantly at a premium over the warnings by international institutions to return to orthodox finance. Only in the last 4–5 years have serious efforts been made to put the deficit under control with some structural measures, like the reform of pensions in 1995 and the process of privatization of public enterprises that was launched in 1992 by the Amato government (but effectively got under way only in 1994). Modest results were, however, achieved up to 1996, when the big decision was taken to meet the Maastricht requirements for the 1997 deficit (3 per cent of GNP). This has been achieved through a substantial increase in taxation and cuts in public spending, particularly on some privileged aspects of the welfare state.

The real burden of public debt (measured as a percentage of GNP), however, did not immediately grow steeply, because of the process of inflation that was unleashed after the demise of fixed exchange rates in 1973 (see Figure 19.1). But this very high inflation was perceived, in spite of the contemporaneous devaluation of the lira, as an obstacle for the country to continue her tight economic and political relationships with the European Community, and three historical decisions were taken that would finally succeed in bringing inflation down.

The first was the entry in March 1979 into the European Monetary System (EMS), which was an agreement to keep fixed, though adjustable, exchange rates among the currencies of the Community. Everybody in Italy understood that it would have been ludicrous for the country to belong to the EMS without trying to put inflation under control. But the instruments were still missing. The second important step forward was made in the summer of 1981 and was the 'Treasury–Bank of Italy divorce',[7] which, through the elimination of the obligation by the Bank to absorb all the state bonds not subscribed by the public, gave more freedom to the Bank of Italy to limit the growth of money supply. Indeed inflation started slowly to come down the same year. The third equally important step was taken in 1984 when the government decided to drastically limit the impact of wage indexation, that had been contributing to inflation especially after the revision of 1975 which was very favourable to labour. In 1986 inflation reached a floor of 5–6 per cent around which it fluctuated up until 1995; then it further declined in 1996, reaching less than 2 per cent in 1997.

In focus: Living with a High Public Debt

Italy is not a country with a bad historical record in the field of public debt. As a unified country, she had only three episodes of climbing public debt before the present one, two of which were connected with the two world wars. In both of these last cases, inflation, plus negotiations with the American and British governments after the First World War, allowed a swift liquidation of the debt. Only the first episode that took place immediately after Italy's unification in 1861 was more difficult to put under control, but the élite of the time proved willing to raise taxation enough to cover the budget deficit and put an end to the accumulation of debt within the span of 15 years.

Why is it proving so difficult at present to find a solution? One reason for this is paradoxical, and it is certainly the high propensity to save shown by the Italian people that has allowed the financing of most public debt domestically with only a marginal contribution by foreigners and with relatively modest effects of crowding out of other types of productive investments. This fact has made the solution of the problem of climbing debt less pressing, because neither the international position nor the domestic viability of the country were jeopardized, and has allowed the political class to muddle through and postpone radical measures.

Another reason for the persistent budget deficit has been the difficult political equilibrium of the last years of the first republic, in the second half of the 1980s, when no government dared to adopt radical measures of increase in taxation and/or cut in public spending for fear of provoking an explosion, which came anyway when widespread corruption was uncovered by 'Clean Hands'.[1] The 'technocratic' governments that followed the demise of the old political class have tried to reverse the previous trend and have succeeded in diminishing the deficit in terms of some percentage points of GNP, without, however, having the authority and the time to project a complete reabsorption of it. Only the Prodi government with full political responsibility has done a lot in bringing the deficit in line with the Maastricht requirements and has given a big push to privatizations, two measures that will bring debt too under control. Meanwhile the country has had to live with constantly higher interest rates and a supply of credit to private activities below demand, which are factors that have undoubtedly made life difficult for Italian entrepreneurs and made usury more widespread, so much so that a law against usury had to be passed in February 1996 to allow at least more effective prosecution of usurers.

1. 'Clean Hands' (*Mani pulite*) is the name of the pool of prosecutors of corruption activities by politicians whose discoveries roused the Italian people against the ruling parties.

The lira stopped devaluing repeatedly and between 1986 and 1992 remained fixed within the EMS, passing from a band of fluctuation of 12 per cent (6 per cent on each side of the par value) to a narrow band of 5 per cent in 1990. However, in 1990 the capital markets were freed in the European Union, and they did not take long before realizing that the lira was overvalued as a result of the cumulative positive differential between Italian inflation and the average inflation of the Community core countries. In the summer of 1992 there was a strong speculative attack against the lira that not only had to devalue, but had to get out of the EMS and freely fluctuate, an event which greatly helped in restoring the competitiveness of Italian exports. At the end of 1996, Italy went back again into the EMS, as required by the Maastricht treaty, though at a much devalued exchange rate.

The process of 'disinflation' of the 1980s had an unintended implication on the side of public debt.[8] The real burden of it, no longer relieved by inflation as had happened in the 1970s, started to climb steeply from a modest level below 50 per cent of GNP to as much as 124 per cent of GNP. This is the only Maastricht requirement for European monetary unification (namely, a public debt below 60 per cent of GNP) which has not yet been met by Italy at the time of writing. The rise of public debt also meant a substantial rise in interest payments, which had a negative feedback into the budget deficit, especially when interest rates had to be kept high, as has often been the case after the freeing of capital markets to avoid the flight of capital in search of the highest real interest rates.[9]

Between Political Turmoil and Major Economic Changes (1990s)

In the 1990s, with the dawn of the hegemony of the Christian Democratic Party (DC) that was literally swept away as a result of corruption and the revolt by public opinion against the old political system, Italy has found itself in the midst of major political changes. At the same time, the acceleration of the process of European integration called for far-reaching economic adjustments. The introduction of the Single European Market, projected in 1986 and achieved in 1992, required a number of institutional changes of crucial importance.

The first is in the field of banking, where the post-war practice had been shaped by the 1936 banking bill, that had abolished universal banking in Italy[10] and acknowledged the existence of public banks. Indeed, public banks had come during the fascist years to control over 80 per cent of banking assets and the situation did not change in the post-war period. Specialization and fragmentation were other features of the Italian banking sector. With the introduction of the Single European Market in banking, competition was expected to increase and Italian banks had to equip themselves to face it. It is in this context that the Amato–Carli banking bill was approved in July 1990, providing for the reintroduction of universal banking in Italy, the granting of merger incentives to foster the formation of larger banks and the setting up of a legal background to the process of privatization. The expected changes in the Italian banking sector are indeed taking place, and many mergers and privatizations have already been achieved, though the process is still very much under way at the time of writing and there have been some difficult cases to be sorted out, like that of the Banco di Napoli that has suffered high losses.

The second institutional change has to do with more transparent markets and the support of competition. In October 1990 an antitrust bill was passed by Parliament with the creation of an Antitrust Authority. It must be noted that this was really an epochal change, given that in Italy there had never been a sensitivity to the questions of fair competition and the transparency of the market. Again, the introduction of this bill is due to European pressure and the almost contemporary introduction of antitrust legislation at the European level that made national legislation inevitable. The new Italian Antitrust Authority has worked very intensively, but the country has not yet got rid of unsatisfactory situations of monopoly or oligopoly in existence before the Authority started its activity, like the public–private duopoly in the field of mass media that is still causing much political upheaval.

Finally, the process of privatization has concerned not only the banking sector but all government holdings with the exception of the railways and the Post Office. There, however, a more managerial type of administration has replaced the previous, highly bureaucratic one. EFIM was liquidated in the summer of 1992 as a result of bad management; ENI, which is presently a highly profitable holding, has been privatized already; IRI is selling bits and pieces and has already liquidated most banks, steel and telecommunications; ENEL is lagging behind because of difficulties in shaping the process of privatization, but projects are now ready; and INA (the public insurance company created in 1912) is also being privatized. When the process is completed, the Italian stock exchange will see a much larger volume of transactions and probably cease to be one of the smallest stock exchanges in the world.

Presently, most of the attention of Italian economic policies is polarized around the question of the monetary union and the Maastricht requirements. As has been emphasized already, Italy has made a big successful effort to curb inflation and interest rates, to get back in the EMS and bring the deficit in line with Maastricht. But this has entailed large cuts in public spending and increased taxation; this marked a major discontinuity with previous policies and has not been accepted without protest by the population, causing difficulties to the Prodi government, which, however, at the time of writing seems well in command of the situation.

The excessive concentration on the Maastricht issues has delayed other reforms in various fields that have been waiting for too long and are strategic to improving the long-run economic performance of the country. Among them are the addition of at least two more years of compulsory school (there are only eight presently); decentralization of government in several fields, especially education and fiscal matters; increased effort in the field of R & D; an adequate law on non-profit institutions; and a better conceived policy of development of the south. But above all, Italy needs constitutional reforms that would allow more effective governance of the country with more stable governments.

Why Italy Does Not Enjoy a Good Press

In spite of Italy having shown great economic dynamism and a capability to reach and remain in the club of the most advanced countries in the world, the country has never enjoyed a good press internationally. Its economic achievements are frequently considered more the result of good luck than of the entrepreneurship and the economic policies that Italy has been able to express; its political life is more often than not ridiculed as a knot of incomprehensible moves and counter-moves with contradictory or ineffective results. It must be said that the Italians themselves are in the front line when it comes to criticizing their institutions and governments and this certainly strengthens a foreign critical view of the country.

Besides the low profile of Italian foreign policy and the modesty of her military apparatus, can this low reputation be traced back to some particular features of the Italian economy? I think it is useful in this context to review the most apparent differences the Italian economy shows in comparison to other advanced countries. First and foremost, the size of its enterprises is on average very small by international standards. This does not mean that they are necessarily inefficient or technologically backward; on the contrary, technological jewels highly competitive in international niche markets can often be found among such firms; but it certainly means that they are normally unable to carry out much original basic research, while being excellent in imitating foreign ideas with new design and some additional functional qualities. It also means that their financial power is very limited and therefore they usually cannot invest abroad, so that overall Italy has a low level of foreign investment. What all this implies is that Italian firms can be quite profitable, but are in no position of dominance in international markets, neither technologically (the standards are determined by other economies) nor financially, especially in the sectors where scale- and research-intensive goods are produced. Indeed Italy has very few big corporations and even fewer multinationals and in general has not shown much talent for managing large corporations, in spite of the efforts to imitate the American models of management. Moreover, the impact of political life has worked against big business, because both the predominant Communist and Catholic traditions were more favourable (for different reasons) to family firms than to large private managerial corporations. Now that both traditions have changed their emphasis and some technologically advanced firms have grown larger and are in need of a new economic context, it might be the right time to achieve a turnaround, helped by mergers taking place in the banking sector too. But I think that only over the very long run could Italy reach some substantial compacting of her economic fabric.

Up to the recent privatizations, the relatively small sector of big corporations in Italy was composed of private, public and foreign firms in about the same proportions. The split between private and public was another powerful factor that did not help to strengthen Italian big business, because of the frequent rivalry between public and private firms. This was especially the case in the field of chemicals, where the fight between the chemical branch of the public enterprise ENI and the private chemical company Montedison has weakened Montedison up to the point of being taken over by another private firm and then sold in bits and pieces in the market, mainly to foreigners. Another struggle, between the public car company Alfa Romeo and the private one Fiat, ended up with Fiat taking over Alfa Romeo, but only in 1986, after heavy losses by Alfa Romeo.

Another typical feature of the Italian economy has been the weak lira. After the demise of the Bretton Woods system in 1973, Italy has let the lira devalue all the time, partly as a result of the increased inflation deriving from excessive money supply growth due to deficit spending, partly as an intentional policy of competitive devaluation. This means that the lira has not been considered a reserve asset and has never played an international role, but has instead been several times the object of speculative attacks leading to further devaluation and lately, as has been pointed out above, to exit from the EMS. This behaviour has indeed allowed Italy to support successfully its growth rates in relative terms, but has been a reason for the loss of reputation of the country in international circles. Here too, if Italy insists in pursuing the target of participating in the European monetary union, a major turnaround is in sight.

In the financial field, two other differential features of the Italian economy are notable: the small size of banks and of the stock exchange. The first aspect is part of the general problem of the small size of firms in Italy, but it entails a weak presence of Italian financial institutions in international markets; the second has to do both with traditions and with the limited number of companies quoted. Up to 1933 Italy had a universal banking system that, as is well known, makes the financial system bank-oriented rather than market-oriented; no change took place after the abolition of universal banking in 1936, mainly because of the persistence of family firms that normally do not want to be quoted on the stock exchange. For this reason Italy's stock market remained one of the smallest and internationally least important in comparison with those of other advanced countries.

One final typical feature of the Italian economy is the profound dualism between north–centre and south, a dualism that is rooted in the history of the country and that is not in the process of closing, with all its negative impact at the economic, institutional and social levels (think, for instance, of the very high rates of unemployment in the south). Dualism is accompanied by widespread crime, which features so prominently in the international news. This is one of the long-lasting problems of the country, that has also polluted political life through the mafia and camorra support of political leaders. The pathological impact of 'clientelism' in the south is also due to the economic difficulties of the place and the lack of an adequate supply of jobs.

This list of differential features of the Italian economy cannot overlook the problem of unstable governments, which is the factor usually charged with having rendered Italian economic policies ineffective. It is indeed true that Italian governments have generally had a short duration, but the negative effect of this on projecting and putting into effect major policies has been greatly diminished by the fact that the coalitions running the governments were the same for long spans of time, always led by the same party, the DC: at first coalitions of centre parties, including the liberals at the right; then since 1963 centre–left coalitions, including the socialists (and sometimes also the liberals) up to the breakdown of the system in the early 1990s as a result of 'Clean Hands'. Often ministers simply moved from one ministry to another, remaining in charge for long spans of time across several governments. The views of the different governments were hardly different, if we except the major change from centre to centre–left in 1963. After 'Clean Hands' and the breakdown and dissolution of the DC and the Socialist Party, political instability increased considerably and it has become the major issue of Italian politics, causing the 1993 referendum that changed the electoral system from a proportional to a majority one, as well as the recent decision to introduce some form of presidentialism.

On the whole, though, Italy has shown that it is possible to prosper economic-ally not only without playing any major international role, but with a very low international reputation. Moreover, the very many shortcomings of her political and economic life have not been as serious as to strangle growth. The country, however, could certainly have done better if its economic system had been brought more in line with those of the world leaders.

Bibliographical Note

A general overview of the Italian economy in the post-war period can be found in the two final chapters of V. Zamagni, *An Economic History of Italy, 1860–1990* (Oxford, 1993); a more lengthy treatment up to the 1970s is given in D.C. Templeman, *The Italian Economy* (New York, 1981). An informed regional survey is provided by R. King, *Italy* (London, 1987); industrial policies are dealt with in M. Baldassarri (ed.), *Industrial Policy in Italy 1949–90* (London, 1993). On monetary and fiscal policies, there are two recent volumes: F. Padoa Schioppa, *Italy: the Sheltered Economy* (Oxford, 1993) and M. Baldassarri (ed.), *The Italian Economy: Heaven or Hell?* (New York, 1994). The golden age of the Cassa per il Mezzogiorno is accounted for in G. Podbielski, *Twenty Five Years of Special Action for the Development of Southern Italy* (Rome, 1978), but a good general account of the rise and fall of public intervention in the south is missing. On the relationships between Italy and the European Union, see F. Francioni (ed.), *Italy and EC Membership Evaluated* (London, 1992). A general treatment of the problem of Italian public debt is offered in F. Giavazzi and L. Spaventa (eds), *High Public Debt: the Italian Experience* (Cambridge, 1988). On the most recent years, see H.M. Scobie, S. Mortali, S. Persand and P. Docile, *The Italian Economy in the 1990s* (London, 1996).

Notes

1. 'Social capabilities' is a concept developed by M. Abramovitz, 'Catching up, forging ahead and falling behind', *Journal of Economic History*, 46, June 1986, to explain why certain countries are able to imitate the leader and others are not.

2. See R.M. Stern, *Foreign Trade and Economic Growth in Italy* (New York, 1967).

3. The best volume in English on the Italian industrial districts is E. Goodman and J. Bamford (eds), *Small Firms and Industrial Districts in Italy* (London, 1986).

4. The typical views and aptitudes of small entrepreneurs are surveyed in E. Kurzweil, *Italian Entrepreneurs* (New York, 1983).

5. See F. Spinelli and G. Tullio, *Monetary Policy, Fiscal Policy and Economic Activity: the Italian Experience* (Aldershot, 1983).

6. A review of the relationships between Italy and the EC can be found in F. Francioni (ed.), *Italy and EC Membership Evaluated* (London, 1992).

7. On this and on other important institutional changes, see P. Lange and M. Regini (eds), *State, Market and Social Regulation: New Perspectives on Italy* (Cambridge, 1989).

8. On public debt, see F. Giavazzi and L. Spaventa (eds), *High Public Debt: the Italian Experience* (Cambridge, 1988).

9. Real interest rates are interest rates deflated by the respective inflation rates. Where inflation is higher, interest rates must be higher to avoid capital flight.

10. Universal banking was abolished on the grounds that it had proved incapable of resisting major crises and had needed repeated operations of bailing out, the last of which ended with the creation of IRI in 1933.

20 Scandinavia

Rolf Ohlsson

In the early nineteenth century the Scandinavian countries were among the poorest in Europe,[1] and they were little affected by the fundamental economic changes which were going on in the United Kingdom and continental Europe during the first half of the century. Today the Scandinavian countries are highly industrialized. From an economic standpoint they are affluent societies, and they are considered by many to be the most advanced welfare states in the world.

The economic expansion which has resulted in this dramatic transformation can be traced back to the middle of the nineteenth century. The industrial expansion from this period onwards was especially marked in Sweden, which enjoyed faster economic growth than any other European country during the second half of the nineteenth century. Denmark and Norway also showed remarkable growth rates during this period, while Finland's industrial breakthrough occurred after the liberation from Russia in 1917.

In all the Scandinavian countries, a growing international demand for their products, especially raw materials and semi-manufactures, was an important engine of growth underlying this outstanding economic performance: iron and steel in Sweden's case, timber and shipping in Norway's, processed agricultural products in Denmark's, and timber and butter in Finland's. But structural and organizational changes in the agricultural sector, along with concomitant increases in productivity and rising purchasing power, also played an important part in the growth process of the four countries.

A Common Denominator: the Scandinavian Welfare State

A common denominator of the Scandinavian countries which revealed itself after the Second World War was the growth of a special exemplar of the welfare state, sometimes called the Scandinavian model, the Swedish model or the social democratic model, since social democratic ideology has been the dominant political force behind social reforms in all the Scandinavian countries. Social democrats have also held political power during the major part of the post-war period.

Some would argue that this exemplar is the most advanced of the various versions of the welfare state that exist. It is a model in which the policy pursued aims to promote an equality of the highest standards, not an equality of minimum needs as pursued in other models of the welfare state. To quote one observer: 'All benefit, all are dependent, and all should feel obliged to pay.'[2]

There are some differences between the four countries, where Sweden can be seen as the most extreme case, but the following may be said to be the salient features of the model:

(1) A progressive 'socialization of the family'. The welfare state takes direct responsibility for children, the aged and the helpless by large transfer payments and the supply of public services. With a little exaggeration one might say that instead of socializing the 'means of production' as in the planned economies of eastern Europe, the Scandinavian welfare model socialized consumption.

(2) A heavy social service burden, not only to meet family needs but also to allow women to choose work in the open labour market rather than work at home. The result is that Scandinavia now shows the highest propensity in the world for women to go out to work. In some age groups this propensity is as high as for men.

(3) A fusion of welfare and work, in which full employment was for a long time an almost sacred goal of economic policy. The costs of maintaining a solidaristic and universalistic welfare system have been high. The policy pursued has been to maximize incomes (and therefore public revenues) by having as many people as possible working.

(4) A full employment policy. In practice this has meant an overheated labour market in the Scandinavian countries during much of the post-war period, making the system very sensitive to inflation. It has also created strong tendencies for Scandinavian countries to devalue their currencies in periods of crisis to enable full employment to be sustained.

(5) Combination of full employment with active labour market policies and a 'solidaristic' wage policy, resulting in remarkably small wage differentials between low- and high-skilled labour. Wage differentials between men and women are also small, viewed in an international perspective. This small wage differential is one important reason why women show a high propensity to work in the open labour market.

(6) High taxes in general. In 1990 the tax–GDP ratio was 56 per cent in Sweden and 50 per cent in Denmark. These high tax–GDP ratios have been the other side of the coin. The question whether these high taxes have been an obstacle to economic growth has been a topic for some debate, especially during the 1980s and 1990s.

An overall consequence has been rising public expenditures, with Sweden in the lead and Denmark close behind. Public expenditures, including transfer

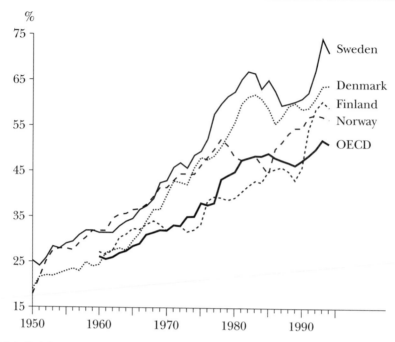

Figure 20.1. Public expenditure as a percentage of GDP in Sweden, Denmark, Finland, Norway and OECD-Europe, 1950–94. *Source:* OECD, *National Accounts, Economic Outlook,* June 1995.

payments, amounted to 71 per cent of GDP in Sweden in 1995 (Figure 20.1), while the average for OECD-Europe was 51 per cent. The somewhat lower growth of the expenditure rates for Norway since 1980 than in the other Scandinavian countries can be attributed partly to higher economic growth, while the generally lower rates for Finland are partly due to a younger age structure.

Growth Performance since the Second World War

The aggregate growth performance of the Scandinavian economy since the Second World War has followed the same broad pattern as experienced in most other countries. The overall growth of the period has been quite close to the average of the European OECD countries, with high growth until the beginning of the 1970s and a slow-down thereafter (Table 20.1). The reasons underlying this changing growth pattern are discussed elsewhere in this book and will therefore not be treated here (see Chapters 4 and 5).

However, the profile of growth has been somewhat different in the Scandinavian countries and the growth performance has also varied between them. This is illustrated in Figure 20.2, where the main deviations from the OECD average have been the following:

Table 20.1. Growth and unemployment in Scandinavia, 1950–94

	Sweden	Denmark	Norway	Finland	OECD
(a) Average annual percentage changes in GDP					
1950–73	3.8	4.0	4.0	4.9	4.5
1973–94	1.3	1.7	3.4	2.1	2.1
1950–94	2.6	2.9	3.7	3.5	3.3
(b) Average unemployment rates (%)					
1950–73	1.8	2.6	1.9	1.7	2.4
1973–94	3.2	8.1	3.1	6.2	6.1
1950–94	2.5	5.2	2.5	3.9	4.2

Note: OECD figures are average for 12 countries (UK, France, Germany, Austria, Sweden, Denmark, Norway, Finland, Italy, Belgium, Netherlands, Switzerland).

Sources: OECD, *Economic Outlook,* various issues; A. Maddison, *Dynamic Forces in Capitalist Development* (Oxford, 1991).

(1) A considerably lower growth in Sweden after 1973 and especially in the 1990s.

(2) A slightly slower growth in Denmark and Norway in the 1950s.

(3) A higher growth in Norway after 1973.

(4) A more violently fluctuating growth pattern in Finland until 1980 and a strong negative growth after 1989.

An attempt is made below to identify country-specific problems in economic structures, economic performance and the economic policies pursued by the respective Scandinavian countries. The point of departure for the analysis has been the different growth profiles in Figure 20.2. The main emphasis is on Sweden, as the largest and the the most 'mature' of the four economies. Moreover, it has been the 'ideological' leader with regard to the welfare state among the Scandinavian countries.

Sweden

Sweden's industry found itself in an exceedingly favourable position at the end of the war as a result of Sweden's having managed to avoid taking part in it, unlike Denmark, Norway and Finland. In the war-torn countries of Europe, whose production apparatus and infrastructure had been wholly or partly destroyed, there was a great need for imports, while the production capacity of Swedish industry was greater than it had ever been. Moreover, prices had risen less in Sweden than in other countries. There were therefore good prospects of a massive expansion of exports. In addition, there was a latent need in Sweden itself both to consume

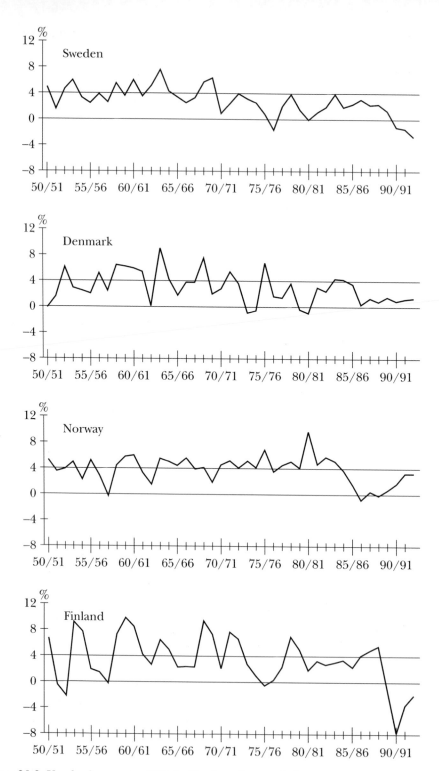

Figure 20.2. Yearly changes in GDP in Sweden, Denmark, Norway and Finland, 1950–93. *Sources:* OECD, *National Accounts, 1950–1968, Historical Statistics;* OECD, *National Accounts,* 1960–93.

and to invest after the controls of wartime, and this manifested itself in a strongly rising home demand.

The need to import production and transport equipment, in conjunction with the reconstruction of industry in the war-ravaged lands, had beneficial repercussions on developments in Sweden's engineering industry and shipyards. But in addition, the limited nature of import competition, in combination with a buoyant home and international demand for consumer goods, furnished the scope for a significant expansion of the textile, ready-made clothing, shoe and leather industries. The result was a strong growth in the 1940s.

In the 1950s the foodstuffs industry declined in relative terms because home market demand was limited, while the textile and clothing industry was soon faced with increasingly fierce international competition which squeezed profit margins and led to reductions in the volume of production and employment. Instead it was export branches such as shipbuilding, motor cars, engineering and the steel industry that became the powerhouse of industrial expansion during the 1950s and 1960s. The expansion was facilitated by the market integration which was taking place under the auspices of the General Agreement on Tariffs and Trade (GATT), the European Economic Community (EEC) and the European Free Trade Association (EFTA).

Vigorous house-building activity also played an important role in the 1950s, 1960s and early 1970s. This was the result partly of a pent-up demand, partly of the motoring revolution and partly of housing policy, which aimed to implement the so-called 'million programme' between 1964 and 1974 under which one million dwellings were to be built within a 10-year period. All these factors had a stimulating effect on housing construction. On the other hand the policies pursued also made it expensive.

Thus, the period from the end of the war to the beginning of the 1970s was a period of industrial expansion marked by high economic growth. A continuance of industrialization, involving a flow of surplus labour from agriculture and its subsidiary occupations into industry and those parts of the rest of the economy which were being developed in close interaction with it, was the main engine powering the fast growth rates. The average rise in GNP between 1947 and 1970 was 4.3 per cent per annum. Industrial growth was even higher at times, notably during the first half of the 1960s, which have been characterized as the 'golden years'. This must be regarded as a very good growth performance, bearing in mind that Sweden had a high income level compared to the OECD average and consequently benefited from a small catching-up effect.

This economic and industrial expansion resulted in a permanent excess demand for labour. Part of this demand was met by means of an increase in the female labour supply, while another part was met by large-scale immigration of labour into Sweden up to the beginning of the 1970s. Between 1950 and 1970 more than 600,000 persons migrated to Sweden – the total population of Sweden is today almost nine million inhabitants – of whom more than 95 per cent came either to work or in company with an immigrant worker. The immigrants came mainly from Finland, but in the 1960s quite a substantial number came from southern Europe. Thus, Sweden imported labour and used its internal labour reserve to a high degree. The question whether Sweden instead should have imported capital to promote growth in the long run has been a topic for some debate.

During this period economic policy, along with housing policy, caused demand to increase considerably more than it would otherwise have done. The devaluation of 1949 started the process. This resulted in an undervaluation of the Swedish krona, which imparted a considerable stimulus to large parts of industry. The effects were greatly reinforced by the international price rise triggered by the outbreak of the Korean war in 1950. Economic policy encouraged a rapid rise in demand from that time on, quickly bringing prolonged inflation along with upward pressure on industry's costs, so that there were soon no positive effects left from the earlier devaluation of the krona. However, since so many other conditions were favourable this did not lead to any serious problems until the end of the 1960s. The deterioration of the relative cost situation was offset by the fact that the products being manufactured were in heavy demand on world markets.

It was during this period that the so-called 'solidaristic' or 'wage equalization' policy, the backbone of the Swedish model, was introduced. The principle of equal pay for equal work was established. This policy was supplemented by an active labour market policy, which increased labour mobility. Other economic policy measures of what can be described as a mainly Keynesian stamp were also brought in.

The industrial sector's relative significance in the total national economy diminished rapidly after the early 1970s. Towards the end of the 1960s, the industrial sector including building construction accounted for 46 per cent of GNP; by 1990 the figure had dwindled to 27 per cent. The impact of the fall in demand for labour is thrown into stark relief by the fact that it was not only relative but absolute. Thus, by the early 1990s, 300,000 fewer people were working in the industrial sector than had been the case 20 years earlier, despite the fact that the total labour force had increased by 800,000.

Also in terms of overall growth Sweden lagged behind the rest of the OECD countries after 1970. During the period from 1970 to 1992 the growth rate of GDP was considerably lower than the OECD average: 1.7 per cent per year compared with 2.9 per cent for the OECD countries.

In parallel with the relative decline of industry (an international phenomenon among highly developed economies), an intensification of competition was becoming increasingly noticeable in Sweden. By the middle of the 1960s the reconstruction of European industry had been more or less completed. The currency system had been restored, the national and international credit markets put in order and great free trade areas established, giving rise to increased investment, new factory installations, modern production equipment and well-adapted organizations all over Europe. By this time Swedish industry, both exporting firms and those aligned towards the home market, was beginning to encounter considerably more severe international competition than before. Moreover, this competition was coming not just from European countries but also from Japan and later from newly industrializing countries in the Third World, the so-called NIC countries. This international competition brought large sectors of Swedish industry, including textiles and clothing, shipyards, the mining and steel industries and parts of the engineering industry, under heavy pressure for change. Some years into the 1970s the business climate also deteriorated for the many home-market firms which depended on building activity. The crisis which hit Sweden in 1973/74 after a long era of high growth resulted not merely from increased oil prices, excessively high wage costs and ordinary cyclical marketing difficulties: it was a structural crisis!

Some economic policy measures were introduced in response to the changing circumstances. The Investment Bank was established as a source of finance and National Enterprise as an umbrella organization charged with the task of promoting industrial development. At the same time less emphasis began to be placed on mobility-promoting labour market policy and more on regional policy instead.

The most important of the changes in Sweden was that the public sector began to grow even bigger than before. Taxes had to be increased, putting upward pressure on wage levels. This upward pressure was boosted by the increased labour requirements of the public sector, where wage settlements were insensitive to weakening economic conditions. Another problem was that the public sector employed a disproportionately large share of the labour force with higher and theoretical education.

Economic policy took a Keynesian turn with the introduction of so-called 'bridging' measures in the middle of the 1970s. These measures included heavy state subsidies to the most vulnerable industries and an expansionary fiscal policy that was supposed to counteract the fall in foreign demand. This policy can be regarded partly as an alternative to devaluation. Another change resulting from the structural crisis was that monetary policy entered upon a long period of significantly higher interest rates. Nevertheless these measures could not solve the underlying structural problems of the economy. This resulted in devaluations of the Swedish krona, starting in 1977 and ending in 1982 with a devaluation of 16 per cent. These measures made it possible to hold unemployment down and keep alive the sacred cow of jobs for all.

The positive effects of the krona's undervaluation were still present at the middle of the decade, but excessive inflation thereafter had almost extinguished them by the early 1990s. In the late 1980s Sweden also abolished regulation of the credit system and scrapped its barriers to the free movement of capital across the national frontiers. These new departures, along with a tax reform which was introduced a couple of years later, aimed to improve industry's opportunities and competitiveness in the long run. Unfortunately the short-run effects of these measures were negative and made industry's situation worse.

Due to the fact that inflation was higher than in most competitor countries, interest rates were increasing to a high level in an international perspective. At the same time actors on the Swedish financial and property markets became large-scale borrowers, speculating heavily on the rapidly rising prices of real assets. This ended with a crash in the autumn of 1990. Many property companies and finance companies collapsed. Building construction was paralysed and heavy credit losses were recorded in the banking system. All these events aggravated the difficulties of especially the many small and medium-sized industrial companies.

Thus, a combination of several factors can explain the bad performance of the Swedish economy in the 1990s. First, an unresolved structural crisis dating back to the 1970s but concealed by several devaluations and rendered worse by house-building and financial crises. Second, a tremendous efflorescence of public sector expenditure not offset by any equivalent restraint upon the demands of households and resulting in heavy foreign borrowing. These factors compelled Sweden to abandon an economic policy centred on the maintenance of full employment. Instead economic policy had to concentrate on bringing interest rates down, checking inflationary tendencies and stabilizing a floating currency while allowing unemployment rates to rise from 1–2 to 8–9 per cent.

However, during later years these changes enforced a structural transformation of industry which involved a sharp decline in certain branches while others have been able to adapt more easily to the new conditions. For most industries the more intense competition meant that efforts had to be made to squeeze costs by reducing personnel, increasing efficiency and implementing organizational changes. This structural transformation has also brought increased investment in knowledge-intensive and high-technology production, the most successful manifestations being in mobile telephone equipment (Ericsson) and pharmaceuticals (ASTRA).

Denmark

Denmark entered the post-war period as a traditional major exporter of agricultural products, while industrial exports played a minor role. More than 60 per cent of Denmark's exports consisted of agricultural produce during the period 1946–49. Market conditions were extremely favourable, resulting in big increases of production and productivity in Danish agriculture. The terms of trade were likewise favourable during the 1940s, and this brought rising incomes.

During the 1950s these conditions changed because of the exclusion of agricultural products from the liberalization of international trade. Many countries protected their agriculture by means of high tariffs or other restrictions. This caused reduced demand for agricultural commodities in the international arena; prices fell and the terms of trade deteriorated. Wages went up and prices of farm implements rose, so that Danish farmers' incomes fell compared with other groups. This led to vociferous demands for public subsidies, which were introduced in 1958. Ten years later, in 1968, these subsidies accounted for 34 per cent of total agricultural incomes.

Because of these worsening market conditions Denmark tried to reduce its dependency on agricultural commodities by diversifying production, switching the emphasis to industry instead. However, the country lacked the requisite raw materials and capital for an industrial expansion. Danish industry was dependent on imported raw materials, and these imports had to be paid for with income either from agricultural exports or from export industries processing imported goods. Chronic problems associated with the balance of payments were thus generated, since the transfer of resources to the urban sector and the subsequent expansion of existing markets and creation of new ones for Danish industrial exports would necessarily take some time.

Theoretically, these problems relating to the balance of payments could be solved in two ways. One way was to adopt a restrictive economic policy aimed at controlling the balance of payments, where total domestic demand had to be reduced in order to keep imports down. But this would in turn mean dampened growth rates. The other way was to import foreign capital to cover the deficit and expand the industrial production apparatus.

In the 1950s the former alternative was applied and, as a result, economic growth in Denmark was lower this time than in most other European countries, with the exceptions of Belgium and the United Kingdom. On a number of occasions negative developments in the balance of payments triggered a contraction of economic policy, thus restraining growth. International price movements had negative effects during the Korean War and the Suez crisis. On both these occasions the repercussions were quickly felt in an economy which depended to a very high degree on imported raw materials and power. The stop–go policy pursued by the government caused economic growth to be irregular and rather slow. On the other hand net foreign debt was almost non-existent by the end of the 1950s.

In spite of the economics pursued, manufacturing production and exports increased in the 1950s, mainly light industries, and in 1960 exports of manufactured goods exceeded those of agricultural products. However, it was mainly small-scale firms that were generated.

From 1957 onwards the second alternative was applied to a greater degree and the government took a more active role in promoting foreign borrowing. Possibilities for financing an external deficit had broadened, and attitudes towards running a balance of payments deficit had changed too. The new approach was rationalized in terms of the need to accelerate the ongoing structural reorientation from agriculture to industry. This shift of policy resulted in a considerably higher growth rate than in the 1950s. But other factors were also important. The ranks of the unemployed as a result of the earlier slow growth rates, including migrants out of agriculture, supplied ample labour with which to lay the foundations of an investment boom, especially in the form of machinery and equipment, lasting from the late 1950s to the mid-1960s. Expansion began in the public sector, and in building and construction. These became the dominant factors in the continuance of high, though decreasing, growth rates. The public share of GDP around 1960 was the same as in other western European countries, but by the 1970s it was among the highest in Europe. The building boom showed the same characteristics as in Sweden, reflecting both a rapid increase in pent-up demand and substantial direct and indirect subsidies.

However, rising wages and a higher rate of inflation than in most competitor countries caused a steady deterioration after 1960 in international competitiveness.

The international recession triggered by the first OPEC shock in 1973 had very grave repercussions on the Danish economy, bringing a shift to high and protracted unemployment, with little or no growth. The oil price increases hit Denmark harder than many other countries because of the relatively large energy imports. In 1972 oil amounted to 94 per cent of all energy consumption in Denmark – the highest figure in western Europe. The collapse in house-building after 1973 and the rapid growth of the interest payments on foreign debts accentuated the economic problems. Accordingly Denmark was forced to abandon the Scandinavian model as early as 1974 in one important respect, namely the goal of full employment.

Income policy measures and devaluations of the currency were applied several times, but structural problems in the Danish economy precluded the possibility of returning to full employment. From 1973 to the beginning of the 1980s the Danish economy displayed low growth, high unemployment, low investment ratios, high inflation, recurrent balance of payment problems and stop–go policy. The only substantial recovery after 1973 occurred during a brief period of the 1980s but was halted in 1986 by another intolerable deterioration of the foreign debt position.

Since 1986 Denmark has managed to keep inflation down and maintain a balance on current account by adopting an economic policy of austerity, often called the 'potato cure'. However, at an average of 9.9 per cent over the last 10 years, unemployment has remained high, although economic growth has shown a tendency to rise in the most recent years.

Denmark joined the EEC along with the United Kingdom in 1973. One important reason was that during the 1960s agricultural exports from Denmark were restrained because Danish EFTA membership meant free trade only in industrial goods. It was hoped that an EEC membership would imply that Danish farmers would be able to compete successfully on the large EEC market. Success seems to have been achieved in this. Average growth in agriculture in the 1980s was higher than in the preceding decades.

Norway

The years immediately following the war can be regarded as a reconstruction phase in Norwegian economic development. During this period an expansive economic policy was introduced where full employment, low inflation and high investment ratios were the main goals. One recurrent problem in the Norwegian economy after the war has been the conflict between ambitious goals of full employment along with external balance on the one hand, and the need to hold the lid down on wages and costs on the other. In pursuit of the latter end, the government in this earlier period interfered extensively in wage negotiations. This interventionism, combined with the regulation of the credit supply, was on such a scale as to justify describing the Norwegian economy during this period as a partial command economy. It has been claimed that Norway had a more extensive and more detailed system of price controls than any other democratic country.

Plate 20.1. The Seaway Swan oil rig looming over traditional houses at Haugesund, Norway. From the 1970s onwards, oil production became a major sector in Norway's economy and an important source of government revenue.

The period 1952–73 can be characterized as a long and continuous boom, although the Norwegian growth rate was a little lower than the average for the OECD countries (Table 20.1). But unemployment rates too were somewhat lower than the OECD average. Heavy investments were made in capital-intensive branches such as shipbuilding and energy-intensive industries. Exports, especially shipping but also paper, chemicals and metallurgical products, functioned as the engine of growth during this period. Inflation was kept in check by an umbrella of price controls and quantitative regulations. Price-freeze was used no less than eight times from 1956 to 1975.

During this period Norway had some success in shifting its production and exports from primary products and raw materials to industrial goods and refined products. A new layer of medium-sized producers of more advanced means of consumption and production, such as electronics, developed. Fish and fish products continued to decline in relative terms, as did paper and pulp, while ore, metals and engineering products maintained their share of exports. Shipping was also an important source of export income, its share of the total being in the region of 40 per cent. However, in Norway the industrial structure and exports continued to be more dependent on capital-intensive heavy industry, which produced raw materials and semi-manufactures, than in other Scandinavian countries. One positive effect of this has been that employment has been quite insensitive to international trade cycles compared with countries where exports have been more dependent on labour-intensive industry. This is one important reason why fluctuations in employment in Norway after the war have been less accentuated than in most other western European countries.

The shift of emphasis to refined products was accomplished without any major problems relating to the balance of payments, thanks to high savings and investment ratios along with imports of foreign capital. Norwegian investment ratios have long been the highest in Scandinavia and among the highest in Europe and have continued to be so after the war. This has helped Norway to achieve a faster structural realignment of production, and of the economy at large, than the rest of Scandinavia. Stringent income and fiscal policies along with a high level of private and public savings have been important factors underlying the high investment ratios. However, Norway had lower growth during this period than could be expected considering the country's high investment ratios. It has been claimed that the quite low contribution to growth from investments had to do with special structural features in the Norwegian economy and the low rent monetary policy that was pursued.

Between 1952 and 1962 real wages were almost exclusively determined through labour–capital negotiations, where branchwise negotiations dominated in the 1950s, while the central organizations took over in the 1960s. As the Norwegian government's first priority was to avoid inflation, stalling excessive wage growth became crucial. Consequently, the government took an active part in central negotiations on several occasions in the 1960s and the 1970s. In spite of this, wage costs rose more than in most competitor countries, which worsened the Norwegian economy's competitiveness and resulted in a lower growth than the average for the OECD countries. Nevertheless the trade balance could be maintained partly through high export incomes from shipping.

Growth rates in most European countries were considerably lower after 1973 than before. In contrast to this, the growth rate in Norway continued at the same level as before, and since 1973 it has been considerably higher than the average for the OECD countries (Table 20.1). This higher growth rate can be attributed in large part to the growing importance of the oil sector. Oil was discovered off the Norwegian coast in 1969; production started in 1971 and has increased every year since then. The increase was especially vigorous during the latter half of the 1980s. Taxes and fees paid by the oil companies have formed a most important source of public revenue. In addition, the state became directly involved in oil production after 1985.

Just as in Sweden, 'bridging' measures were introduced to counter the effects of the slump after 1974. These measures included heavy state subsidies and loans to shipping and industry, but the revenues from oil facilitated the growing commitments from the state. Other consequences of oil were problems associated with higher price and wage increases than in other OECD countries, which forced the government to use price and wage freezes on several occasions in the 1970s and 1980s and also to devalue the Norwegian krone. Nevertheless the buoyant oil revenues have made it possible to stabilize the exchange rate and also to deregulate foreign exchange controls. The most important effect of the flow of money from the oil sector has perhaps been that Norway has been able to keep its economy in balance, thus avoiding the high unemployment rates which have characterized most European countries, including Denmark, since the mid-1970s and Sweden and Finland since the beginning of the 1990s.

Finland

Three special features characterized Finnish economic performance in the three decades following the Second World War.

The first was that Finland entered the post-war period burdened by heavy war reparations, which had to be paid to the Soviet Union in the form of metallurgical and engineering industrial goods. This forced Finland to increase its imports in order to meet its obligations to the Soviet Union. The immediate result was a chronic balance of payments problem which compelled Finland to devalue its currency three times in 1945, twice in 1949 and once in 1952, with further devaluations in 1957 and 1967. Thus Finland set forth early along the route of monetary accommodation. Deteriorating profitability was repeatedly countered by exchange rate adjustments. The Finnish markka was devalued no fewer than nine times between the end of the Second World War and 1973. As a result unemployment was kept relatively low, but the price paid was high inflation and low credibility of the exchange rate.

The mechanisms which usually came into play were these. In the short run devaluation would result in an improved trade balance and increased revenues for exporting firms. Private consumption would be forced back at the same time as investment in industry increased, bringing about a rise in employment. This in turn resulted in a new deterioration of the trade balance because of increased consumption and imports, eventually leading to a fall in employment. This pattern was repeated regularly, causing a constant conflict in economic policy between the aims of low unemployment and trade equilibrium. This conflict made it difficult to accomplish extensive structural change in the Finnish economy and was one important reason behind the strong annual variations in economic growth (see Figure 20.2).

The second special feature was the specific problems that Finnish agriculture had to solve after the war. More than 400,000 Finns were repatriated after the war, over half of them farmers. Many small farms were created with low productivity and had to be sheltered by a protectionist agricultural policy. In 1950 employment in agriculture amounted to 40 per cent of the total labour force. Labour and capital were thus tied up in a low-productivity sector, much more so than in other Scandinavian countries, and this hampered structural change and economic growth. In this way a large and relatively backward agricultural sector came to be highly protected and subsidized. By the 1980s these subsidies represented about three-quarters of value-added in the agricultural sector.

Thirdly, industry occupied a position in the economy differing from that which it enjoyed in other west European countries, chiefly because of its backwardness at the end of the war but also in that the structural transition of recent decades has been directly from agriculture to services. The share of GNP accounted for by industry never achieved the same dimensions as it did at its peak in Sweden. Thus an industrial sector which had limited possibilities of growth, in combination with a protected, low-productive agricultural sector, created a surplus of labour mainly in the form of underemployment. This surplus of labour resulted in a sizeable flow of emigrants to Sweden, especially in the 1960s and the beginning of the 1970s.

Post-war industrial growth in Finland was the same as the European average until the oil crisis of the 1970s, although the annual variations were considerably larger. Since the end of the 1970s, however, Finnish industry has grown faster than the European average. The fact that exports of manufactured products to the Soviet Union remained stable helped in this respect. At times of economic downturn in the West, Finland was able to continue eastward exports based on long-term trade agreements. Growth was sustained during the early part of the 1980s because the eastern trade made up for the weakness of demand for Finnish exports on the western market.

After a good economic performance during the first half of the 1980s with a lower unemployment rate than the OECD average, Finland experienced a very strong boom in the second half, resulting in overheating of the economy. Three factors contributed to this: financial market liberalization, a sharp worsening of the terms of trade, and an economic policy inadequately geared to resist overheating. The boom faded rapidly and ended in a crash, as in Sweden. The Finnish economy suffered an acute loss of momentum. GDP fell by 10 per cent, open unemployment reached a record high of 15 per cent by the end of 1992, and the Finnish markka depreciated by 35–40 per cent. International and domestic factors both contributed to these events. A slow-down of the international economy had serious repercussions on the Finnish economy, notably the collapse of Finnish trade with the centrally planned economies generally and with the former Soviet Union in particular. Nominal and real interest rates rose to extremely high levels which had a depressing effect on economic activity. A banking crisis loomed in 1991 and deepened in 1992. Consequently the national debt grew rapidly. All these factors forced Finland to adopt an economic policy of austerity and reconstruction even tougher than that in Sweden.

Historiographical Debate

In 1990 the tax–GDP ratio was 56 per cent in Sweden and 50 per cent in Denmark. These ratios were considerably higher than the OECD average. The question whether the high taxes have been an obstacle to economic growth has been a topic for an intensive political and scientific debate, especially in Sweden during the 1980s and 1990s.

Two empirical observations have been the point of departure for the more scientific debate.[3] First, Swedish economic growth has been lower than in other comparable countries, and secondly, the Swedish tax–GDP ratio has been higher than in these countries. It has then been argued that there exists a causal link between the two phenomena. The high tax–GDP ratio – which first and foremost can be attributed to the generous size of social security transfers (pensions, child allowances, sickness, parent and unemployment insurances, housing allowances, etc.) – has been seen as responsible for the decline in economic performance. The main argument put forward for this negative relation between taxes and growth has been that high taxes and tax wedges introduce undesired rigidities in the functioning of the labour market and reduce the labour supply. Accordingly, cuts in social transfer spending and corresponding lowering of taxes have been regarded as prerequisites for a return to the era of full employment and high economic growth that existed in Sweden in the 1950s and 1960s.

The first controversy in the debate has been if Sweden really has had a lower growth rate than other countries. The following are some of the issues that have been dealt with in this controversy. How should GDP and productivity be measured? Which difficulties in measuring growth have been caused by the index number problem? How can internationally comparable measures of production and productivity, especially in the public sector, be created? Should Sweden be compared to all OECD countries or just the highly industrialized countries? Which period should be taken into consideration? At the end of the day there seems to have emerged some kind of general agreement that Sweden has had a lower growth than comparable countries since 1970. However, the decline in growth cannot be interpreted to be as dramatic as was claimed by those who started the debate.

The second controversy has concerned the empirical evidence on the relation between growth and the tax–GDP ratio, where the evidence has been based on comparative macro-level data. In a review article Anthony Atkinson reports and comments on nine studies, where cross-section and time-series analysis of available OECD statistics for different countries have been used.[4] Two of the studies find an insignificant effect of social security transfers on annual growth rates, four studies find that the welfare state variable is negatively associated with average growth, and three studies find a positive relation. However, the calculated elasticities are small in all studies, and the general conclusion seems to be that there is no reliable international relation between growth and various indicators of taxation and the size of the public sector. In particular, two problems have been discussed in this context: first, the omitted variables problem, concerning discussions whether all relevant variables have been included in the models on which the econometric calculations have been based; and secondly, the causation problem, concerning whether the causation mainly runs from growth to the size of the public sector and not the other way round. It is also possible that an unknown factor has caused both growth to decline and social security transfers to increase.

The third controversy has been on theoretical issues and how the empirical results should be interpreted. Should we expect slower economic growth in rich countries due to 'catching-up', in which poorer countries usually embark on a catching-up process by applying modern techniques transferred from the richer and more advanced countries, while richer countries experience a slow-down in productivity due to the decline of the industrial sector? Or should we expect higher economic growth in the richer countries according to 'new growth theory', where investments in knowledge and education and in research and development are considered to be crucial for long-term economic growth and where, furthermore, the returns to these investments in human capital are assumed to be constant or even increasing? It should be pointed out that research with the aim of discriminating between the two competing hypotheses has recently begun.

Two general conclusions seem to have emerged from the debate. These conclusions can also be seen as points of departure for current research within the field. First, in order to understand the relationship between the welfare state and economic growth the theoretical framework has to be set out explicitly before more empirical work can be done. Secondly, the country-specific institutional structure of the welfare system has to be studied in more detail, from both an economic and a historical point of view, and then with a microeconomic approach.

Bibliographical Note

Most of the literature on Scandinavia's economic history since the war has been published in the Scandinavian languages. An overview of Sweden in English can be found in E. Dahmén, 'Sweden's economic development after the war', in L. Jonung and R. Ohlsson (eds), *The Economic History of Sweden since 1870* (Cheltenham, 1997); of Denmark in P. Pedersen, 'Postwar growth of the Danish economy', in N.F.R. Crafts and G. Toniolo (eds), *Economic Growth in Europe since 1945* (Cambridge, 1996); of Norway in F. Hodne, *The Norwegian Economy 1920–1980* (London and Canberra, 1983); and of Finland in R. Hjerppe, *The Finnish Economy 1860–1985* (Helsinki, 1989).

Notes

1. In *Essay on the Principle of Population* (second edition, 1803) Thomas Robert Malthus after visiting Sweden in 1799 commented on the situation in the country in the following way: 'The sallow looks and melancholy countenances of the peasants betrayed the unwholesomeness of their nourishment.'

2. G. Esping-Andersen, *The Three Worlds of Welfare Capitalism* (Cambridge, 1990), p. 28.

3. For an overview of the debate in English see the articles by Korpi, Henrekson, Agell and Dowrick in *The Economic Journal*, vol. 106 (1996), no. 439.

4. A.B. Atkinson, 'The welfare state and economic performance', *National Tax Journal*, vol. XLVIII (1995), no. 2.

21 Spain, 1939–96[1]

Jordi Catalan

Autarky and Failure in Reconstruction, 1939–50

Although Spain did not participate in the Second World War, its reconstruction process was the most unsuccessful in western Europe: Spanish GDP per capita remained below its pre-Civil War maximum (1929) until 1954. Only in Greece was economic recovery achieved at an even later date, but that country had experienced the most dramatic fall in activity of all during the international conflict and subsequently went through civil war.[2] While Spanish per capita output increased by 1.4 per cent on annual average during 1939–45, by the end of this period it was still well below its 1929 level. Hence Spain's economic performance during the war years compares unfavourably with that of neutrals such as Sweden, Switzerland or Portugal.

It could be tempting to attribute Spain's poor growth record to damage inflicted on the capital stock during the Civil War (1936–39). However, the extent of physical destruction was much less dramatic than that caused by the Second World War in France or Italy, for example. The central problem in Spain was not destruction but a low level of utilization of the existing productive capacity.

The Spanish pattern of slow recovery derived mainly from the interaction of four factors: a lack of raw materials, bottlenecks in the supply of energy, a fall in labour productivity and the negative effects of policy choices made by the early governments of General Francisco Franco. Those factors prevented full recovery not only during 1939–45, but also during 1945–50 when output growth decelerated even further (see Figure 21.1).

The scarcity of raw materials resulted, first of all, from the reduction in the volume of imports of goods such as cotton, scrap, leather, paper pulp, phosphates and nitrogenous fertilizers. Imports of raw materials remained below 60 per cent of the 1935 level throughout the forties, mainly because of a lack of foreign currency. The slow recovery of agriculture forced the authorities to devote scarce foreign exchange to importing food. Moreover, the new regime showed a clear preference for autarky and hostility to inflows of foreign capital. Finally, international resentment of Franco, due to his cordial attitude towards

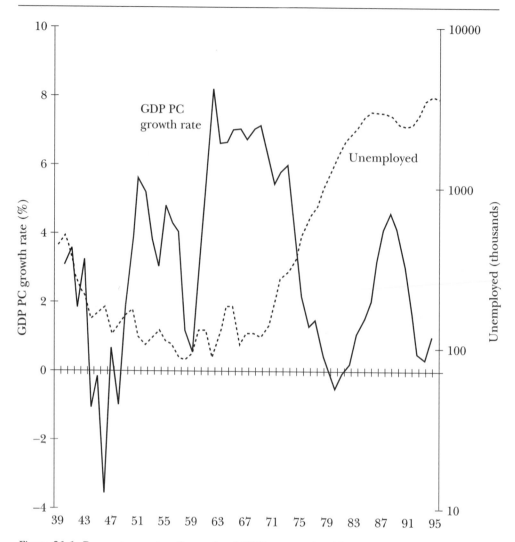

Figure 21.1. Percentage rate of growth of GDP per capita (three-year moving average) (solid line, left scale) and unemployment (dotted line, right scale), Spain, 1939–95. *Sources:* A. Maddison, *Monitoring the World Economy, 1820–1992* (Paris, 1995); INE, *Encuesta de Población Activa.*

the Axis powers, led to the closure of the French border in 1946 and Spain's exclusion from the Marshall Plan in 1947.

The problem of scarcity was aggravated by the system of resource allocation. Price controls and compulsory deliveries of agrarian products and raw materials remained in force until the fifties. Official agencies directly supplied basic inputs to firms. Allocation priority was given to those firms involved in projects related to the military, the recently created 'Instituto Nacional de Industria' (INI) and activities orientated towards self-sufficiency in case of war. Prices of official supplies were fixed far below the point of equilibrium and, as a result, black markets

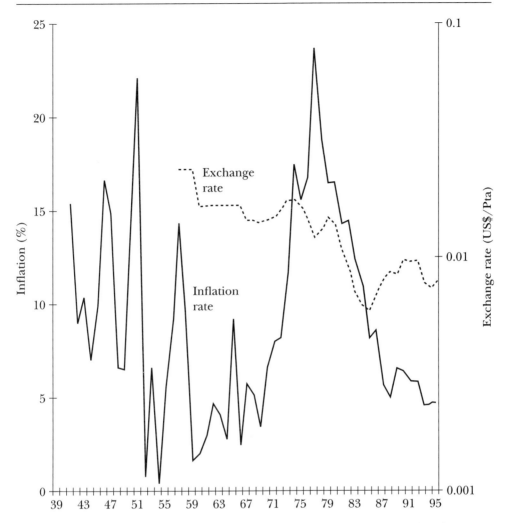

Figure 21.2. Percentage rate of inflation (solid line, left scale) and nominal exchange rate (U$/Pta) (dotted line, right scale), Spain, 1939–95. *Sources:* INE, *Anuario Estadístico;* OECD, *Historical Statistics.*

flourished. As late as 1949, black market prices of cotton and scrap in Barcelona, for example, were three times as high as official prices. Black market dealings, instead of production, became the main source of profit.

Low levels of imports of coke and fuels and their administrative allocation contributed to the stagnation in manufacturing and in the transportation system. In addition, electricity prices were frozen since 1939. Given the scarcity of other sources of energy, this meant that demand for power outstripped supply throughout the decade. The authorities' response was to ration the supply of electricity, i.e. to impose cuts. In 1949, for example, these were equivalent to as much as one-third the level of total demand for electricity.

Plate 21.1. Visit of Franco to the 'La Maquinista Terrestre y Maritima' factory in
Barcelona, 1947. Note the workers in the background, watching less than
enthusiastically.

The productivity of labour declined for several reasons. The human exodus
caused by the Civil War had decreased the stock of knowledge and technical skills
available. In addition, there were few incentives to intensify work because of the
permanent reduction in real wages: in 1950 the net real pay of labour remained
26 per cent below that of 1935. Finally, restrictions on imports of equipment
and a reduction in the relative cost of labour encouraged the use of less
capital-intensive techniques of production and entailed a decline in the degree
of mechanization. One positive outcome, though, was a fall in the number of
the unemployed from more than 670,000 in 1936 to about 160,000 in 1949 (see
Figure 21.1).

Misguided policy choices meant that production bottlenecks were more severe
and long-lasting than in the rest of western Europe. The Italian and German
experiences of the mid-1930s prevailed in the orientation of Spanish economic
and social policy. Direct allocation of inputs sacrificed consumer goods industries
in favour of those producing for the military and increasing self-sufficiency.
The Ministry of Labour fixed nominal wages and workers lost the right to strike.
Moreover, they were forced to join entrepreneurs in compulsory industry-unions.
INI was created in 1941 as the Spanish version of the Italian public holding IRI
and initially wasted precious resources in war-orientated projects. Foreign trade
remained under strict licensing and operated in bilateral terms, while foreign
exchange controls took an extreme form and were taken out of the hands of the

central bank. Although multiple exchange rates were introduced in 1948, the peseta became increasingly overvalued between 1939 and 1950.

During most of the 1940s, both monetary and fiscal policies were extremely expansionary. Throughout this period Spain ran large fiscal deficits which were financed mainly by money creation with highly inflationary consequences. In 1946, for instance, prices rose by as much as 17 per cent (see Figure 21.2). This contributed to a foreign exchange crisis which was handled with further import restrictions, an increase in interest rates and fiscal restraint. However, in 1950 Spain was the west European state devoting the largest share of its government budget to defence (32 per cent).

Acceleration of Growth and Instability, 1950–59

Compared to the previous period, economic growth accelerated sharply in the early 1950s. GDP per capita expanded at an annual rate of more than 5 per cent during 1950–55, that is seven times faster than in 1945–50. The change in performance was made possible by substantial increases in the supply of energy, a rise in imports of raw materials and efficiency gains in the allocation of resources.

In less than three years the production of electricity and imports of raw materials increased by more than 50 per cent. Power generating capacity expanded in response to the revision of prices and investments undertaken by INI firms. The substantial increase in imports derived from better export performance, the availability of new sources of finance and a partial change in the orientation of policies. The dollar value of Spanish exports increased about 40 per cent during 1950–53. On the demand side, impulses came first from the fast growth of German and French imports of Spanish agrarian products, and secondly from the Korean War which had a stimulating effect on the production of strategic raw materials. Moreover, the United States' attitude to Franco changed with the outbreak of hostilities in the Far East which, ultimately, led to the provision of American aid.

The change within the Francoist government in 1951 brought about the separation of the ministries of industry and commerce. The latter was headed by a reformer, Manuel Arburúa, who reduced price controls and the central allocation of goods and allowed larger imports of raw materials. Rationing and some direct controls were abolished, resulting in a transitory peak of inflation (22 per cent in 1951), but also in a noticeable increase in the supply of all kinds of goods. Agricultural prices were raised and so encouraged food production. Lower needs of food imports, in turn, allowed for an increase in imports of raw materials and contributed to industrial recovery.

The Spanish economy continued to grow rapidly up to 1959, when a stabilization programme was finally launched. Over the decade as a whole, per capita output expanded at a rate of 4.8 per cent per annum. The fastest rates of growth were recorded in the production of transport equipment, energy, chemicals and metal products. The most significant contribution to productivity and employment

In focus: The Stabilization Programme of 1959 – From Foreign-Exchange Crisis to Rapid Growth

In spite of the generous American help which Spain enjoyed during the fifties, its foreign reserves of gold and convertible exchange declined from 224 million dollars at the end of 1955 to about 54 million dollars in mid-1959. Spain had reached a situation of virtual foreign default. This led to the adoption of a radical programme of stabilization in July 1959.

The package was prepared by the Research Director of the Bank of Spain, Joan Sardà, under the supervision of the International Monetary Fund which Spain had joined in 1958. The programme included both stabilization measures and those orientated towards structural reforms. Its objectives were twofold: to reduce internal and external disequilibria by provoking a short-term contraction of aggregate demand and to promote growth in the medium to long term by changing the structure of economic incentives.

The first group of measures included monetary and fiscal restriction as well as devaluation. Fiscal measures included an increase in taxes on petrol and tobacco and in duties. Public expenditure was subject to drastic cuts in the remaining months of the year and was frozen during 1960.

Monetary restriction had to deal with the lack of adequate tools such as liquidity coefficients or open-market purchases. The alternative was to impose quantitative restrictions on credit growth. Upper credit limits were assigned to both public sector and private borrowers. In addition, the official rates of discount and interest were tightened. A compulsory deposit of 25 per cent of their value was imposed on imports. The government also suspended the emission of public debt that was automatically discountable at the central bank.

The remaining multiple-exchange rates were unified at a rate of 60 pesetas per dollar and the Spanish currency became convertible. Both measures aimed at alleviating the trade deficit and promoting a structural transformation of the foreign sector.

The government abolished quotas on the bulk of Spanish foreign trade. Liberalized imports were no longer subject to price administration and the direct assignation of raw materials was to end as well. Finally, a new law permitted foreigners to participate in Spanish firms with up to 50 per cent of the capital invested.

The stabilization programme of 1959 was a clear policy success. Its short-term objectives were achieved rapidly. The trade deficit declined substantially during the second half of 1959 and the current account showed a surplus by the end of the year. The wholesale price index rose by only 2 per cent between June 1959 and February 1960. Foreign reserves improved sharply, reaching 360 million dollars in May 1960. The programme also brought about a brief recession, but already in 1961 GDP per capita expanded again at a rate of almost 11 per cent.

growth came from the mechanical engineering industries, especially automobile production. Public firms created by the INI, such as SEAT and ENASA, accounted for the largest shares of production in their respective markets of cars and trucks.

The long-term acceleration of Spanish economic growth during the fifties can be explained by the low initial level of per capita income, the externalities generated by the development of the mechanical engineering industries, the performance of exports and the relatively large size of the domestic market which made import substitution a seemingly viable industrialization strategy. Nevertheless, the growth of exports remained below its potential. This was mainly a consequence of the persistence of severe restrictions on imports of raw materials and machinery for the production of consumer goods, the weak bargaining position of Spain in its main markets and the overvaluation of the peseta. The large trade deficit, around 300 million dollars per year during 1956–58, exhausted the foreign exchange reserves and forced a change of policy in 1959. The discrimination of industrial policy against consumer goods industries contributed to the poor relative performance of Spanish export products such as processed food, textiles and footwear. Moreover, non-membership of the OEEC made it more difficult for manufacturing exports to compete in the European markets whereas agricultural products were confronted with high protectionist barriers in the traditional French market.

The recovery of the early fifties brought about budget surpluses, but deficits reappeared during the second half of the decade. Inflation, which had fallen after 1951, accelerated again after 1955. A substantial loss of competitiveness occurred despite the government's downward adjustment of (multiple) exchange rates to compensate for rising inflation. The discount rate was increased in 1956 and a new government, which came into office the following year, modified the tax system in order to raise fiscal income. There was also an attempt to unify the exchange rate and further increases in interest rates were approved. However, the foreign disequilibrium remained so vast that more radical steps had to be taken in mid-1959.

Catching-Up and Stability, 1960–73

After the stabilization, *long-term* growth accelerated again (see Figure 21.1). During 1960–73, Spain's GDP per capita grew at the historically unprecedented annual rate of 7.4 per cent on average. One of the outcomes was significant catching-up with western Europe.

Some of those factors that accounted for growth during the previous decade made an even stronger impact during the 1960s. First, in 1960 the potential for catching up continued to be high because Spain's per capita income still reached only half of the western European average. Second, large private and public investments in mechanical engineering, chemicals and energy production led to substantial productivity growth. The mass consumption of automobiles, electrical appliances, plastics, new fibres and pharmaceutical products became, for the first time, a feature of the Spanish economy. Diffusion effects were substantial because these goods enjoyed a high elasticity of demand and increasing returns in production. Third, although the process of industrialization continued to be based on the domestic market, the new tariff law of 1960 implied a shift from a protectionist policy based on quotas to one based on duties. Such a move decreased discrimination against consumer goods industries and firms with weak links to the administration. Finally, exports performed the double role of increasing the import capacity and allowing efficiency gains through the realization of economies of scale.

However, while post-1959 economic policy was more conducive to stable growth than that pursued in the 1950s, Spain, as a Mediterranean country, also benefited from the rapid transformation of the world economy and particularly that of western Europe. Mass tourism rocketed, the number of foreign visitors to Spain climbing from four million in 1959 to 33 million in 1973. Moreover, during Europe's 'golden age' there was an increase in demand for foreign labour which offered new opportunities to surplus labour in Spain's most backward regions. Finally, the dynamic and relatively large domestic market together with the more liberal legislation on foreign investment encouraged transnational capital inflows. These developments helped preventing the reappearance of serious balance of payments problems.

The removal of barriers to imports of raw materials and capital goods together with the increasing availability of sources to finance them resulted in substantial modernization of manufacturing processes. Many firms producing consumer goods could renew their equipment for the first time since the 1930s. Thus the purchase of up-to-date foreign machinery allowed them to capture large productivity gains. In addition, exchange rate policy became more responsive to the needs of long-term development since 1959. A further devaluation took place in 1967, solving transitory imbalances in the foreign sector.

Spain also benefited from the reduction of American tariffs agreed in the GATT rounds and from the Preferential Agreement with the EEC signed in 1970. Between 1964 and 1973 the share of manufactured consumer goods rose from 12 to 27 per cent of total Spanish exports. The share of capital goods increased from 9 to 19 per cent while that of foodstuffs decreased from 53 to 29 per cent of exports. During this period, Spain left the club of primary-commodities exporters to join that of manufacturers.

Stagflation and Transition to Democracy, 1973–82

The country made its political transition to democracy immersed in a dramatic economic crisis. Franco died in 1975. The centre–right party of Adolfo Suárez (UCD) won the first democratic elections of 1977, when inflation rocketed to 24 per cent. Unemployment climbed steadily from 2 per cent of the working population in 1973 to 16 per cent in 1982. By that time, Spain had become the country with the highest level of unemployment in the OECD. The vigorous growth of the sixties had turned into long-lasting stagnation. Spain's GDP per capita grew by only 0.9 per cent per year during 1973–82, a rate significantly below the west European average, and the process of economic catching-up reversed. Three main features account for the particularly severe impact that the international oil crisis of 1973/74 and its aftermath (see Chapter 5) had on Spain: structural weaknesses in the industrial sector, mistakes in macroeconomic management and expectations of economic agents.

At least five structural deficiencies should be considered. First, in 1973 the relative size of industrial branches with weak demand prospects in the OECD markets remained significantly higher in Spain than elsewhere in western Europe. This was particularly the case in coalmining, shipbuilding, and the manufacture of steel, textiles and footwear.

Second, some capital-intensive activities had until then overexpanded due to negative real interest rates, far–reaching intervention in the financial system and preferential access to public funds. In particular, INI firms in the coal, steel, shipbuilding and fertilizer sectors suffered enormous and sustained loses throughout the seventies and eighties.

Third, although the previous period of rapid economic expansion favoured the re-emergence of an organized working class, the dictatorship always refused the setting of a new framework of industrial relations. An important opportunity was lost to create the basis of a regulatory system for the bargaining process between entrepreneurs and employees.

Fourth, Spain's technological dependency remained extremely high, mainly because of a lack of investment in human resources. For instance, in 1973 the rate of scientists, engineers and technicians engaged in research and development was only 3.3 per 10,000 inhabitants in Spain whereas comparable countries such as Italy and Ireland stayed above 10 per 10,000 inhabitants. Spanish public expenditure on education as a percentage of GNP was below 2 per cent, whereas the corresponding share in most European countries was above 4 per cent.[3]

Last but not least, at the time of Franco's death Spain stood out as the west European country with the lowest tax revenue out of GDP (see Figure 21.3). This constituted a fundamental barrier against the improvement of technical skills and the supply of public infrastructure. It also implied the underdevelopment of the Spanish welfare state. Finally, it made it difficult to use fiscal restraint as a tool of economic policy.

However, macroeconomic mismanagement since the first oil shock played a part as well. The authorities, with the *placet* of the International Monetary Fund, decided in 1974 to maintain a high level of demand by following expansionary fiscal and monetary policies and reducing domestic taxes on oil. This fostered price increases and delayed the adjustment in energy consumption. As a result, the inflation rate climbed from 9 per cent in 1972 to 17 per cent in 1974. Such a performance stimulated wage-earners' claims at a time when the dictatorship appeared particularly weak. The balance of payments deficit nearly tripled in two years and activity declined in export-orientated activities, a problem aggravated by the peseta's temporary appreciation against the US dollar in 1973–74.

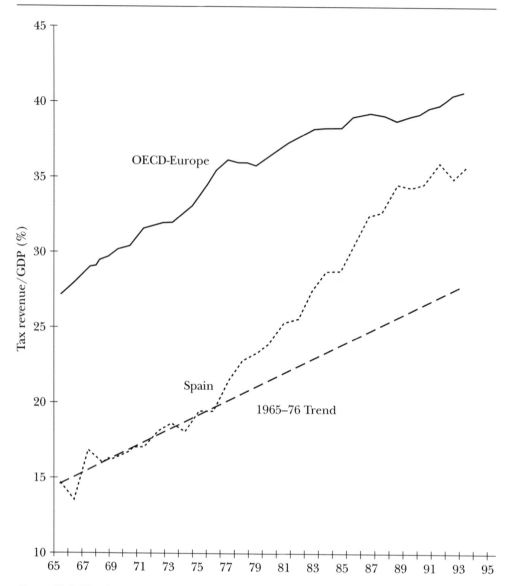

Figure 21.3. Total tax revenue as a percentage of GDP, Spain and OECD-Europe, 1965–95. *Source:* OECD, *Revenue Statistics.*

Although macroeconomic policies became more restrictive during the follow-ing two years and the peseta was allowed to depreciate in 1976, the only serious attempts to correct disequilibria were taken after the first democratic elections of June 1977. They were followed by a 20 per cent depreciation of the exchange rate in July and the signing of the so-called Moncloa Pacts in autumn. The agreement between the government and the main political parties looked at promoting wage moderation in exchange for political and economic reforms. This programme resulted in a successful reduction of the foreign imbalance and

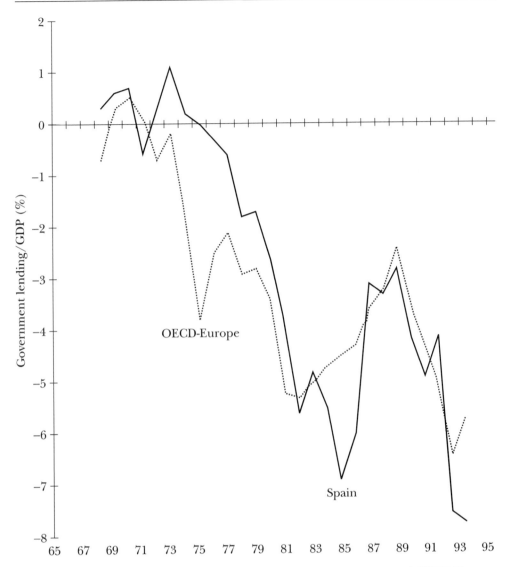

Figure 21.4. Net government lending as a percentage of GDP, Spain and OECD-Europe, 1965–95. *Source:* OECD, *Historical Statistics.*

inflation (see Figure 21.2). It also implied a fiscal reform which led the level of tax revenue in Spain to converge with that elsewhere in western Europe (see Figure 21.3). Nevertheless, the severe monetary restriction between the last months of 1977 and mid-1978 was associated with a sharp rise in interest rates, leading to widespread defaults of firms and a sharp contraction of real investment.

After 1978 macroeconomic policy was based on restrictive monetary and income policies and expansionary fiscal policy. The public deficit climbed from 0.6 per cent of GDP in 1977 to 5.6 per cent in 1982 (see Figure 21.4). Real interest rates became positive. The number of private defaults went on increasing,

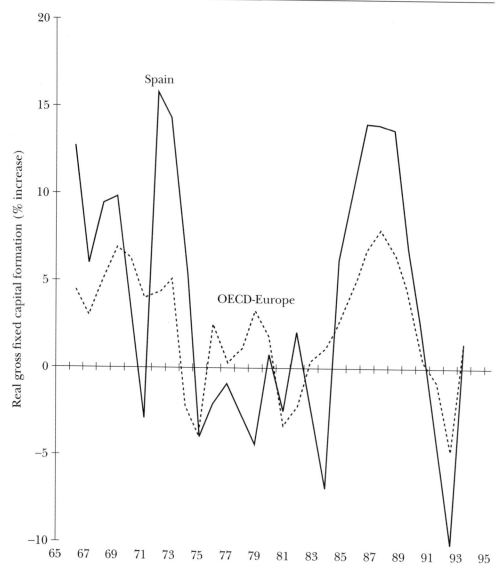

Figure 21.5. Percentage increase in real gross fixed capital formation, Spain and OECD-Europe, 1965–95. *Source:* OECD, *Historical Statistics.*

crowding-out took place and capital formation continued to decline (see Figure 21.5). Compared to most of western Europe, the second oil shock of 1979 was more painful because of the insufficiency of previous price-policy and energy-saving measures.

However, an important part of the fall in investment derived from the attitude of many employers who missed a world without legal unions. Moreover, after the first oil crisis, workers tried to shift the burden of adjustment to entrepreneurs by pushing wages up, whereas the latter aimed at achieving the opposite by increasing prices. At the same time, negative interest rates encouraged the rise in firms' indebtedness. However, since 1977, when a restrictive monetary policy was adopted, such a strategy appeared fruitless and the subsequent bankruptcies worsened expectations even further. The second jump in oil prices (1979), the attempted military coup in 1981 and the increasing difficulties of some financial institutions had a negative effect on investment decisions.

Restrictive fiscal policy might be thought of as a less painful alternative to cope with inflation, but such an option had few chances given the expectations that were associated with the transition to democracy. The working class expected the extension of welfare benefits, so there was little room for decreasing public expenditure. On the contrary, between 1977 and 1982 public sector outlays rose from less than 23 to more than 32 per cent of GDP. This increase was partly facilitated by the fiscal reform of minister Francisco Fernández Ordóñez, which resulted in a change in tax revenue trends from 1977 on (see Figure 21.3). Nevertheless, this was not enough to prevent the rapid growth of the public deficit (see Figure 21.4). However, the process not only reflected increasing social expenditure but also growing subsidies to large firms, both public and private, which were accumulating enormous losses.

Social-Democratic Recovery and Integration in the European Community, 1982–96

The administration of Prime Minister Felipe González and the Spanish social-ist party, PSOE, took over in December 1982 and lasted until April 1996. The inflation rate, which still remained at 14 per cent in 1982, declined to 5 per cent in 1995 while unemployment rose from 16 to 23 per cent of the working population. GDP per capita expanded at an average of 2.4 per cent per year during 1982–95, i.e. at a rate two and a half times that for 1973–82.

In terms of economic growth, the socialist era in Spain went through three very distinct phases. Up to 1985 per capita income increased by a modest 1.5 per cent per year. During the following five years, though, the economy experienced a boom with an average rate of expansion above 4 per cent, only to slow down again during 1991–95, with a recession reaching its nadir in 1993 (see Figure 21.1).

During the first phase (1982–85), the new administration had to deal with further reductions in private investment (see Figure 21.5). The government refused to adopt expansionary policies and nationalizations, being aware of the failure of such a strategy in Mitterrand's France. Priorities focused instead on the fight against internal and external disequilibria, the restructuring of the industrial sector, the preparation of accession to the European Community and the change in the composition of public expenditure.

A moderate depreciation of the currency in December 1982 contributed to halving the balance of payments deficit during the following year. The policy against inflation led to a severe control of money supply growth and, ultimately, the 1983 and 1985 agreements between unions and employers on wage restraint.

In spite of rapidly growing unemployment, the rise in the public deficit was relatively modest while inflation decreased markedly from 14 to 9 per cent (see Figures 21.1, 21.2 and 21.4).

The pressing issue of industrial restructuring was addressed in a new law (1984) which aimed at reducing excess capacity in industry and provided public funds in exchange for adjustment. As a result, many firms in various industrial sectors returned to being profitable again around 1985. However, steelworks and ship-yards, which absorbed around two-thirds of public subsidies, continued to run enormous losses. Another means to foster restructuring was the privatization of public firms controlled by INI which began in 1985. Initially, the most important sale was that of the car producer SEAT to Volkswagen, but the programme also included public firms in electronics, textiles, car equipment, food processing, chemicals and petrochemicals, papermaking, aluminium, tourism and banks.

Spain's accession to the European Community in 1986 opened a period of rapid growth up to 1990 which was encouraged by cheaper imports and a rush of foreign investment. Domestic firms took the opportunity to modernize their equipment and, as a result, obtained substantial gains in efficiency. During 1985–88, inflation fell from 9 to 5 per cent and the rate of unemployment decreased from 22 to 19 per cent. While inflation picked up again during the last two years of the boom, unemployment continued to fall until 1990. The international recovery, the fall in oil prices and the liberalization of housing rents also contrib-uted to the upswing. However, the previous trade surplus with the Community turned into a deficit after 1985. The surge in imports, which was not compens-ated for by a sufficient increase in exports, revealed a loss of comparative advant-age in some branches of industry such as textiles and footwear, food processing, woodworking, paper and printing, plastics and transport equipment.

Membership in the European Union created by and large favourable con-ditions for Spain's convergence to the productivity levels of her trade partners. This process of convergence, though, was temporarily interrupted during the recession in 1991–94. The severity of this downturn was partly an outcome of policy decisions made in the late 1980s and early 1990s. Liberalization of rents and large tax allowances for investment in housing fostered real-estate specula-tion in the second half of the 1980s. In spite of already rapid growth, fiscal policy became even more expansive after 1987. Yet monetary policy remained restrictive as real interest rates were maintained at historically high levels. This contributed to attracting more foreign capital than ever with the final result of the overvaluation of the peseta. In June 1989 Spain joined the European Monetary System with an over-optimistic parity and up to 1992 the government was prepared to sacrifice any other economic objective to maintain it. The overvaluation of the domestic currency made Spanish exports relatively more expensive and imports relatively cheaper and, therefore, explains at least part of the mounting trade deficit be-tween 1987 and 1991. Although the recent adoption of value-added tax had helped initially in alleviating public finance problems, the sharp increase in public spend-ing associated with the forthcoming 1992 celebrations raised the budget deficit from 3.1 per cent of GDP in 1987 to 4.9 per cent in 1991 (see Figure 21.4).

The peseta collapsed some weeks after the Olympic Games of Barcelona and before the International Exhibition of Seville had closed its doors. Between September 1992 and March 1995, the rate of exchange and its bands of fluctuation were revised five times. In addition, the government was forced to adopt fiscal restraint during the recession, which meant a further check to the already sluggish growth of aggregate demand. Partly as a result, unemployment reached its climax in 1994 at more than 24 per cent. The budget deficit continued to rise despite the attempts to curtail public expenditure. At the beginning of 1996, Spain did not fulfil any of the Maastricht criteria for membership in the planned European Monetary Union.

Nevertheless, the long-term benefits of 13 years of social-democratic government seem to outweigh the costs. In terms of income and productivity levels, Spain was gradually catching up with other countries in the European Union. The shares of education and welfare in the budget rose significantly, whereas those of defence and capital transfers decreased (see Figure 21.6). The rate of staff in research and development went above 10 per 10,000 inhabitants for the first time. Social security contributions lost in importance as a means of public finance, while the opposite holds for taxes on income, property and corporate profits. The country finally joined the European club and consolidated its democracy. In 1993 Spain enjoyed the tenth position in the ranking of the United Nations' Human Development Index.[4]

Debates and Interpretations

The economic performance of Spain since 1945 appears as a long-lasting attempt to recover the relative income levels reached before the Civil War. According to Maddison's data, Spanish GDP per capita accounted for 72 per cent of the west European average in 1932. In the early nineties, Spain still had not exceeded this level (see Table 21.1).

Although there is a rather wide consensus among Spanish scholars over the adverse consequences of post-Civil War economic and social policies, the reasons for the choices made remain controversial. Three main interpretations can be found in the literature. Some authors argue that autarky and extreme intervention were the final outcome of a process of inward-looking development which began with the move to extreme protectionism in 1891. A second group of scholars maintain that they resulted from the adverse external circumstances brought about by the Second World War and the unexpected isolation of Franco's regime during the second half of the forties. The third group sees the pattern of reconstruction of the Spanish economy as a consequence of deliberately following policies in line with the German and Italian totalitarian examples.

There is much evidence indicating that, in fact, early Francoist policy choices were strongly influenced by the attempts of Nazi Germany and Fascist Italy to centralize the economic system, discipline labour, encourage heavy industry and prepare for war. If this is true, it is misleading to identify the post-war pattern of

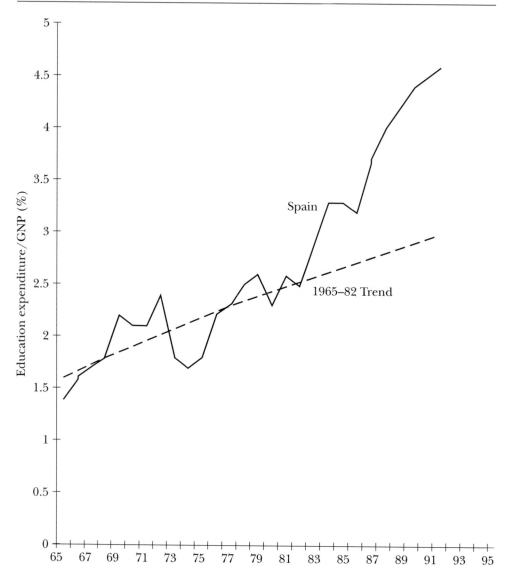

Figure 21.6. Public expenditure on education as a percentage of GNP, Spain, 1965–95.
Source: UNESCO, *Statistical Yearbook.*

Spain's reconstruction as a typical case of industrialization led by import substitution. Post-war Spain moved far away from pre-Civil War protectionism and became something similar to a war economy. Military priorities and administrative allocation of resources distorted the economic incentive structure. This situation lasted for more than two decades and produced a fundamental change in the nature of Spanish capitalism. Whereas the successful pre-war entrepreneur made his profits mainly from innovation in the production sphere, the post-war capitalist derived his income from black-market speculation and preferential access to

Table 21.1. Long-term economic growth in Spain and western Europe, 1914–92

	GDP per capita (1990 G–K dollars)		Rate of growth (%)		Relative GDP per capita (%)
	Spain	W. Europe	Spain	W. Europe	Spain/W. Europe
1914	2,255	3,704	–	–	60.9
1932	2,772	3,851	1.1	0.2	72.0
1950	2,397	5,123	−0.8	1.6	46.8
1962	4,125	8,271	4.6	4.1	49.9
1973	8,739	12,288	7.1	3.7	71.1
1983	9,601	14,474	0.9	1.5	66.3
1992	12,498	17,384	3.0	2.1	71.9

Note: GDP per capita in 1990 Geary–Khamis Dollars. These are dollars of parity of purchasing power. The method corrects the underestimation of GDP of poor countries derived from the use of market exchange rates in international comparisons.

Source: Maddison, *Monitoring the World Economy.*

rationed inputs, machinery and foreign exchange. The reduction in real labour cost resulted in a trend towards full employment, but also led to the adoption of techniques with low level of mechanization.

The sixties can be seen as a partial return to the pre-Civil War economic policies. Protection was now mainly exerted through tariffs, and firms no longer faced quantitative restrictions on imports of raw materials and equipment. A realistic parity of the peseta helped prevent bottlenecks derived from foreign imbalances. The public sector was financed in a non-inflationary way and public firms in some branches such as automobiles and energy made a positive contribution to technological change. Indicative planning, although ineffective, did not significantly interfere in the expansion of the private sector.

Such a change of policies encouraged the process of catching up with other European economies. The potential for catching up was very large because of the low point of departure in 1959. At that time, many firms were operating with an outdated capital stock that was last renewed during the pre-Civil War industrial upsurge. The removal of import restrictions after 1959 allowed for rapid modernization of the machinery and equipment used in Spain's industrial sector, greatly enhancing productivity. Within a framework of high tariff protection, structural transformation of Spanish industry took place and some manufacturing branches such as footwear and transport equipment were able to develop comparative advantages in the world market.

However, the very success of the 1960s and early 1970s meant that reforms of the tax and financial systems, labour relations, education and the public industrial sector were delayed. The process of liberalization of foreign trade also lost momentum. No significant step was made towards political democratization. The postponement of such changes at a time of rapid growth made their implementation more painful during the 1973–85 crisis. The interruption of vital reforms during 1965–76 was partially responsible for the new phase of economic divergence from western Europe which lasted up to 1985. Nevertheless, the severity of the economic crisis and the intensity of social demands to extend the welfare state forced the resumption of reforms after 1977. These were completed during the eighties by the PSOE administration. However, while Spain after 1985 recovered some of the ground lost in terms of output and productivity growth relative to other western European countries, the high level of unemployment remained a major economic, social and political problem.

Economists give four different explanations for Spain's top position in the European unemployment rank: real wages, institutions, structure and macroeconomic management.

To begin with classical interpretations, unemployment is often considered as a result of excessive wage demands. The historical evidence indicates that, in the mid-seventies, a real wage explosion took place, causing a profit squeeze and a loss of jobs, particularly in some labour-intensive branches in which Spain used to have a comparative advantage. On the other hand, empirical data also suggest that since the late seventies labour costs per unit of output have tended to decrease steadily without inducing a corresponding increase in employment.

Spain inherited from Francoism a labour market with permanent labour contracts, severe restrictions on dismissals and relatively heavy employers' contributions to social security. In addition, subsequent democratic administrations extended unemployment benefits. Such an institutional framework could have resulted in a reluctance to hire labour and low incentives to seek jobs. The evidence of recent years suggests, however, that although labour market flexibility increased markedly and firms' relative social security contributions decreased, this did not lead to a significant reduction of long-term unemployment. It is also true that, to some extent, Spanish unemployment has institutional origins. This is especially the case in southern Spain where particularly advantageous subsidies to agrarian workers slowed down the traditional outflow of surplus labour.

The structural interpretation of Spanish unemployment sees it as a result both of the initial pattern of specialization of the Spanish productive system in 1973 and of the rapid rise of labour productivity. In fact, Spanish growth since the sixties is better explained by the contribution of increases in productivity than by capital and labour accumulation. Since the mid-seventies the rapid rise in productivity within a framework of slow growth of GDP has resulted in increasing levels of unemployment. In addition, counter-factual analysis indicates that, given the structure of Spanish employment in 1973 and assuming a sectorial evolution of productivity within the European average, current unemployment should be even higher, mainly because of the large initial supply of agrarian labour.

Finally, Keynesian economists focus their attention on the evolution of expectations that govern investment and on mistakes in macroeconomic policy. Much of the present unemployment derived, first, from the low levels of confidence of entrepreneurs during 1973–84 and, secondly, from the impact of restrictive monetary policies which aimed at controlling inflation. In addition, during the late eighties budgetary policy was pro-cyclical. This meant that the economy received further stimuli when it was already overheating, while fiscal restraint was imposed during recessions, thus worsening the employment situation. At the same time, the overvaluation of the currency implied a loss of foreign demand for Spanish goods and so reduced the scope for job creation.

Both structural and Keynesian approaches agree on the existence of involuntary unemployment as a result of sluggish demand for labour. The dramatic rise in redundancies during 1992–94 suggests that, in fact, a large part of Spanish unemployment is not voluntary.

Bibliographical Note

The main surveys in English, covering substantial parts of the period under consideration, are the following: J. Fontana and J. Nadal, 'Spain 1914–1970', in C. Cipolla (ed.), *The Fontana Economic History of Europe*, Vol. 6 (Glasgow, 1976); E. Merigó, 'Spain', in A. Boltho (ed.), *The European Economy: Growth and Crisis* (Oxford, 1982); J. Harrison, *The Spanish Economy: From the Civil War to the European Community* (London, 1993); and L. Prados and J. Sanz, 'Growth and macroeconomic performance in Spain, 1939–1993', in N. Crafts and G. Toniolo (eds), *Economic Growth in Europe since 1945* (Cambridge, 1996). It is also worth taking into account the articles reprinted in P. Martín-Aceña and J. Simpson (eds), *The Economic Development of Spain since 1870* (London, 1995).

The basic books in Spanish are: J. Muns, *Historia de las relaciones entre España y el F.M.I. 1958–1982* (Madrid, 1986); J. Nadal, A. Carreras and C. Sudrià (eds), *La economía española en el siglo XX: Una perspectiva histórica* (Barcelona, 1987); J.L. García Delgado (ed.), *Economía española de la transición y la democracia* (Madrid, 1990); L. Prados and V. Zamagni (eds), *El desarrollo económico en la Europa del Sur: España e Italia en perspectiva histórica* (Madrid, 1992); A. Argandoña and J.A. García-Durán, *Macroeconomía española: Hechos e ideas* (Madrid, 1992); J. Catalan, *La economía española y la segunda guerra mundial* (Barcelona, 1995); R. Marimón (ed.), *La economía española: Una visión diferente* (Barcelona, 1996); and O. De Juan, J. Roca and L. Toharia, *El desempleo en España: Tres ensayos críticos* (Cuenca, 1996).

Notes

1. The author thanks the Spanish Ministry of Education for its financial support through the project grant PB94–0853.

2. A. Maddison, *Monitoring the World Economy, 1820–1992* (Paris, 1995).

3. See UNESCO, *Statistical Yearbook* (Louvain, various years).

4. See United Nations Development Programme, *Human Development Report 1996* (New York, 1996).

22 Conclusion: The Post-War European Economy in Long-Term Perspective

Max-Stephan Schulze

After five decades of almost uninterrupted economic growth, Western Europeans at the end of the twentieth century enjoy per capita incomes that are about three and a half times as high as they were in 1950. Moreover, the income gap between 'rich' and 'poor' countries in western Europe is now much smaller than it was then. This rise in material welfare was associated with increasing integration and interdependence of the European economies with each other and with the rest of the world.

However, post-1945 growth was part of a process with origins stretching back into the eighteenth century. Similarly, 'economic integration', which features so prominently in current debates, is not a phenomenon confined to the late twentieth century. Again, there is ample evidence of progressive cross-border economic integration taking place from the early nineteenth century onwards. Yet the long-run processes of economic growth and integration were subject to massive shocks such as the two world wars and the Great Depression. The discussion in this concluding chapter, therefore, serves to place western Europe's economic development since 1945 in its broader historical context.

Economic Growth and Convergence

By the last quarter of the nineteenth century, almost all European economies were in the throes of a process which Simon Kuznets identified as 'modern economic growth'.[1] That is, they were experiencing high rates of growth in output and population and, most importantly, a *sustained*, irreversible rise in output *per person*. Growth became sustained once the upward trend in economic activity was

Table 22.1. Employment structure in western Europe (per cent of total)

	Agriculture	Industry	Services
1870[a]	50.0	26.5	23.5
1950	24.7	38.1	37.2
1973	9.7	38.5	51.8
1987	6.1	31.3	62.6

[a]Excluding Denmark and Switzerland.

Note: The data are unweighted averages for 12 countries (Austria, Belgium, Denmark, Finland, France, Germany, Italy, Netherlands, Norway, Sweden, Switzerland, United Kingdom; all adjusted for boundary changes).

Source: A. Maddison, *Dynamic Forces in Capitalist Development* (Oxford, 1991).

no longer 'overpowered' by the impact of short-run fluctuations. The proximate source of this expansion has been the rise in labour productivity which, in turn, was based on technological innovations, on major breakthroughs in human knowledge.

However, advancing technology is only a permissive source of economic growth, a necessary condition. Its effective exploitation depended on the ability to implement institutional and ideological adjustments needed to accomodate change. Modern economic growth involved a high rate of structural transformation in the societies where it occurred. This included, for instance, a shift of resources from agriculture into non-agricultural sectors such as manufacturing and services, an increasing scale of production and a rise in impersonal forms of business organization, rapid urbanization and secularization. Table 22.1 demonstrates the extent of structural change since 1870. Once dominated by agriculture, the European economy today is characterized by high shares of service sector employment (see Chapter 6).

Another major element of modern economic growth is its international dimension. During the early nineteenth century, modern economic growth had spread from Britain, where its essential features were already present in the eighteenth century, to Belgium, France, Switzerland and the western regions of Germany. Interregional commodity and factor flows constituted the transmission mechanism through which growth impulses were diffused further in a broadly easterly and southerly direction across the European Continent.

Over the last 130 years, western Europe's real GDP has increased at an average rate of 2.3 per cent per annum, or about 1.7 per cent when measured in per capita terms (Table 22.2). Taking these rates as indications of the secular trend, one can readily see that during certain sub-periods the European economy diverged markedly from its long term growth path. Two such sub-periods stand out: First, the years from the outbreak of the First World War to the immediate aftermath of the Second World War (1913–50), during which on every measure the European economy under-performed relative to the long term trend and compared to the previous four decades. Second, the post-Second World War period

Table 22.2. Growth in western Europe, 1870–1994 (per cent per annum)

	Real GDP	Population	Real GDP per capita	Real GDP per hour worked	Export volume
1870–1994	2.3	0.6	1.7	2.2[a]	3.3[a]
1870–1913	2.1	0.7	1.3	1.6	3.2
1913–1950	1.4	0.5	0.9	1.3	–0.1
1950–1973	4.7	0.8	3.9	4.8	8.4
1973–1994	2.1	0.4	1.7	2.4[b]	4.1[b]

[a]1870–1992 [b]1973–1992

Note: GDP, population, hours worked and exports are aggregates for the 12 European countries listed in Table 22.1.

Sources: A. Maddison, *Monitoring the World Economy, 1820–1992* (Paris, 1995); own output estimates for Austria 1870 to 1913. For 1950 to 1992 data for hours worked have been amended, using N.F.R. Crafts, 'The Human Development Index and changes in the standard of living: some historical comparisons', *European Review of Economic History* 1 (1997).

up to 1973 when aggregate output, income per head and labour productivity rose at, historically, unprecedentedly high rates.

The causes and main characteristics of Europe's economic expansion during the 1950s and 1960s are explored in greater detail in Chapter 4. Here it suffices to say that the marked widening in the technological and productivity gap separating the European and US economies by the end of the Second World War created the scope for rapid catch-up growth in Europe. In comparison with this period of exceptionally rapid expansion, the European economy appears to have performed poorly since. Not only has the rate of income and productivity growth nearly halved, but Europe is now struggling with high levels of unemployment (see Chapter 5). However, when placed in long-term perspective, the post-1973 period looks markedly better than the comparison with the 'Golden Age' alone would suggest. First, at 1.7 per cent on annual average, the rate of per capita output growth was on a par with the secular trend rate and well above the rates of expansion achieved in the late nineteenth century. Second, this holds true even if comparison is made with the particularly dynamic increase in economic activity during the *belle époque* of the international economy between about 1890 and the outbreak of the First World War.[2] Third, in terms of labour productivity growth, or changes in GDP per hour worked, the late twentieth century European economy was still doing well, surpassing by far the rates achieved before 1914 and, even more so, those prevalent during the inter-war years.

It has been pointed out in Chapter 4 that, in general, there was a strong *inverse* (or negative) correlation between the initial level of per capita and an economy's subsequent growth performance during the Great Boom. This inverse relationship is at the heart of the concept of poor economies *catching-up* with rich economies. The scatter plots of per capita GDP against growth presented in Figure 22.1

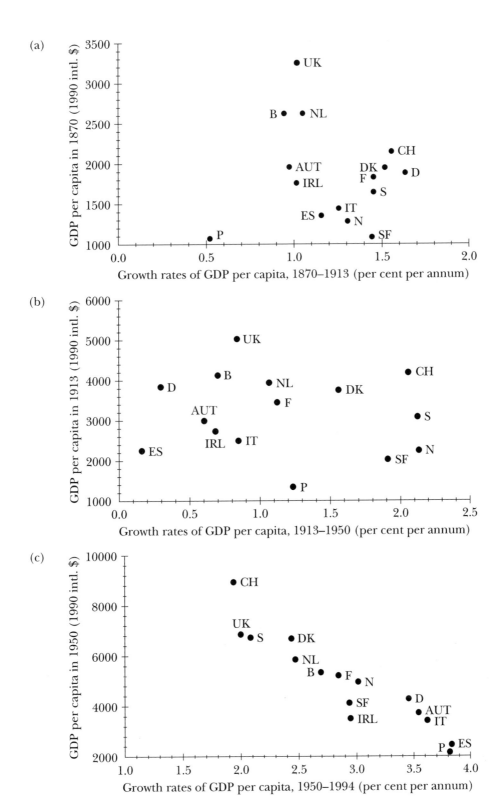

Figure 22.1. Levels and growth rates of GDP per capita.

show that, compared to the second half of the twentieth century, this association was markedly weaker between 1870 and 1913 and virtually absent in the inter-war years. If there were a strong inverse correlation, this should show in a graph that, broadly, depicts income-growth combinations clustering around an imaginary line that falls from the upper left hand corner to the lower right hand corner of the diagram. This is the case only for the post-1945 data.

The graph would therefore suggest that, without further qualifications, the initial level of productivity as such is not necessarily a good predictor of subsequent growth. While, in principle, being low down the productivity 'league' leaves an individual economy with greater scope for catch-up growth, the ability to exploit this scope varies markedly between economies and over time. The most extreme case for the late nineteenth century seems to be that of Portugal. In terms of per capita GDP, she was the poorest of the 15 west European economies surveyed here; yet the Portugese economy also had the lowest rate of growth up to 1913.

Other economies, too, did not expand at rates that were broadly commensurate with their relative income or productivity position. Think, for instance, about Austria's growth, which failed to keep pace with the expansion achieved in economies such as Denmark, France and Germany, all of whom had similar per capita income levels in 1870. Or Switzerland, on the other hand, which achieved high rates of growth from a relatively high initial income level. This is not the place to go into the details of what exactly accounts for the diverging performances of countries. The main point here is that country-specific factors such as institutions, skill and educational attainment levels, the policies pursued by governments, or the degree of openness to international trade, to name only a few such factors, matter. Varying 'social capabilities' for growth and catch-up, to use Abramovitz's well known term, disturb the simple correlation between initial productivity levels and subsequent growth across a range of individual economies.[3]

During the late nineteenth century, growth rates of per capita income and labour productivity in different European countries varied within a relatively small range. This was to change dramatically during the years from 1913 to 1950. Two world wars and the inter-war depression had different effects on individual economies which, moreover, responded in different ways to these massive shocks. Not only was overall income and productivity growth markedly slower than during 1870–1913 (see Table 22.2), but the divergence between different economies in terms of their growth rates increased greatly (Figure 22.1). Moreover, the growth gap between the economy which expanded most rapidly and that which grew most slowly over the period 1913–50 was much wider than during the late nineteenth century. Though the post-Second World War period would see a return to a much smaller degree of growth variation among the European countries, it is noticeable that variation has remained slightly higher than it was prior to 1913. To some extent that may be an outcome of some economies being able to exploit their catch-up potential only after the end of the Second World War.

The economic disintegration that started with the outbreak of the First World War broke up many of the national structures and international economic rela-

Table 22.3. Coefficients of variation

	Real GDP per capita		Real GDP per hour worked	
	12 countries	15 countries	12 countries	15 countries
1870	0.308	0.325	0.344	–
1913	0.257	0.313	0.267	–
1929	0.252	0.324	0.278	–
1938	0.211	0.322	0.218	–
1950	0.289	0.375	0.273	0.350
1973	0.165	0.234	0.136	0.203
1994	0.091	0.165	0.120	0.180

Note: Data refer to 12 countries as in Table 22.1; '15 countries' includes, in addition, Ireland, Portugal and Spain.

Sources: See Table 22.2.

tionships that had permitted the cross-border diffusion of growth impulses in the late nineteenth century. As a result, the already far from perfect inverse correlation between initial productivity levels and subseqent productivity growth declined even further in the 1920s, 1930s and 1940s. Hence there were not only country specific, but also period or time specific factors at work: the conditions prevalent in the inter-war years were not conducive to facilitating catch-up, as initial differentials in productivity had even less bearing on the rates of growth than before 1913. This development was reversed only afer the end of the Second World War.

The question that now arises is: was the long-run process of economic growth associated with *convergence*, that is, did the gap between rich countries and poor countries in Europe decline over time (at least in percentage terms)? To achieve this, initially poorer economies must grow faster than richer ones.[4] Here we shall look again at GDP per capita and also GDP per hour worked as measures of economic activity.

Convergence as defined above implies a consistent diminution of variance in per capita income or productivity among individual economies. The coefficient of variation is a measure that allows us to check whether average incomes or labour productivity in Europe have 'converged' over time. The greater the coefficient of variation, the greater the extent of dispersion or variance. Thus, convergence should be reflected in a decline of the coeffcient of variation over time.[5]

Unfortunately, the evidence is less conclusive than one would wish for (see Table 22.3). Looking at the 12 countries sample only, four observations on the dispersion in *levels* of per capita income and labour productivity among European countries can be made: first, between 1870 and 1913, dispersion gradually declined; second, the First World War and its aftermath interrupted this process, though by the late 1930s it had resumed again; third, as an outcome of the war, income and productivity levels in the immediate post-Second World War years had dispersed again. Furthermore, the ratio between the highest and the lowest per capita incomes declined between 1870 and 1913, had risen slightly again by 1950 and fell rapidly thereafter, especially up to the early 1970s.

However, the picture looks less clear cut if a larger number of countries is examined. Adding Ireland, Portugal and Spain, for instance, leads to the conclusion that there was no convergence in the levels of per capita incomes in western Europe before 1950. In fact, the degree of income dispersion in 1950 was higher than in 1870! Apart from a temporary dip in the 1930s, the ratio between the highest and the lowest per capita incomes in western Europe actually rose to a peak in 1950. Thereafter, though, the gap between the richest and the poorest nation narrowed rapidly.

The evidence presented here would suggest four main conclusions: first, after the end of the Second World War, per capita income and productivity differentials among European countries became progressively smaller, with a particularly fast reduction in income dispersion during the 'Golden Age' (1950–73). In this sense we can say that post-war growth was accompanied by a process of convergence. Second, encompassing the two world wars and the inter-war depression, the period from 1913 to 1950 as a whole was one of *divergence* rather than convergence. By 1950, variation in income and productivity levels among the European countries was higher than in 1913. Third, any statement on the presence or absence of convergence in late nineteenth-century Europe depends critically on the range of countries included in the sample. While the marked fall in the coefficients of variation among the income and productivity levels of the 12 economies lends credence to the notion of convergence, the same cannot be said if the net were cast wider, in our case, to include 15 European countries. This result finds support in the recent literature which argues that there were so-called convergence 'clubs', that is, groups of economies within which convergence is observable, rather than global convergence.[6] The next section asks to what extent the European growth experience is mirrored in the record on economic integration.

The Integration of the European Economy

Sidney Pollard distinguishes three major phases of European economic development and industrialization since the eighteenth century: first, a phase of progressive liberalization and integration up to the early 1870s; second, a period of accelerating economic disintegration that set in with the rise of neo-mercantilist policies in the late nineteenth century and encompassed the collapse of the international economy in the inter-war years and the Second World War; finally, a period of economic reintegration into *two* Europes, that is, West and East, since 1945.[7] Here, in contrast, it will be argued that despite the increase in the use of protectionist measures by European states after 1870 the period up to 1914 should still be interpreted as one of continuing economic integration. This view is based, first, on the evidence that relates directly to the extent of economic integration during the late nineteenth century and, secondly, on the comparison with the incidence of economic disintegration during the inter-war years. In short, rising protectionism does not necessarily translate into economic disintegration though the two issues are, of course, closely related.

Here, economic integration refers to *international* economic relations, that is, to the varying extent to which the national economies of sovereign states are combined into one entity. Hence integration is understood, first, in a *dynamic* sense as the *process* of eliminating economic frontiers between states. Second, in a *static* sense integration represents a *condition*, that is, the degree to which national economies are no longer separated but function as one larger unit. In the literature, two types of integration are usually distinguished: first, the cross-border integration of goods and factor (i.e. capital and labour) *markets* and, secondly, *policy* integration which goes further and also involves the formation of economic and/or monetary unions. However, explicit international policy integration among the European states played only a relatively minor role prior to 1945.[8]

The main channels of interaction between national economies, and ultimately, their integration into one larger unit, have been cross-border trade in goods and services, cross-border migration of people, cross-border flows of capital, the transfer of technology and knowledge, and the payments and transport systems facilitating such movements. Conversely, economic integration has often been held back by an unfavourable geography where high transportation costs reduced the volume of goods traded internationally. Cultural and linguistic barriers impeded commercial exchange. More often than not, tariffs and non-tariff barriers such as quotas and currency restrictions were introduced so as to protect domestic producers from import competition or to avoid balance of payments deficits. In any case, they undermine the integration of product markets. Similarly, the free flow of labour and capital was frequently hindered for a multitude of economic and non-economic reasons.

What, then, is the nature of the relationship between economic integration, growth and convergence? Suppose there were fully integrated commodity markets where all barriers to trade have been removed (i.e. a situation of free trade). National or regional economies are then in a position to specialize in making those goods in whose production and exports they enjoy a comparative advantage. And they will import goods of which they are less efficient producers than other economies. The ability to specialize in the production of only a relatively small range of goods encourages the most efficient allocation of production factors such as labour and capital and will thus have a positive impact on economic growth. Moreover, exporting to other economies implies an increase in market size; this, in turn, allows for the realization of economies of scale and specialization that accrue from lower costs per unit of output. Integration of goods markets thus widens the scope for growth. The same type of reasoning applies to service markets, though, typically, services tend to be traded less than goods. The integration of factor markets is important for output and productivity growth because it allows for a more efficient *international* resource allocation. In the absence of restrictions to free movement, labour and capital are likely to move to where they receive their highest returns. This has far-reaching consequences for the growth of *individual* economies. For instance, borrowing from the residents of other countries may enable a developing or industrializing economy that is short of capital to build up its infrastructure and to purchase technology abroad. Access to foreign capital thus permits increasing imports that are crucial for raising productivity levels. This, in turn, opens up longer term export opportunities and specialization along the lines of comparative advantage. Hence international capital flows play an important role in the expansion of international trade.

Trade, factor and knowledge flows are also the main international transmission channels that permit catch-up and convergence. If it is differences in (broadly defined) technology that account for most of the gap in incomes between poor countries and rich countries, then any barrier to the transfer of technology is likely to slow down the closing of this income gap. Similarly, convergence is fostered if factors of production can move from where they are relatively abundant to where they are relatively scarce. In the absence of counteracting forces, this is likely to reduce income differentials between economies. For example, emigration from a relatively poor country with a labour surplus to a rich country with a labour shortage should lead to an increase in labour productivity and wage growth in the poor country relative to the rich. In short, those measures that impede international trade and factor flows are also likely to reduce the incidence of 'convergence' in per capita income levels.

Western Europe's economic history is characterized by distinctly different phases of economic integration and disintegration. Here it is argued that those periods which displayed either significantly increasing market integration or relatively high levels thereof coincided broadly with periods of high rates of growth and a comparatively strong incidence of catching-up and convergence among the European economies. Conversely, the economic disintegration during the years between the outbreak of the First and the end of the Second World War was associated with slow growth, an interruption of the process of catching-up of the poorer with the richer European economies and, broadly, economic divergence.

International trade is perhaps the one most significant conduit for the interaction between economies. The data in Table 22.2 show that, measured over the whole of the last 130 or so years, the volume of exports rose at a faster rate than aggregate output. As a result, the share of exports in West European GDP increased from about 10 per cent in 1870 to almost 30 per cent in 1992.

During the late nineteenth century the European economy became increasingly trade intensive. This holds despite the marked rise in protectionism from the late 1870s and the associated slow down in the rate of export growth compared to the previous half century. Even though tariff rates went up in Europe, often by quite significant margins, and may thus have slowed down the rise in the share of trade in total output, this did not lead to a reversal of the trend towards more openness. Before the First World War, imports and exports in most European countries expanded at faster rates than national income. The United Kingdom was an exception from the general pattern where trade was primarily carried out among European countries; that is, most of Continental Europe's foreign trade in the nineteenth century was intra-European. The expansion in international trade was aided by a multilateral payments system which relied on fixed exchange rates under the gold standard. Whatever the shortcomings of the pre-1914 international gold standard, it broadly worked (though there is much debate why that was so). This was in marked contrast to the inter-war period. Most countries that joined the system managed to stay on at an unchanged parity in the late nineteenth century. This was important for several reasons. First, the currencies of the major economies were fully and readily convertible into each other, easing the cross-border flows of both goods and capital. With currency convertibility, trade deficits with one country could be offset by a surplus in trade with other countries which fostered specialization in production. Second, Britain was at the centre of this network. Not only was she the world's largest exporter, she was also the largest importer, offering a readily accessible market to the exports of other countries. She also continuously 'recycled' her current account surplus in the form of capital exports, of which she was the largest source in the late nineteenth century, ahead of France and Germany. By 1914, these three economies provided about 75 per cent of the world's foreign capital and about one quarter of this was invested in Europe. Ready access to these funds, thirdly, made it possible for capital importing countries to run deficits on their current accounts. That is, they could continue to import more than they exported, as long as their earnings of foreign exchange were sufficient to service their debts, without facing serious balance of payments crises. That was vital not only for the growth prospects of these individual economies, but also for the international economy at large, since it helped contain protectionist pressures.

Craig and Fisher argue that by 1913 the national economies of western Europe were so integrated in most important aspects of economic life that they constituted a 'European economy'. National economies were interacting through their sharing of product markets (export and import) and capital markets. This interaction was reflected in a high degree of cyclical integration among the real economies of the major *industrial* countries. In short, there was a 'Pan-European' business cycle.[9]

The inter-war years mark a stark deviation from the long term pattern and the experience of the pre-1913 and post-1950 periods. International and thus European trade contracted sharply in the widespread economic dislocation following the First World War. By 1929, western Europe's exports had just reached again the 1913 level. During the 1920s, governments at least tried to restore some of the international economic stability and commercial exchange that was prevalent before 1914 and that was so badly lacking after the war. They saw a return to gold as a means to achieve these ends and, broadly, sought to limit the extent of protectionism. That was to change dramatically under the impact of the Great Depression and world financial crisis in the early 1930s. The collapse of international lending, the abandonment of gold convertibility of the major currencies, the introduction of exchange controls and the raising of tariff and non-tariff barriers to trade meant that by the early to mid-1930s the multilateral trade and payments system had disintegrated. Even after the international crisis had passed, there was no return to multilateralism. Instead, foreign trade became increasingly organized along bilateral lines and within *regional* currency areas. In the case of Nazi Germany, trade and exchange policies were geared towards autarky and preparation for war.

European exports contracted sharply and did not reach again their 1929 peak before the outbreak of the Second World War. Over the whole period 1913 to 1950, the volume of European exports declined in absolute terms (see Table 22.2) and, as a result, we observe a pronounced decline in the share of exports in national income. In other words, cross-border trade played an increasingly less significant role in the European economy. It is, of course, difficult to say whether economic growth generates trade or whether trade generates economic growth. Yet the decline in international trade appears to be a major factor in explaining the poor performance of the European economy between the wars. For once, slow growth in the inter-war period was associated with a reversal of the long term pattern that saw European exports grow faster than total output. In no other period of comparable length since the early nineteenth century did foreign trade expand at such a low rate and so much slower than output. Whatever economic recovery there was after the Great Depression of the early 1930s, it was not a recovery of the international or European economy. Rather, it was a recovery of individual national economies.

However, the impact of the Second World War on the European economy made an *immediate* return after 1945 to multilateral trade and payments, and the potential for growth that this entailed, impossible. As Chapters 3 and 7 have shown, the severe material shortages and balance of payments problems that Europe faced after the war did not permit the speedy removal of barriers to trade and the re-establishment of currency convertibility, as many had hoped for. On the contrary, bilateral trade agreements remained widespread. Hence new institutional arrangements such as the European Payments Union had to be found in order to progressively remove the main obstacles to an expansion of trade. Yet once the liberalization process got under way and the clearing union allowed for the multilateralization of payments at least *within* Europe, intra-European trade accelerated rapidly.

Probably the most significant difference between the nature of the pre-1914 and post-1945 economic integration processes is the rise of policy integration after the Second World War. Apart from the constraints that adherence to the international gold standard imposed on participating countries, 'national economic sovereignty' remained more or less intact during the late nineteenth century. There were no supra-national institutions such as, for instance, the European Coal and Steel Community or the European Union with comparable tasks of implementing specific policies with a view to 'harmonizing' economic conditions in member countries and pooling resources (see Chapters 3 and 9). However, this does not mean, of course, that market integration was less important after 1945 than it was before 1914. On the contrary, the share of foreign trade in national income in western Europe is now much higher than it was a century ago.

The 'Standard of Living'

So far, the discussion has focused on long term changes in income and productivity. But, obviously, living standards are affected by more factors than simply income. One concept that has been developed to capture at least some of these factors is that of the Human Development Index, or HDI, which also takes account of life expectancy and educational attainment.[10] The importance of demographic and educational change in post-war Europe has been explored in Chapters 10 and 12. What are the effects on our measurement of 'well-being' if these factors are accounted for, especially taking a long term perspective?

Viewing human development as a process of expanding choice, the HDI is composed of three elements: longevity, schooling and income. These are combined with equal weights into a single index by measuring each of them as a percentage of the *distance* travelled between an assumed minimum and maximum value.[11] Of course, there is an element of arbitrariness in giving equal weights to the three components included in the index and zero weight to other aspects of welfare, some of which may be regarded as equally or even more important. However, the HDI offers at least some indication of what it means in terms of welfare comparisons over time and between societies, if measures other than per capita income are taken into account as well.

Table 22.4 presents a comparison of GDP per capita and HDI levels for 12 European countries since 1870, including their ranks. Several observations can be made. First, in 1870 the United Kingdom was the leading economy by a large margin in terms of per capita income. Yet at the same time, despite their significantly lower income levels, Denmark and Switzerland scored slightly higher in terms of the HDI on the grounds of their better performance in schooling and/or life expectancy. Thus the choice of 'welfare' indicator affects strongly the ranking among different economies. This point is further emphasized by the cases of Belgium and Austria, high income economies which performed poorly on HDI in 1870. By 1913 Denmark, Norway and Sweden rank four or five places higher on HDI than on GDP per capita, while Belgium continues to rank as many as six places below on HDI than she does on income. Second, with the exceptions of Austria, Finland and Italy, by 1913 all economies had reached a markedly higher level in HDI than the United Kingdom had in 1870, irrespective of whether they had also achieved income levels as high as those for the United Kingdom in 1870. In 1913, the unweighted average per capita income in Europe was only slightly higher than British income in 1870, but the average 1913 HDI was more than 25 per cent above the British HDI level in 1870. In other words, many of the nineteenth century 'follower' countries compared more favourably with the 'leader' Britain in terms of more broadly defined living standards than they did in terms of income. Third, much of the comparatively better HDI performance of poor countries since 1870 is explicable in terms of the decline in mortality. Rather than from increases in per capita incomes, improvements in mortality have primarily resulted from scientific advances and better public health care. These, however, have been available to *both* poor and rich countries. Fourth,

Table 22.4. Levels of GDP per capita and Human Development Indices

	1870		1913		1950		1992	
	GDP pc	HDI	GDP pc	HDI	GDP pc	HDI	GDP pc	HDI
Austria	1,971	0.184	2,986	0.336	3,731	0.562	17,160	0.863
	(5)	(10)	(9)	(10)	(11)	(10)	(7)	(9)
Belgium	2,640	0.312	4,130	0.432	5,346	0.597	17,165	0.864
	(2)	(9)	(3)	(9)	(6)	(7)	(6)	(7)
Denmark	1,927	0.367	3,764	0.507	6,683	0.640	18,293	0.873
	(6)	(1)	(6)	(1)	(4)	(3)	(3)	(5)
Finland	1,107	0.109	2,050	0.301	4,131	0.551	14,646	0.835
	(12)	(12)	(12)	(12)	(10)	(11)	(12)	(11)
France	1,858	0.322	3,452	0.455	5,221	0.581	17,959	0.882
	(8)	(6)	(7)	(8)	(7)	(9)	(4)	(3)
Germany	1,913	0.316	3,833	0.458	4,281	0.591	19,351	0.893
	(7)	(7)	(5)	(7)	(9)	(8)	(2)	(2)
Italy	1,467	0.129	2,507	0.331	3,425	0.512	16,229	0.837
	(10)	(11)	(10)	(11)	(12)	(12)	(10)	(10)
Netherl.	2,640	0.334	3,950	0.496	5,850	0.638	16,898	0.870
	(3)	(5)	(4)	(3)	(5)	(4)	(9)	(6)
Norway	1,303	0.316	2,275	0.477	4,969	0.620	17,543	0.877
	(11)	(8)	(11)	(6)	(8)	(6)	(5)	(4)
Sweden	1,664	0.343	3,096	0.490	6,738	0.641	16,927	0.864
	(9)	(4)	(8)	(4)	(3)	(2)	(8)	(8)
Switzerl.	2,172	0.364	4,207	0.486	8,939	0.657	21,036	0.922
	(4)	(2)	(2)	(5)	(1)	(1)	(1)	(1)
UK	3,263	0.349	5,032	0.497	6,847	0.628	15,738	0.833
	(1)	(3)	(1)	(2)	(2)	(5)	(11)	(12)

Note: Ranks are given in parentheses. GDP per capita (GDP pc) is measured in constant 1990 international dollars.

Sources: Crafts, 'Human Development Index' with Austria (1870, 1913) adjusted; Maddison, *Monitoring.*

from 1950 individual economies' ranks in terms of income and HDI corresponded generally much more closely to each other than they did in the earlier period. This was largely an outcome of the rather similar levels of life expectancy and literacy that they had achieved by then. For instance, in 1870 the highest life expectancy was more than twenty years above the lowest within the group of 12 European countries; by 1950 the difference had shrunk to seven years. Similarly, the ratio between the highest and the lowest literacy rates declined from 8.5 in 1870 to 1.2 in 1950. Though remaining slightly higher, differences in school enrolment narrowed to a comparable degree. As a result, most of the divergent levels in HDI between European countries after the Second World War have been due to remaining differences in per capita income.

In summary, by the beginning of the twentieth century most western European countries had progressed further towards modern standards of living as measured by HDI than a comparison based solely on per capita income would indicate. Moreover, after 1913 differences in living standards between economies appear to have been significantly smaller when measured in terms of 'human development'.

Conclusions

On the evidence from Europe's recent economic history, growth, convergence and integration appear as closely interrelated processes. In general, phases of rapid economic growth coincided with periods of increasing integration. Viewed over the course of the late nineteenth and twentieth centuries, convergence in income and productivity levels was not a universal, but a group and period specific phenomenon. Moreover, international economic integration developed at varying speeds over time and proved reversible. The European economy moved through a period of progressive integration during the nineteenth century. The inter-war years, however, witnessed rapid and far reaching disintegration, culminating in the emergence of regional trading blocs, moves towards autarky, and, ultimately, the outbreak of war. In the post-Second World War period the response was to focus not only on *negative* integration in the form of removing obstacles to interaction in product and factor markets, but also on explicit *positive* integration. Economic policies were, to varying extents, formulated and implemented within an agreed supra-national institutional framework in efforts to find joint solutions to commonly shared problems.

Bibliographical Note

H. van der Wee, *Prosperity and Upheaval: The World Economy 1945–1980* (London, 1987) is a very good non-technical introduction to international economic history since 1945. The origins and early history of western European integration after 1945 are explored in two important books by A.S. Milward, *The Reconstruction of Western Europe, 1945–51* (London, 1984) and *The European Rescue of the Nation State* (London, 1992). The most up-to-date and detailed treatment of western Europe's post-1945 growth experience is offered in N.F.R. Crafts and G. Toniolo (eds), *Economic Growth in Europe since 1945* (Cambridge, 1996). C.H. Feinstein, P. Temin and G. Toniolo, *The European Economy between the Wars* (Oxford, 1997) is a readily accessible, well-structured synthesis of the economic history of inter-war Europe. On the nineteenth century, unfortunately, no comparable work is available. Addressed to the non-specialist, F. Capie, *Tariffs and Growth. Some Insights from the World Economy 1850–1940* (Manchester, 1994), is a good introduction to the problem of protectionism. A rather technical analysis of the process and extent of economic integration in the late nineteenth century is L.A. Craig and D. Fisher, *The Integration of the European Economy, 1850–1913* (London, 1997). A. Maddison, *Monitoring the World Economy, 1820–1992* (Paris, 1995) is a much used compilation of international long term data and offers a brief overview of the major phases of economic development since the early nineteenth century. For an introduction to the economics of integration see W. Molle, *The Economics of European Integration. Theory, Practice, Policy* (Aldershot, 1990).

Notes

1. S. Kuznets, *Modern Economic Growth: Rate, Structure and Spread* (New Haven, CT, 1966).

2. Rates of growth in western Europe (per cent per annum):

	Real GDP	Population	Real GDP per capita
1870–1890	1.8	0.7	1.2
1890–1913	2.3	0.8	1.5

See Table 22.2 for sources.

3. M. Abramovitz, 'Catching up, forging ahead, and falling behind', *Journal of Economic History* 46 (1986).

4. In the literature on economic convergence, perhaps the most important distinction is that between *unconditional* convergence, where economies are expected to move towards the same productivity or income levels, and *conditional* convergence, where allowance is made for those factors such as, for example, different literacy levels that may at least partially offset the forces which make for convergence. In other words, productivity or income levels are not expected to be completely equalized across economies. In the following discussion, the focus is on the most basic evidence on unconditional convergence.

5. This formulation of the problem is often referred to as sigma-convergence, while the inverse relationship between the initial productivity level and the subsequent rate of productivity growth is labelled beta-convergence. Note that beta-convergence, though necessary, does not guarantee sigma-convergence as, for instance, the absolute difference in productivity levels between two countries can increase even while it may decrease in proportional terms. Moreover, dispersion in productivity or income levels may be increased as a result of shocks having a differential impact on different economies, over-powering catching-up effects that may be present.

6. Cf. S.N. Broadberry, 'Convergence: what the historical record shows', in B. van Ark and N.F.R. Crafts (eds), *Quantitative Aspects of Post-War European Economic Growth* (Cambridge, 1996); G. Williamson, 'Globalization, convergence, and history', *Journal of Economic History*, 56 (1996).

7. S. Pollard, *Peaceful Conquest. The Industrialization of Europe 1760–1970* (Oxford, 1981).

8. Monetary unions in nineteenth-century Europe include the Latin Monetary Union encompassing Belgium, France, Greece, Italy and Switzerland, and the Scandinavian Monetary Union of Denmark, Norway and Sweden. Both of these, however, involved the maintenance of separate national currencies which were legal tender in all member states and national central banks. Though in operation until after the First World War, they lost in significance during the late nineteenth century as members went

onto the international gold standard. Moreover, they did not involve a common monetary policy where the principal decisions are taken collectively.

9. L.A. Craig and D. Fisher, *Integration of the European Economy* (London, 1996).

10. The following discussion relies on Crafts, 'Human Development Index'.

11. The HDI as presented in Table 22.5 is calculated as (indexed life expectancy + indexed educational attainment + indexed adjusted income)/3 . For each of its components, the indexed figure lies between 0 and 1. To illustrate its derivation, the example of Denmark in 1870 is used. Life expectancy is assumed to fall between a maximum of 85 and a minimum of 25 years. Life expectancy in Denmark was 45.5 years, which yields an index for life expectancy of $(45.5 - 25.0)/(85.0 - 25.0)/3 = 0.342$. For educational attainment a weight of 2/3 is given to the literacy rate and a weight of 1/3 is given to the combined primary, secondary and tertiary education enrolment rate. Both rates are taken to lie between a minimum of 0 and a maximum of 100 per cent. Given the relevant data for Denmark, the educational attainment index is $[2*(0.81) + 0.390]/3 = 0.670$. Indexed real per capita income is expressed as the percentage of a maximum that is taken to be the US income level in 1992: 1,927/21, 558 = 0.089. The HDI for Denmark in 1870 is thus $(0.342 + 0.670 + 0.089)/3 = 0.367$.

Key Dates and Events

1939   End of Spanish Civil War after Franco's troops enter Madrid.
Italy conquers Albania.
Germany conquers Czechoslovakia; Slovakia declared independent state.
Germany conquers Poland and partitions it with USSR.
France and Britain declare war on Germany.
Systematic racial persecution of Jews and others extended from Nazi Germany to German-occupied territories.

1940   Germany conquers Denmark, Norway, the Netherlands, Belgium and Luxembourg and France.
Italy declares war on Britain and France, and invades Greece.

1941   Lend-lease agreement between USA and UK.
German army conquers the Balkans.
Germany invades the USSR.
Germans begin mass extermination of European Jews that continues until the last days of the war.
Japanese attack on Pearl Harbor brings USA into the war.

1942   Germany defeated at El Alamein.
Vichy France occupied by Germans.
Intensive Allied bombing of Germany begins.

1943   Italian government surrenders to Allies but German resistance in Italy continues.
German forces at Stalingrad surrender.
USA, UK and USSR agree to found United Nations.

1944   Allied 'D-Day' landings in Normandy.
Bretton Woods Conference (agreement to set up World Bank and International Monetary Fund).

1945 Russians capture Berlin; European war ends.
USA drops atomic bombs on Hiroshima and Nagasaki; Pacific war ends.
Expulsion and emigration of Germans from central and eastern Europe.
Election of first majority Labour government in Britain.

1946 Introduction of economic planning in France with Monnet Plan for re-construction and modernization.

1947 Declaration of Marshall Plan by USA.
Establishment of the General Agreement on Tariffs and Trade (GATT).
Sterling made convertible; decision reversed after six weeks.
Threat of hyperinflation in Italy is brought under control and the economy is stabilized.

1948 Commencement of Belgium–Netherlands–Luxembourg customs union.
Establishment of the Organization for European Economic Cooperation (OEEC).
Congress of Europe and formation of the European Movement.
Currency reform in the western zones of Germany.

1949 Formation of North Atlantic Treaty Organization (NATO).
Formation of the Council of Europe.
Foundation of Federal Republic of Germany (West Germany).
Devaluation of sterling and other European currencies against US dollar.

1950 Announcement of Schuman Plan on the organization of the European coal and steel industry.
Formation of European Payments Union (EPU) to allow multi-lateralization of trade in western Europe.
Beginning of trade liberalization under OEEC auspices.
Outbreak of Korean war.

1951 Belgium, France, West Germany, Italy, The Netherlands and Luxembourg ('the Six') sign the Treaty of Paris, establishing the European Coal and Steel Community (ECSC).
Special agency set up in Italy to foster investment in the country's poor south (Cassa per il Mezzogiorno).

1952 Signature of European Defence Community (EDC) treaty.
Beginning of ECSC operations.
First commercial flight of a jet plane (Comet).
End of Marshall aid programme.

1953 End of Korean war.

1954   France rejects EDC.
West European Union (WEC) treaty signed.

1955   WEU starts to operate.
Messina conference of 'the Six' discusses full customs union.

1956   Suez crisis.

1957   'The Six' sign Treaty of Rome, establishing the European Economic Community (EEC) and the European Atomic Energy Commission (Euratom).
First container ship service.

1958   Beginning of EEC and Euratom operations.
Revolt of French settlers and army in Algeria causes fall of the Fourth Republic and brings de Gaulle to power.
New constitution in France ('Fifth Republic').
European currencies made convertible.

1959   Economic stabilization programme in Spain.

1960   European Free Trade Area (EFTA) established among Austria, Denmark, Norway, Portugal, Sweden, Switzerland and the United Kingdom.
OEEC reorganized into Organization for Economic Cooperation and Development (OECD).
Sustained growth in the rich economies of western Europe in the 1950s and 1960s leads to large-scale immigration from poor southern Europe.

1961   Denmark, Ireland and the United Kingdom apply for EEC membership; Norway follows in 1962.
Revaluation of Dutch guilder and German mark.

1962   First commercial telecom satellite launched (Telstar).

1963   French President de Gaulle vetos British EEC membership; Irish, Danish and Norwegian applications suspended.
Syncome, first satellite in geostationary orbit.

1964   Common Agricultural Policy comes into operation.
Kennedy round of GATT (to 1970).

1965   Creation of the European Community (EC) from the merger of EEC, ECSC and Euratom.

1966   The Luxembourg Compromise, EC member states are allowed to veto proposals which threaten 'special national interests'.

1967   Denmark, Ireland, Norway and the United Kingdom re-apply for EC membership; British application again opposed by de Gaulle.
Devaluation of sterling.

1968   Widespread student protests in western Europe, especially in France where they combine with mass strikes against de Gaulle's government.
Removal of internal customs duties and introduction of common external tariff by EC 'Six'.

1969   First attempt at Economic and Monetary Union (EMU) launched.
Devaluation of French franc and revaluation of German mark.
Widespread expression of social discontent in Italy during the 'hot autumn'.

1970   Werner Report on EMU.
First commercial flight of Boeing 747 ('jumbo jet').
First VCR on the market.

1971   Smithsonian Agreement to shore up fixed exchange rates.
Beginning of commercial North Sea oil exploitation by Norway.

1972   Formation of the 'Snake' currency arrangement.
Sterling floats against other currencies.
Miners' strike in Britain leads to large-scale power cuts.

1973   Denmark, Ireland and the United Kingdom join the EC, Norway rejects membership in referendum.
Collapse of Smithsonian Agreement, European currencies float against the US dollar.
Tokyo round of GATT (to 1979).
First oil price shock.

1974   Shelving of EMU scheme at Paris summit.
First commercial flight of supersonic airliner (Concorde).
Increase of inflation across western Europe.
Beginning of long-term rise in European unemployment levels.

1975   United Kingdom confirms membership of EC by referendum, Greece applies for EC membership.
Death of Franco, Juan Carlos becomes King of Spain.

1977   First free elections in Spain since 1936.
Portugal and Spain apply for EC membership.
Optical fibres first used in telephone communications.
Davignon Plan of EC providing for the rundown of capacity and co-ordinated price increases in the European steel industry.

1978   'Winter of Discontent': industrial action in many sectors of the British economy.

1979   Launch of European Monetary System (EMS) and Exchange Rate Mechanism (ERM) after agreement at 1978 Bremen summit.
Conservative government under Thatcher elected in United Kingdom, committed to radical change in economic policy.
First direct elections to European Parliament.
Second oil price shock.

1981   Greece joins the EU.
First commercial journey of high speed train in Europe (TGV Paris–Lyons).

1985   Publication of the Commission White Paper on the completion of the EC internal market, agreement at Luxembourg summit on Single European Act, defining 1992 as date of completion of frontierless market within EC.

1986   Single European Act signed by EC member states (effective from July 1987).
'Big Bang': deregulation of London's City institutions, fuelling subsequent boom of the economy.
Spain and Portugal join EC to complete the 'Southern enlargement' and establish the 'Twelve'.

1989   Publication of Delors Report on the establishment of Economic and Monetary Union (EMU) in three stages; agreement that first stage of EMU would begin on 1 July 1990 with all twelve members adhering to ERM.
Spain joins ERM.

1990   Stage 1 of the Delors blueprint begins.
Britain joins Exchange Rate Mechanism (ERM) of EMS.
Unification of East and West Germany.
Intergovernmental conferences on EMU and political union among EC member states.
Process of far-reaching institutional reform in Italy initiated in early 1990s.

1991   Maastricht Treaty on European Union (EU) and timetable for EMU signed, effective from November 1993 following national ratification; the EC becomes one of three 'pillars' of the EU, along with a Common Security and Defence Policy and a Common Internal Affairs Policy; Britain secures an 'opt out' on EMU and social charter.

1992   Single Market (or 1992) programme completed at the end of the year.
Speculative pressures on their currencies force Britain and Italy to leave ERM.
Norway applies for EC membership.

1993   Devaluations of Irish, Portugese and Spanish currencies.
        Second Danish referendum supports amended Maastricht Treaty providing for Danish 'opt-outs'.
        Britain ratifies Maastricht Treaty but refuses to commit itself to single European currency.
        ERM bands widened to 15 per cent.
        EU comes formally into existence.

1994   European Economic Area established, extending the single market to EFTA members.
        Stage 2 of EMU begins; establishment of the European Monetary Institute (EMI).

1995   Sweden, Austria and Finland join EU; Norway and Switzerland reject membership in referendums.
        Schengen Convention comes into effect, seven out of 15 EU member states remove border controls.
        Italy rejoins ERM.

1996   Preparations for Stage 3 (adoption of a single currency) of EMU programme begin; timetable for single currency by 1999 confirmed at Dublin summit.

1997   Labour victory in British general election, followed by outline acceptance of social charter by the new government.

Notes on Contributors

Max-Stephan Schulze is Lecturer in Economic History at the London School of Economics. He has published on the economic history of the Habsburg Empire, including *Engineering and Economic Growth: The Development of Austria-Hungary's Machine-Building Industry in the late 19th Century* (1996), and is currently working on income convergence in Europe.

Peter Howlett is Lecturer in Economic History at the London School of Economics. He has published several articles on the British economy in the Second World War and, with the Central Statistical Office, is the author of *Fighting with Figures* (1995). He is currently working on a book on the long run impact of the war.

Till Geiger is Lecturer in European Studies at Queen's University Belfast. He has written several articles and book chapters on the history of post-war European integration. He is currently writing a book on American military aid to western Europe.

Nicholas Crafts is Professor of Economic History at the London School of Economics. He has written extensively on economic growth in Britain and Europe. Among his recent publications are the edited volumes, with G. Toniolo, *Economic Growth in Europe since 1945* (1996) and, with B. van Ark, *Quantitative Aspects of Postwar European Economic Growth* (1996).

Nicholas Woodward is Lecturer in Economic History at the University of Wales, Swansea. His main interests are in the area of macroeconomic history since 1945. He is the co-editor, with N.F.R. Crafts, of *The British Economy since 1945* (1991) and, with R. Coopey, of *Britain in the 1970s: The Troubled Economy* (1996).

Maurice Kirby is Professor of Economic History at Lancaster University. He has published widely on themes of British economic and business history. His most recent book is *The Origins of Railway Enterprise: The Stockton and Darlington Railway,*

1821–1863 (1993). He is currently writing a history of operational research in the UK.

Catherine Schenk is Senior Lecturer in Economic History at the University of Glasgow. She is the author of a book and several articles on Britain's international economic relations, as well as the post-war financial history of East Asia. She is currently engaged in research on the Eurodollar market and the origins of Hong Kong as an international financial centre.

Paul Johnson is Reader in Economic History at the London School of Economics. His publications include *Saving and Spending: The Working Class Economy in Britain* (1985) and, with Jane Falkingham, *Ageing and Economic Welfare* (1992). He is the editor of *20th Century Britain: Economic, Social and Cultural Change* (1994) and currently works on laws and markets in Victorian England.

Valerio Lintner is Senior Lecturer in Economics at London Guildhall University. His recent publications include, with Sonia Mazey, *The European Community: Economic and Political Aspects* (1991) and, with D. Edye, *Contemporary Europe: Economics, Politics and Society* (1996). He is co-editor, with Michael Newman and Frank Brouwer, of *Economic Policy Making and the European Union* (1994).

Dudley Baines is Reader in Economic History at the London School of Economics. He previously taught at the University of Liverpool and has held visiting appointments at the University of Monash, Melbourne and the University of California, Berkeley. His publications include *Migration in a Mature Economy* (1986) and *Emigration from Europe, 1815–1930* (1991). He is currently working on the analysis of the labour market in inter-war London.

Martin McLean is Senior Lecturer in Education at the Institute of Education, University of London. He has written extensively on comparative education issues. His publications include *The Curriculum: A Comparative Perspective*, with Brian Holmes (1989), and *Britain and a Single European Market: Prospects for a Common School Curriculum* (1990).

John Armstrong is Professor of Business History at Thames Valley University, London, and editor of the *Journal of Transport History*. He is interested in all aspects of transport history, especially British coastal trade. His latest book is *Coastal and Short Sea Shipping* (1996).

William Lever is Professor of Urban Studies at the University of Glasgow. His numerous publications include the edited volumes *The Global Economy in Transition*, with P.W. Daniels (1996), and *The Spatial Impact of Economic Changes in Europe*, with Antoine Bailly (1996).

Peter Solar is Professor of Economics at Vesalius College, Vrije Universiteit Brussel. In addition to his work on twentieth-century Belgian economic history, he has published numerous articles on early modern poor relief, the Irish economy in the nineteenth century, and the European linen industry.

Jim Tomlinson is Professor of Economic History at Brunel University. He has published extensively on British economic policy in the twentieth century. His recent publications include *Government and Enterprise since 1900: The Changing Problem of Efficiency* (1994) and *Democratic Socialism and Economic Policy: The Attlee Years, 1945–1951* (1997).

Alain Guyomarch is Lecturer in European Politics and Deputy Director of the European Institute at the London School of Economics. His main research area and publications cover public administration in France and in the EU, as well as political parties, elections and institutional changes in France. He is co-author, with H. Machin and E. Ritchie, of *France in the EU: Politics and Policy* (1998).

Christoph Buchheim is Professor of Economic History at the University of Mannheim. He has written widely on German economic history. His publications include *Die Wiedereingliederung Westdeutschlands in die Weltwirtschaft* (1990) and he is the editor of *Wirtschaftliche Folgelasten des Krieges in der SBZ/DDR* (1995).

Vera Zamagni is Professor of Economic History at Bologna University. She has published numerous articles and books on the development of the Italian economy. Among her recent publications are *The Economic History of Italy 1860–1990* (1993) and the edited volume, with Peter Scholliers, *Labour's Reward: Real Wages and Economic Change in 19th- and 20th-Century Europe* (1995).

Rolf Ohlsson is Professor of Economic History at the University of Lund. His research interests are economic history of the twentieth century, population economics, economics of education and the growth of the welfare state. He is the co-editor, with Lars Jonung, of *The Economic Development of Sweden since 1870* (1997).

Jordi Catalan is Associate Professor of Economic History at the University of Barcelona. His publications on Spanish economic history include the volume, co-edited with Jordi Nadal, *La cara oculta de la industrialización española* (1994) and *La economía española y la Segunda Guerra Mundial* (1995).

Index